"Huzza!"

"Huzza!"
Toasting a New Nation, 1760–1815

Timothy Symington

McFarland & Company, Inc., Publishers
Jefferson, North Carolina

LIBRARY OF CONGRESS CATALOGUING-IN-PUBLICATION DATA

Names: Symington, Timothy, 1967– author.
Title: "Huzza!" : toasting a new nation, 1760-1815 / Timothy Symington.
Description: Jefferson, North Carolina : McFarland & Company, Inc., Publishers, 2023. | Includes bibliographical references and index.
Identifiers: LCCN 2023040454 | ISBN 9781476693156 (paperback : acid free paper) ⊗ ISBN 9781476650562 (ebook)
Subjects: LCSH: United States—History—Revolution, 1775-1783. | United States—History—1783-1815. | Toasts—United States—History—18th century. | Toasts—United States—History—19th century.
Classification: LCC E210 .S97 2023 | DDC 973.3—dc23/eng/20230912
LC record available at https://lccn.loc.gov/2023040454

BRITISH LIBRARY CATALOGUING DATA ARE AVAILABLE

ISBN (print) 978-1-4766-9315-6
ISBN (ebook) 978-1-4766-5056-2

© 2023 Timothy Symington. All rights reserved

No part of this book may be reproduced or transmitted in any form or by any means, electronic or mechanical, including photocopying or recording, or by any information storage and retrieval system, without permission in writing from the publisher.

Front cover images © 2023 Shutterstock

Printed in the United States of America

McFarland & Company, Inc., Publishers
  Box 611, Jefferson, North Carolina 28640
    www.mcfarlandpub.com

To the memory of my father.

Table of Contents

Acknowledgments ix

Preface 1

Introduction 5

1. *"Ridiculous Formality"* 9
2. "May our Mother never oppress her dutiful children," 1763–1774 23
3. "His Excellency General Washington and the Armies of America," 1775–1783 32
4. "May the Wisdom of 1775 pervade the Councils of 1787!" 1784–1788 43
5. "The Rights of Man throughout the world," 1789–1793 53
6. "Hypocritical Federalism and Malignant Toryism," 1793–1796 64
7. "John Adams … the Rock and Strength of our political Salvation…," 1797–1798 81
8. The "*double curse*" of John Adams, 1798–1800 96
9. "Thomas Jefferson, the polar star of republicanism," 1801–1804 111
10. "The embargo—a deformed bantling of democracy…," 1805–1808 133
11. "James Madison—'tho last, not least'…," 1809–1811 155
12. "…War.—The offspring of an *adulterous* intercourse…," 1812–1815 168

13. "The American Fair—May every Mother give a WASHINGTON to her Country," 1760–1815	188
14. Red Savages and Our National Curse, 1760–1815	202
Conclusion	216
Chapter Notes	219
Bibliography	245
Index	255

Acknowledgments

No author writes a book solo. There are many people who assist in various ways. I have been incredibly lucky to get help from a community of friends, teachers, colleagues, and family. Some people were able to proofread several chapters and then offer valuable advice on my writing, while others gave me suggestions as to what rocks to look under for information and resources. Friends and family kept track of my progress or listened with interest (feigned or not) while I prattled on about toasts. Each of the following deserves more than a simple thank-you, and I would need perhaps two bottles of wine to toast them all properly.

First, I would like to thank Elizabeth Foxwell, Rhonda Herman, and the editorial staff of McFarland & Company, Inc. I am incredibly grateful that they decided to take a chance on my book. I could not be happier nor have a better publisher.

Denver Brunsman gets the credit for being the one responsible for giving me the idea of doing anything about toasts. His online lecture, in which he read off a list of toasts from Rhode Island, intrigued me enough to want to learn more. Denver was always able to answer any questions I had about doing research for both my master's thesis and this book. I hope that he continues to get more students interested in a topic that they will seek out further.

Joseph J. Ellis gave me invaluable advice on history and the world of publishing. Mining his books for information and anecdotes was a pure pleasure. He was eager to learn about my progress all along the way, constantly pushing me to continue. He was kind enough to be the first one to read the original manuscript and give me his honest thoughts. Most importantly, he never let me forget that I am my father's son.

Tom Nichols gave me important advice on the book-writing process. I appreciate the time he took to answer my many questions on a topic that he is certainly an expert on. I hope that he finds my book to be as interesting as his are. Intelligence runs in the family.

Christian Di Spigna befriended me at the Fort Plains American

Revolution Summer Conference in 2021. He is a walking resource himself, and I appreciate his willingness to both share his knowledge and introduce me to other writers and historians. Christian also encouraged and guided me when it came time to find a publisher.

Liz Covart, the host of the podcast *Ben Franklin's World*, held a group discussion "roundtable" in the spring of 2021. Some of the participants were able to workshop some of the chapters of my manuscript and make suggestions. I found their words of wisdom to be important, and I am indebted to them. It was a great experience!

Nancy Fletcher, a relative from my wife's family, always asked me how the book was coming along. Every time I saw her, she wanted to know if it was finished. Her enthusiasm helped me when I doubted whether I would ever finish. I hope that the finished product meets all her expectations.

Brian and Jennifer Symington served as my muses from the beginning. They were the ones who thought that my thesis should be extended, giving me the idea of turning it into an actual book. Their encouragement and constructive criticism (as only family members can give) meant a great deal to me. This entire project would not have been possible without their support.

My mother gets a special glass raised to her because she instilled in me a passion for history. She turned me on to the classic musical *1776* when I was a child, and I am glad that I got to share *Hamilton* with her as an adult. Mom never really knew what it was I was writing, but when she read it, she deemed it "brilliant." Of course, mothers know best. Thanks for all the love you have given me.

My children were always there to raise my spirits when I went through periods of doubt regarding this project. They both mean the world to me, and I cannot thank them enough for their presence in my life. As happy as I am to have completed this book, they are the source of my greatest joy.

Finally, my wife. She has been my rock. Words will never do justice to how much she has done to keep me going. I would not have been able to begin and finish this project without her. She listened to my ideas, read through some of the text, translated anything in French, and patiently put up with all of my craziness. I may be her "Sweet Babboo," but she is my life, pure and simple.

Preface

I gave a toast only once. I was honored by my older brother when he asked me to be his best man in October 1991. Fumbling through an awkward introduction, I had the guests raise their glasses to "Peace, love, and a sense of fun." Your typical wedding benediction. And that was the extent of my toasting experience for a while. Writing a book about toasts was as unlikely as a Beatles reunion.

My knowledge of toasts changed in the fall of 2016 when I took some graduate courses online, courtesy of the Gilder Lehrman Institute and Adams State University. One of the courses was on the American Revolution, led by Professor Denver Brunsman of George Washington University. In the eighteenth lesson, "Ratification and the Anti-Federalist Legacy," Professor Brunsman stated that, like songs, drinking toasts reflected the attitudes of society. He then proceeded to quote from a list of toasts given at the Wise Tavern in Alexandria, Virginia, and printed in the July 3, 1788, issue of the *Virginia Journal*:

1. The Convention of Virginia: May the Constitution of the United States of America be executed with the wisdom and integrity with which it was framed.
2. The States which have ratified the Constitution: May their example be followed by those who are yet to decide.
3. His Most Christian Majesty: As the effects of his friendship will be immortal, so may the gratitude of America never cease.
4. The memory of those heroes who, in the late war, laid down their lives on the altar of freedom.
5. The Marquis La Fayette: May the services he has rendered America be engraven on the hearts of her citizens.
6. Our worthy Representatives in the present Convention, Dr. David Stuart, and Col. Charles Simms.
7. The Potomack: May its navigation be improved to its sources, and its trade flourish to the degree bountiful nature intended.

8. The learning, agriculture, manufactures, and commerce of America.

9. The majesty of the people of America: Let the nations of the world look to them as an example, where, on mature deliberation, and with one accord, they have laid down one form of Government and accepted another.

10. Union and harmony among the members of the federal empire: May its various natural resources be improved to make the people happy and the nation glorious.

Professor Brunsman naturally became more animated with each toast, no doubt mimicking the 1788-era celebrants whose inebriation increased each time they drank.

I was taken aback by the toasts. They did not say anything profound, but I had never heard toasts given in that fashion. I had no idea that toasts were such an important ritual, being carefully written, edited, revised, and then selected specifically for publication. I did not know that they were used to unify the new nation by spreading American ideals, nor that they became effective political weapons for propaganda.

When the time came to choose a topic for my master's dissertation, the toasts had not left my mind. I contacted Professor Brunsman to ask if toasts were a "thesis-worthy" subject. He suggested that I do a longitudinal study of toasts given in one specific place. Since I am a Massachusetts native and resident, I chose to research the toasts of Revolution-era Massachusetts. I successfully defended the finished work in the spring of 2018, making sure that I brought glasses and sparkling grape juice so that the committee could raise their glass and drink to my success.

Having learned so much about toasts of Massachusetts, I was curious about the toasts of other regions of the country. Did Virginians drink to different people and events? Was there a big difference between the toasts of Federalist New England and the rest of the nation? Who else was toasted across the nation? Some of my colleagues and family encouraged me to continue the research. I broadened my scope so that I covered all the states from the start of the Imperial Crisis in 1763 to the end of the War of 1812 in 1815.

Finding the thousands of toast lists was not terribly difficult. Luckily, we live in an age of digital resources. The sites newspaperarchives.com and genealogy.com were instrumental in helping me find the newspapers of each state, toast lists, and commentary. I was also able to access documents from the American Antiquarian Society. If I used secondary sources and a toast was mentioned, I searched for the newspaper, diary, or letter that the toast came from. I was fortunate to be able to continue my research when the coronavirus hit and libraries and museums shut down.

Preface

The toasts, I discovered, were like cannon blasts over the battlefield: suddenly very loud, and then completely gone. They captured moments of public sentiment; they changed when the mood of the populace changed. Looking up the toasts by year helped me stay on a narrative path that told the story of the Early Republic. Familiar figures feature prominently in toast lists (no list would be complete without drinking to George Washington), and I "watched," through toasts, as some people rose in favor, fell from favor, and rose again later. To my disappointment, the local event that contributed to the calling of the Philadelphia Convention, Shays's Rebellion, did not merit a single toast in any newspaper.

There was one important problem with the toasts I read. They reflected the sentiments of only one group of Americans: wealthy white men. How did women feel about the events and people in the toasts? What about Native Americans? Or African Americans, whether free or enslaved? The toasts put public sentiment on display for only one segment of the population. It is the white viewpoint that the toasts capture, since white men were the ones celebrating at banquets and drinking healths.

The book, begun in 2018 and finally completed in the summer of 2022, went from being a study of a ritual to a historical narrative. There are several books that showcase toasts, such as Len Travers's *Celebrating the Fourth: Independence Day and the Rites of Nationalism in the Early Republic* (1997), Simon P. Newman's *Parades and the Politics of the Street: Festive Culture in the Early American Republic* (1997), and the excellent book by David Waldstreicher, *In the Midst of Perpetual Fetes: The Making of American Nationalism, 1776-1820* (1997). Each of these books mentions toasts as a part of national celebrations. *"Huzza!": Toasting a New Nation, 1760-1815* focuses only on toasts, and I tell the story of the early United States through that unique medium. This is not a book for people looking for toasts to use at specific events, although there are plenty to choose from. There are, and have been, many books containing toasts for a variety of occasions. My book is a historical narrative, the first that uses toasts as a guide through the taxation crises of the 1760s, the American Revolution, the creation of the Constitution, the first four presidential administrations, and the end of the War of 1812. Heroes and villains abound in the thousands of toasts: King George III, John Dickinson, Joseph Warren, John and John Quincy Adams, Thomas Jefferson, Alexander Hamilton, James Madison, John Jay, Aaron Burr, Benedict Arnold, Massasoit, Napoleon, Martha Washington, William Henry Harrison, and Andrew Jackson. Other people will be new to the reader.

The toasts were given in celebration. The United States was an infant nation, so many Americans had reason to gather and honor people or commemorate special events with a glass of their favorite wine or ale.

The toast, a form of literature, is a long-forgotten and unappreciated ritual that brought people together to speak with a united voice. The newspapers carried the toasts all over the country, uniting the different regions with shared ideas and values. Drinking became a patriotic act, and woe to the celebrant who refused to join in and shout "Huzza!" at the mention of Washington, or Jefferson, or the king of France. It has been a fascinating way to look at American history.

Introduction

There are countless journals, diaries, letters, and books that include public opinions about the events concerning the creation of the United States. Toasts were given at celebratory dinners and reflected the attitudes people had toward people, virtues, patriotic events, and politics. In a way, drinking toasts was the original Twitter: brief statements made about contemporary events and people to promote a specific viewpoint. Unlike tweets, however, toasts *"emanated in moments when the heart contemplated no disguise; and may be considered as the leading sentiments of those from whom they proceeded."*[1] They were given in commemoration of good fortune, although by the late 1790s they became effective propaganda weapons. They were carefully planned and edited for proper delivery; just as Twitter followers check for the latest tweets, lists of toasts were anticipated by newspaper patrons. The public was eager to find out who was or was not toasted, and newspapers issued apologies if the lists were either unavailable or incomplete.

Reading through the lists of toasts is like looking through a time portal. The changing feelings and opinions of people (mainly white property owners) living during the tumultuous events of the late eighteenth and early nineteenth centuries are displayed. Twenty-first-century readers can learn about who or what was considered worthy of praise or damnation before and during the Revolution and the Early Republic. Toasts evolved as a form of literature, going from a simple one such as "King GEORGE the Third, may his Reign be long and prosperous"[2] to "May the helm of Government ever preserve an intermediate course between the *shoals of* SLAVERY, and the rocks of LICENTIOUSNESS; the SCYLLA and CHARYBDIS of the *political channel!*"[3]

Newspapers throughout the nation printed extensive lists of toasts when describing dinners or celebratory events, being the perfect conduit for the transmission of these moments because they gave ordinary people a way to get information almost daily. Almanacs and newspapers unified the nation as an actual entity, no longer existing only in the imagination of its early citizens.[4] *"Huzza!" Toasting a New Nation, 1760–1815* explains who and what was important in the toasts given at various events and describes the popular political trends of the new United States. The toasts, found in newspapers, letters, and official correspondences, will serve as the medium.

The first chapter, *"Ridiculous Formality,"* explores the history of toasts. What does it mean to drink to the health of someone? What happens if one does *not* raise a glass? What are "bumpers"? How was the ritual perceived by the New England Puritans?

The second chapter looks at the toasts of the antebellum period: "May our Mother never oppress her dutiful children," 1763–1774. The events leading up to the Revolution are viewed from the perspective of the toasts offered, paving the way for the next chapter, "His Excellency General Washington and the Armies of America," 1775–1783. Chapter 4, "May the Wisdom of 1775 pervade the Councils of 1787!" 1784–1788, examines what was said at dinners and celebrations immediately after the Revolution, during the Confederation Period, the Philadelphia Convention of 1787, and the issues concerning ratification of the Constitution.

The use of toasts as political weapons is clear in Chapter 5, "The Rights of Man throughout the world," 1789–1793, and Chapter 6, "Hypocritical Federalism and Malignant Toryism," 1793–1796. The events of these chapters involve the competing visions people had for the nation, and the toasts reflected the conflict. So many things happened during the presidency of John Adams that his administration is divided into the seventh and eighth chapters: "John Adams … the Rock and Strength of our political Salvation…," 1797–1798, and The *"double curse"* of John Adams, 1798–1800. Chapters 9, "Thomas Jefferson, the polar star of republicanism," 1801–1804, and 10, "The embargo—a deformed bantling of democracy…," 1805–1808, cover both terms of President Jefferson, going from enthusiasm over Republican victory to anger over the Embargo Act. The events leading up to another war with Great Britain are examined through toasts in Chapter 11, "James Madison—'tho last, not least'…," 1809–1811. Chapter 12, "…War.—The offspring of an *adulterous* intercourse…," 1812–1815, covers the War of 1812, ending with the toasts of 1815.

The final two chapters are devoted to the groups who rarely gave toasts and were only occasionally mentioned in some. Chapter 13, "The American Fair—May every Mother give a WASHINGTON to her Country," 1760–1815 is about the toasts given to celebrate American women, who were prevented from the toasting ritual. Libations were offered to their many virtues by the male celebrants. Chapter 14, Red Savages and Our National Curse, 1760–1815 attempts to find out what was said about these often ignored populations. Since they typically did not participate

Introduction

in the toasting ritual, they did not figure in most toast lists. Conflicts with Native Americans were remembered with some toasts. Slavery was a topic that was rarely mentioned in toasts, unless it referred to the North American colonists being slaves of the British government or American sailors captured on the high seas and held in captivity.

I will be referring to many individual toasts throughout the book. Some are amazing works of literature, elegantly written and presented. Please keep in mind that the toasts are printed here exactly as they appeared in the newspapers and other original sources. Grammatical errors are included if they were from the source. There is apparently no rhyme or reason as to why eighteenth- and nineteenth-century printers capitalized some words or put others in italics. The quotations and toasts in this book appear exactly as they did in the original sources. Please sit down, pour yourself a glass of your favorite beverage, and enjoy learning about American history captured in very brief moments of celebration.

In the country villages it is rare that both political parties celebrate the day in the vicinity of each other. The toasts should therefore be framed so as not to give offense to the minority who may possibly unite in the celebration. It is so easy to express sentiments of patriotism on such occasions, without invidious party distinctions and odious epithets, that it is to be regretted these points are not more attended to. The harmony of social life should not be disturbed on trivial grounds. Good neighborhood and social affection is often preserved by a little attention to this, and often lost for want of such attention.

It would be well for those appointed to deliver addresses and orations, to pay some attention to the latter particular. He is the best patriot who does most to heal the divisions of his country.

"HINT TO TOAST MAKERS"
Columbian, 6-30-1815

Chapter 1

"Ridiculous Formality"

"Wass bael!"[1]
"Go fetch me a quart of sack; Put a toast in't."[2]

A party would not be the same without toasts. Giving or drinking a toast brings revelers into a community with a common sentiment. Receiving a toast is a noble experience. Offering one can be either honorable or embarrassing. The best man at any wedding might dread the toast because he must deliver a decent, funny, tender-hearted, and sentimental blessing in front of a large crowd. What if a mistake is made, and then nobody raises a glass? *Seinfeld*'s George Costanza gave what became known as the "Curse Toast" at a wedding, and people were so shocked at his language that no one drank.[3]

In 1804, an anonymous article appeared in the South Carolina *Charleston Courier*, explaining the utility of raising glasses in a toast:

> Of all the means which human creatures adopt for the purpose of amusing themselves, and flattering their hopes, their hatreds, their likings or their wishes, the drinking of toasts seems to be the weakest and most inefficacious. There are few things in which human infirmity displays itself more visibly than in men imagining that they give efficacy to a wish, or force to a prayer by compressing it into a concise epigrammatic form, and offering it up with the fumes of distempering wine.[4]

What exactly is a toast? Why is it even called that? Toasting was an important ritual to early communities. Toasts celebrated individuals, events, and national ideals. There were spontaneous at times, especially given as "volunteers," but were more often carefully planned and edited before being delivered.[5] They could be sentimental, lyrical, lewd, cynical, humorous, or rebellious.[6] The toast affirmed one's loyalties and political ideals. They enhanced the mood of the occasion, drawing people together in an egalitarian setting. Social boundaries became less clear as people raised glass after glass after glass, usually forgetting about these boundaries altogether. The order in which these tributes were drunk was determined by custom, but once the drinking started it could go on for hours. It was not uncommon for more than twenty toasts to be drunk.[7] The alcoholic haze allowed people to share feelings that they normally would not make public.[8]

Toasts were not only used as an excuse to drink more alcohol, although that was one of the reasons people participated. Strangers of various ranks were included in a "fellowship" that reinforced social unity during the American Revolution, when it was often necessary to verify one's loyalties.[9] The ritual was once referred to as "health drinking" because the health of the recipient was the aspiration. Peter Thompson, in his article "The Friendly Glass," wrote, "The toasts ran the gamut of contemporary rhetorical devices—being by turns formal, provocative, learned, repetitious, and digressive."[10] Toasts stated political beliefs, made veiled threats, lauded good, aroused anger or suspicion, advocated patriotism, labeled treason, pledged loyalty, and established both regional and national ideals.[11] Richard Hooker's article, "The American Revolution as Seen Through a Wine Glass," pointed out that the toasts publicized "every notable feeling that appeared in the years" leading up to independence:

> In these sentiments Americans were reminded of their heritage of freedom, inspired by glimpses of their glorious future, credited with the noblest characteristics, and encouraged to think and act as one people, as a nation entrusted with a sacred mission during a significant moment in history.[12]

George Washington loved to raise his own glass of madeira at dinner. John Adams, brought up in a much more rigid society, appreciated and understood the importance of printing lists of toasts in the struggle against British imperial authority.[13] Adams would also be the subject of many toasts, but they would be far different from those for Washington.

One of the most popular early collections of toasts, J. Roach's 1793 *The Royal Toast Master*, begins with a description of the purpose of toasts:

> A Toast or Sentiment very frequently excites good humour and revives languid conversation; often does it when properly adapted and applied, cool the heat of resentment, and blunt the edge of animosity. A well-applied Toast is acknowledged, universally, to sooth the flame of acrimony, when season and reason oft used their efforts to no purpose.[14]

The seriousness of a celebration was often measured by the number of toasts given.[15] At least fifteen toasts were planned, and those who could still raise their glasses frequently offered "volunteers."[16] Since the toasts were spoken, they relayed messages and symbols across a wide spectrum of participants. Both the literate and illiterate could understand what was being said.[17] Most important, toasts brought all levels of society together in a symbolic acceptance or denigration of a person or an abstract value.[18]

1. "Ridiculous Formality"

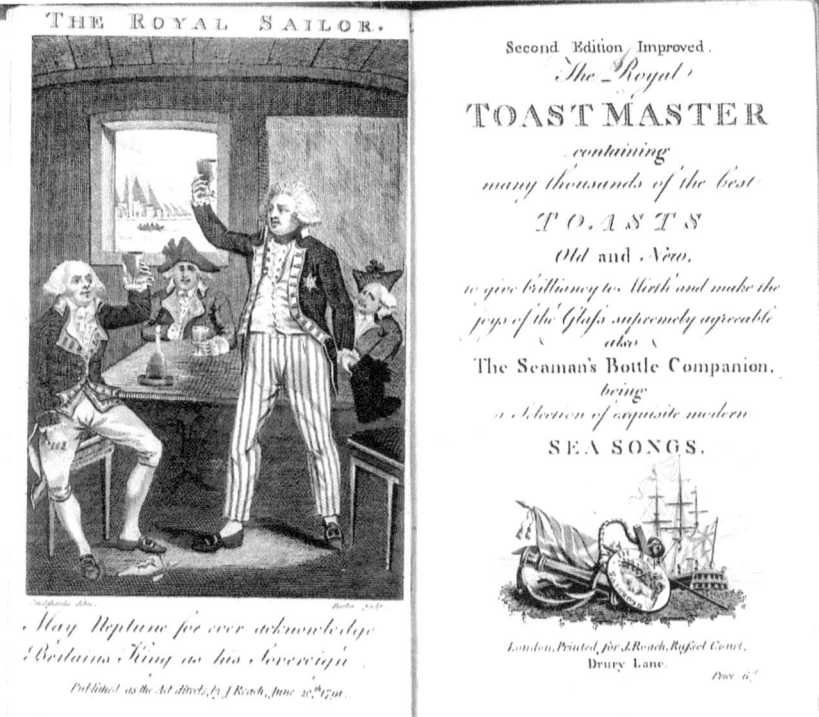

"The Royal Sailor." Four naval officers raise their glasses to each other on the inside cover of *The Royal Toast Master,* published in London in 1791. Books such as this were very popular in Great Britain and the United States, offering many toasts for various occasions (Library of Congress).

The heroes of America received praise and honors, while others were consigned to slavery, hunger, disappointment, contempt, misery, infamy, destruction, and "due punishment."[19]

Drinking to another's health once permeated the worlds of the Greeks and the Romans. Each culture grasped the social importance of the toasting ritual. The giving of toasts was an opportunity for men to compete in the arts of oratory and improvisation. Leading the crowd in a good toast became a badge of honor.[20] The Greeks proposed toasts to fallen comrades, war, peace, leaders, women, and their own health.[21] The main figures in their toasts were Hermes, the Graces, and Zeus.[22] Homer writes of Odysseus drinking to the health of Achilles in *The Iliad.* Warriors drank toasts to the gods before going into battle, no doubt hoping that this would ensure their success. Greek libations were offered in religious rituals. The person offering the toast stood up and spoke, prompting the audience to likewise stand. The person giving the toast to someone present had to look that person directly in the eye, and then the person honored had to acknowledge the toast with a nod or a bow. After that, everyone took a sip of their drink. Cups and glasses were then "clinked" to ward off evil spirits.[23]

The Romans adopted the ritual from the Greeks and made it their own. The Roman Senate decreed that all men should drink to the health of Emperor Augustus at every meal, and later Fabius Maximus insisted that no Romans could drink without first drinking to his own health.[24] Edward Gibbons, in his 1776 epic *The Decline and Fall of the Roman Empire*, describes a toast once offered to Attila the Hun:

> The Romans, both of the East and of the West, were twice invited to the banquets, where Attila feasted with the princes and nobles of Scythia. Maximin and his colleagues were stopped on the threshold, till they made a devout libation to the health and prosperity to the king of the Huns; and were conducted, after this ceremony, to their respective seats in a spacious hall.[25]

The English custom of health-drinking was a holdover from the Roman occupation of Britannia. The first recorded instance of a toast given in Britain was in 450 by King Vortigern to his Saxon allies: "*Wass bael!*," translated as "Be healthy!"[26] After the Danish invasion of Britain in the tenth century, drinking to someone's health was necessary to protect the drinker, as there was a fear that a Dane would cut the throat of a Briton as he tossed his head back to drink. Pledging the health of the drinker was a promise to prevent such a threat.[27] It was also a good way to prove that a drink shared among everyone was safe for consumption.[28] Putting a piece of spiced bread or charred toast into the drinking vessel was something that the English started doing by the beginning of the seventeenth century. It is possible that the Romans had done this to reduce the acidity of their wine. Perhaps the morsel improved the flavor of the drink, or it might have been included as a token nourishment.[29] Whatever the reason, the drinking cup or bowl was passed around for everyone to take a sip until it was returned to the host, who then ate the bread.[30] By the 1600s, toasting in England was immensely popular. Celebrants drank excessively by this time, drinking healths to each other and to absent friends. Men in Scotland waited for the women to leave the party before they started to drink their toasts.[31]

The North American British colonies, a society saturated with alcohol, easily kept the ale flowing and the glasses clinking. Glasses filled up to the brim were referred to as "bumpers," since the glass appeared to swell at the top.[32] Almost all occasions and social events were opportunities to drink. Drinking pervaded American life and crossed all social lines.[33] Benjamin Franklin praised wine when he wrote to his friend André

Morellet in France: "Behold the rain which descends from heaven upon our vineyards, and which incorporates itself with the grapes to be changed into wine; a constant proof that God loves us, and loves to see us happy!"[34]

Pledging the health of everyone in attendance at parties and feasts became compulsory.[35] Some people did not care for the practice and saw health drinking as a danger to society. Louis XIV of France outlawed the practice when he saw its effect upon the people.[36] William Penn's first tavern in Pennsylvania forbade toasting because the Quaker religion equated toasts with taking oaths, which was blasphemous.[37] Puritan New England was even stricter:

> Drinking and discussing politics *were* disruptive to the social order—and made even more dangerous by groups trying to impress one another with both orator and drinking prowess. The war on toasts and efforts to keep bawdy drinking songs out of taverns was part of an attempt to redefine drinking into two categories—healthful drinking and drunken fits.[38]

The Puritan minister Increase Mather claimed that "healthing" obliged men to drink to excess, while Massachusetts Bay Colony governor John Winthrop viewed health drinking as a danger that was tearing the colony apart.[39] A reformation of personal and public behavior would succeed, the Puritan ministers believed, if taverns were strictly controlled and all adhered to temperance.[40] The giving of healths, considered a "useless ceremony," was banned between 1639 and 1645 in Massachusetts Bay Colony in an effort to reform behavior, speech, and attitude.[41] Puritan leaders in the 1680s were concerned about excessive drinking impairing the mental faculties of their congregants and promoting a dangerous sense of camaraderie that blurred the divisions between social classes.[42] Over time, toasting became more of a refined, civilized, and intellectual endeavor. One person writing to the *New York Chronicle* in July 1769 elaborated on his problem with the use of alcoholic drink with toasts:

> To the PRINTERS.
> OF all the vices which debase mankind, Drunkenness is the meanest, the most ridiculous, and one of the most pernicious. Its too general influence is not a little extended, by the unmeaning custom of drinking healths. Many a sober inclined man is forced into excesses he dreads and detests, by fear of offending the company, or appearing wanting to the sentiment the toast conveys. For who can decline drinking to this Gentlman's best beloved, or that friend's fire-side? Who shall refuse the King, in a bumper? Or who more bold will hazard being kicked out of company, if a band of Patriots, take it in their heads, to drink 45 rounds to Wilkes and Liberty!
> If drinking toasts would procure the completion of the wishes they express, I would stand foremost of the frantic train. I would sacrifice my constitution to the good of my country, and my reason to the happiness of my friends.

The setting sun should see me staggering, under the prosperity of poor Old England and the Colonies, and the rising morn, find me wallowing in the over flowing bliss of the woman I love; but, alas! there is not the most distant connection between the draught and the wish; and hogsheads swallowed to health and prosperity, will not keep off sickness, or ruin a moment.

Yet ridiculous as is the custom of toasting in itself, pernicious, as it is a promoter of Drunkenness; these are not my only pleas against it; it introduces that worst of fiends, the spirit of party, even to our repasts. When the wisest, elevated by wine, and jovial converse, are a little off their guard, and the expanded breast is but too ready to kindle a political sentiment, not universally resisted, may change the festive harmony to riotous anger productive of the worst consequence.

Another (and not the least frequent) kind of toasts, are expressly and professedly calculated to promote the true interests of what (to give it the softest name) we will call pleasure; yet even this end is not answered, for the true taste of pleasure, is as averse to grossness of expression, as Chastity herself. Obscene toasts, therefore, only serve to disgust the sensible, to disconcert the modest, and to expose the depravity of taste as well as manners, of the few how are brutes enough to relish them.[43]

A new way of writing and delivering toasts was evident by the 1760s. Although most of the toasts up until then had been impromptu, the planning, editing, and revising of toasts was necessary to ensure maximum publicity and unity among the revelers.[44] The toasts were prepared in advance and presented to a toastmaster. Toasting expert Paul Dickson, author of *Toasts: Over 1,500 of the Best Toasts, Sentiments, Blessings, and Graces*, enumerated several guidelines to keep in mind when toasting: keep the toast short, be sincere, stand up when giving the toast, always alert the guests to join in, clink your class before drinking, never use the toast to complain or vent emotions, never refuse to participate in a toast or exclude someone from doing so, and respond appropriately to being honored with a toast.[45]

The gathering of people at civic feasts was an important component of popular culture, allowing for everyone present to make their sentiments known.[46] If there was one thing that the British colonists in North America liked to do, it was to get together to celebrate. They partied for Pope's Day and the birthdays of the King and Queen. Anniversary Day was a special festival for the ministers before the opening of the Massachusetts General Court. Forefathers' Day recognized the landing of the Pilgrims at Plymouth.[47] Colonists got together for merchants' dinners, charitable society dinners, St. Patrick's Day dinners, Masonic dinners, artillery election dinners, dinners on board vessels of war and commerce, and dinners observing the close of the school year.[48] Military celebrations became the most important political festivities displaying Revolutionary War values.[49]

1. "Ridiculous Formality"

Impressive ceremonies frequently accompanied toasts: the firing of cannons, volleys from small arms, music and cheering.[50] It was common practice to fire off a shot for each toast, and newspapers included how many were given. The revelry ended in tragedy in Savannah, Georgia, in 1806:

> A melancholy accident happened while celebrating the 4th of July in this place. About five o'clock in the afternoon, whilst firing to one of the toasts, Mr. Jacob Fox, one of the corps, acting at the time as gunner to the field piece, neglected to spunge properly, and left some wad on fire in the piece, putting in the cartridge it caught about half way the unextinguished wad, whilst he was cramming it home, and went off, the spunge carrying off one arm and one hand, and broke the remaining arm in three places. Young Master Robert Greer was passing very imprudently, about ten steps in front of the field piece at the time; the spunge staff took him on the left side and came out in front, carrying away with it his heart and some of his entrails! He fell and expired without a groan![51]

Participating in the celebrations enabled people to put the ideas and values of the nation into practice.[52] At the very least, the ceremonies allowed for large groups of people to learn, invent, and practice a common language that could be transformed later for other civic and political uses.[53] In early colonial celebrations, the message of a shared "'legacy of freedom'" reverberated among the people and affirmed their dignity and political empowerment.[54]

The message conveyed in each toast needed to be reinforced by the audience. Toasts defined who "the people" were and what they believe in.[55] Remaining silent during a toast was more than just a simple faux pas. Sharing in a toast bound the drinker to a group, so not acknowledging it caused conflict and could lead to fights.[56] Refusing a toast in a tavern also led to suspicion.[57] The Rev. Richard Valpy French published *The History of Toasting, or Drinking of Healths in England* in London in 1881, explaining the social violation of refusing a toast: "To take a glass of wine during dinner without previously dedicating it to the health of some one, was a breach of etiquette that few would care to be found guilty of, and anyone so offending would have been thought either eccentric or exclusive."[58]

To illustrate the danger inherent in proposing "controversial" toasts, two men were tarred and feathered in antebellum Charleston, South Carolina, because their toasts called for the damnation of the local committee of correspondence.[59] Later, one Pennsylvania soldier at the end of the war was charged with mutiny because he spoke disrespectfully of General Washington and the Congress, then drank to the health of King George III. He received 100 lashes and was drummed "out of the Army with a halter around his Neck."[60] Benjamin Rush described in a letter to John Adams a certain Dr. Zubly, who turned his glass upside down and refused to drink to a toast to the "'Commonwealth of America.'"[61]

Occasionally people were caught in an awkward situation due to a toast. During the Revolution, the HMS *Experiment* captured the American privateer *General Arnold* after a brief firefight in June 1779. The commander of the *Experiment*, Sir James Wallace, was so impressed by the bravery of the *General Arnold*'s captain, Moses Brown, that he invited the American into his cabin for drinks. The toasting ritual turned the convivial atmosphere into something inimical:

> Conversation turned to the larger conflict. Wallace proposed a toast to "George the Third, and the Royal Family!" Although taken aback, Brown nevertheless didn't protest and took a draft of the wine. When Wallace invited Brown to deliver a toast of his own, the proud American did not hesitate: to "George Washington, the Commander-in-Chief of the American forces!" What kind of toast Wallace expected Brown to utter is not clear, but his he perceived to be an act of defiance. Incensed, Wallace lowered his glass and said, "Do you mean to insult me, sir, in my own ship, by proposing the name of that arch-rebel?" "No," replied Brown, "if there was any insult, it was by your giving [a toast to] George the Third, which, however, I did not hesitate to drink, though you must have known it could not have been agreeable to me, who at this moment am a guest, though a prisoner." To his credit, Wallace realized that Brown was right and apologized. He then drank to General Washington, however bitterly.[62]

The use of the toast as a method of patriotic upmanship was well understood by many Americans. During the War of 1812, a British commanding officer invited an American officer, who had crossed over to British lines under a flag of truce, to dinner. The British officer "being called upon for a toast, gave Mr. Madison, 'dead or alive,' which the Yankee drank without appearing to notice. When it came to the American's turn to give a toast, he gave the Prince Regent, 'drunk or sober...'" The British officer said that the toast was an insult. "'No sir,' answered the American very coolly, 'it is only a reply to one.'"[63]

Quarrels often played out in the media over what was said in toasts. If a toast was considered slanderous, then the gloves came off and people were ready to fight. In 1805, the *Boston Chronicle* printed one such toast, and someone wrote to the *Centinel* about how "*blasphemous and wicked*" it was. The toast was in such poor taste that the writer would not even repeat it:

> —and the cause the Editor is anxious to support,—to aver, in the most solemn manner,—that every word of the charge or insinuation, or his having uttered the toast, is FALSE; and without the least foundation in truth for its support:— That so blasphemous a thought never entered his mind, much less issued from his mouth or pen—nor had he the most distant recollection of ever hearing that so infamous a toast had ever been given:—And he has taken and will undeviatingly pursue, measures to bring the libellers before a tribunal proper to try the truth or falsehood of the monstrous accusation.[64]

It was improper to propose a toast that might put someone on the spot and tempt him to refuse to participate.[65] Perhaps the most famous example of this occurred at an 1830 celebration for Thomas Jefferson's birthday. President Andrew Jackson was angry over South Carolina's threats to nullify federal law. He looked at his vice president, John C. Calhoun of South Carolina, raised his glass, and said, "Our Federal Union. It must be preserved." Calhoun responded with a toast of his own: "The Union—next to our liberty the most dear. May we all remember that it can only be preserved by respecting the rights of the states and distributing equally the benefit and burden of the Union."[66]

Toasts by the late eighteenth century took on a political form since almost all parades, feasts, and festivals were part of the new American popular political culture.[67] Toasts spread revolutionary ideology and promoted national and local pride.[68] There were three sorts of pledges given in toasts. The first was of faithfulness to the present body and its concerns: toasts to the group and to its associated luminaries. Second, toasts to the civil authority, such as the government, demonstrated the attachment to the larger body of the state or nation. Finally, toasts made to timely and topical abstractions (such as agriculture, trade, the fisheries, manufacturing, etc.) promised adherence to certain perceptions and ideals.[69]

The acceptance of the toast as a political platform was eloquently stated by the unknown writer "Z" in the New York newspaper *Balance* in 1801, who described the customs associated with drinking, and how women were toasted. "Z" concluded:

> I am not able to say at what period the practice of drinking toasts began to be used as an expression of *political sentiments*. But however, or whenever it commenced, the practice is now become general in our country; and it is usual, particularly on the anniversary of our national independence, to drink a number of toasts, equal to the whole number of the confederated States. This custom, though well enough in itself, is liable, like everything else, to abuses. When such toasts are merely *sentimental*, or are only expressive of approbation of particular men and measures, no mischief can arise from them; but whenever they are in such a sense *personal*, as either expressly or implicitly to question the integrity and thereby wound the feelings and the characters of people of the opposite political sentiments, they serve but to inflame rancour, which it should be the endeavor of every good man to assuage. And it is sincerely hoped, that in the public toasts on the approaching anniversary all insulting and irritating personalities may be carefully avoided.[70]

Despite the popularity of the ritual, some still did not seem to comprehend the value of toasts. Abigail Adams believed that observing the custom was too much for her. She wrote to her son John Quincy in 1788 that the ritual was a type of enslavement:

Ridiculous formality. Then there must be, every two minutes, Mam will you do me the Favour to drink a Glass of Wine with me, which obliges some to say, with pleasure, when in reallity they never drink any thing but Water and had rather be excused. And then the additional formality of drinking Healths and toasts which above all things I detest, and will not now nor henceforward for evermore do it. In short once cannot consult their ease and pleasure but must be enslaved with fashion and customs.[71]

The following anti-toast rant appeared in the *Daily Advertiser* in August of the same year:

HEALTHS AND TOASTS.
"*They order the matter better in France*; each one drinks when he pleases, without diverting the attention of his companions, or obliging any to join when they are not athirst"—"They order the matter better,"—as the rules of hospitality not only excuses the patron from intoxicating his guests, but the practice is viewed as highly shameful. It is a maxim in the world, that if a man drinks in private he is a sot.—In France every man at the table is equally free as if he was in his own chamber—A Frenchman therefore feels his national honor wounded when he sees his countrymen in foreign parts inebriated in circles of conviality? at home he would spurn him from his room as a brute.

Why then don't we order the matter as well in America? For what custom is more ludicrous? What more debasing than our *unmeaning Healths and Toasts?*—At our entertainments 'tis an unhappiness for a man to be distinguished in life; at best he is but the puppet of the dinner, and nods at the deceitful wishes of folly—in the midst of eating he experiences the truth of that saying, "*there is many a slip between a knife and the lip.*" If unhaply he should be an epicure, what efforts must he make when saluted, to gorge the mouthful and cascade his thanks—At the close of the feast, when toasts upon toasts are given, how changed are the guests; their eyes projected, their tongues swollen, and their countenances reddened with intemperance.—'Tis the palace of folly and the lazar house of disease.—Strange that we should dare a revolution in our government, deliberate in our reform in our police and have not the courage to throw off any British shackles of ancestral manners.[72]

One French visitor to the new United States, the Marquis de Chastellux, had plenty to say in his observations of the toasting ritual, describing it as "'a sort of refrain punctuating the conversation, as a reminder that each individual is part of the company and that the whole forms but one society.'"[73] He found the practice to be both "'absurd and truly barbarous,'" complaining that after hearing one toast after another, a man "'could die of thirst, whilst he is obliged to inquire the names, or catch the eye of five and twenty persons' before taking the quenching gulp."[74] Another observer, Mathew Carey, referred to the custom of filling the glass up to the top, known as a "bumper toast," as "'savage and barbarous … worthy of Creeks and Cherokees.'" People unable to finish their glass had to withstand the ridicule of the crowd.[75] The usual number of toasts that followed the dinner started off at thirteen to represent the original number of states. That number increased as new states entered the union, contributing to the "'hilarity'" often observed in descriptions of patriotic events.[76]

The Marquis de Chastellux appreciated how toasting brought members of a group together. He described Washington dining with the officers considered to be his "family" at Morristown, New Jersey, in 1780:

> I accommodate myself very well to the English mode of *toasting* [and] I observed that there was more solemnity in the toasts at dinner: there were several ceremonious ones; the others were suggested by the General, and given out by his aides-de-camp, who performed the honors of the table at dinner.... The toasts in the evening were given by Colonel Hamilton, without order or ceremony.[77]

The obvious setting to witness people heartily drinking toasts was the local tavern. Taverns provided liquor and were often the only places where travelers could get a bite to eat and a bed to sleep in.[78] Taverns were used by informal clubs, committees, public councils, and acted as a headquarters on muster days.[79] Visitors included rich male citizens, clerks, artisans, master craftsmen, laborers, and occasionally wives and sweethearts.[80] People came together to conduct business, discuss local and national events, see friends, read newspapers, and drink. Free white men in eighteenth-century America went to the taverns and coffeehouses to exchange views and discuss politics, expressing their shared identity.[81] Drink helped with the communication between officials and their constituents, making taverns part of the growing political tradition in local government.[82]

Ironically, colonial taverns licensed by the Crown became the centers for seditious activities.[83] Educated and uneducated men discussed the ideas that fueled resistance to British policies.[84] Samuel Adams felt completely at home in a tavern, but his distant cousin John saw them as destabilizing forces. John's legacy, however, would be defined by the revolutionary forces unleashed in taverns.[85] Since toasts galvanized public curiosity, any that were given at a formal occasion or political event in the tavern were recorded and given to newspapers for publication.

During the summer of 1798, when the XYZ Affair turned many Americans against the French, someone writing as "NESTOR" explained the purpose of political toasts, allowing him to question toasts made to Thomas Jefferson. However, the beginning of NESTOR's editorial is an important description for such toasts:

> WE derive the custom of drinking *healths* and *toasts*, at dinners in *private* families, and on *public* occasions, from our *British* ancestors. The practice of drinking *healths*, was ancient in England, and has prevailed with the addition

of giving *toasts*, in private houses, and in public assemblies for some centuries. I approve the fashion in public as well as in private, and wish it to be continued; but like other good customs, it is sometimes abused by mistaking *its subject and design*. The *real* intention of giving *toasts* in America, at *public dinners*, which are given to celebrate great events, or to shew respect to illustrious characters, is to express the POLITICAL opinions of the company, to declare their approbation or disapprobation of *particular* acts or conduct of their legislature, executive, heads of department, public ministers, or other great officers of government. In *general*, the opinion of the people at large, may be collected from the sentiments delivered at respectable meetings of citizens on great occasions; it is not a *certain*, but it is a strong evidence of their impressions of public men and public measures. It is the duty of *public* characters, to *respect* the sentiments of their fellow citizens, and experience proves, that *good* men are often encouraged to persevere in patriotic conduct, and *bad* men are sometimes deterred from committing actions, by the public approbation or censure. Public toasts are considered, in some measure, as a *mask of honor*, or a *stamp of infamy*; and frequently operates as a *beacon* to direct the opinion, and the suffrages of the people.[86]

Newspapers were crucial in getting the toasts to the public. Periodicals were the tools of a free society. Samuel Adams once wrote that "'There is nothing so *fretting* and *vexatious*, nothing so justly TERRIBLE to tyrants, and their tools and abettors, as a FREE PRESS.'"[87] People who did not attend ceremonies could still absorb the patriotic messages in the newspapers.[88] Simon Newman, in his book *Parades and the Politics of the Street*, explains how the printed toasts needed to reach a wider audience by the time of the Revolution:

> Relatively few of the toasts of the colonial era traveled farther than the rooms in which they were offered. During the revolutionary and early national years however, newspapers played a vital role in broadcasting many thousands of the toasts drunk at civic feasts and celebrations, thereby establishing them as a vital part of eighteenth-century political discourse. These "sentiments" were of considerable significance not only to those who drank them but also to others who then read them: one contemporary observed that these toasts "may justly be denominated the criterions of sentiment and truth," while another acknowledged that toasts were "indications of the public sentiment."[89]

The printed word carried its own authority, and the influence of a public address more than doubled when it was printed in a newspaper.[90] Newspapers joined sermons, monuments, parades, and songs in giving meaning to the violence of the Revolution, documenting the shared sacrifices of citizens.[91] While the celebrations were frequently local affairs, the printing of toasts in newspapers turned them into national events for the purpose of spreading specific viewpoints.[92] When they were printed, they were taken seriously enough to warrant follow-ups, rebuttals, reviews, and

1. "Ridiculous Formality"   21

commentaries.[93] The following passage came from an article titled "THE UTILITY OF NEWSPAPERS," printed in a London newspaper in 1791:

> In fine every passion is put in motion by a Newspaper—It is a bill of fare, containing all the luxuries, as well as the necessaries of life. Politics, for instance, have of late been the roast beef of the times—Essays the plumb pudding, and Poetry the fritters, confections, custards, and all the &c. of the table, usually denominated trifles—yet the four winds are not liable to more mutability than the vehicles of those entertainments;—for instance, on Monday it is whispered, on Tuesday it is rumoured, on Wednesday it is conjectured, on Thursday it is probable, on Friday it is positively asserted, and on Saturday it is premature!—But notwithstanding this, some how or other all are eventually pleased; for as the affections of all are divided among Wit Anecdote, Poetry, the prices of Stocks, the arrival of Ships, &c. a Newspaper is a repository where every one has his hobby-horse; without these, Coffee-houses, &c. would be nearly depopulated, and the country villages, the Curate, the Exciseman, and many others, lose the Golden opportunities of appearing as wise as OLD QUIDNUNC.[94]

The number of newspapers increased nationwide after the Revolution. Over forty papers served three million colonists at the start of the Revolution, and that number rose to one hundred by the early 1790s, doubling to more than two hundred by 1800. The editors of these many papers included descriptions of festivals, celebrations, and parades from all over the young nation.[95] And of course, they printed lists of toasts. Groups and organizations published toasts in newspapers to proclaim their loyalties, celebrate their deceased and living heroes, and "advertise aims while threatening enemies."[96] Readers offered their own commentaries about toasts given at some of these events. One Massachusetts newspaper spent several weeks attacking the political toasts offered at one event, devoting each consecutive issue to a single toast. During the highly charged political tensions of the 1790s, toast lists were used as political party platforms, stressing what ideals and figures were considered worthy of honor, effectively demonstrating who or what was not valued. The omissions were just as important.[97]

It was important that editors printed the toasts correctly because a great deal of work went into preparing them. They were written by committees and then edited. The *Petersburg Intelligencer* of Virginia explained the simple process at the Festival of Freedom: "The committee of toasts reported that they had performed their duty; which report was taken into consideration, and after several amendments, adopted by the meeting."[98] If something was noticed in the toasts that could cause offense, the editor had to take responsibility for printing it. The editor of the Vermont newspaper *Farmer's Library* had to make an apology for not overseeing the way the toasts were laid out by one of his workers:

To the Committee appointed to draught Toasts, to be drank on Christmas eve, at Burlington:

Gentlemen,

I ACKNOWLEDGE the receipt of a letter from one of the Members of your Committee, together with a friendly reprimand for alterations made in your toasts.—Being necessarily absent on a journey, I left my business in the care of a young workman, who, in order to crowd the toasts into that paper and oblige those concerned, undesigningly curtailed some of the most lengthy, as he informed me on my return, but he having mislaid the original, I never had the perusal of it:—I acknowledge myself culpable on this occasion, and am exceedingly sorry to merit the displeasure of any of my customers; should the committee conceive the alterations consequential, I would beg they might redraught and transmit them, by the post to me, and if possible I will do them justice.

I am Gentlemen your humber servent, the EDITOR.[99]

Before the Revolution, there was a common template for the giving of toasts. The first toasts affirmed the colonists' allegiance to the King, the Queen, and members of the royal family. The colonists wanted their toasts to show that they were loyal subjects. Then toasts were given to members of Parliament in gratitude or praise for whatever actions they took to benefit the colonies. Finally, there were "formulaic" toasts to the prosperity of the colonies and the British empire: "May the interest of Great Britain and her Colonies be always United."[100] Soon, however, the toasts given at the end of the 1760s and the beginning of the 1770s would be deemed disloyal and treasonous by royal officials. Members of the Sons of Liberty, tax evaders, and smugglers would gain respectability in the taverns of colonial America, and the King would no longer be praised first, if at all.

Toasts were used to celebrate events and people, a tradition that began in the worlds of ancient Greece and Rome and was continued by the English, eventually making its way to the British colonies of North America. The giving of toasts became an important ritual that was prepared with care because making the wrong toast or not drinking to a toast could be socially problematic. Some people had their political sentiments publicly "announced" if they did or did not drink to a toast. Before and during the American Revolution, toasts were effectively used to spread propaganda, and newspapers became a vital method of disseminating national ideals throughout the new United States.

Chapter 2

"May our Mother never oppress her dutiful children,"[1] 1763–1774

> "Those illustrious personages, and friends to Liberty, who distinguished themselves in obtaining a repeal of the Stamp Act, on constitutional principles."[2]
>
> "May the last Agreement of the Boston Merchants, respecting Non-importation of British Goods become general throughout America."[3]
>
> "May the persecuting Genius of Liberty find a lasting Asylum in America."[4]

Loyalty to the King was the theme of toasts given during the years preceding the American Revolution. The most important civic holidays at the start of the 1760s were King George III's birthday in June and the anniversary of his coronation in September.[5] The conservative leaders of colonial communities, who led the parades and gave the toasts, did their best to make sure that the festivities were orderly and tasteful.[6] However, newspapers were spreading scandalous and seditious toasts to a very receptive audience by 1774.

A crowd of over 200 revelers gathered in Boston's Faneuil Hall on August 15, 1763, to applaud the proclamation of peace at the conclusion of the French and Indian War. Their toasts were like many others given throughout the colonies:

> The King.—The Queen, Prince of Wales, and Royal Family.—His Majesty's Ministers of State.—The Duke of Bedford, and all other his Majesty's Ministers who assisted in conducting and concluding the glorious Peace.—Prosperity to the Province.—His Majesty's Forces by Sea and Land, and in the Memory of their Country in the late War.—May the Peace be lasting.—May Internal Peace prevail thro'out His Majesty's Dominions.—Prosperity to the British Empire in North-America, and may it be well Peopled to its utmost Bounds.[7]

The King always received the first toast. This was ironic, for George III wrote a letter to his sons in May 1778 referring to the "'bad custom of toasting.'"[8] His family was next, then his ministers. The colonists were often quite specific with these healths, honoring only those individuals whose actions had benefited the colonies during the war. The theme of the celebrations was British loyalty and pride. The French were no longer a threat or an obstacle to westward expansion, and the might of the Empire was unquestioned.

These loving sentiments changed in 1765 when the British Parliament, plagued by the debt incurred to win the war, unwisely decided to tax the colonists directly to raise revenue. To most people in Great Britain, this was not an unreasonable expectation. The victory over the French meant security for the colonies. The tax burden on people living in Britain was heavier, so the colonists had very little to complain about. On March 22, 1765, Parliament enacted the Stamp Act. All paper goods, such as playing cards, documents, and newspapers, had a duty that was to be paid upon purchase. The item would then receive a "stamp." Even Benjamin Franklin, working in London, did not think the tax was excessive, but he was out of touch with the feelings of the colonists. They strongly resented being taxed by a government so far away. Their anger over this violation of their liberties led to violent demonstrations. A new political organization in Boston, the Sons of Liberty, led by the brilliant organizer Samuel Adams, took charge of the demonstrations against the Stamp Act.

King George III engraving by William Pether in 1762; printed in London by H. Parker and E. Bakewell. George III, the king of Great Britain, was always the first person toasted in the colonies before the American Revolution: "The KING, and many happy Days to him" (Toast #1, *Pennsylvania Gazette*, 6-12-1766) (Library of Congress).

2. "May our Mother never oppress her children," 1763–1774

On August 14, 1765, an effigy of Boston's tax agent, Andrew Oliver, was hung from a tree on Boston Common.[9] August 14 became a new annual holiday in Massachusetts, and now fourteen toasts were given at most banquets. On the first anniversary of the riot, the fourteenth toast drunk at a dinner at Liberty Hall in Boston was "May the everlasting Remembrance of the 14th of August, serve to revive the dying Sparks of Liberty, whenever America shall be in danger of Slavery."[10]

Toasts were used to directly attack the hated law. People drank to "Liberty, Property, but no Stamp Duty," and hoped "That America might always be free; and the promoters of the stamp duty be slaves—."[11] On March 7, 1766, a militia company in New Jersey hosted a dinner and offered toasts that called for "Confusion and Disappointment to the Promoters of the Stamp-Act" and "Horror and Conviction to the Authors of it."[12]

Economic pressure and colonial intimidation led to the repeal of the Stamp Act on March 18, 1766, which became another day of celebration. Those in Parliament who supported the colonists and worked hard to get the hated tax repealed were toasted:

> *May the British* House of Lords *ever support the just Prerogative of the Crown without suffering the least Infringement on the Liberty of the Subjects.*[13]
>
> May the kind Protector of Great-Britain continue to produce Love and Gratitude in the Colonies; May the Loyalty of Americans ever be the Measure of their Happiness.[14]
>
> May the Manufactures of Great-Britain, the Population of the Colonies, and the Cultivation of their Lands, for ever increase, to the mutual Interest of both.[15]

The Boston Fire Club offered fourteen toasts at a celebration in August, acknowledging the efforts made by other colonies in the fight against the Stamp Act:

> The noble VIRGINIANS, who first asserted their RIGHTS with *decent Firmness.*
>
> The *generous and public-spirited* CAROLINIANS, who chose rather to share the Fate of AMERICA, than accept a *partial Exemption.*[16]

The euphoria over the repeal of the Stamp Act would be temporary. Charles Townshend, Chancellor of the Exchequer in 1766, pushed a series of revenue laws through Parliament that imposed duties on manufactured goods sold to the colonies, such as glass, lead, and paper. These laws have become known as the Townshend Acts.[17] The colonists were now crying out that they were being treated like "slaves." At one August 14 anniversary celebration in Boston in 1767, revelers at Liberty Hall raised their glasses to "that Day which sees America submit to Slavery, be the last of her existence."[18] However, even the yoke of British slavery did not stifle their enthusiasm at being British. In fact, it was true to form for all Britons to object to "tax" slavery: "May an Abhorrence of Slavery still and ever remain the best Criterion of a true British Subject."[19]

Between 1767 and 1768, John Dickinson of Pennsylvania wrote a series of essays titled *Letters from a Farmer in Pennsylvania to Inhabitants of the British Colonies*, using them to elaborate on the violation of British law that Parliament was committing by taxing the colonists. Parliament, according to Dickinson, could only regulate trade.[20] Dickinson became a hero and was toasted throughout the colonies as "The Farmer of Pennsylvania." Toasts were still given first to the King, the Queen, and the royal family, but the Townshend legislation and the anger it aroused was changing sentiments.

Following the example set by Dickinson, Samuel Adams and attorney James Otis drafted the Circular Letter, which was approved by the Massachusetts General Court in February 1768 and then circulated throughout the colonies. The Letter repeated the claims that direct taxation by Parliament was unconstitutional. Resistance to taxation was proposed. The Massachusetts House of Representatives was pressured to rescind the Letter, but ninety-two members refused.[21] Although James Otis and John Dickinson received most of the toasts offered at celebrations, the "Ninety-Two Anti-Rescinders" were now included. They were "'The Glorious Ninety-Two, who defended the Right of America, uninfluenced by the Mandates of a Minister, and undaunted by the Threats of a Governor.'"[22]

Ninety-two was not the only celebrated numeral. By the mid–1760s, many toast lists either included a toast to the number forty-five or there were forty-five toasts in all. This number referred to the forty-fifth issue of the London publication *North Britain*, written by an influential member of Parliament, John Wilkes. Wilkes supported the liberties of all Englishmen, including the colonists, and wrote that the recent tax legislation targeting the colonies violated basic British rights. Wilkes received toasts on nearly every possible occasion in the colonies between 1768 and 1771, becoming a living symbol of resistance.[23] The Boston Sons of Liberty wrote to Wilkes and praised his continued support: "Your health your friends and cause were the toasts of the evening. We congratulated ourselves on our well plac'd confidence, and presumed much on the exertions of such a Martyr to universal Liberty."[24] Toasts to Wilkes and other supporters of colonial rights, such as Edmund Burke and William Pitt, no doubt bolstered American morale. On the third anniversary of the Stamp Act protests, Bostonians offered forty-five toasts, including Wilkes and Pitt, the "'glorious NINETY-TWO,'" and "'The Sons of Liberty throughout the World.'" It was clear many wanted the British government to remember the limitations of its power: "'Prosperity and Perpetuity to the *British Empire*, on Constitutional Principles!'"[25]

The toasts did not cross over into the realm of treasonous behavior. Even the most radical of the Sons of Liberty did not yet consider independence from Great Britain. Instead, they wanted to be treated as true British subjects. The *Connecticut Gazette* printed the following toasts on July 29, 1768:

> May the present Union of the Colonies ever subsist.
> May the Grumbletonian Sons of Slavery ever be disappointed in their Designs against our happy Constitution.
> Magna Charta preserv'd inviolable to the latest Generation.[26]

Diners in Roxbury, Massachusetts, went back even further to remind each other of Britain's ancient principles: "*Spartan, Roman, British Virtue, and Christian Graces conjoined.*"[27]

Paschal Paoli, the Corsican patriot who had been fighting for the island's independence since 1764, received many colonial toasts by the end of the 1760s. He represented the colonists' own struggle for liberty in his fight against France.[28] Toasts praising Paoli included the following: "Success to General Paoli, and the brave Corsicans" and "Paschal Paoli and his brave Corsicans—May they never want the support of the Friends of Liberty."[29] Paoli's birthday was celebrated by a "Number of Gentlemen" in Philadelphia in 1769, and some of their toasts mirrored colonial sentiments regarding unfair British policies:

> May the Corsican Virtues prevail over French policy.
> The Spirit of Paoli to every American.
> May the Attempts of France upon Corsica meet with the same Fate of those of Persia upon Greece—repulsed with Shame.[30]

The struggles for liberty in other parts of the world were closely watched by the colonists. The situation in Ireland was embraced as a cause célèbre by most colonists who had Scotch-Irish blood. New Yorkers toasted "The Friends of Liberty, and Enemies of Oppression and arbitrary Power in Great-Britain, Ireland, and elsewhere" at the house of Edward Smith on March 23, 1769.[31] The Sons of St. Patrick met in Philadelphia on the same day and drank to "all the authors who by their writings support the cause of Liberty be introduced into Heaven by St. Patrick."[32] Toasts to the Irish patriots and Dr. Charles Lucas, who advocated Irish autonomy and freedom of the press, were later included at many banquets.[33]

The colonists were at least united in their efforts to prove their loyalty to their sovereign. The "friends of Liberty" in Boston still reserved their first toasts for members of the royal family and other court officials, but then drank to "The patriotic Assembly of Connecticut, Rhode-Island, New-York, Pennsylvania, Maryland, North and South Carolina, and Georgia."[34] The members of the Virginia House of Burgesses finished their business on May 17, 1769, and drank toasts first to the King, then the royal family. Virginia's prosperity was the third toast, but the fourth expressed hopes for "A speedy and lasting Union between Great-Britain and her Colonies."[35] The toasts made it clear what was most important to the colonists. In a July 1769 jubilee in Dorchester, Massachusetts, the crowd toasted the daughters and sons of liberty, the freedom of the press, members of Parliament, American manufacturing, and the perpetual union between Great Britain and the colonies. The forty-fifth toast, referring to the British officers who ordered the arrests of "troublesome" colonists, received loud cheers: "*Strong Halters, Firm Blocks*, and *Sharp Axes*, to all such as deserve either."[36]

By the end of the decade, more toasts were to the protest movement. The Boston Sons of Liberty toasted America, Wilkes, the colonies' friends in Great Britain, and a "'Speedy Deliverance to the illustrious PAOLI, and the brave Corsicans.'"[37] New Yorkers celebrated November 1 as "The Day on which the Inhabitants of this Colony nobly determined not to surrender their Rights to arbitrary Power, however august," and offered the following toasts at the house of Mr. De La Montagne:

> May the last Resolutions of the Great and General Court of Massachusetts Bay, and the Commons House of Assembly of South Carolina, in not granting Supplies to the Troops, be universally adopted in North America.
> The Printers who nobly disregarded the detestable Stamp-Act, preferring of the public Good to their private Interest, in 1765.[38]

Violent events challenged the colonists' allegiance to Britain. Colonists were aware of the deadly street riot in Boston on the night of March 5, 1770, thanks to the propaganda machine set up by Samuel Adams and Paul Revere. Included in a list of toasts drunk at Newport, Massachusetts, on the anniversary of the Stamp Act's repeal was a pledge to honor "The Memory of the massacred Martyrs to British and American Liberty, Alien, Snider, Caldwell, Attucks, Gray, and Maverick! May swift impartial Justice overtake the murderous Hand." The thirteenth toast expressed a desire to get the colonies to unite in condemning the bloodletting: "May every Town thro' this Continent deeply sympathize with the Town of Boston, and feel on Account of the Blood there cruelly and inhumanly spilt, as if it were drawn from their own Bowels."[39]

James Otis, whose fiery rhetoric alarmed even his colleague John Adams, had been receiving almost as many toasts as "The Farmer of Pennsylvania." Otis was forced to end his career and participation in the events in and around Boston in 1769 after being assaulted by a British official, and toasts to Otis in 1770 hoped for a better fate for the unfortunate lawyer: "Confirmed Health to the Patriot OTIS."[40] Paschal Paoli had gone into

2. "May our Mother never oppress her children," 1763–1774

exile in London after losing his struggles for Corsica in 1769. Toasts continued to be made to "The glorious, tho unfortunate General Paoli."[41]

The year 1773 ended with the destruction of the tea in Boston on December 16. Although the protest has been recognized as a seminal event in the Revolution, at the time it was widely condemned. For a time, the protest was not recognized in public rituals or celebrations, and there is no mention of it in any toasts given in 1774. The dumping of the tea was too outrageous an action for even the boldest radicals. Since the participants had taken an oath of secrecy, no individuals were recognized by name. They understood that the consequences of such a dangerous action would be severe. "The colonists had not merely resisted government; they had wantonly destroyed private property. They must be brought to heel, and those who had lawlessly ruined so much good tea must be brought to the bar of justice."[42]

Lord Frederick North, Britain's prime minister, pushed punitive legislation through Parliament in 1774, shutting down Boston Harbor, severely limiting city government, and allowing for a change of venue for British soldiers who committed any crimes in the colony.[43] Pouring gasoline on the fire, Parliament then passed the Quebec Act, restoring the old boundaries of the province of Quebec and recognizing French law and Roman Catholicism.[44] Lord North and his "Intolerable Acts" became targets for the Sons of Liberty throughout the colonies. The seventeenth toast given at a dinner of the Independent Military Society in Boston demanded "a speedy Repeal of the Boston Port-Bill, the Murder Act, and the Charter Annihilating Bill."[45] The *Norwich Packet* of Connecticut printed a toast calling for "Confusion to the Authors of the Canada Bill."[46] When North received a toast at one Boston gathering, Bostonians hissed while British soldiers cheered: "Someone called out 'Damn him!'" In response, the toastmaster shouted, "Bless him!" The shouting continued and intensified, until the commander of the grenadiers gave the order to disperse the crowd and clear King Street. The King's own grenadier complied, with fixed bayonets.[47]

Another consequence of the Tea Party was the royal appointment of General Thomas Gage as military governor, replacing the unpopular Thomas Hutchinson. Gage sincerely hoped to keep the peace in the colony. He arrived on May 13, 1774, and spent some time discussing the situation with Hutchinson. He got a glimpse of the city's temperament when he attended a formal dinner at Faneuil Hall four days later, when someone proposed a toast to Hutchinson: "all he got in response was a loud hiss."[48]

The British troops in Boston were going up against a well-organized resistance movement that controlled all the printing presses and militia units in the colony. The colonists were fanatically committed to their cause, demanding that others follow their example. Doubters and critics were not to be tolerated in their ranks. Toasting the King was now dangerous, and anyone who dared to do so faced persecution.[49] John Adams and a group of attorneys were dining at the home of a "Tory" judge in the central Massachusetts city of Worcester. The judge offered a toast to "the King." Many of the dinner guests were upset with this, and Adams responded with his own toast to "The Devil": "As the host was about to resent the indignity, his wife calmed him, and turned the laugh upon Mr. Adams, by immediately exclaiming 'My dear! As the gentleman has been so kind to drink to our King, let us by no means refuse in our turn to drink to his.'"[50]

John Adams, knowing he was a witness to history, frequently wrote about many events. He was chosen to attend the meeting of what would become the First Continental Congress in Philadelphia on September 5, 1774, representing the colony of Massachusetts. Before the first day of the proceedings, Adams joined other delegates and dined at the home of Mr. Thomas Mifflin. The toasts Adams described demonstrated that the delegates were not interested in liberty from the British crown, but rather a more beneficial relationship with the mother country:

> [Benjamin] Harrison gave us for a Sentiment "a constitutional Death to the Lords Bute, Mansfield and North." [Thomas] Paine gave us "May the Collusion of british Flint and American Steel, produce that Spark of Liberty which shall illumine the latest Posterity." Wisdom to Britain and Firmness to the Colonies, may Britain be wise and America free. The Friends of America throughout the World. Union of the Colonies. Unanimity to the Congress. May the Result of the Congress, answer the Expectations of the People. Union of Britain and the Colonies, on a Constitutional Foundation—and many other such Toasts.[51]

Feelings of allegiance were sporadic, however. Adams later described a toast given by a Dr. Cox on September 27, 1774: "May the fair Dove of Liberty, in this Deluge of Despotism, find Rest to the Sole of her Foot in America."[52]

The congressional delegates blamed the problems on the King's ministers. When they met at Philadelphia's City-Tavern on September 19, they toasted, "May the Cloud which hangs over Great-Britain and the Colonies, burst *only* on the heads of the present Ministry."[53] The delegates wanted to allay any fears that they were acting rashly, but only to protect themselves and help the "much injured town of Boston." They later raised their glasses to "No unconstitutional standing armies" and hoped that "British Swords never be drawn in defence of tyranny."[54] Massachusetts toasts also desired peace and reconciliation:

> All the Promoters of the Militia, who have no sinister ends in view. Restoration of peace and harmony between Great-Britain and America.

2. "May our Mother never oppress her children," 1763–1774

A happy establishment of virtuous freedom and good order throughout the British Empire.[55]

Such sentiments were futile. The King and Parliament were incensed that the "illegal" Continental Congress called for more colonial boycotts of British goods and then recommended that colonial militias prepare for defense against possible British aggression. Individuals who had been honored for their efforts on behalf of the colonies, such as John Dickinson, John Wilkes, Edmund Burke, John Hancock, and the venerable Dr. Benjamin Franklin were unable to prevent the escalation of tensions. The "Happy Reconciliation" would soon become a fantasy. Toasts went from being hopeful for better relations with Britain to advocating rebellion and independence.

Toasts at the beginning of the 1760s honored the King first, as expected, but they soon reflected a disruption in the connection between the colonies and Great Britain after the passage of the Stamp Act. The Stamp Act's repeal led to many celebratory toasts the reaffirmed loyalty to the monarchy. As time went on and the Imperial Crisis intensified, figures who stood for liberty started appearing in the toast lists in colonial newspapers: John Wilkes, John Dickinson, Paschal Paoli, the Ninety-Two Rescinders, the Boston Massacre victims, and the persecuted of Ireland. Parliament's harsh reaction to the Boston Tea Party, called the "Intolerable Acts" by the colonists, led to more toasts that demanded a restoration of British liberties. The toasts still did not demand a separation from the mother country, but rather a return to the protective relationship the colonists had benefited from before the Stamp Act.

Chapter 3

"His Excellency General Washington and the Armies of America,"[1] 1775–1783

"Perpetual Itching without benefit of scratching to the enemies of *America*."[2]

"The bright luminary of America, his Excellency General Washington."[3]

"May the Memories of those Heroes who have bled in the Glorious Cause of Freedom be transmitted with Gratitude to future Ages."[4]

The British colonists in 1775 still hoped that their monarch would protect them, considering themselves to be his "children," and so they were shocked when blood was shed at Lexington. The colonists found themselves having to choose sides: commit treason and support the rebels, or remain loyal to the King and risk persecution. It was becoming too difficult to remain neutral in what was essentially a civil war.

Toasts were used effectively to unite people behind the "Glorious Cause." Toasts and other public rituals did their best to make sense of the violence. Sarah J. Purcell underlines the need for such commemorations during the war in her book, *Sealed with Blood: War, Sacrifice, and Memory in Revolutionary America*:

> Americans could witness and take part in many different forms of commemoration during the war years. In addition to reading almanacs like George's, they could read other forms of commemoration newspapers, broadsides, and books. Patriots, especially those living in or near towns like Lexington, Massachusetts; Bennington, Vermont; or Charleston, South Carolina, could attend celebrations, church services, parades, and picnics, all of which dramatized in public form the message of shared sacrifice for the newly created

patriotic cause. This popular participation became the basis for the future postwar democratization of memory, although for the time being the democratic consequences of the actions of average citizens remained veiled. During the war, heroic offices were the objects of praise, but "the people" also became potentially important, not necessarily for their own heroic deeds but for their own ability to offer proper patriotism and memory in return for the hero's sacrifices.[5]

The Continental Congress gathered in emergency session in Philadelphia in May 1775, after Lexington and Concord. People expected their delegates would do their best to secure peace with the mother country. Fort Ticonderoga was captured at the same time in a surprise raid led by Ethan Allen and Benedict Arnold. To celebrate their accomplishment, they fired off their muskets and gave many loyal healths to the Congress.[6] However, not everyone wanted Congress to succeed. Loyalists at one dinner also drank to Congress, or rather "To the Pimps," and offered the toast in the form of song.

Benjamin Franklin wrote to Jonathan Shiply in June 1775 and explained that his primary concern was for an end to all fighting: "Many I meet with are so warmly and heartily your Friends and some whose constant Toast is Success to the Americans, in which, to own the Truth, I cannot join. My Toast is, Success to neither Party, but Peace and Good Will to both."[7]

"MASSACHUSETTENSIS" wrote a scathing letter "to the perfidious, the truce breaking THOMAS GAGE," which appeared in the *Connecticut Gazette* on July 16, 1775. Gage was called a monster for letting loose the "DOGS OF WAR." The letter referred to toasts that Gage had once given when he first arrived in New England, pledging to do good in Boston:

> Witness your toasts on the last Election day at Boston; the first was—A good choice of Counsellors—the second, Prosperity to the town of Boston—when your professed design in coming to America was to destroy both—This is evident, especially to those who heard you profanely swear, that *you* came to put the acts of the British parliament in execution, and, *By God you would do it.*

Israel Putnam of Connecticut, who led the rebels at Bunker Hill in June, was one of the first to be singled out for honors when the war began. The *Connecticut Gazette* printed toasts from a July 25 dinner in London attended by the Freeholders of Middlesex. General Putnam was toasted "and all those American Heroes, who, like men, nobly prefer death to slavery and chains."[8] Sons of Liberty leader Dr. Joseph Warren, who was killed on the battlefield, received the following toast from the Field Officers of the Sixth Brigade in Cambridge: "Immortal Honor to that Patriot and Hero Doctor *Joseph Warren*, and the Brave American troops, who fought the Battle of Charlestown on the 17th of June 1775." This list of toasts, appearing in the August 21, 1775, issue of the *Boston Gazette, or Country Journal* started with a toast to the Continental Congress instead of to the British monarch. The officers raised their glasses instead to all the colonies, the Stamp Act riots, Lexington and Concord, and an end to the "present unhappy Disputes." Dr. Warren would be a consistently toasted figure into the early 1800s.

George Washington replaced George III as the main recipient of toasts, becoming the most toasted individual in the new nation. The King was now the enemy.[9] Even English supporters of colonial rights, such as John Wilkes and Edmund Burke, were replaced by American military heroes.[10] English support for the rights of the colonists, however, had not disappeared. The *Virginia Gazette* printed toasts the London Association made in October 1775. Association members wished for "axes and halters, at public expence, to all those who attempt to trample on the liberties of their fellow subjects, either in Great Britain or America," and that "kings remember that they were made for their subjects, and not their subjects for them."[11]

The former British corset-maker Thomas Paine brilliantly explained why the colonists should no longer rely on the King to protect their liberties. His pamphlet, *Common Sense*, demanded that Americans free themselves of Britain's control. Paine wrote that "One of the strongest *natural* proofs of the folly of hereditary right in Kings, is that nature disapproves it, otherwise she would not so frequently turn it into ridicule, by giving mankind an *Ass for a Lion*."[12] His words reached everyone in the colonies, and so he and his work were toasted: "May the INDEPENDENT principles of COMMON SENSE be confirmed throughout the United Colonies."[13]

Most colonies had already taken Paine's advice to heart and declared themselves to be independent states. Members of the Virginia convention calling for a resolution for national independence gave toasts in May: "*The American independent states*" and "*The Grand Congress of the United States, and their respected legislatures.*"[14] Washington attended a feast at the Queen's Head Tavern in New York City, where toasts were given to the Continental Congress and the American army, and to the memory of General Richard Montgomery, killed in the disastrous invasion of Quebec in December 1775. The final toast was "to 'Civil and religious liberty to all mankind'—mankind, that is, except Tories."[15] Tories, the conservative supporters of the Crown, received extra abuse in the Patriots' toasts: "Sore Eyes to all Tories, and a Chestnut Burr for an Eye Stone."[16]

Toasts could quickly identify people whose loyalties were still to the King, and so the Loyalists had to be careful when glasses were raised around them. Kenneth Silverman, author of *A Cultural History of the American Revolution*, wrote that Loyalists "had long been compelled 'in a *whisper* to toast Church & King'":

> We whisper'd for fear, Sir, and faith! we had reason,
> When Honor was Baseness, and Loyalty Treason.
> And truly!, 't was no very laughable thing
> To see Faction in triumph defy Church and King....

Now, however, Tories gathered at Hull's Tavern or the King's Head to sing out loyal sentiments uninhibited—secure in Clinton's protective might and relaxed by toasts "To the Pimps" (Congress):

> True Souls drink and sing,
> Remember the King,
> With Loyalty, good Will and fervour;
> So while we can stand,
> The Flaggon command,
> To GEORGE his Empire for ever.[17]

The signing of the Declaration of Independence ushered in a wave of intense patriotism, and the July Fourth holiday could not be matched in enthusiasm by either the King's birthday, the anniversary of his coronation, or even the repeal of the Stamp Act. The new Independence Day festivities brought people together as proud Americans. Toasts praised the leaders of the Revolution, including the Declaration's signers: "From this act of treason against the British Crown sprang a chart of Liberty and Emancipation broad as the universe and filled with glad tiding and a good will towards men. They who periled their lives by this noble act will live and be cherished in the hearts of free men."[18] Independence Day was also ripe for political manipulation. David Waldstreicher's online article "The Invention of the Fourth of July" explains how Americans quickly made use of the event:

> These patriots focused on what unified them and on a glorious national future that would follow from their victories, rather than on the British past that they had once actively remembered at such occasions but which they now left behind. The need of the revolutionary movement to simultaneously practice policies and create national unity only raised the stakes of the celebrating national holidays. The trend in the early republic would be for July Fourth, and other celebrations modeled on the Fourth, to spread nationalism and at the same time, to provide revenues for divisive political expression. In this way, Americans learned to be American and to practice partisanship without any sense of contradiction. Just as they blamed the British while claiming and using British traditions, they used the Fourth of July to praise and criticize their governments and each other, in the process struggling over who, and what, was truly American.[19]

Members of the Upper and Lower Houses of Assembly in Providence, Rhode Island, wished in an August toast that "the Crowns of Tyrants be crowns of thorns" and that "the Union of the States be established in justice and mutual confidence, and be as permanent as the pillars of nature."[20] Captain William Watson made a similar toast at the Eagle Tavern of East Poultney, in the future state of Vermont, in reference to those "enemies" who sympathized with Tories: "May these have cobweb breeches, a porcupine saddle, a hard trotting horse, and an eternal journey."[21] At the same time, the *New Hampshire Gazette* published an article written by "AMICUS PATRIAE" about a dinner given in New York by the Provincial Congress. "AMICUS" pointed out one toast that should "be drank by every gentleman, in his family throughout the continent, in perpetuam rei memoriam, VIZ. MAY PLACEMEN AND PENSIONERS NEVER FIND SEATS IN AMERICAN SENATES.—":

> It is wholly owing to a fatal influence *of this nature*, in the British Parliament, that Britain has lost the AMERICAN COLONIES, and if she continues to suffer the same, she will not long remain a kingdom, but will become a province of France. And will America split upon the same rock? Forbid it, Heaven! Rather let her guardian angels (the Continental Congress) be ever watchful over those rights and privileges, which her SONS should defend, and transmit to the latest posterity a system of political government, founded on a basis which can never be shaken, exempted from those defects and errors that have subverted other states. I could have wished to have seen another toast added, viz. MAY THE LEGISLATIVE AND EXECUTVE POWERS NEVER BE LODGED IN THE SAME HANDS—such a measure is unconstitutional, impolitic, oppressive and absurd. From the same principle, we may as well admit the civil and military powers to center in the same persons, which seems to be allowed by all is unconstitutional, but whether it does not still exist in *some colonies*, may be a pertinent inquiry.[22]

Opinion in England was divided. Many supported the cause of the rebels. Elizabeth Wright wrote to Benjamin Franklin on February 13, 1777, and described the reaction of diners in London when someone gave as a toast: "'Damnation to all Americans' to which Mr. Plat Reply'd that No Gentlemen of Honour or Goodness could drink such a Toast as it was Repugnant to the Rules of Society, on which the other grew warm as well as some of the Company, and Mr. Plat fearing a Quarrel imediately Withdrew."[23] Dr. Samuel Johnson, the famous writer and committed Tory, had nothing but contempt for the rebels. He was especially irate about the fact that the Americans called for freedom and independence for themselves but continued to keep African slaves in bondage: "We are told, that the subjection of Americans may tend to the dimunition of our own liberties; an event, which none but very perspicacious politicians are able to foresee. If slavery by thus fatally contagious, how is it that we hear the loudest yelps for liberty among the drivers of negroes?"[24] Hoping that the Americans would one day suffer a fitting punishment, he famously raised his glass at a dinner in September 1777 and toasted, "'Here's to the next insurrection of the negroes in the West Indies.'"[25]

The first anniversary of the signing of the Declaration became a model for future observances. Festivities combined serious ceremonies, such as military displays and solemn toasts, with disorderly behavior, including bonfires and vandalism against Loyalists.[26] In Philadelphia, "After dinner a number of toasts were drank, all breathing independence, and a generous love of liberty, and commemorating the memories of those brave and worthy patriots who gallantly exposed their lives, and fell gloriously in defense of freedom and the righteous cause of their country."[27] South Carolinians combined their Independence Day celebrations with their own Palmetto Day, honoring the June 28, 1776, victory at the Battle of Sullivan's Island. They drank to General William Moultrie, Sergeant William Jasper, and hoped that "American Troops, in the Day of Battle, remember the 28th of June."[28]

Some leaders of the Patriot cause were not happy with Washington's performance by the fall of 1777, blaming him for the loss of New York City. Washington and John Adams desperately wanted to go on the offensive. Washington was forced to adopt a "Fabian" strategy: keeping the army alive long enough for the British to become exhausted and abandon the fight. Adams wrote to his wife Abigail on September 2, 1777, about his hopes for a quick victory: "The Officers drink a long and moderate War. My Toast is a short and violent War. They would call me mad and rash &c. but I know better. I am as cool as any of them too, for my Mind is not inflamed with Fear nor Anger, whereas I believe theirs are with both."[29]

The entrance of the French into the war would make three things available: money, troops, and naval power. The most popular toasts in Philadelphia in the fall of 1777 were to the French.[30] The surrender of John Burgoyne's army to General Horatio Gates in October opened the gates to French aid. Congressional delegates now praised Gates over Washington, and Gates received his share of toasts: "The brave Major-General Gates who with effect, said to the vaunting Burgoyne, 'hiterto shalt thou come and no further.'"[31] The young French aristocrat Marquis de Lafayette defended his beloved superior. He attended a dinner with Gates and the toasts given at the conclusion included some to Congress and the United States. Lafayette said, "'Gentlemen—you seem to have forgotten to drink to the health of General Washington.'" Lafayette later recalled that the diners refilled their glasses to toast Washington, "'but not with much exuberance of feeling.'"[32] The Patriot performance at the Battle of Monmouth Court House in June 1778 improved Washington's reputation. Writer Francis Hopkinson offered the following poem as a toast to the General:

> 'Tis Washington's health-fill a bumper all round,
> For he is our Glory and Pride;
> Our Arms shall in battle with Conquest be crown'd,
> Whilst Virtue and He's on our Side.³³

The British had their own celebrations. At one dinner attended by British soldiers, an orchestra played "God Save the King" while the soldiers toasted the royal family, Admiral Richard Howe, and his brother, General William Howe. John André, who would meet the hangman's noose for his role in Benedict Arnold's treachery, "claimed that those sitting near them could see on their faces 'a generous emotion' in reply to 'the undissembled testimony of our love and admiration.'" After toasts to the army, navy, and German mercenary detachments, "they were no doubt ready to toast anyone, even General Washington."³⁴ The Ancient York Masons, Lodge #210, held a dinner at the Shakespeare Tavern in British-occupied New York City in celebration of St. John the Evangelist on December 30, 1779. They raised their glasses to the King, General Sir Henry Clinton, and "His Majesty's Fleet against the Fleets of France and Spain." Remembering the plight of the Loyalists, they offered success "to all true hearted Refugees who endeavour to crush the Rebellion."³⁵

The French alliance allowed for royalty to be embraced and toasted once again. The American Coffee-House hosted an event lauding the French alliance on April 23, 1778, and the third toast was to King Louis XVI of France.³⁶ It seemed that Americans could not completely disregard the importance of a monarch, be it English or French. And while most Americans were fiercely Protestant, they embraced the French king and then the king of Spain, both Catholic. The *New Jersey Gazette* reported on a dinner in Philadelphia in honor of the French minister, where toasts were made to:

> His Most Christian Majesty.
> The Queen of France.
> His Most Catholic Majesty.³⁷

Toasts to Louis XVI were like those offered to George III before the Declaration of Independence. Thomas Paine's arguments in *Common Sense*, however, had taken root in the minds of many of the former colonists: "*Let every citizen remember he is a king, and worthy his dignified condition.*"³⁸

Americans also drank to "Success to the French and American Army and Navy" and "Perpetual Union between France and the United States of America." Dr. Franklin, instrumental in getting French support, was considered in this toast: "May the Names of those glorious Men, who have framed and concluded the Alliance between France and America be immortalized in the Annals of the World."³⁹ On July 5, 1779, Franklin hosted several American and French friends at Passy, France. The guests dined under a portrait of George Washington, who was holding copies of the Declaration of Independence and the Franco-American Treaties of Alliance. The first toast called the French king "the illustrious Protector of American Liberty." Lafayette, the king of Spain, the Congress, and the American military high command were likewise honored with 136 "pintes" of wine.[40]

By 1781, the military campaign turned southward, and the toasts followed: "Success to the present Expedition to the Southward" and "General Greene and the Southern Army."[41] Boston's *Independent Ledger* printed the toasts offered by American army officers at the American Coffee-House at an Independence Day gathering. Daniel Morgan saved Nathaniel Greene's army at Cowpens, South Carolina, in January, earning him praise from the group: "An endless eclat to the fame of the enterprising Gen. Morgan, and his gallant FEW, who so admirably distinguished themselves at Cowpens, in South Carolina." Washington was referred to as "His Excellency," which would remain his title in countless toasts. General Benjamin Lincoln was also praised despite his recent defeat at Charleston: "The heroic and incomparable opposition at Charlestown in South Carolina, tho successless and felicity to Gen. Lincoln, and his brave band."[42]

Benedict Arnold was by now a detested figure. Toasts once praised him, but now they wished a bitter end to his existence: "May that Traitor Arnold, and all his accomplices, be suspended between heaven and earth, as unworthy of either."[43] Arnold would set the bar for all evildoers in toasts for years to come.

The final battle was fought at Yorktown, Virginia, in October 1781. The surrender of Lord Cornwallis and his army to the French and Americans was cause for many parades, bonfires, and toasts throughout the United States:

> The memorable 16th and 19th of October, and the action of the Eutaw Springs.[44]
> May the lilies of France and the stripes of America wave in triumph from shore to shore.[45]
> The illustrious Count de Grasse.[46]

Congress, the American army, and General Washington were always honored, and then they were joined by Louis XVI, General Rochambeau, Admiral de Grasse, and the peace commissioners in Paris. The toasts not only expressed joy, but also explained the American victory. Nobody drank to British leaders or military officials. The British lost the war, and so lost any honorable mention in toasts.[47]

The postwar joy was not universal. Hessian prisoners in Frederick,

Pennsylvania, threw a party in their barracks when they received news of their impending release. Their toasts to King George angered the American guards, who reacted by killing four of the prisoners.[48] Other toasts identified those "sunshine patriots," as Thomas Paine called them in *The American Crisis* (#1). New Hampshire partygoers in 1783 singled out such characters: "'May the degenerate sons of America, who shrunk at the clouds of her distress, never bask in the rays of her glory.'"[49]

George Washington became a larger-than-life hero. He was praised as "His Excellency General Washington. May his fame be immortal, as his virtues are unrivaled."[50] People from Georgia to New Hampshire were united in their affection for Washington, whose name was a powerful cultural symbol that helped create one "coherent Union."[51] Washington's birthday was a golden opportunity to toast the General and values of the Revolution, such as these given in Milton, Massachusetts: "May this revolving day be ever celebrated in gratitude to our illustrious chief!" and "May tyranny and oppression be blown from the earth by the breath of liberty." The Milton gathering toasted "freedom to the slave," which was arguably one of the first toasts to promote the abolition of African American slavery.[52]

Benjamin Franklin contributed to the Washington cult of personality in Paris while he was negotiating the peace treaty. One of his most famous toasts was given at the Palace of Versailles. The British ambassador offered a toast to his own sovereign, as expected: "'George III, who, like the sun in its meridian, spreads a luster throughout and enlightens the world.'" The French minister, in response, said, "'The illustrious Louis XVI, who, like the moon, sheds his mild and benevolent rays on and influences the globe.'" Franklin, refusing to be undone, toasted Washington: "'George Washington, commander of the American armies, who, like Joshua of old, commanded the sun and moon to stand still, and both obeyed.'"[53]

The French alliance joined Washington in many after-dinner healths: "May the union between powers in alliance ever continue on the basis of justice and equity."[54] When news of the Treaty of Paris reached the American shores, people gathered to recognize all who contributed to the American success and the treaty's generous terms:

> The Marquis De LaFayette, and all such distinguished patriots.[55]
> The King of Spain and the other powers of Europe who have discovered a friendly disposition to this country in its late struggle.
> His Most Christian Majesty. May that great and good monarch live and die with the exalted character of being the friend of mankind.[56]
> His Excellency the Chevalier de la Luzurne, Minister Plenipotentiary of his Most Christian Majesty at Congress.[57]

Many toasts established the vision of one nation: "An increase of arts, agriculture, and manufactures and commerce, in America; and may republican virtue and frugality take place of monarchical luxury and extravagance."[58] Washington himself was looking toward a future of rest and relaxation at Mount Vernon after eight years. He hosted a party for 500 guests at West Point in late May 1783 and "favored a toast raised to 'a new edge to our swords, until they have opened the way to independence, freedom, and glory; and then may be converted to the instruments of peace.'"[59] However, the signs of division were already threatening the prospect of the states working together. A celebration in Pawtucket, Rhode Island, foreshadowed the upcoming difficulties when people toasted the needs of their state over those of the federal union: "The State of Rhode Island, and their Delegates in Congress who nobly opposed the raising an unconstitutional Revenue."[60]

Keeping the states together in a union was necessary if the nation were to survive. Those who had fought and sacrificed for the new nation were hopeful that the union would be perpetual. One Independence Day toast from Wilmington, Delaware, pleaded, "May the present confederation of the United States be lauded down inviolate to the latest posterity."[61] A show of strength to the rest of the world was crucial to the confederation's survival. Revelers wished that the American navy would "be more successful in their future marine operations than heretofore," and that the states "exceed the republics of Sparta, Athens, and Rome, in Public Virtue, Learning, and Military Glory."[62]

By the fall of 1783, Washington was more concerned with the deteriorating condition of his soldiers. He offered toasts calling for the support of the veterans and that their sacrifices would not be forgotten. The governor of New York hosted a dinner for Washington at Fraunces Tavern in November, and one toast was in line with Washington's sentiments: "May our country be grateful to her military children."[63] A toast given at a dinner in New Brunswick, New Jersey, in December followed suit: "May the spirit of gratitude pervade the breasts of Americans."[64] Washington was involved with the creation of an organization that would look out for veterans: the Society of the Cincinnati. This hereditary organization was named after the Roman leader Cincinnatus, who walked away from power and returned to a life tilling the soil. Officers in the Continental Army formed this exclusive club, "an avowedly elitist enterprise designed to sustain the aristocratic ethos of superior officers in the Continental army had been harboring since Valley Forge."[65] It was founded "'to perpetuate ... the remembrance of this great event [and] the danger, and in many instances cemented by the blood of the parties.'"[66] Members of the Society, Washington included, looked backward to the Revolution for examples of political action and toasted "'the dear memory of those illustrious patriots who shed their blood in the cause of freedom,' and 'the rising generation; may they, like their fathers, love their country.'"[67]

Washington was a farmer above all other things, and he saw himself as the modern-day Cincinnatus. Meetings of the Cincinnati included banquets and drinking. Members toasted "'the dear memory of those illustrious patriots who shed their blood in the cause of freedom,' and 'the rising generations; may they, like their fathers, love their country.'"[68]

Washington bade his soldiers farewell at Fraunces Tavern on December 22, 1783. He drank to the new nation, France, liberty, and the future: "'To the memory of those heroes who have fallen for our freedom!' And: 'May America be an Asylum to the persecuted of the earth!' And finally: 'May the remembrances of the day be a lesson to princes.'"[69] After making a controversial political point when he raised his glass to the "'competent powers to Congress for general purposes,'"[70] he was ready to wish his men well. He offered his drink and said, "'With a heart filled with love and gratitude, I now take leave of you,'" then, "'I most devoutly wish that your latterday may be as prosperous and happy as your former ones have been glorious and honourable.'"[71] With that famous exit, Washington returned to Virginia.

The war had been fought and won, and Americans substituted their English king with a beloved Virginian general in their toasts. Independence Day was now a national and American event, replacing all previous celebrations in importance and passion. America appeared to be truly united, and one toast from a New York City dinner in December 1783 expressed the wish that there would be no future divisiveness: "May the spirit of Faction be chained in the regions of darkness."[72] "Faction" would soon tear apart the infant nation's government.

The toasts of the American Revolution started with calls for continued loyalty to the British sovereign, but events left George III out of toasts. His place was taken by General George Washington, who became a regular in toast lists throughout the nation during and after the Revolution. People who were loyal to the British "tyrant" could be singled out if they did not drink the correct toasts. The new Fourth of July holiday became the most popular of all national holidays, and patriotic toasts were the norm. After the French joined the war on the side of the Americans, toasts included the French monarch and commanders. The end of the war led to toasts that pushed for a strong national union, which was in danger once the common enemy was defeated at Yorktown.

CHAPTER 4

"May the Wisdom of 1775 pervade the Councils of 1787!"[1] 1784–1788

"The United States—may the benign influence of the thirteen states be shed on every quarter of the world."[2]

"May all the states of America join heartily in adopting and making effectual the proposed federal government."[3]

"May the Members of the Grand council of America be endowed with Wisdom to hold the Reins of Government, in a Manner the most conducive to the public Weal of this infant, but growing Empire."[4]

While the ink on the Treaty of Paris of 1783 was still damp, little could dampen Americans' enthusiasm for their having defeated the strongest military force in the world. Ceremonies of gratitude took the form of parades, fireworks, triumphal arches, and sermons.[5] Winning the war was the easy part. Now, how to keep thirteen separate entities together as a nation? King George III united the colonies twice: when he was the loving parent, and then when he was the hated tyrant. There was very little that united the states after 1783. European powers were interested in what would happen next in America.

The Second Continental Congress, which became the Confederation Congress after the Articles of Confederation were ratified in 1781,[6] succeeded in getting the United States through the Revolution. Once the war ended, the states fiercely protected their sovereign status because they feared a strong central authority. Many appreciated the weak Articles because the power belonged to the states. Popular toasts regarding the Articles included "'Cement to the Union' and 'A hoop to the barrel.'"[7] Washington hoped that the government would at least be able to accomplish the simplest tasks in a toast he made in Annapolis: "'Competent Powers to Congress for general purposes.'"[8]

The July Fourth holiday at least united the states, connecting Americans to their past and creating a national identity that went above local and regional concerns. The celebrations helped to hide the social and political conflicts that would eventually surface by the end of the 1780s.[9] Merchants could count on doing some brisk business on the Fourth because various groups were gathering in taverns to eat and offer toasts to the nation. The number of toasts mirrored the number of states, but additional "'voluntary' toasts often swelled the number of glasses raised to twenty or more—no doubt contributing substantially to the general 'hilarity' so frequently observed in newspaper accounts."[10]

Toasts that appeared in newspapers gave the impression that they were the sentiments of the American "people" and represented the feelings of "'the most respectable characters.'"[11] Some of these characters belonged to fraternal organizations in the 1780s: the Masons, the Sons of St. George (known for helping indigent British immigrants), the Sons of St. Patrick, and the Sons of St. Andrew. The Sons of St. Tammany invented a Native American heritage, complete with sachems and headquarters called wigwams.[12] Tammany Society toasts were given to the president, or "Great Sachem," and to the federal government, called the "Council Fire." These citizens were portrayed as being above the "crowd." There were no reports of drunken behavior. Their celebrations were filled with decorum and order "worthy of virtuous republicans."[13]

Gordon S. Wood wrote that the group that best embodied the ideals of the Revolution, sociability, and cosmopolitanism was the Freemasons:

> It would be difficult to exaggerate the importance of Masonry for the American Revolution. It not only created national icons that are still with us; it brought people together in new ways and helped fulfill the republican dream of reorganizing social relationships. For thousands of Americans, it was a major means by which they participated directly in the Enlightenment.[14]

Masonic lodges served the community with their charitable activities in the absence of nonprofit organizations or government welfare programs. They also offered social connection outside of the church and government.[15] The Freemasons claimed Washington as a member, and toasts were given to him, other famous Masons, and the virtues associated with masonry. Glasses were raised every December 27, the anniversary of their patron saint, St. John the Evangelist. Some of their typical toasts were to "All Nobles, Princes and Potentates, that ever propagated the excellent art," "All the Fraternity round the globe," and "The Right Worshipful the Grandmasters of Ancient Masons."[16] The values of the Grand Lodge of Masons in Philadelphia were on full display at a December 1786 dinner:

4. "May the Wisdom of 1775 pervade...!" 1775-1783

> The President our venerable Brother Franklin, and the land we live in.
> Our illustrious and beloved Brother *George Washington*.
> May virtue, happiness and brotherly love, the pure offspring of Masonic excellence, rest in this New World.[17]

One of the most famous of the fraternal organizations was the Society of the Cincinnati. The *Massachusetts Centinel,* on July 14, 1787, reporting on the Fourth of July toasts of the Society, described its conviction that American democracy was the salvation of the civilized world:

> Who can calmly reflect on the American Revolution, and not be convinced of its *importance—a revolution* which clearly demonstrates that PATRIOTISM and UNANIMITY can alone effect miracles—a revolution which has not only given the *blessing* of *freedom* to this Western World; but has enlightened nearly all Europe, with respect to the *natural rights of mankind.*

Society members held their anniversary meeting at Cape's Tavern in New York City on July 8, offering toasts to their colleagues in France and the American soldiery. The final toast was to "the day; and may the Society of the Cincinnati be as permanent as the designs of its members are virtuous and patriotic."[18]

American eyes looked toward Europe in many 1784 toasts, either in gratitude or for political direction. Toasts honored the alliances with Spain and the United Provinces (the Netherlands). Washington drank a toast in Philadelphia to the persecuted island off the English coast: "May the people of Ireland enjoy the freedom of Americans."[19]

France continued to receive special attention. When a dinner was given at the house of the French consul in Philadelphia on King Louis's name day, the French monarch received the first toast: "The King of France and the other sovereigns of the House of Bourbon." After toasts to the U.S., Pennsylvania, and General Washington, the majority of the remaining healths were devoted to France. The final toast was to "all Princes, who like Lewis the XVI have advanced the prosperity of their subjects by promoting that of other nations."[20] The Marquis de Lafayette almost eclipsed Washington and the king of France with the number of toasts he received as he toured the nation in 1784. He was also toasted as "The AMERICAN FABIUS" in Marblehead, Massachusetts.[21]

Some Americans were alarmed by the many toasts given to the French king and George Washington, especially when they were given precedence over those to the Congress. Samuel Adams and other "'old fashioned Whiggs' regarded it as a portent of approaching military tyranny."[22] Wherever Washington traveled, he was feted and praised. People at one such public dinner in Annapolis, Maryland, called for "long health and happiness to our Illustrious General."[23] The dinners and fireworks taking place to honor Washington's birthday included many military toasts, perhaps justifying Adams's earlier concerns:

> His Excellency George Washington, Esq. may his disinterested patriotism be handed down to the latest posterity as a lasting monument of his memorable achievements.
> Baron Steuben; may his unexampled skill in military discipline prove an honor to the profession of a soldier.
> General Knox and the late American army.[24]

Since the federal union was tenuous in 1784, many toasts celebrated local and regional people, events, issues, and concerns. The toasts given in Portsmouth, New Hampshire, on June 19 showed that people were more devoted to the state than the nation. The first toast was to the "State of New-Hampshire," and the second was a wish: "May the citizens of this State, long experience the happy effects of their new Constitution." The seventh toast turned attention to the nation: "May the Federal Union be increased and strengthened over time."[25] Fourth of July toasts in the southern states praised states first. After Georgians toasted their state, the twelfth was for the nation: "May the American Eagle bear the Thirteen Stripes to the remotest corners of the earth."[26] South Carolinians praised the agriculture, commerce, arts and sciences, and the memory of dead soldiers.[27] Traders in the state were preoccupied with financial issues:

> [F]irst, Addition to our trade, multiplication to our manufactures, subtraction to our taxes, and reduction to useless places and pensions.—The second, a cobweb pair of breeches, a porcupine saddle, a hard trotting horse, and a long journey to the projectors of the American war, and its appendage the Shop-tax.[28]

The many dinners, feasts, and celebrations still had a sense of national unity. Not everyone agreed that drinking toasts was the best way to establish this. The following letter appeared in the *New-York Packet* in May 1784:

> Mr. PRINTER,
> I have, agreeable to what I hinted sometime since, sent you the following curious edict, against drinking healths or toasts, as it is called—I must confess it is time to leave this foolish custom, as it is become quite worn out, and seems to carry with it too much stiffness and unsociability; not on account of its being attended with the horrid consequences mentioned in this decree; for I have never conceived such mischief could possibly arise from it. (Though let us beware of changes, for they are dangerous; and this has been a practice for more than a century, under the present constitution of this town.) What sort of genius, our fore-fathers possessed, is not easy to determine, unless we judge from this specimen; and then we should suppose them children or worse—
> Can it be supposed in drinking to a persons health, that a challenge was meant

and a duel was fought, from whence proceeded bloodshed; or, could it be the custom in the days of yore, to do it just at the time murder was intended? How could it be the "occasion of the much waste of the good creatures?" I always thought drink was a liquid! What sort of good creatures, Mr. Printer, did those persons drink? Were they camels or gnats? If drinking of to anothers health was sin in former days,—thanks to Heaven, we can do it now a days without sinning, in good humour, friendship, without getting drunk, and without quarrelling, uncleanness, &c. or any other of those develish consequences, with which it was attended in former times.

One of you [sic] Constant Readers.[29]

Toasts given by the mid-1780s showed people the weaknesses of the nation. People still believed in the supremacy of the state governments and held out hope that the Confederation would continue to recognize their liberties: "May the Union of the confederated States be as durable as the fields on which their citizens fought them free."[30] Fourth of July toasts given in Savannah, Georgia, not only hoped that "Georgia never need exertion to comply with her confederated engagements," but also that "Congress never want support to maintain the Liberties of the States."[31] Members of the Society of the Cincinnati in Albany, New York, likewise promoted the success of the Confederation government: "May the Splendor of the American Confederation (like the pillar of fire of old) conduct those who are endangered to the land of liberty," while Society members in Philadelphia added to their toasts "May the Union, Friendship and Happiness of these States be for ever uninterrupted by local prejudices, or local interests" and "confidence in our Continental councils, and an Increase of Energy to our Federal Government."[32]

Other toasts presciently warned about the formation of factions in government. Toasts given at Mr. Gordon's Tavern in Providence, Rhode Island, called for "a speedy Abolition of Party," and "May the base Designs of private Interest (in Opposition to public Good) never operate in the Councils of America."[33] A dinner held at the Bunch of Grapes tavern in Boston on October 23, 1786, included toasts to John Adams, the Commonwealth of Massachusetts, and one that cried out, "May the Herculean arm of Government destroy the Hydra Faction."[34] Worries about factions would later have a place in many toast lists.

The event that finally forced Americans to address the weaknesses of the Articles of Confederation occurred during the winter months of 1786–1787. Farmers in western Massachusetts had been facing foreclosures and debtor's prison since the end of the Revolution. Increasingly high taxes were imposed on them from the commercial elite of Boston. The farmers subsequently organized and marched on the country courthouses, shutting them down to prevent the farmers' lands being confiscated due to nonpayment of debt. Pelham farmer and Revolutionary War veteran Daniel Shays, who had once been honored with a ceremonial sword by Lafayette,[35] was recognized as one of the leaders of what has become known as Shays's Rebellion. The high point of this agrarian insurrection was a standoff at the federal armory in Springfield. Shays and his followers faced forces led by Revolutionary War general Benjamin Lincoln, who came out of retirement and was hired by the Boston commercial establishment. Four insurgents were killed before the "Shaysites" scattered.

Shays's Rebellion was brief, gaining only sporadic support throughout the sparsely populated region of western Massachusetts. Since most formal toasts were usually written and given by those in positions of power or influence, there were no toasts honoring Shays in the newspapers of the time. Most Massachusetts papers were printed and distributed in Boston and Worcester, which were both more commercial than the western communities. One of the first toasts to refer to the insurrection was given in Rhode Island in 1788, serving as a warning to future troublemakers: "May we never have a Shays without a Lincoln." The memory of Shays would still have a future in the partisan toasts of the 1790s. In 1787, the Shaysites were ridiculed in verse for claiming the Revolutionary tradition to support their movement:

> Huzza my poe bankers! No taxes we'll pay!
> Here's a pardon for *Wheeler, Shays, Parsons* and Day.
> Fix green boughs in your hats and renew the old cause.
> Stop the courts in each County and bully the laws.[36]

The protest may not have been viewed as more than a skirmish to Massachusetts residents, but Benjamin Lincoln and Henry Knox wrote to Washington and decried the violence that had taken place, painting a picture of mob rule and a complete turnover of the social order. Washington feared that the principles he had espoused against the British would be used against the United States government. The propertied classes in all the states were concerned. Shays's Rebellion historian Leonard Richardson wrote of their fears: "They too had concluded that the whole nation was in danger, that if government in Massachusetts gave way to anarchy, governments throughout the new republic would give way to anarchy.... If the people in Massachusetts could erupt in disorder, what lay in store for the other twelve states?"[37]

Washington used his influence to get people to consider revisions to the Articles of Confederation, and by May 1787 state delegates gathered in Philadelphia in what would become the Constitutional Convention. Expectations were high for the Convention to produce a government that would remedy the nation's problems. Many throughout the states raised their glasses to the Convention's success on the Fourth of July in 1787:

4. "May the Wisdom of 1775 pervade...!" 1775-1783

May each citizen of the United States, prefer the national dignity of America to the inferiour distinctions of country or of state.[38]

The Federal Convention—May the wisdom of their debates, and the salutary effects of their decisions, like the secrecy of their counsels, resemble the decrees of Fate.[39]

The federal Convention—may the results of their meeting be as glorious, as its members are illustrious.[40]

Delegates in all the represented states received their share of toasts. Rhode Island, however, did not send any delegates to Philadelphia. One toast in the July 24 issue of the *Massachusetts Gazette* took issue with the small state's non-participation: "May Rhode Island be excluded the union until they elect *finest* [sic] men to rule." Other Americans were angry with the small state, including "A Writer" for the *Providence Gazette*:

> The Citizens of that State, one Day, view the Governor sitting in the Chair of Government, and the next Day may see his EXCELLENCY in his BLACKSMITH's Shop, completely equipped for a hot *Engagement!*—At the Celebration of the Anniversary of American Independence, in New-Jersey, the Sons of Liberty it is said had express Orders from the Governor to fire but TWELVE CANNON, and to drink but TWELVE TOASTS!!—'Till a Reformation takes Place, may they meet with similar CONTEMPT from the TWELVE UNITED STATES!!![41]

When the Convention concluded its business in September 1787, witnesses to their celebrations heard self-congratulatory toasts that emphasized a desire for union over region: "The toasts given were truly conciliatory, and were, we believe, drank with sincerity by every one present—all appeared willing to bury the hatchet of animosity, and to smoke the calumet of union and love."[42] The next step to true union was that the resulting document had to be ratified by the states. The *Maryland Journal* printed toasts given in Baltimore by the Artillery of Massachusetts that praised Washington's role as president of the Convention, and declaring that anyone who was opposed to the Constitution "be marked as an Enemy to the Liberties of America."[43] Diners at Mr. Eppelle's tavern in New York City toasted, "May the Citizens of America display as much wisdom in adopting the proposed Constitution to preserve their liberties, as they have shewn fortitude in defending them."[44] It frightened emerging factions that the reality of a federal union might weaken the powers and identities of the thirteen states. The Pennsylvania newspaper *Independent Gazetteer* published a letter to a Mr. Oswald in which the writer had a problem with the concept of individual states within one nation:

> Some of the toasts that were drank, were middling, but most of them were not to the purpose; for we should now forget our past national transactions; and it will be ridiculous to give 13 toasts hereafter, as we are all *to be* united and

bound together into 1,—for the same reason it was wrong to fire 13 guns, *one great gun* ought only to have been fired; and we must immediately alter our flags and remove the 13 stripes and stars, and in their places insert the spread eagle, or some other great monster, emblematical of our future unison.[45]

The ratification of the Constitution by each state added stars to the American constellation. Political cartoons showed pillars, each representing the states, attempting to hold up the federal edifice. Toast lists acted as a tally as each state formed a convention to debate the Constitution. The Massachusetts newspaper *Independent Chronicle* published toasts that counted down the progress of the states:

> The patriotick State of Delaware.—As her conduct has been, may it still be exemplary to her sister States.
> The State of Pennsylvania,—may the new Constitution render her as unrivaled in agriculture, as she has been in commerce.
> The State of New-Jersey—may the adoption of the Federal Constitution, make them as happy in peace, as they have been distinguished for their patriotism, and intrepidity in war.
> The State of Connecticut—may the fertility of her soil, render her virtuous citizens happy, while human beings are permitted to inhabit the globe.
> The State of Georgia—may her designing opposers of the Federal Constitution, meet the same fate, the savage opposers of all government have met, from the gallantry of her citizens.
> The State of Massachusetts—may her virtuous citizens, that raised the sixth pillar, by cementing themselves, become an emblem of union to America.
> May the virtuous citizens of New-Hampshire be as forward in adopting the Constitution, as her military sons have been, in preparing themselves to defend her rights.[46]

Each time a state ratified the Constitution, newspapers described the many celebrations and toasts given. "A speedy Ratification" was offered as a toast to the first five states that approved the document, then the sixth state, then the seventh, and so on. Meanwhile, Rhode Island continued to stand alone. Her situation was constantly referred to in many toasts. For example: "The citizens of *Rhode Island*—may the scales be removed from off their eyes, and may they join the Federal Edifice under the banners of *truth* and *justice*."[47] The pressure to ratify was constant: "Perpetual infamy, shame and confusion be to all those who seek to dissolve the federal union."[48]

Nine states were needed to ratify the Constitution for it to be official. New Hampshire became the ninth by June 1788, and Portsmouth residents were extremely proud: "The State of New-Hampshire—may the glory of putting the great political machine in motion, render her citizens immortal."[49] Most federal celebrations therefore only included nine toasts.

4. "May the Wisdom of 1775 pervade...!" 1775–1783

A group of revelers in Brooklyn, New York, "attacked" those who were against ratification in their ninth toast, hoping that "continual disappointment and never-dying remorse, pain and poverty [may] ever attend those antifederalists who, through motives of interest, stand opposed to a government, formed for the good of their country." They ended their toasts on a more optimistic note: "May the United States, cemented by the new constitution, rise beautiful as a Phoenix from the ashes of contempt; and may commerce, in all its branches, flourish unrestricted under its auspices, as long as America has a name amongst the nations."[50]

The supporters of the Constitution were known as the Federalists, while those opposed to ratification were called Antifederalists. The Antifederalists were concerned about the loss of state liberties and sovereignty. A strong central authority was undemocratic and too much like the British monarchy. Antifederalist toasts in the *Carlisle Gazette* in July 1788 expressed their concerns: "May the designs of such endeavour to enslave the citizens of America, prove abortive"; "May America remain free from tyranny, anarchy, and consolidation."[51] One toast given in Keene, New Hampshire, held out hope that Antifederalists would eventually come around and support the federal government: "The Antifederalists—may they read the Constitution without prejudice, have wisdom to understand it, become good subjects, and enjoy the blessings of it."[52]

There was already an effort by some states to amend the new constitution to make it more acceptable for ratification. The citizens of Carlisle, Pennsylvania, gave this toast on Independence Day: "If the new federal government is not altogether perfect, may it speedily receive such amendments as will reconcile to it every citizen who has objected to it from virtuous principles."[53] An Antifederalist judicial committee met in Newport, Rhode Island, and raised their glasses to "[t]he old Confederation, with proper amendments," and "May each State retain their sovereignty in the full extent of republican governments."[54] Antifederalists still did not have the numbers to prevent Virginia from becoming the tenth state to ratify the Constitution, but Federalists hoped that they would realize the inevitability of ratification: "May the Minorities in the different States be disappointed in their Fears, behold their Error, and Rejoice with the Happy."[55] The *New-Hampshire Spy* reprinted a list of toasts that honored the many "Bearers of the Flags, in the Procession formed to celebrate the *progress* of the new Constitution—They are besides being federal, superior to any of the *technical toasts, sentiments,* &c. so celebrated, and so often recorded in European celebrations." Each toast honored the many groups representing the people and occupations of the nation: farmers, masons, bricklayers, watch makers, bakers, tailors, coppersmiths, printers, carpenters, blacksmiths, saddlers, shoemakers, tobacconists, tanners, weavers, butchers, gunsmiths, brewers, barbers, coopers, rope makers, surveyors, merchants, lawyers, and physicians.[56]

George Washington was getting ready to take the helm of the new government as its first president in 1788. Many looked to Washington to lead them through the unknowns of a new government: "May the United States never fail of having a President who shall be possessed of the spirit and temper of a Washington."[57] Within the next decade, the nation would split into factions, and the toasts, once used to unify, would instead become weapons of division.

After the American Revolution, there was a concern that the lack of a common cause among the states would cause the union to cease. This worry was reflected in toasts. Americans were appreciative that the end of the war had come, and many toasted the return of the commercial relationship with Great Britain. People also drank to the Confederation Congress, but was that enough to keep the nation together? Toasts were made more to local concerns of the states than those of the nation. Washington was still the most toasted individual, so he was a symbol of national unity. The western Massachusetts conflict known as Shays's Rebellion finally got delegates from the states to gather in Philadelphia and create a new federal constitution. Toasts were made in the hopes that the states would approve the new government, but some worried that the federal constitution was either too weak or too strong.

Chapter 5

"The Rights of Man throughout the world,"[1] 1789–1793

"Our ILLUSTRIOUS PRESIDENT, may calmness, peace and felicity, bless the evening of his life, as his youth and middle age have been glorious by the most exalted achievements of military renown."[2]

"The French Nation—may they have temperance and firmness to accomplish the glorious Revolution they have begun."[3]

"President WASHINGTON—transcendent of royalty, SAVIOUR of his country, enemy to tyranny, and friend to mankind."[4]

George Washington was inaugurated as the first president in April 1789. As he traveled from Mount Vernon to New York City, Americans flocked to see him pass through their towns, honoring him with triumphal arches, flowers, dinners, and toasts. Some compared him to Moses, for he led the American people out of political slavery.[5] His Excellency was "The Illustrious WASHINGTON, in the triple Capacity of Citizen, Soldier and Statesman."[6] Even his vice president was praised: "Mr. Adams—May he deservedly keep that honor as Vice-President, which he gained as an Ambassador."[7] The Fourth of July toasts in 1789 overflowed with nationalist and military sentiments. The residents of Portsmouth, New Hampshire, praised Washington as the "Protector of their Liberties."[8]

Enthusiasm and national fervor were high, so the sentiments people drank to were very generous. The newly elected members of the Boston Artillery offered a toast to Rhode Island and North Carolina, in the hope they would soon join the "Eleven Confederated" states that had already ratified the Constitution. Then, in a spirit of forgiveness, their volunteer toasts were given to the British:

We must not forget to mention, that among the *voluntaries*, their Most Christian and Britannick Majesties' healths were drank:—Nor to omit mentioning the polite and pleasing deportment of the officers of her Britannick Majesty's frigate—who heartily joined in the universal hilarity—and who received from every one present all due attention, agreeably to the spirit of our memorable Declaration of Independence, which declares that *we hold the King and subjects of Great Britain, as we do the rest of the world*, ENEMIES *in* War, *in* Peace FRIENDS.[9]

Events in Europe endangered the high expectations Americans had of Washington and his cabinet. The French economy was bankrupt, so King Louis XVI called the Estates General in May 1789. During the meetings of the new National Assembly, foreign mercenary troops surrounded the city of Paris. On July 14, 1789, the angry people of the city sought gunpowder and entered the courtyard of the massive Bastille prison, which was a symbol of royal oppression. Rumors about the foreign troops circulated wildly, and the Parisians decided to defend themselves with weapons stored in the Bastille. After a day-long siege, the fortress was overtaken and its superintendent brutally decapitated. The French Revolution had its violent beginning.[10]

Americans believed that their own fate as a new republic was intertwined with that of France. Although geography separated them, they believed that they understood what the French were going through because they had experienced firsthand the power of revolution.[11] Stanley Elkins and Eric McKittrick, in their magisterial work *The Age of Federalism: The Early American Republic, 1788-1800*, wrote that the events in France served two purposes for the Americans:

> The main one, the value of which is still almost beyond calculation, lay in the nourishment it gave to Americans' own opinion of themselves. The Revolution began at the moment at which America, having already shown the world with its own Revolution what a liberty-loving people could do, was venturing upon its career as a constitutional republic in 1789, still needing every sanction of legitimacy it could lay hold of for its past and present course, and for its very character. The other function for America, though this did not appear until the Revolution was well advanced, was a major point of reference for domestic political partisanship, just as partisanship was first public emerging.[12]

The Marquis de Lafayette was closely involved with the events in Paris, later sending the key to the Bastille to Washington. Future Supreme Court Chief Justice John Marshall wrote, "'We were all strongly attached to France—more strongly than myself. I sincerely believed human liberty to depend in a great measure on the success of the French Revolution.'"[13] Toasts continued to praise the French king: "Louis the 16th the defender of freedom."[14] The German Society of Pennsylvania ended the year with

5. "The Rights of Man throughout the world," 1789–1793

a hopeful toast: "May the altar of freedom, now erecting in France, prove as eminent and illustrious as that established in America."[15] New Hampshire residents celebrating the Fourth of July holiday in 1790 toasted "the National Assembly of France and the asserters of freedom throughout the world" and "May the powers of Europe, now at war, soon enjoy the blessings of peace, and be as free as America."[16]

It was easy for Americans to support the actions of the people in Paris. They were kindred spirits separated only by an ocean. It is interesting that the French king was still frequently toasted, even during the early stages of the Revolution. Americans were fiercely anti–Catholic, and so it seemed that Louis XVI's faith was either ignored or conveniently forgotten. The following anecdote from Massachusetts proved that even a misinterpreted toast regarding Catholicism almost led to trouble:

> GOV. SHIRLEY of Massachusetts, while on a public commission in France, married a French woman: On his return to his government, at a public entertainment, after the King and Royal Family were toasted, he gave the *Earl of Holdrenesse*, who was then Prime minister. The Door-Keeper, who at that time announced the toasts, said, "His Excellency gives his Holiness"; The Governor with astonishment and indignation vociferated, "you rascal, I did not." Col. P____ being present, and at the time Sheriff of the county, started up, and repeating the toast as it was really delivered, calmed the agitation the company was thrown into by the accident; and from that time this service always devolved on the Sheriff for the time being.[17]

Some were still concerned about Rhode Island's reticence to ratify the Constitution. A toast given by grand jury members in the District of New York was for "the Convention of Rhode Island—May their wisdom and integrity soon introduce our stray sister to her station in the happy national family of America."[18] Rhode Island finally ratified in May 1790. The *Newport Mercury* printed a list of toasts given by the inhabitants of Tiverton, Rhode Island, on March 26, 1789, because "it must afford our readers a pleasing reflection, that there yet remains a virtuous few, daily increasing, who are firm friends to good government, and detest *unrighteous laws*." Two toasts demonstrated both the hopes and fears of the Federalists (supporters of the Constitution): "May the Wheels of the Federal Superstructure turn to the honor of our infant Empire"; "An utter destruction and speedy annihilation of Antifederalism."[19] The state's hesitation was not appreciated by others: "The state of Rhode Island—May her former errors teach her a better mode of conduct in future."[20] The Augusta, Massachusetts (District of Maine), chapter of the Tammany Society, which frequently used Native American imagery and symbols in its rituals, attacked Rhode Island in a toast given just before the small state ratified: "May the Seminoleans of Rhode-Island see their error, and be no longer styled wanderers."[21] All seemed to be forgiven when President Washington toured Rhode Island later that summer. He attended a dinner in Newport on August 19 and the toasts extolled Rhode Island's cautious integrity:

> May the Virtues of her citizens equal their Valor and Wisdom.
> May they be as zealous in support of the present Government, as they were in the Defense of their Liberties.
> *May the Last be the First.*[22]

The visit by the president thrilled the citizens of Rhode Island and they enthusiastically praised him:

> This visit was as gratifying to the citizens as it was unexpected. All classes vied with each other in demonstrations of joy, respect and admiration: The pleasing affability and gracious manners of the President, and his polite attention to the great number of citizens who were successively presented to him, added, if possible, to that love, which was felt before. When he withdrew from table at Newport, the company rising, drank the following toast—*The man we love!*—and never was a toast drank with more sincerity—When *"the President of the United States"* was given at Providence, the huzzas, plaudits, and shouts of the company within and without the town hall continued for some time. There never was, perhaps, a greater exhibition of sincere public happiness than upon this occasion; every individual thought he beheld a friend and patron; a father or a brother after a long absence; and, on his part, the President seemed to feel the joy of a father on the return of the prodigal son. We have little room to doubt that his visit to the state of Rhode-Island will be productive of happy effects, for whatever aversion the citizens of that state may have hitherto had to the new government, they must now feel a confidence in the administration of one who professes their universal esteem, and of whose virtues and patriotism they have upon numerous occasions had the strongest pledges.[23]

By 1791, the number of toasts given had increased to fifteen with the addition of two states: Vermont and Kentucky. The New York Society of the Cincinnati offered a volunteer toast to both: "The new states of Vermont and Kentucky. May our stars increase in lustre as they do in number."[24] Citizens at William's Inn in Bennington, Vermont, were thrilled to be a part of the federal union, demonstrated by the following toasts:

> The union of Vermont with the united states,—may it flourish, like our pines and continue unshaken over our mountains.
> May the new states soon rival the old in federal virtues.
> May the federal officers of the district of Vermont act with integrity and merit the confidence of the people.[25]

A toast given later by Vermont troops in 1792 was to "the memory of Ethan Allen & all the deceased patriots of Vermont, may their children remember their offspring and survivors copy their good deeds."[26]

5. "The Rights of Man throughout the world," 1789-1793

Washington's national tour brought him into contact with many Americans. Traveling through South Carolina in May, he was feted with sumptuous feasts. The following passage was reprinted in South Carolina's *Columbian Herald*, taken from a Boston newspaper. The writer stressed that the most effective way to truly honor Washington was by drinking toasts:

> OF TOASTS
>
> The ebulitions of convivial hours, may justly be denominated the criterions of sentiment and truth. If this position is well-founded, human nature is not so depraved as some moralists endeavour to insinuate. Where can be found a fuller flow of the sweet "milk of human kindness"—than in the majority of toasts given on political and festive occasions?—*Happiness to all mankind*, contains a sentiment that volumes, in expression, cannot exceed. Our fair friends too universally attract a particular notice. Our gallant allies—and of them their patriot KING—and *Liberty's Viceroy*, FAYETTE—not to mention the distinguished characters, "who first respired our native air"—always receive the tribute due to their worth—and though *wit* is not easy to be courted—and *Pleasantry*, good natur'd slut as she is, will not come at a call— we frequently find in toasts a very happy brilliancy of expression. The first toast drank a few days since, at an entertainment given by the sons of St. Tammany at New-York—was, "The *grand sachem* of the *thirteen United fires*—may his declining sun be precious in the sight of the Great Spirit—that the mild lustre of the departing beams, may prove no less glorious than the effulgence of the transcendant splendour of his meridian greatness."—after this, what can *we* say?[27]

Masons all over the country glorified Washington, a brother Mason himself: "Our brother, George Washington—With the honors of Masonry."[28] The laying of the cornerstone of the new Federal District on the banks of the Potomac River was cause for Masonic euphoria. Commissioners of the project toasted the event in the Alexandria, Virginia, Masonic lodge in late May:

> May the Stone which we are about to place in the ground remain an immovable monument of the wisdom and unanimity of Northamerica.
>
> May "Jealousy, that green eyed monster," be buried deep under the work which we have this day completed never to rise again within the Federal district![29]

John Adams was overshadowed by Washington's fame and stature, but he was still the recipient of many positive toasts: "The vice president of the united states. May he long bless his country with ability and integrity that has hitherto characterized him."[30] Bostonians gave the following toast to Adams, praising him for his role as a peace commissioner in Paris after the Revolutionary War and the generous trade terms he negotiated: "'*The persevering and successful Negotiator for the* FISHERIES *of our country—the* VICE-PRESIDENT *of the United States.*'"³¹ Fishing was of the utmost importance to Adams's native state. It was "the Staple of *Massachusetts.—*may she ever remember, '*That with every fish she draws out of the ocean, she draws out a piece of silver.*'"³²

Alexander Hamilton, once General Washington's most important aide-de-camp, was recognized for his work as the treasury secretary. Merchants in Charleston, South Carolina, were especially eager to honor him and his financial program, which benefited them:

> The national bank, a general diffusion of its happy effects throughout the united states.
> The secretary of the treasury; may his fame increase with the rising credit of his country.³³

Some toasts were used to eulogize heroes who had passed on. Early patriots such as Dr. Joseph Warren and Richard Montgomery, who were both killed in battle in 1775, continued to be toasted well into the 1790s. Benjamin Franklin passed away in May 1790, and the Tammany Society of New York City, on May 14, 1791, drank to "the memory of our immortal countryman, Benjamin Franklin, whose Philosophy drew electric fire from Heaven, and whose Patriotism cherished the first sparks of that freedom which now blesses his native land."³⁴ There were many toasts in the southern states to the brilliant General Nathaniel Greene, who died in 1786:

> The memory of our late brother, general Greene, and all those who have fallen in defence of our nation.³⁵
> The memory of gen. Greene.³⁶
> The memory of general Greene. May his name inspire us with gratitude, so long as his military achievements excite our applause.³⁷

The Fourth of July celebrations in 1791 throughout the country "fully confirm this sentiment, that Independence, Freedom and Government are dear to the citizens of this great Republic," according to a letter published in the *Gazette of the United States*.³⁸ France was included now in Independence Day toasts. France's Declaration of the Rights of Man and the Citizen was adopted in August 1789. Thomas Paine wrote a pro–French pamphlet in May 1791, *The Rights of Man*.³⁹ Banquet participants in Braintree, Massachusetts, toasted "the King of Frenchmen, and the National Assembly, may the Revolution, cause a [illegible] fire, whose effulgence, shall irradiate the nations, which are now wrapt in the gloom of slavery; and whose heat shall dissolve the chains, with which the victims of tyranny are bound," and "PAINE, and the RIGHTS of MAN."⁴⁰ Paine was "the citizen of the world"⁴¹ and "The Clarion of Freedom."⁴²

5. "The Rights of Man throughout the world," 1789-1793

Americans toasted the day when "'the Rights of man shall become the supreme law of every land, and their separate fraternities be absorbed in one great Democratic Society comprehending the human race.'"[43]

The situation in France caused an ideological split in Washington's cabinet. The president, Adams, and Hamilton were shocked by the violence and speed of the French Revolution. A strong federal central government brought stability, they believed, and so they were known as Federalists. Thomas Jefferson supported the Parisians who wanted to establish a republic, and so he and his followers became Republicans. They distrusted a strong national government and anything remotely "British." Republicans saw themselves as the true defenders of liberty and the national government:

> Federalists, they claimed, were wolves in sheep's clothing: would-be aristocrats, Anglophiles and "new Tories" who used the Constitution to protect the interests of their "class." The same Boston militia company that toasted their "Gallic Allies" also proclaimed: "May the emanations of *Federalism* be as a *Pillar of Fire* to true Republicans, and as a Cloud of Darkness to Aristocrats." Republicans lost no opportunity to identify Federalists with aristocracy, linking them to images of opulence, greed, and corruption. "However pleasing the ideas of Monarchy may be to *some* people," wrote a Philadelphia correspondent concerning the 1791 celebrations, "the citizens of Philadelphia are too strongly attached to the arguments that are broached in favor of arbitrary government, and hereditary succession."[44]

The fourteenth of July became a new holiday: Bastille Day. Toasts given for this new celebration were to the events and people of the French Revolution: the King, the National Assembly, and new French liberties (freedom of the press, religious tolerance, and trial by jury).[45] The residents of Sandgate, Vermont, gave this elaborate toast: "The distinguished patriots of the French nation composing the national assembly of France, may their glorious exertions for the establishment of the rights of conscience and of citizenship be crowned with success, and may their generous toils merit the approbation of all lovers of freedom throughout the world."[46] Even New York City's Evacuation Day, November 25, was an opportunity for Republicans to take advantage of the pro–French attitudes of many Americans. The Tammany Society toasted "'those heroes of France whose patriotic virtues have caused Columbian flame to consume the Gallic yoke of despotism.'"[47]

King Louis XVI, bowing to popular pressure, formally accepted the new French constitution in September 1791. A large gathering of French citizens took place at Mr. Gray's Public Gardens in Baltimore, Maryland, to celebrate this highly anticipated event. Their toasts could only offer a "faint Idea" of "the joy that pervaded every Heart, and filled every Mind."

The French nation, the King, and the National Assembly took the top positions on the toast list, with Washington and Congress in fifth place. La Fayette and all who contributed to the Revolution in Paris were toasted next. The seventh toast recognized the civil clergy of France, who had taken a loyalty oath to the new government: "May the Light of Reason drive Fanaticism from their Hearts; and teach them that the Citizen's Duties towards Religion and his Country are inseparable." After wishing general prosperity to both France and the United States, the fourteenth toast offered forgiveness to those who held different opinions regarding the ideals of the Revolution or had fled France in fear: "The general Amnesty; may those that have erred from a Difference of political Opinion, recover from their Error, re-enter their Country, and may they be reconciled in its Bosom in a Manner that will forever make them cherish it."

The Federalists did not view the French Revolution with eagerness and joy. Some were becoming increasingly concerned about the radical actions of the Jacobins and the sansculottes. In a February 19, 1792, letter to Thomas Brand Hollis, Vice President Adams questioned the motives of radicals like Thomas Paine and expressed his own moderate conviction:

> Pray, how go the rights of man? The wrongs of Nobles, Priests and Kings? Pray how do you like the Author of the Rights of Man? Do you find him a holy man, fit for an Apostle of Republicanism? The spirit, and System of Rational Liberty to all Nations, Is a favorite Toast with me, but I deprecate the rashness of desperate adventurers, and detest the Articles or unprincipled impostures.[48]

By July 1792, people were equating support for the French Revolution with "true" support for the principles of the American Revolution. The following comment on toasts appeared in the *Federal Gazette*:

> If a judgement may be justly formed from the various Toasts that have been drank this year on the *fourth* or *fourteenth* of July, the republican spirit is very fast raising in this country, to re-assume its former elevation on the political thermometer; and the cause of France, if an opinion may be formed from the universal effusions in favor of the patriotic cause, is become in a great degree our own.[49]

One toast given by a Vermont militia company condemned aristocracy while highlighting republicanism: "May the American states be long defended from the inundation which is threatened by the increase of aristocrats, who wish for a rich metropolis and a poor peasantry; want a great personage's head on the current coin, and are advocates for keeping shut the doors of the Senate."[50] Members of the Tammany Society in New York City later joined French gentlemen who had gathered on the third anniversary of Bastille Day, toasting, "May the heroes of the *Bastile* and the American 'Mahawks' be ever honored is the forlorn hopes of universal freedom."[51]

5. "The Rights of Man throughout the world," 1789-1793

Jefferson and his Republican supporters believed that the bloodthirsty means used in France were justified. The new French republic "heartened American republicanism and undercut Hamiltonian 'monocrats.'"[52] The pro-British critics of the French Revolution's radicalism were described as being anti-republican Francophobes. Federalists feared the violent excesses of uncontrolled democracy,[53] refusing occasionally to read the Declaration of Independence at some celebrations because of the anti-British sentiments. The phrase "all men are created equal" prompted fear of egalitarianism. The right of revolution especially frightened Federalists. The spiraling tumult in France justified their fears.[54]

Federalist toasts tended to focus on the achievements of the federal government. The Friends of Liberty in Carlisle, Pennsylvania, gathered on July 11, and their toasts were to "National Credit—the palladium of National Greatness." They also included a toast to Thomas Paine as "the scourge of Tyrants."[55] Celebrants at Mr. Gibson's farm on July 14, also in Carlisle, toasted both the Senate and the House of Representatives, reminding both chambers to uphold the interests of their constituents.[56]

Alexander Hamilton wrote an editorial under the pseudonym "An American" to John Fenno, the editor of the *Gazette of the United States*. Hamilton criticized Thomas Jefferson, warning the public to question Jefferson's motives:

> If to National Union, national respectability Public Order and public Credit they are willing to substitute National disunion, National insignificance, Public disorder and discredit—then let them unite their acclamations and plaudits in favour of Mr. Jefferson: Let him be the toast of every political club, and the theme of every popular huzza. For to those points, without examining his motives do assuredly tend the political tenets, real or pretended, of that Gentleman.[57]

Meanwhile, during the spring of 1792, voters in New York were dealing with a situation in the gubernatorial election. Governor George Clinton, running for reelection, was certified as the winner only because the ballots from Otsego County were rejected. If the ballots had been accepted, according to supporters of Clinton's opponent, John Jay, Jay would have won the election with a comfortable majority: 300-103. People were understandably angry, evidenced by their toasts. Jay's supporters drank the following toasts in Poughkeepsie on June 21:

> John Jay, (Governor) by the voice of the people.
> The patriotic four who protested against the rejection of the ballots of Otsego.
> May the electors of Otsego, act like freemen, and display a spirit ever ready to assert their privilege.[58]

Jay's supporters meeting at Mechanics Hall in New York City on the Fourth of July expressed their outrage:

> May the contempt of every free patriot light upon the men who by a pretended respect to the letter have omitted all regard to the spirit of the law; violated the Constitution and intentions of the Legislature.
>
> May his Excellency Geo. Clinton, by resignation, convince the world that neither the last of power or gain have effaced from his mind the duty he owes to the peace and happiness of his country.[59]

Pro-Clinton toasts appeared at the same time in the *Diary* newspaper on Independence Day, attacking those who tried to prevent Clinton's reelection and questioned the election results:

> The independent electors, who have secured their re-election, and who, in their suffrages, were unawed by the menaces of aristocrats, and the impotent, vulgar threats of a braggadocia judge.
>
> May their determination upon the law in the judicial capacity in which they acted, be an example to other judges, not to be intimidated by the threats of disappointed faction.
>
> May the cry of the privileges of the people no longer be used by aspiring demagogues, as a pretext for encouraging licentiousness, and for concealing ambitious views.[60]

An ironic toast that appeared in the South Carolina paper *City Gazette* deserves attention. It was given by the American Revolutionary Society, and it praised South Carolinians' ability to support the laws of the federal government: "The state of South Carolina—may her citizens ever be the first in supporting federal measures, and the last in submitting to lawless usurpation."[61] The nullification crisis of Andrew Jackson's presidency and actual secession from the Union in 1861 were several decades away.

By the fall of 1792, France was fighting several foreign enemies on its eastern borders, such as Prussia, Brunswick, and Austria. A Prussian military force took the fortress town of Verdun, but they were later defeated by the French General Charles-François Dumouriez at the Battle of Valmy in September.[62] Toasts given on Columbus Day that year in New York City pledged support for the French armies:

> May the liberty of the French rise superior to all the efforts of Austrian despotism.
>
> A Burgoyning to the duke of Brunswick.[63]

The French military victories excited the American public, reminding them of their own revolutionary past. The victory at Valmy and the retreat of the German forces were cause for celebrations that mirrored those glorifying Bunker Hill, Saratoga, and Yorktown. Virginians in Alexandria

5. "The Rights of Man throughout the world," 1789–1793

raised their glasses to the Duke of Brunswick's defeat at Valmy: "May the Duke of Brunswick always receive in France a *Treat* as will make him wish for a *Re-Treat*."[64] The victorious General Dumouriez was lauded as the hero of the day:

> As Joshua, the son of Num, did to the children of Ammon, so may Dumourier do to all tyrants.[65]
>
> Dumourier and the heroes of the French army—May they still be characterized by the same courage and perseverance which has already produced effects so brilliant.[66]
>
> Dumourier—may this hero of liberty teach princes, who traffic in human blood, to prize their subjects Liberty.[67]

Praises for Dumouriez would be short-lived because he deserted the French army and joined up with the Austrian forces in March 1793. Toasts later compared him with the despised traitor, Benedict Arnold:

> May France have no more Dumouriers, and may the United States never produce another Arnold.[68]
>
> Arnold and Dumourier; may they wander comfortless through the deserts of Arabia, and their names handed down to posterity to perpetuate their baseness.[69]

Although patriotism was high at the beginning of Washington's second term, the few years remaining before his retirement would bring division and intrigue. The French monarch lost his head and France entered a violent stage in its Revolution, but revolutionary enthusiasm never abated for many. The American people would later attack Washington's negotiator for bringing back an unpopular treaty with their detested enemy, Great Britain. The toasts that welcomed Washington to office were indicative of one American vision. Toasts would be very different by the time he left office.

The beginning of Washington's administration was full of inspirational toasts, all hoping for a successful future. By the start of the 1790s, events in France led to toasts that pledged support for the new revolution. Bastille Day became an occasion for celebrations. George Washington, John Adams, Thomas Paine, and Alexander Hamilton made their presence known in toasts throughout the nation. Rhode Island, meanwhile, received many toasts that were unforgiving for the state's late ratification of the Constitution. The unity that Washington hoped for in his cabinet started to come apart as factions formed regarding support for the French Revolution. Toasts were used to capture the ideals of both factions (Republicans and Federalists), and in New York the toasts supported opposing sides in a controversial election.

CHAPTER 6

"Hypocritical Federalism and Malignant Toryism,"[1] 1793–1796

"The Rights of Man, the liberty of the press, and trials by Juries, be the happy privilege of the citizens of America, from the Gulf of St. Lawrence, to the river Mississippi."[2]

"The President of the United States—may he deliberate with coolness, that he may determine with firmness, to withhold his signature from the treaty with Britain."[3]

"His excellency, JOHN JAY, Esq. governor and commander in chief of all the militia, & admiral of the navy of the State of Doctor of Laws, &c. &c. &c, late chief justice to the United States of America, envoy extraordinary, and minister plenipotentiary to the king of Great-Britain—*may he and his treaty be for ever politically d----d.*"[4]

George Washington's second term did not begin with the same enthusiasm as his first term. His hopes for a unified cabinet were devastated. Treasury Secretary Alexander Hamilton was the leader of the commercial pro-northern, pro–British faction, while the agricultural pro-southern, pro–French faction was led by Secretary of State Thomas Jefferson. Jefferson and Hamilton partnered to pressure Washington to remain for another term. He was still the personification of national union, and Jefferson wrote to Washington that "'North & South will hang together if they have you to hang on.'"[5]

Although France had entered a violent phase by 1793, support was still strong for America's "sister republic." People understood the debt they owed France for the victory over the British, so it was important to many to embrace France's efforts to establish a republic. The March 15, 1793, issue of Philadelphia's *General Advertiser* printed a lengthy reminder of this fact, addressed to the "citizens of America," and approved by the "ghosts of WARREN, MERCER, & MONTGOMERY":

Had the French, when we were struggling for our liberties, expressed their approbation of our conduct by splendid and sumptuous banquets, & by quaffing bumpers of Champaine, accompanied with florid toasts. I say, had the French done this, and left us to our own feeble efforts, where would been the freedom of America? Long before France, as a nation, declared herself in our favour, how many of its magnanimous and intrepid heroes had already dyed our shores with their blood? And whom have we put in the balance against these defenders of our freedom? One brave, one generous, one truly patriotic citizen.[6]

Americans saw it as their responsibility to be the harbingers of democracy to the world and be the asylum for all victims of tyranny in England, Scotland, and Ireland.[7] On Washington's birthday in 1793, the people of Portland, Massachusetts (District of Maine), drank to "'Brave Irishmen! May the sword of justice, once drawn, never be sheathed till they have obtained equal liberty and laws.'"[8] The neighbors to the south were also not forgotten: "The colonies of South America: may they become happy and free as we are."[9]

Poland's fight for independence was recognized in the Fourth of July toasts in 1793. Poland's King Stanislaus was toasted as "the only patriotick King; may the Poles be reanimated and enabled to establish a free constitution."[10] One volunteer toast in Philadelphia expressed a common hope: "May the Poles unite their strength, and with the assistance of the friends to universal freedom, oblige those ambitious, rapacious land-jobbers, and land-robbers of Russia and Prussia, to restore the stolen property to the right and lawful owners, with damages—and the royal thieves be condemned to undergo a total and eternal obscuration, by the sun of liberty."[11]

The Marquis de Lafayette ran afoul of both the monarchy and the radicals in Paris. The radicals became known as the "Jacobins," taking their name from the religious order that leased their meeting space in Paris.[12] The Jacobins believed that Lafayette was too close to the royal family and could not be trusted, but Lafayette also lost the favor of Queen Marie Antoinette. He was forced to leave France in August when a warrant was issued for his arrest. It was a shocking turn of events. The Marquis was a man who had been able to unite the different factions of the country, and both Hamilton and Jefferson considered him to be a close friend.

Toasts to Lafayette reminded Americans of his efforts on behalf of the United States and the early stages of the French Revolution. They also pleaded for merciful treatment and his speedy release from an Austrian prison cell:

> LA FAYETTE.—May his patriotick virtues be rewarded with blessings of Liberty, and his restoration meet the welcome of a free people.[13]
> LA FAYETTE, whose torch first enkindled the flame of Liberty in France.[14]

FAYETTE—May every true patriot survive the calumnies of his enemies, and meet the reward of his merit.[15]

The Marquis De la Fayette—May the people of America forever pay to him the just tribute of gratitude, and may they continue to esteem him in his adversities, as they justly loved and admired him in the splendor of his fortunes.[16]

The Committee of Public Safety in France was established in April 1793. The violent repression of anti-revolutionary activities known as the Reign of Terror began in September. Lafayette was lucky to be imprisoned in Austria, since he undoubtedly would have met the guillotine. The *Columbian Herald* of South Carolina reprinted an excerpt from a French paper that was critical of Americans' constant support, obvious through the use of toasts, for someone the French radicals viewed as a traitor:

> It is a pity, that having thrown aside the pompous strappings of their old government, they should still return trifling decorations which can only sit easy on the shoulders of puppies, and neglect the honorable title of *Citizen*. The phrase citizen has made, we are told, many Americans smile; wise men, however, its has set a thinking. We find nothing that is a better criterion of the general sentiments of the Americans, than their toasts published in the newspapers. From these it is wonderful to learn, that they still hesitate to pronounce La Fayette guilty of treason against the nation![17]

The pro–French demonstrations reached their zenith when the new French ambassador arrived in Charleston, South Carolina, on April 8, 1793: Edmond Charles Eduoard Genet, or simply Citizen Genet. Genet intended to end American neutrality and then get the government to provide him with loans and a privateer navy.[18] An ambitious man, he was astonished by his reception. He catered to the Republican faction by calling Washington a monarchist and criticizing him for seeking a strong commercial relationship with England. Genet cried out, "In the United States, men still exist who can say, 'Here a ferocious Englishman slaughtered my father; there my wife tore her bleeding daughter from the hands of an unbridled Englishman,' and those same men can say, 'Here a brave Frenchman died fighting for American liberty; here French naval and military power humbled the might of Britain.'"[19]

Washington was rather cool to the Frenchman. Genet attended a dinner at Oeller's Hotel with Republican supporters, and toasts were drunk to "'the guillotine and all tyrants, plunderers and *funding* speculators' and 'The persecuted Citizen Genet: may his country reward his honest zeal, and the shafts of *calumny* levelled against him, recoil upon the *Archers*.'"[20] Later in June he was again at Oeller's Hotel and participated in several Gallic toasts:

> The Republics of France and America—may they be forever united in the cause of Liberty.

> May France be an example to the World, that the balances of government depend more upon knowledge and vigilance than upon a multifarious combination of its powers.
>
> In complaining of the temporary evils of revolutions, may we never forget, that the greater evils of Monarchy and Aristocracy are *perpetual*.[21]

The eighth toast given at that dinner was to "the spirit of seventy-six and ninety-two—may the citizens of America and France, as they are equal in virtue, be equal in success." The reference to ninety-two was for 1792, when France declared itself a republic. This toast prompted a printed response, titled "THE OBSERVER, No. 1," which argued that the toast was "forcing" Americans to side with the radical factions in France:

> If it is the intention of this doughty toastmaker, merely to *compliment* France at the expense of his country, we must all feel ourselves disposed to join in a tribute of praise for his extreme complaisance; but if by this sentiment he meant to express either his own opinion or that of the public, we must either wish a happy majority to this unripened judgement, or a more competent knowledge of the sentiments of his fellow citizens. Is there no American who would be willing that the glorious and genuine spirit of liberty, which actuated our countrymen in *seventy-six* should be debased by the most distant comparison, with that spirit of anarchy and sedition which at present so strongly predominates among the French? Believe me, the one is as different from the other as the mild dictates of charity and benevolence are from those of malice and revenge.[22]

King Louis XVI, whom Jefferson himself had called "'a good man'" and "'an honest man,'" was beheaded on January 21, 1793. Adams, Hamilton, and Washington were worried that the Revolution in France was out of control.[23] Washington's Neutrality Proclamation was his attempt to protect the nation and keep revolutionary fervor overseas in check. Many people supported the Proclamation. Fourth of July celebrants in Norwich, Connecticut, saw the wisdom of avoiding war and expressed it in an original toast: "'May a horses nightcap be the reward of every one who wishes to involve the United States in war.'"[24] A regiment in Bristol, Rhode Island, expressed the same hope later in October: "May the President's Proclamation be considered and obeyed as the supreme law of the land."[25]

British subjects were likewise relieved at the American government's neutrality. A group of them gathered in Philadelphia at Mr. Richardet's Tavern on Tenth Street with local merchants to celebrate George III's birthday. They toasted, "May the heart that dictated, and the head that proposed it, live long to enjoy the blessings of all the friends to humanity." They also raised their glasses to such sentiments as:

> The prosperity of Great-Britain and America—may their interests be reciprocal, and those interests protected.

"Mort de Louis XVI, le 21 janvier 1793 Place de la Concorde—on voit à gauche le socle de la statue de Louis XV déboulonnée." King Louis XVI of France was once embraced by all Americans as a beloved ally, but by 1793 he was a deposed ruler who lost his head in the French Revolution: "The guillotine—May it be laid aside after every crowned head has received a parting embrace" (Toast #8, *New Jersey Journal*, 7-15-1795) (Library of Congress).

> All good Americans—May moderation be their principle; neutrality their resolution, and industry their motto.[26]

Unsurprisingly, the pro–British toasts given at Mr. Richardet's Tavern caused an uproar. One article appeared in Philadelphia's *National Gazette*, demanding to know if it was prudent to print such toasts in four local newspapers. Was it really discretion "to obtrude their sentiments on the public"? After all,

> The people of the United States wish to see the world purged on kings, for they consider them the *pests of the human race*. Toasting, is a method which societies have lately adopted, to rehearse the articles of their *political faith*. What then shall we say to men who dare to drink in this country, "The red coats of London." Who are these red coats of London? Are they not the same British hirelings whose progress in the United States but a few years since was marked by devastation, burning, rapes, and murder, who at this present time are employed in cutting the throats of all who deny the divine, indefeasible, hereditary right of kings, passive obeisance, or non-resistance?[27]

Responding to this complaint, "A FRIEND TO PEACE" penned a letter two weeks later and argued that it was nobody's business as to how the British toasted their king. If they included a toast to the president, which they did (toast #14), it was done out of decorum. The British revelers drank to Washington as a token of good will. It was no question that they were going to toast their own monarch first: "for they all do what gives you so much offense, that is they give their sovereign saint, nation or patron, for the first toast, after which *most* of them give the President of the United States."[28]

Republicans were increasingly more successful in manipulating the Independence Day festivities to advocate ideals. Thomas Jefferson was toasted prominently because of his link to the Declaration: "'Jefferson, chairman, of the committee that reported the declaration of American independence.'"[29] Some of their toasts were offered to the "leader" of the people in the House of Representatives, James Madison.[30] Washington was still venerated, although the policies of his administration were increasingly unpopular. The Federalists still deified Washington, and the president and his administration were compared to classical virtues and figures in the following Federalist Independence Day toasts:

> May every nation on the Globe, boast like America, a Washington, who has the *shield* of FABIUS, the *sword* of MARCELLUS, and the helmet of SCIPIO!
> May the helm of Government ever preserve an intermediate course between the *shoals* of SLAVERY, and the rocks of LICENTIOUSNESS; the SCYLLA and CHARYBDIS of the *political channel!*[31]
> Heaven forbid! that the name of Washington should ever be assumed, like that of Caesar, to consecrate villainy, or deify ideocy.[32]

Republicans saw the value in claiming Washington as a symbol of their own ideology. Doing so was a complex task, since his perceived pro–British feelings were viewed by them as a character weakness. The *National Gazette* printed a letter written under the pseudonym "PHILOGENET" that emphasized Washington's increasing unpopularity, saying "that when 'The man of the people' was toasted in the presence of the person to whom it was *intended* to apply, those warm emotions were not excited in the breasts of the many citizens who were present, that the same circumstance would have produced some time ago." The writer then argued that Washington surrounded himself with the wrong people, and if that bad influence continued, then the people "will withdraw their esteem and confidence" in his government. The final line was a plea: "May our long esteemed Washington speedily disentangle himself from the counsels of the aristocratic *friends* who surround him, become the active friend of our generous allies, and command the *universal* regard of his countrymen."[33]

If people did not support truly "republican" values, they were accused of embracing aristocracy, monarchy, and despotism. Farmers in Vermont, for example, toasted Washington as a reproof instead of praise. They acknowledged his "'well-earn'd fame,'" but then hoped that he would die "'before his heart shall be enchained or contaminated, by tyranny or despotism.'"[34] Others were on the lookout for inappropriate toasts, such as "A Friend to Truth," who read Federalist toasts given on February 4, 1794, at Cooperstown, New York, and wrote to the printer of the *Diary* newspaper: "It is not less curious than disgustful, to observe the most pitiful subterfuges adopted by a dying party of aristocrats to keep alive their vile opposition to the liberty and tranquility of this country."[35]

Citizen Genet's star was losing its luster due to his dangerous intrigues. Even Jefferson tried to distance himself from the ambassador. A witness in Morris County, New Jersey, described the reaction of the crowd to a toast to Genet: "After a number of toasts were drank, Citizen G---- was proposed, but met with such opposition, that it was withdrawn—This is a sure evidence that his conduct is not generally approved among us—and we hope he may be recalled before any further mischief ensues."[36] Still, Genet's supporters were still active. When members of the Republican Society of Charleston, South Carolina, got together on to commemorate the anniversary of the French Alliance of 1778, they made several toasts honoring Genet:

> The firm patriot and true Republican, Citizen Genet.
> Citizen Madison, and the Republican party in Congress.
> The guillotine to all tyrants, plunders and funding speculators.
> May the flags of France and America be ever combined against regal tyranny.[37]

"A CITIZEN" wrote at length in the *Daily Advertiser* about each of these toasts. First, the writer took issue with calling Genet a "firm patriot." Genet's conduct was endangering the country, and he was even denounced by the leader of the Paris radicals, Maximilien Robespierre. Next, it was crucial to point out that James Madison was a member of a deliberative body that represented many viewpoints, not just those of the Republicans. The toast praising the guillotine appeared to be the most upsetting for "A CITIZEN," and his dismay is clear:

> I read in this sentiment, neither the benevolence of christians, nor the magnanimity of freemen. Such cruel wishes uttered in the bosom of peace, and amidst the hilarity of joy, do no credit to the moderation and benignity of the American character. But who are we to understand by Funding Speculators? It can mean only the dealers in the funded debt; and for this lawful and innocent traffic, they are denounced as deserving death, the ultimate punishment of political justice. And it deserves in this place to be remarked, that while some of our best patriots and philosophers, are endeavouring by their persuasive reasoning, to soften the edge of our penal codes, these Republican Societies are wishing to arm them with tenfold terrors, by introducing among us the bloody spectacles of the guillotine.

6. "Hypocritical Federalism and Malignant Toryism," 1793–1796

The second volunteer toast given by a Newark, New Jersey, artillery regiment on Washington's birthday showed that people were disillusioned with France's chaotic radicalism: "May reason and philosophy preserve sacred the Rights of Man—but may they never be dependent on Democratic or Jacobin factions."[38] A group of "*patriotic* Gentlemen" drank to Genet's removal: "Citizen Genet's end to all the sons of faction."[39]

While Republicans drank to Jefferson, Madison, and the French Jacobins, Federalists praised the members of the Washington administration. A correspondent for the *Independent Gazette* asked why Alexander Hamilton and John Adams were not honored at a celebration in Newark:

> Could the toasts, which were drank at Newark, flatter Mr. Hamilton and the Vice-President; could they even communicate a ray of comfort to them? They must surely serve as a melancholy memento of departed popularity, and entombed ambition—Like an exception to a general rule that serves to render the rule more strong, the remembrance of those gentlemen at Newark, has the wine sparkled to the health and virtue of those gentlemen? In what other corner of America have bumpers and cheers greeted the patriotism of [John] Jay and [Rufus] King? Solitary indeed must be that virtue, must be that republicanism, which cannot find more than one spot of an immense territory to render homage to them![40]

Just as there were complaints about Republican toasts, it stands to reason that there would be some regarding Federalist toasts. A letter on March 12, 1794, to the editor of the *New-Jersey Journal*, claiming to speak for "Many of your Subscribers in this County," expressed anger about the printing of Federalist toasts and the recognition of such men as John Jay and Rufus King. The subscribers, allegedly, were "of the opinion that such anti-republican examples have a dangerous tendency; for by how much such publications can influence our political manners, by so much have you counteracted our hopes and wishes as a republican printer." The threat of boycotting the paper was made if the editor could not, or would not, provide reasons as to why the paper "is open to publications so opposite to the principles of our government."[41]

Republican toasts included the concepts of Reason: "May it successfully counteract the baneful effects of executive influence, expose the insidious arts of judicial sophistry, and preserve inviolate the purity of legislation"; and Knowledge: "May every citizen be so learned as to know his rights and so brave as to assert them."[42] Republicans wanted their ideals to match those of America's revolutionary past. The Bunker Hill anniversary in Massachusetts was a perfect opportunity for Republican sentiments:

> Americans, forget not your HANCOCK; ye sons of freedom venerate his name.
> The fifteen states of America; prosperity to their Agriculture, Manufactures,

and Commerces; may they suffered no more diminution by robbery and insult abroad, or tyranny at home.

Madison and all the victorious Republicans in Congress.[43]

Independence Day toasts in 1794 were different from those of previous years because of the French Revolution. Toasts supporting the people and policies of the Federalist government then in power were fewer in number.[44] One toast in Providence, Rhode Island, was for national improvements: "May the Spirit for establishing Turnpike Roads, Bridges, and Canals, pervade the Union."[45] Celebrants in Dumfries, Pennsylvania, toasted the "Intrepid Congress of 1776": "may their virtues and valour be a lasting example for our posterity to follow, and their remembrance be engraved on the heart of every republican, till the ardent love of liberty shall expire in the breasts of Americans."[46] Sticking to domestic issues pleased one writer in Hartford, Connecticut:

> It is with great pleasure we remark, that the 4th of July has been much more extensively celebrated this year than usual.—And it is with equal pleasure we observe the spirit of federalism, peace and moderation, which breaks through the multitude of toasts drank on this anniversary. Saving a few toasts, of a few party clubs and societies, the above remark is almost universally just. What a happy prospect has this country, when, amidst the convulsions of Europe, the errors of weak and mistaken, or the attacks of desperate and wicked politicians in her own bosom, a general opposition to war, bloodshed and anarchy, pervade our enlightened citizens. The rational joy of the inhabitants on every return of the DAY OF INDEPENDENCE, proves their strong attachment to real liberty; while their moderate and peaceful sentiments, evince their thorough acquaintance with their own best interests—PEACE and GOOD GOVERNMENT.[47]

American seamen who had been taken captive in the Mediterranean Sea in 1794 received many toasts. Pirates from the Barbary States had been doing this since the early 1790s. The Americans were being held for ransom and forced to work as slaves in Algiers, infuriating the freedom-loving white, Christian American populace. Toasts called for comfort and liberty for the sailors and revenge against the Algerians:

> The Guillotine to the traitors who have traduced the cause of liberty, and to those who have armed the Algerine Pirates against our own American brethren; and may eternal Vengeance overtake such French Republicans.[48]
>
> To our unfortunate Brother Mariners in Algiers—may the justice and generosity of their country speedily emancipate them from the chains & stripes of infidel barbarians.[49]
>
> To our Brethren at Algiers:—Sympathy and Affection, with a liberal and speedy Provision for their Support and Ransom.[50]

6. "Hypocritical Federalism and Malignant Toryism," 1793–1796

Trouble on the high seas was not just limited to the Barbary pirates. The British navy was seizing American vessels in retaliation for America's refusal to assist the British in its war against France. Washington sent the chief justice of the Supreme Court, John Jay, to London to negotiate a favorable trade agreement that would bring peace between the United States and Great Britain. Toasts were given in Jay's honor, hoping for a positive outcome:

> May the embassy of John Jay, be conducted with that manly firmness and persevering integrity, as shall be satisfactory to the people of the United States.[51]
>
> May the result of Mr. Jay's mission give general satisfaction and confirm to the United States a long continuance of peace and public prosperity.[52]
>
> The Chief Justice of the U. States, Envoy Extraordinary to the Court of London.—May his mission be successful; otherwise may America be unanimous in asserting her honor and avenging the unprovoked insults towards her citizens.[53]
>
> May the issue of John Jay's negotiations prove as honourable, and advantageous, as the policy which sent him was wise and patriotic.[54]

Domestic troubles contributed to Washington's worries when farmers in western Pennsylvania rose in rebellion. As part of Hamilton's financial program, a tax on whiskey was passed by Congress in 1791 to raise revenue. Protests were especially strong in Pennsylvania's rural counties, and tax collectors faced the same abusive treatment that was meted out by the Sons of Liberty in pre–Revolutionary Boston. A large force of insurgent farmers gathered to challenge federal authority in August 1794. Washington quickly sent 13,000 troops to end the insurrection.[55] Those in power did not toast the rebels of what became known as the Whiskey Rebellion, but instead praised the federal government's response:

> May our western brethren see the necessity of conforming to the Constitution and Laws of our Country, before the sword of equality, is unleashed against them; and thereby, convince the world that men are capable of governing themselves;—and may every emigrant to this country become a real American in principle.[56]
>
> May the Insurgents of Pennsylvania resign their arms to the legal and constitutional modes of redress, and harmony be speedily restored, without the effusion of human blood.[57]
>
> May the event of the late insurrection prove to the world that the militia of the United States are always ready to suppress insurrections and repel invasions; and be a lasting monument of the virtue efficiency and flexibility of our Republic.[58]

Both the Republicans and Federalists were trying to control the Revolutionary narrative, making sure that the "Spirit of '76" matched their own values. This was obvious at the Evacuation Day festivities in New York City:

> Significantly, militia members on both sides of the political fence chose to celebrate the anniversary of the British evacuation, but they did so with their own purposes in mind. Each side recognized the importance of coming together to celebrate memory that confirmed national identity, but when they adjourned for toasting, their political ideas diverged. Although the commemorative parades, tributes, and toasts were familiar in their forms, their meanings were shifting as real contests for political power were carried on in their midst.[59]

Although the Reign of Terror in France ended with the execution of Maximilien Robespierre in July 1794, the pro–French public still considered the Terror to have been a necessary instrument to establish republican rule. The guillotine received radical toasts, much to the disgust of Washington and the Federalists:

> The guillotine—May it be laid aside after every crowned head has received a parting embrace.[60]
> The guillotine—May it maintain its empire till all crowned heads are laid in the dust.[61]

On Washington's birthday in Massachusetts, a Federalist stronghold, some toasts had a different view of the Terror: "May a divine respect for the preservation of life, take place of that cruel spirit of destruction which has soiled their Revolution under the Robesperian administration,"[62] "May the contempt be the guillotine of the Robespierres of America."[63] The March 6, 1795, issue of the *Massachusetts Mercury* further commented: "On the celebration of the Birthday of the President breathed the purest sentiments of Federal Republicanism; and demonstrated, explicitly, That Jacobinism, Licentiousness, and blood thirsty Democratism, has become as unfashionable in *America* as in France."

The *Federal Intelligencer* of New York printed an extract, titled simply "REPUBLICAN TOASTS," from the *Gazette Francaise*. The writer attacked two particular toasts, which "are the most sarcastic—but not the most humane": "'To the French Cock and the American Eagle—may the first tear out the eyes of the British Lyon, and may the second, if insulted by him, knock at his teeth, as he has cut off his claws in 1783'"; "'May the guillotine not be laid aside until it has given the *farewell clipping* to all crowned heads.'" The writer was incensed by these toasts, asking:

> How can a people, who exist *only* by the benefits of peace, wish for the fall of all crowned heads; who, however guilty they may be, cannot fall without involving millions of innocent souls in their destruction? Ought they not be *blush* at professing such sentiments in cool blood, of which they boast in the delirium of their public revels?[64]

6. "Hypocritical Federalism and Malignant Toryism," 1793–1796

John Jay, meanwhile, continued to negotiate what he hoped would be a decent treaty. He was bargaining from a position of weakness, hoping to get conditions that would ensure that there would be peace between the two nations. However, peace was not a goal for the British. Jay wrote to Washington on March 6, 1795, describing toasts given at a dinner he attended with British merchants:

> You have doubtless heard, that the merchants concerned in the american Trade gave me a Dinner—the principal cabinet ministers were present, and about 200 merchants—many Toa[s]ts were given—when "the President of the united States" was given, it was proposed to be with three cheers, but they were prolonged (as if by Pre-concert, but evidently not so) to six—Several other Toasts passed with great acclamation—particularly "the wooden walls of old England"—almost every Toast referable to america, and manifesting a Desire of Concilition and Cordiality, met with general and strong marks of approbation—Towards the conclusion of the Feast, I was asked for a Toast—I gave a *neutral* one—vizt "a safe & honorable Peace to all the belligerent powers"—You cannot concieve how coldly it was recieved, and tho civility induced them to give it three cheers, yet they were so faint and single, as most decidedly to shew that Peace was not the thing they wished—these were *merchants*—Mr Pinckney was struck as forceably by it as I was; and we both drew the same Conclusions from it.[65]

The results of Jay's efforts culminated in what has become known as simply the Jay Treaty, which arrived in Philadelphia on March 7, 1795. Even before knowing what the treaty contained, people refused to support any agreement negotiated with their former enemy, viewing it as a betrayal of America's primary ally, France. A man identifying himself as "FRANKLIN" wrote a lengthy complaint to the *City Gazette* of Charleston, South Carolina:

> Heretofore it has been usual, on all *public* occasions, to remember the French republic; but since the issue of the negociation, French successes seem no longer to interest us. At the entertainment given to the *Ex Secretary of the Treasury*, in New-York, the French republic was thought unworthy of a place among their toasts, and here the enemies of France were toasted! When all these circumstances are viewed in the aggregate, and as explanatory of each other, what must be the emotion excited in the breast of French republicans?[66]

The two-thirds majority vote needed in the Senate to ratify the treaty occurred on June 24, 1795. The terms that John Jay was able to achieve were far from ideal, but they accomplished Washington's main goal of averting war. However, the Jay Treaty "created a neocolonial status for the United States within the British Empire."[67] British naval supremacy over the Americans was established, but war was avoided and the economic ties to America's strongest commercial trading partner were strengthened. As an equal and independent nation, the United States was able to negotiate with Great Britain.⁶⁸ Support for the treaty, Jay, and the Senate majority was strong in Federalist circles, demonstrated by these congratulatory toasts:

> The treaty with Great Britain: may the American "tonnage" never be limited, but by the growth of her forests!⁶⁹
>
> Our late Envoy to Great-Britain—May the satisfactory amendment of the 12th Article in the Treaty, bring it into speedy operation, and secure us the fruits of talents and exertions.⁷⁰
>
> Confusion to the usurping Demagogues, who opposed the Treaty—May their late contest with the friends of peace and order prove the dying struggles of a disorganized Faction.⁷¹

The supporters of the Jay Treaty were in the minority, however, because when news of the terms was leaked to the press, people went wild with disbelief and anger. Jay claimed that he could walk along the entire eastern seaboard at night because all his burning effigies would light the way.⁷² The treaty was viewed as a betrayal of the American ideals of independence, republicanism, liberty and equality. Americans pleaded with Washington to refuse to sign the treaty, while the senators who voted against the treaty were revered as heroes. Senator Aaron Burr of New York worked diligently with nine other senators to stop ratification. Republican civic groups "drank toasts to the 'ten virtuous, wise, and independent Senators,' the *'Patriotic Ten,'* who had 'refused to sacrifice their country's commerce, rights, and honor.'"⁷³

It seemed as if the sacrifices that Washington had made throughout his public life for the good of his beloved country were being ignored. Just as he had replaced King George III in prominence in drinking toasts, he was now being tossed aside:

> The unpopularity of Washington's policies was ever more central to many of these celebrations. In Boston, amid the usual bell-ringing and cannon fire, those who attended a civic feast pointedly drank no toast to Washington, an unusual omission by these "bigoted democrats" that drew the wrath of Federalists as far away as Charleston. In Portsmouth, New Hampshire "a large number" did drink a cursory toast to "The President of the United States," but they made their partisan sympathies clear with lavish tributes to "The mighty Republic of France," "genuine republicanism," "All American friends to the French revolution," "Thomas Jefferson the American Statesman, Philosopher and Patriot," and "James Madison, the distinguished patriot of America."⁷⁴

One anti-treaty toast in Virginia crossed a line that was thought to be impossible: "'Speedy death to General Washington.'"⁷⁵

Republicans took advantage of the public outrage. Toasts were used as a reliable method to communicate those emotions: "The feelings of a PEOPLE are best described by a display of *their own* sentiments. And perhaps a

6. "Hypocritical Federalism and Malignant Toryism," 1793–1796

perusal of the TOASTS given the last memorable 4th of July, would be the most impartial mirror in which to look for the TRUTH of the many *party* assertions of the times."[76] Toasts attacking Jay continued into September. Some of the typical expressions of anger included:

> The President of the United States—may he never affix his signature to a Treaty, on whose front is engraved "*Destruction to Liberty and Commerce.*"[77]
>
> The Coalition of Hypocritical Federalism and Malignant Toryism, with its offspring, Justice Jay's treaty—may the *via juncta in uno* be speedily strangled by the genius of liberty.[78]
>
> Mr. Jay's treaty with Great Britain—May it never be ratified by our government, if its support is inconsistent with the independence of our country, or prejudicial to its union with France.[79]
>
> John Jay—May he enjoy all the benefits of a purgatory.[80]
>
> MAY the Cage constructed to coop up the *American Eagle*, prove a *trap* for none but *Jays* and *King birds*.[81]
>
> May the names of all true patriots be honored, while an Arnold, Dumourier and Jay are remembered with detestation.[82]

There were, of course, other topics in the drinking toasts of the mid-1790s, although it seems as if the uproar over the Jay Treaty consumed everyone's attention. Reminiscent of the new French liberties, toasts to the freedom of the press were plentiful:

> Freedom of opinion; may it never be surrendered as long as freemen have a nerve to support it.[83]
>
> A candid and impartial discussion—and may the invader of a free press be considered an enemy to his country, and meet the reward of a traitor.[84]
>
> *The freedom and independence of the press*—May that most noble and useful of all human institutions remain forever devoted to the maintenance of public virtue; and consecrated to the guardian genius of liberty—May it never become prostituted to the support of state intrigue, or perverted to the service of lawless and unconstitutional liberty.[85]

The Tammany Society of Philadelphia had religious freedom on its mind: "The Rights of Conscience—May political tenets never be culminated from the pulpit nor religious opinions be enforced by the sword of the law."[86] Education was also important. The German Incorporated Society for the relief of Emigrants from Germany, meeting at Mr. Weed's tavern in Philadelphia, offered one to "Knowledge. May such a system of public instruction be established, as shall banish ignorance from our country, that the people may be kept in their duty, by a sense of their happiness, rather from the ignoble motives of fear."[87] A successful growing season was the topic of a toast given in Springfield, Massachusetts: "Plentiful harvests, thankful hearts, universal humanity and *good cider* throughout America."[88] Vermonters had a banquet in Windsor to celebrate the construction of a bridge over the Connecticut River, uniting the state with New Hampshire:

> The States of *N. Hampshire* and *Vermont*—May they be as unified by the two grand *arches* of *political* and *brotherly* love, as their boundaries are by two *arches* of CORNISH BRIDGE.
> CORNISH BRIDGE—May the *River Connecticut* ever glide gently under its *arches*; and the PROPRIETORS never have occasion to repent their building it.[89]

Meanwhile, the general assembly of Tennessee, meeting in Knoxville, offered a toast that their access to the Mississippi River would continue: "May the right to the free navigation of the Mississippi be speedily acknowledge, and peaceful residence to the Spaniards on its Western branches."[90]

Due to the unpopularity of the Jay Treaty and other administration policies, Washington was no longer the subject of adoration. His birthday had once been an excellent opportunity for the nation to be truly united. But he was still popular, and the Federalists continued to put him at the center of their festivities. Republican criticism of these events became criticism of the man himself.[91] Republicans had to tread carefully in their efforts to undermine the Federalists, making sure not to insult Washington or seem ungrateful for his contributions to the United States.[92] One correspondent for *Wood's Newark Gazette* reminded the readers how important it was to continue to recognize the president:

> The sentiments of benevolence, that must arise in an ingenuous mind, on a recollection of the unequalled services and unrivalled virtues of our WASHINGTON, (which is a duty entered upon with alacrity on that day) ought not to be repressed or neglected, but should be cherished; for the public acknowledgement of them constitutes one of the most natural, and sweetest rewards of merit.[93]

The *Columbian Centinel* of Massachusetts printed a summary of birthday toasts that idolized Washington:

> Accounts of the celebration of GEORGE WASHINGTON'S birth day arrive by every post. The toasts on these occasions issue from the same feelings, the garbs of genius and erudition. Among the best, are those given at *Petersham*.—May our beloved President, like the Sun, long continue to illuminate our political horizon; and may HIS ENEMIES BE OURS.—May republican virtue shield JOHN JAY from the insidious shafts of his enemies.—May that *hydra*—that offspring of *Robespierre*, the *Jacobin Faction*, ever find a Hercules in a WASHINGTON.—May we *have* a Chief Magistrate in Massachusetts *who shall never join a disorganizing faction*.—May the treaty with *Great-Britain* unite the interests of both countries, and prove its enemies to be *Prophets of Ahab*. These with many others, equally striking, portray the true "*spirit of the times.*"[94]

6. "Hypocritical Federalism and Malignant Toryism," 1793–1796

Abigail Adams frequently mentioned toasts in her letters to her husband. She wrote to him on February 28, 1796: "you will see by the Centinel that the Presidents Birth Day Was celebrated, with more than usual Festivity in Boston, and many other places. in the Toasts drank, they have for once done justice to the VP. it is a Toast that looks, I conceive to a future contemplated event."[95] The toast she referred to was given at the Boston Concert Hall: "May Americans never forget the blessings they owe to his firmness, nor the truths his clients, have explored."[96] She wrote to him later to describe a toast she heard in Ipswich, Massachusetts, which hoped for his success in the upcoming election: "John Adams. May his Virtues, Genius and knowledge long revolve, the first planet from our political Sun."[97]

The Independence Day toasts in 1796 included those for the Jay Treaty, such as "the Treaty with Britain. To its opposers merited mortification, to its friends gratitude, to our country peace,"[98] and those against it: "The friends of the British Treaty—may they be convinced by reason, or converted by the Guillotine."[99] Republicans in Philadelphia were hopeful for the upcoming presidential election, raising their glasses "to 'The Election of 1796—May all the Officers of Government be cast in a pure Democratic Mould.'"[100] Their confidence was encouraged by the Republican nature of many toasts. The editor of the Republican paper *Claypoole's American Daily Advertiser* wrote that he was grateful for such enthusiastic support:

> We have conned over the great variety of Toasts which were given on the late anniversary of American Independence, and recognize with pleasure that the glorious spirit of patriotism still emits its invigorating rays in almost every company, though clouded and rendered contradictory in some by those daring sentiments which the aristocratic prints have so industriously endeavoured to unstill into the minds of the American citizens. *Success to the French Republic* reverberates in nearly all; the preservation of the Republican system seems still to be the general wishes and the conduct of the British towards America emphatically resented by the greater part.[101]

Jefferson's disciples were fearful that the administration of a Federalist meant the loss of civil liberties and, worst of all, a return to monarchy. Massachusetts governor Samuel Adams, a fervent Republican, refused to attend the 1795 Fourth of July ceremonies in Boston because he would have had to consort with Federalist local and state dignitaries. Toasts contained sentiments that required approval of the group to whom they would be given: "Collectively, the sentiments expressed in toasts representing the political creed were purged from the group or discouraged from joining. Instead of uniting Americans, the rites of Independence Day were becoming tools of exclusion and the means of polarizing political allegiances."[102]

In 1796, the Federalist militia company commander, a Captain Laughton, refused to offer a Republican toast on the Fourth of July: "'May no insidious instrument ever consign the liberties of the country into hands of those who oppose them.'" The company voted to publish the toasts as they were originally intended, leading to Laughton's resignation.

The end of the year brought a certain level of national anxiety. Washington was looking forward to his retirement and a return to Mount Vernon. The First Regiment of the Second Brigade in Rehoboth, Massachusetts, wished the great man happier days in retirement: "The PRESIDENT of the UNITED STATES—may his life be useful when retired—may health and quietude attend him thro' the evening of his days, and may his SUCCESSOR follow his footsteps in prudence and virtue."[103] The Marine Society had their annual feast at Boston Concert Hall in November, and their toasts used nautical imagery to express their feelings for the future:

> The President of the United States, our old & faithful pilot—when he quits the helm, may the crew be preserved from mutiny and the ship from breakers.
> The vice-president and congress—may they prosper in their approaching voyage, and continue to take the benefit of the trade winds.
> A leaky ship, heavy gales, lee shore, dark night, and no light house to the enemies of freedom.[104]

Americans still kept a close watch on the progress of the French armies in Europe, celebrating important military victories, and a new name appeared in 1796 in the District of Maine. Celebrating the French success in Italy, the diners offered the fourth toast to "General Buonaparte and all the victorious army of Italy, may their success at the gates of Rome be extended to the Tagus."[105]

The second term of President Washington was not as successful as the first. The events and figures of the French Revolution still occupied many toast lists. People who supported the French Revolution became known as Republicans, and those who were disgusted by the violence were the Federalists. Citizen Genet, the French minister to the United States, was feted all over the nation, but he started to sabotage Washington's policy of neutrality. When Washington sent John Jay to London to negotiate a commercial treaty, people had high hopes. Jay received countless toasts that attacked him because the treaty he arranged, known now as the Jay Treaty, gave Great Britain more concessions than many believed were necessary. Washington achieved his goal of peace, however. Toasts were made to defend His Excellency, but others attacked him as weak and a traitor to the principles of the American Revolution. The next president would have to deal with the mess caused by the events in France and the disunion of the cabinet.

CHAPTER 7

"John Adams ... the Rock and Strength of our political Salvation...,"[1] 1797–1798

"John Adams, President of the U. States—Whilst Americans recollect his zeal, particularly in advocating American independence, 21 years since, let them support him in his present arduous undertaking, in the execution of the laws, which are formed for the safety, honor and dignity of the republic."[2]

"May every cent of tribute ever demanded by France be punctually paid them in red-hot balls."[3]

"The American Navy. While rocked in the cradle of the ocean, and nourished by the breast of finance, may it clean our coast of Pirates and fear no Artillery, but that from the clouds."[4]

George Washington counted the days until his successor was inaugurated. Until then, he continued to deal with the troubling issue of foreign policy. Mania for France bracketed Washington's first term, but the situation was very different by the end of his second term. There were toasts that sought a peaceful end to the events in France: "The Republic of France.—May a frequent recurrence to the original principles of their Revolution, accelerate the blessed reign of peace and the permanent establishment of a government which shall ensure to the French liberty and happiness."[5] Other toasts pledged "confusion to the sons of anarchy ... to cure the plague of Jacobinism."[6]

Washington's last contribution to the nation was his farewell address, in which he stressed the importance of avoiding foreign entanglements. The Richmond, Virginia, Artillery Company toasted Washington five times as "The Patriot," and honored his closing homily in the ninth toast: "The Farewell Address of George Washington, to his fellow-citizens—May its utility compensate for the loss of his services and may it, by forming the basis of American politics, preserve to the latest time that fabric he has been so instrumental in rearing."[7] Revelers in Beverly, Massachusetts, likewise drank to "the President's valedictory address; may it be adopted as the political creed of our country."[8]

While the Republicans used the Fourth of July for their propaganda purposes, Washington's birthday became the holiday of choice for the Federalists. Washington was the military hero, whose battlefield victories "were the currency of national unity, to bolster support for his political achievements, which were fare more controversial," and he was toasted as "'the Hero, who for eight years, through situations in which the boldest might despair, conducted the armies of Liberty to Victory, Independence, and Peace.'"[9] Images of heroic praise were influential in public culture.[10] Washington was feted with many dinners and dances for his many sacrifices, and guests at one of these banquets in Alexandria, Virginia, offered toasts to the new president and vice president, then to the Congress. Following those was one to "'Our Illustrious Neighbor—May he enjoy uninterrupted felicity in Retirement; and may the hears of his cotemporaries, as well as those of succeeding ages never cease to be grateful for his Past Services.'"[11] Leaving the burdens of public life was a goal Washington sought for years. According to the new President Adams, Washington murmured under his breath after the inauguration ceremony, "'Ay! I am fairly out and you are fairly in! See which of us will be the happiest.'"[12]

What was once unthinkable—criticism of His Excellency—was now expected of Republicans. Philip Freneau went after him in his newspaper *National Gazette*. Benjamin Franklin Bache, the editor of the *Aurora*, attacked Washington as "either a senile or a willing co-conspirator in the Hamiltonian plot to establish an American monarchy."[13] The politically divisive atmosphere made it even more difficult for John Adams. Occupying the nation's highest political office after the American Cincinnatus would have turned away lesser men than Adams. He had to deal with the public's anger over the Jay Treaty and the loss of American commercial sovereignty:

> The British Treaty—May it recall to our minds the sufferings of '76, and the seven subsequent years.[14]
>
> May treaties, prohibitions and restrictions no longer shackle the freedom of commerce.[15]
>
> The British Treaty: May it be an awful lesson how to trust to the "justice and magnanimity" of those who ever have, and still do, seek the ruin of our commerce and the destruction of our liberty.[16]

7. "John Adams ... our political Salvation," 1797–1798

Adding to Adams's problems was the fact that there were now two organized and opposing political parties: Federalists and Republicans. They had their own views about which direction the nation should be heading. The Federalists wanted to model the government on that of Great Britain. Regarding foreign policy, England's enemy would become America's, which obviously meant the French.[17] The Republicans hoped to keep the spirit of democracy and revolution healthy. Even reason could not be used to settle the differences between the two parties:

> Each side esteemed the other in terms of one-dimensional stereotypes that precluded rational discussion. To Republicans, Federalists were little more than monarchists intent on subverting American republicanism. Federalists regarded Republicans as "social levelers and anarchists," bent on mob rule. Each thought the other dangerous for different, yet similar reasons: each seemed to its opponents likely to destroy the American republican experiment.[18]

The antipathy the parties had toward each other was played out in the newspapers. One editorial written for the Philadelphia *Porcupine's Gazette* included a list of Federalist toasts given at a Fourth of July celebration in Carlisle, Pennsylvania. Republican Benjamin Franklin Bache criticized the toasts, prompting a strong response:

> I should not have inserted a list of toasts containing one in favour of *myself*, had not the circumstances been misrepresented by that abominable miscreant BACHE. In his dirty poverty-struck Aurora of the other day, he makes his poor stupid readers believe, that "ADAMS, WASHINGTON, and PORCUPINE were the only persons toasted" on this occasion. But my readers will perceive, and I beg those rascals who call me a British hireling to observe, that "the Commonwealth of Pennsylvania,"—"the 4th of July,"—"the heroes of independence,"—"the American envoys";—and "the friends of America throughout the world,"—I would have my envious calumniators observe, that all these toasts were drunk along with the health of PETER PORCUPINE.— Let Noah Webster comment on this.[19]

Since the Republicans identified themselves as the successors to the original rebels, "claiming" the Declaration of Independence, being anti-government was one of the "'genuine principles' of republicanism."[20] Republican diners did not toast President Adams, instead saving that honor for Vice President Jefferson. After all, Jefferson was "'the friend of his country, the framer of the declaration of Independence.'"[21]

The Republicans were the opposite of the Federalists in outlook, sentiments, foreign policy, and economics. They were fiercely against England and any connection to their former mother country. They supported France and the republican ideals of the French Revolution. The Portland Republican Society offered a toast to the Republican governor of Massachusetts, Samuel Adams: "Governor ADAMS—may he live to see Boston once more purged of enemies to the Rights of Man."[22] Whereas the Federalists looked up to the military heroes at their public events, the Republicans were more interested in elevating all Americans, so long as they were white, free and non-Indian.[23]

Besides attacking the Jay Treaty in their toasts, Republicans went after other controversial Federalist policies. A group of Republicans met for Washington's birthday at New York City's Republican Hotel, "alias the Gaol of New-York." Following the first toast to Washington, they then attacked the Federalist banking system:

> May the States of America preserve their rights free from the incumbrance of private banks.
> May bankers, brokers, and usurers be obliged to change situations with debtors, whose misfortunes have been owing to their ruinous system.

After these invectives, they proceeded with typical Republican toasts to France:

> May Citizen Buonaparte be successful against the despots of Europe.
> May the French, in their glorious struggle, attend to the respect due to the rights and independence of other states.[24]

Although the presence of opposing parties appeared to threaten the stability of the Union, many were grateful that the famous pair of Adams and Jefferson occupied the head of the executive branch. Abigail Adams wrote to her husband and described a dinner she attended at Harvard College, where one proposed toast was for "Adams and Jefferson, or Checks and Balances."[25] Jefferson scholar Robert M.S. McDonald, in his unique biographical sketch of Jefferson, *Confounding Father: Thomas Jefferson's Image in His Own Time*, elaborated on the prospect of the two revolutionaries working together:

> Many Americans embraced the union of the men from Massachusetts and Virginia. Congressman William Barey Grove and his friend James Hogg, for example, were North Carolinians who fit neatly into neither of the two developing factions. As Grove informed Hogg, "Mr. Adams is Elected President & Mr. Jefferson Vice—this is as we both wished." He cheered Jefferson's acquiescence to the second post, as well as his magnanimous "satisfied at the Election of Mr. A[dams], whose Character & Patriotism it seems he does and [has] respected." In Chester County, Pennsylvania, celebrants at a banquet honoring Washington toasted "Moderation" and raised their glasses to both "Adams and Jefferson" in hopes that "they, when at the head of the family of the United States, go hand in hand" in their duties. "There is no doubt they will act harmoniously together," wrote Joseph Priestly, "which shall greatly abate the animosity of both the parties." Even the most virulent proponents of Jefferson and Adams hoped to cheer the fruits of their partnership.[26]

7. "John Adams ... our political Salvation," 1797–1798

Eager for a successful "team of rivals," diners on George Washington's birthday in Newburyport, Massachusetts, raised their glasses to the famous duo:

> John Adams, President elect, may our anticipations of the wisdom and energy of his Administration be amply realized.
>
> Thomas Jefferson, Vice President elect, may the man who wrote the declaration of American independence, never fail to support that independence, against the intrigue or assaults of foreign power.[27]

After Washington's exit, the Republicans no longer withheld their attacks on the Federalists. Popular sentiment, however, was becoming more anti–French because of the previous machinations of Citizen Genet and the seizures of American ships, which was France's effort to end American neutrality. A Republican civic feast that took place in Philadelphia on April 12, 1797, to celebrate recent French victories in Europe elicited a strong Federalist reaction in the *Porcupine's Gazette*. The writer was stunned by the overly enthusiastic toasts given to France, and so he recommended that the public not take them seriously:

> The sentiments of the company, which are now published, might reflect dishonour on the country, if it were not well known that there was hardly a respectable character in it, and that the greatest part was mere spectators, whom curiosity to see the preposterous exhibition had drawn together. The occasion ought, nevertheless, to convince the good

Engraving of President John Adams by James Smithers in 1797, based on John Copley's portrait. "JOHN ADAMS, the President-elect.—May the vigour and rectitude of his administration, palsy the viperous tongue of faction, and annihilate those destructive engines to Republican governments, foreign influence and intrigue" (Toast #2, *Columbian Centinel*, 3-4-1797) (Library of Congress).

citizens of Philadelphia, that they have some such seditious persons among them, and that, in case of a war with France, it will be necessary to take proper care of them.

Their toasts for the most part were such a composition of stupidity and malice, that I don't know which most to admire. Indeed they were altogether so mal-apropos that, were not the characters of the convives so well known, for an exclusive attachment to French politics, I should hardly think they they [sic] were serious. The few I send you, with remarks on them, will enable you to judge of the whole. They are all replete with the same wit and spirit, and some of them, if possible, more exceptionable.

The 1st. begins with what is always the uppermost in the minds of these gentry, "The French Republic, whose victories we celebrate—may she never experience a defeat, until her arms be pointed against *liberty*."

REMARKS.—The author of this toast must certainly mean French *liberty*, the sister of French *venality*, two ladies that sanction all the tyrannic edicts of France; for I am sure there is no other liberty under Heaven, whether of body or soul, at home or abroad, that they have not for the last five years been enemies.

2d.—"The American Republic, may the glory of her revolution never *more* be tarnished by base ingratitude, or by a coalition with tyrants."

Remarks.—If I had been present at the entertainment, I would have encored this toast with all my soul; for when I think of poor Louis and his murderers, my mind tells me, we *have been guilty* of both these crimes.[28]

President Adams sent a commission to France in May to negotiate a better relationship, encouraging hope from both parties. Diners at in Alexandria, Virginia, drank to "*Our three Envoys Extraordinary to the French Republic—Health to their persons, Success to their Negociations, and let all the people say Amen!*"[29] Celebrants in Albany, New York, toasted, "Our Envoys to France. May their conciliatory mission speedily terminate in an accommodation of our differences compatible with our rights, and honour."[30] Banqueters in Lansingburg, Pennsylvania, warned the commissioners: "May those statesmen who basely suffer foreign aid or venal speculation, to soil their palms or influence their duty, be consigned to the infamy they merit."[31]

Republicans wanted the relationship with France to be repaired quickly. Advocates for a small government, Republicans discouraged military spending or creating a large army, though they cheered Napoleon's military successes. The pro–British faction was condemned, and Republicans hoped that these "traitors" would not be able to influence President Adams:

> May the misunderstanding at present existing between the United States & the French Republic be amicably settled, and the seed of discord mutually buried between us.[32]

No standing army. May the defense of our rights never be entrusted with a set of mercenary hirelings.[33]

May the *British faction* in the United States, who wish this country to assume the "*erect attitude of Great Britain,*" soon experience the degradation and contempt which awaits a humbled nation.[34]

May the President of the United States disappoint his insidious friends and prove himself as formerly a practical republican.[35]

At the same time, the Federalists continued to attack the supporters of France, classifying them all as "Jacobins." Federalists in Hartford, Connecticut, simply wished that "the Jacobins suffer no greater evil, than governing themselves, on *their own principles.*"[36] Someone writing as "*No Frenchified American*" in the *Porcupine's Gazette* paper was disgusted with the pro–French healths given at a July Fourth dinner:

> The 2d toast. "*The Republic of France.*"
> What cause have we to wish prosperity to this bloated monster that has fattened on the spoils and on the miseries of one half of Europe; and has requitted us its too partial friends with the basest ingratitude—that has insulted our government, with the most studied contempt, and carried on a piratical war against our citizens for four years, with circumstances of uncommon outrage,—that has answered our complaints, by commanding the messenger, who bore them, to depart unheard—and has since published to all Europe, that, unless we will agree to violate our faith solemnly pledged, in a treaty of commerce with Great Britain, it will neither make compensation nor cease from plundering?[37]

The Jay Treaty was hated by Republicans, but Federalists saw its economic benefits. Massachusetts fishermen were thankful for the treaty's influence on their industry. One toast given that summer of 1797 at Boston's Faneuil Hall was to "The Fisheries. May we recollect with gratitude the able and independent negociations of Mr. JAY, and his illustrious *Co-patriot*, which secured to us this important Source of National Defence, and so may be productive of National Prosperity."[38] Diplomacy was working, and Secretary of State Timothy Pickering was recognized: "Timothy Pickering, Regardless of the feeble Malice of his Calumniators, may he continue to ferret Foreign Influence from its lurking places."[39]

There were other topics, events, and people who were toasted during this time. Public virtues were important at a dinner honoring the president in New York City: "PUBLIC GRATITUDE," "PUBLIC GOOD," and "PUBLIC SPIRIT—While it rouses us against Foreign Hostility; may it also secure us against Foreign Intrigue."[40] A yellow fever epidemic hit Philadelphia in September, and one toast was given to the medical personnel who assisted the sick and dying: "The memory of the visiting Physicians who have died in the great cause of humanity during the calamity of 1797."[41]

One short editorial comment inserted in the Connecticut paper *Bee* had this to say about the absence of toasts to Jefferson: "It is remarked that among the toasts drank at the late Presidential feast in New-York, the vice President was taken no notice of. Was this 'paying proper respect to the constituted authorities,' or displaying the meanness of party spirit?"[42]

James Monroe, who replaced Jefferson as the American minister to France, was praised by Republicans for his efforts to maintain favorable relations. He was "the worthy and enlightened patriot, may every statesman, like him, consider honesty as the best policy."[43] One toast given in honor of Monroe in Richmond, Virginia, extolled him as a real symbol of the Jeffersonians: "Health and long life to the true Republican, and perdition to him, who under the pretense of defending the fortress of freedom, attempts to undermine it for the purpose of erecting the bastille of Tyranny in its room."[44] Meanwhile, Federalists lined up behind President Adams and his efforts to stay out of European issues. One Harvard toast at a Washington's birthday celebration promoted Adams as the "American Terminus," who was "the Roman God of boundaries who swore he would not stir one foot for Jupiter."[45]

One Federalist writer made it appear that the Francophile Republicans were no longer influential with the people. In an article titled "DEMOCRATIC DESPONDENCY," in the *Gazette of the United States*, he joyously gloated about the lack of public support for them:

> It is delightful to observe that the few rancorous, inveterate and *Frenchified* democrats who still hang on to their shattered cause, are compelled to confess their weakness and defeat, and shape their sentiments and toasts accordingly. Deserted by the American people, broken up in congress, and staggering to their political graves in shattered and contemptible gangs, they will shortly become objects of public pity or disgust.

The writer then criticized recent Republican toasts, including one to Secretary of the Treasury Albert Gallatin, an immigrant from Geneva. The writer hoped that Gallatin would return to his native home. The second toast mentioned had been made to the Republican minority in Congress:

> Another toast is the *The minority in congress*—Here is the confession of defeat—republicans toasting minorities!—this is pretty work—and wishing that this precious republican minority may not be affected by the *elamore* (to wit. the innumerable and unexpected addresses of approbation and confidence in the government and the universal determination to hold to it against all enemies) excited by the enemies of republicanism.[46]

The partisan atmosphere was so intense that Alexander Hamilton wrote to Washington, his former commander, on May 19, 1798:

In such a state of public affairs it is impossible not to look up to you; and to wish that your influence could in some proper mode be brought into direct action. Among the ideas which have passed through my mind for this purpose—I have asked myself whether it might not be expedient for you to make a circuit through Virginia and North Carolina under some pretence of health &c. This would call forth addresses public dinners &c. which would give you an opportunity of expressing sentiments in Answers Toasts &c. which would throw the weight of your character into the scale of the Government and revive an enthusiasm for your person that may be turned into the right channel.[47]

Shattering news from across the Atlantic in the spring of 1798 caused an uproar that not even Washington's presence could calm. The three American envoys Adams had dispatched to Paris, John Marshall, Charles Pinckney, and Elbridge Gerry, were hoping to meet with the French foreign minister, Charles Maurice de Talleyrand-Périgord, when they arrived in October 1797. Believing that most Americans supported the French cause, Talleyrand felt no pressure to negotiate.[48] He sent his own emissaries to deal with the American delegation. These three agents were known as "X, Y and Z" because their names were never released to the American public.[49] They informed the American delegation that Talleyrand refused to meet with them until certain conditions were met. First, Talleyrand demanded that the American government apologize for an anti–French speech Adams had given to the Congress the previous May. Second, he wanted the U.S. to assume responsibility for any outstanding debts France owed to Americans.[50] Third, the U.S. had to pay for any damages inflicted on American ships by French privateers.[51] Finally, Talleyrand insisted on a ten-million-dollar loan for the French Directory and a bribe for himself in the amount of $250,000.[52] Marshall and Pinckney left Paris in disgust after hearing the humiliating terms; Gerry opted to remain in an effort to try to negotiate.

Between November and December 1797 France threatened to provoke a civil war in the U.S. and use its navy to ravage the American coast.[53] When the American people learned of the XYZ Affair, as it became known, reaction was swift and furious. To be patriotic was to be anti–French, and anger toward the former ally swept through the country. Abigail Adams observed that the French tricolor cockades people once wore disappeared overnight. No one was singing French patriotic songs like "*Ca ira!*" or praising French republicanism.[54] Hamilton rejoiced that people were finally seeing France's true colors, although some Republicans blamed Hamilton for the crisis.[55]

President Adams became the hero of the nation by adopting a resolute and threatening position toward France. He was toasted as "the Rock and Strength of our political Salvation—may Fame waft his Virtues to the

British satire of the XYZ Affair, showing five Frenchmen groping a female "America": "Our late Envoys to the republic of France—May their steady virtue and stubborn integrity be an example to all future ambassadors" (Toast #12, *Albany Gazette*, 7-6-1798) (Library of Congress).

end of time."[56] New Hampshire's *Amherst Village Messenger* was one of several papers that printed this now famous toast to the president: "John Adams—may he, like Sampson, slay thousands of Frenchmen with the jaw-bone of Jefferson."[57] Fourth of July celebrants in Baltimore, Maryland, cheered: "The President—May his wisdom, firmness & integrity, annihilate *French diplomatic skill*."[58] Jefferson, on the other hand, seemed to be out of touch with the national sentiment: "The Vice-President of the U. States—*May his heart be purged of Gallicism, by the pure fire of Federalism, or be lost in the furnace.*"[59]

The immediate response of the Adams administration was to prepare for war, and Congress voted to spend one million dollars on harbor fortifications and cannon foundries. French privateers were now to be seized. President Adams had tremendous public support for spending money to strengthen the defenses of the country, including the creation of a ten-thousand-man army.[60] Toasts to the president lauded his strength, integrity, and firmness:

> The President of the United States—may public gratitude and private affection be the reward of his integrity, discernment and fortitude.[61]
> The President of the United States—a man whose policy and firmness, have placed America in a situation, that will bid defiance and party rage at home, as

well as to the haughty menaces of an imperious & insulting foe—The French Directory.⁶²

Abigail Adams witnessed the changing attitudes toward her husband, and wrote to her son John Quincy, "if we may credit the voice of the people from Georgia to Main, exprest in the Numerous addresses which have overwhelmed the Chief Majestrate for more than two months past, there lives and fortunes are ready at the call of their Country to be offered up in the defence of it. with one voice, they repeat the toast Given—'Millions for defence, but not a cent for tribute—'"⁶³

Building a navy was the main goal of the Adams administration after the XYZ Affair. A new Navy Department, separate from the War Department, ended up being Adams's lasting achievement. Nothing else during his presidency would give him more joy or satisfaction. He brought in his loyal ally, Benjamin Stoddert of Maryland, as the first secretary of the navy.⁶⁴ The American public was enthusiastic about this preemptive move by the president, and their toasts now included the formation of the navy and benediction for its anticipated mission against France:

> The navy of the United States—may its infant efforts, like those of Hercules, be the presage of its future greatness.⁶⁵
> *Sound bottoms to the American navy*, and while engaged in a lawful defence of our Commerce, may heaven send them prosperous gales.⁶⁶
> *The* AMERICAN NAVY:—May the pride of the nation inspire with a principle of honor that will render it invincible.⁶⁷
> The Navy of America, altho' in its infancy—may the valor of our seamen make our FLAG respected; protect our commerce, and guard our coasts from the depredations of avarice and ambition.⁶⁸

Although popular opinion favored war with France, some were hoping that the American envoys could still settle matters. They were all praised for their abilities and surviving the insult to the mission:

> Our three envoys to France, may "diplomatic skill" be ever soiled by American honesty.⁶⁹
> CHARLES COTESWORTH PINCKNEY, JOHN MARSHALL and EBRIDGE: Faithful to excellent instructions, and having nobly vindicated the insulted honor of their country, may the return from a triumph of candor & justice, over meanness and villainy, and read the eulogy in every American face.⁷⁰
> *Our late Envoys*—May the wisdom and firmness they have existed in the French Republic, put its *Talleyrand* to the bluffs, and prepare the way for justice.⁷¹

Secretary of State Timothy Pickering, an avowed Francophobe, "the man whose honesty and integrity cannot be called in question,"⁷² was seen as a victim of French intrigue. His diplomatic efforts were widely praised throughout, and his "incorruptible integrity" stood in stark contrast "with the mercenary Talleyrand and his contemptible coadjutators."[73] Pickering "withstood domestic calumny, and foreign insult,"[74] and it was hoped that he and his colleagues would "return like Noah's dove, with the olive branch of peace."[75]

War fever seemed to be uncontrollable. Gone were the feelings of affection and gratitude many once had for their former ally, without whom their own revolution would have failed. The French Directory became the enemy of America, according to Independence Day revelers in Fryeburg, in the Massachusetts District of Maine: "*The French Directory—until they become sensible of their evil ways, may they be seized with a tight spasm upon the lungs, a strangury upon the neck of the bladder, and an inflammation upon the intestine.*"[76] Republicans were eager that the tension with France would be temporary: "A speedy and honorable treaty between our country and the French republic; may the unhappy controversy terminate in the detection and punishment of all traitors, and enemies to the liberties of man."[77] Patriotic toasts against the French were in fashion:

> The Independence of the United States—May it never be tarnished by Submission to French Rapacity, nor sacrificed at the Shrine of their Ambition.
> The Hydra of France—May the Arm of the U.S. prove a Hercules to smite the Five-headed Monster.[78]
> *The Day.*—May our independence be founded on the *rock* of our *constitution*, and not on the *quick sands* of Gallic *liberty* and *equality*.
> *Our Federal Government.*—Confusion to those vain builders, who would attempt to surmount its lofty pillars, with the *Babel* of French Democracy.[79]

Supporters of France were sometimes suspected of treason. One toast given in Maine warned, "The *Jacobins* of America—May they be expos'd, *naked and hungry*, to all the winds of heaven, and Nebuchadnessor like, feed on *thistles*, and be down upon *thorns*."[80] New Hampshire's *Amherst Village Messenger* printed a collection of toasts "extracted from various papers, drank the 4th of July." Among them was another warning: "For that American who can have the baseness to cleave to *France* in opposition to his country, may Heaven reserve 'some chosen curse, some hidden thunder, red with uncommon wrath.'"[81]

Vice President Jefferson came under fire because of his Gallic leanings. Federalists were already angry when Jefferson criticized the Washington administration in a letter to his Italian friend Philip Mazzei, which ended up being published. This outrage was added to the heated atmosphere brought on by the XYZ Affair. The writer "NESTOR," mentioned in the first chapter, questioned Jefferson's loyalties because the French government would have preferred his own victory over Adams in the election of 1796:

> In the election between Jefferson and Adams, all the *French partizans*, all the *American jacobins*, and all the *violent democrats* supported Jefferson, and opposed Adams; and we recollect the base means they used to elect Jefferson. The letter published from Mr. Jefferson to his friend Mazzei, and which he certainly wrote, is irrefractable proof of his opinion, and condemnation of the administration of president Washington, and his hostile sentiments to all measures of our government, and his predilection of the French government and its conduct. The political principles of Mr. Jefferson have been fully censured and cannot be justified. They stand in direct opposition to those of general Washington, president Adams, and a host of the real and best patriots of America, and by whose virtuous exertions our country must be saved: I hope and believe that the opinions of Mr. Jefferson are, *at this time*, reprobated and condemned by almost the whole of his countrymen. Some men will still adhere to him, but, to Gallatin, Monroe, Maddison, Livingston, and their party; but I hope they will be *few*. But the objection to the toasting of Mr. Jefferson is this, that the *same* gentlemen drink Adams and Washington, and approbate their conduct; and never were the *political* opinions of men more decidedly opposite.[82]

An even stronger condemnation of Jefferson appeared later in the *Federal Gazette*, on July 19, 1798. The *Gazette of the United States* printed a list of Republican toasts that were given in Fredericksburg, Pennsylvania, on July 3. Among the honored were Mr. Gerry in France, the Republican minority in Congress, James Madison, James Monroe, a free press, Mr. Gallatin, and Aaron Burr. The first volunteer toast was for "John Adams—May he recollect that he is the chief magistrate of a free people and not the despotic ruler of slaves." Someone provided "REMARKS" as a criticism of the toasts, which were "undoubtedly the most infamous and insulting to the government of the United States, and the patriotic sentiments of its citizens, that have ever been hatched in the hottest holes of jacobinism." The toasts were "in direct contempt and hostility to the government constitutionally administered." The fact that Jefferson, the vice president, expressed gratitude to these toasts left him open to "be considered and regarded as he is—the declared foe of the government of the United States!"[83]

The former alliance was perceived to be a danger to the country, and French victories in Europe portrayed France was a militaristic juggernaut: "May unanimity pervade our insulted country, and may the unhappy fate of Holland, of Venice, and more than all of Switzerland, be an awful warning to us of the consequences of French fraternity."[84] The *Gazette of the United States* reprinted an article from the Charleston, South Carolina, *City Gazette*, in which article's author, "REPUBESCO," explained the dangers of any political ties to Europe, since peace did not seem to be a European virtue: "What are all the records of their history, but narratives of successful villains, of treasons, usurpations, massacres, and wars." REPUBESCO included a list of toasts given by President Adams at the Independence Day celebration in Philadelphia:

> The following toasts were given by the president, and drank, not with that hilarity which has usually accompanied the effusions of the day; but with a sober seriousness expressive of the struggling emotions of the mind in its conflicting moments. However, every sentiment which bespoke unanimity in defence of our country and our independence, was received with enthusiastic applause from every mouth—from the mouth of cannon also, they were announced, each toast being accompanied by the discharge of a field piece.

The toasts also stressed the need for the public to unite to stand up to the French. The second toast claimed that a strong position had been forced on the nation: "While with heart-felt regret we look back on the first steps which led to our present, contrasted and distressing situation; yet as self-preservation is imposed on us as the first law of nature; May we unite as one man, heart and hand, in defence of our country."[85]

Adams continued to prepare for a possible war with France, finally receiving the adulation he always thought he deserved. He enlarged the army and appointed Washington to be Lieutenant General and "Commander in Chief of the Armies of America, and, it is said, is 'ready to war, if such is the will of heaven.'"[86] Veterans excitedly drank to his return: "GEORGE WASHINGTON, Lieutenant General and Commander in Chief of the Armies of the United States—May he live to convince the few despicable Americans, *whom* envy and base ingratitude, (with French intrigue,) have raised against him, that '*take him all in all*' he has never been equalled in public virtue and patriotism, either in ancient or modern times."[87]

The "American Youth" appeared in toasts given at Federalist Independence Day celebrations in 1798. The younger generation was increasing, so the Federalists took the lead in courting them for support of Federalist policies: "The leading Young Men were Federalists and men of means: but now, instead of proclaiming their respectability or their membership in the merchant or planter elite, they spoke of their youth and their maleness while performing patriotic sentimentalism."[88] Toasts to the young expressed the hope that they would join with their elders in defending the nation and emulate the virtues "acquired by their fathers"[89]:

> The gallant youth of America. May they disdain to hold as Tenants at Will, the Independence inherited from their ancestors.[90]
>
> The Youth of America—May they display the patriotism of their fathers of 1776.[91]
>
> The America Youth—May ardour increase as war and danger appears and

may they like the land of Grecians at the pass in the Mountain, disdain to turn their backs to Xerxe's mighty Army; and may they like them, fall crowned with honor and glory, or conquer and be free.[92]

The XYZ Affair briefly united the politically divided nation. By the spring and summer of 1798, Adams was seen as the necessary leader who would redeem the humiliation that Talleyrand's demands caused. The love that many once had for their former ally and partner in revolution turned to shock and disgust. The strengthening of the navy further increased confidence in America's strength and sovereignty, especially after the immensely unpopular Jay Treaty. Adams had always wanted to be recognized and loved, and he finally received such adoration. This would be short-lived, however, and his legacy would be tarnished by a situation of his own making. To make it worse, his former friend would take full advantage of his undoing, temporarily destroying one of the most important political relationships in American history.

The Adams administration got off to a difficult start. Toasts still honored Washington, in whose shadow Adams had to navigate his own presidency. The political divide between Federalists and Republicans threatened to destroy the country's future. When Adams sent envoys to France to negotiate a better relationship between the two countries, the French foreign minister's demands for unfavorable terms and a bribe for himself led to fierce anti–French toasts. Americans demanded war to save the country's honor, and Adams became a beloved leader when he started to increase spending for a stronger navy. The return of George Washington contributed to national pride and euphoria. Toasts were made to the success of the American navy and Adams was seen as the savior of his country.

Chapter 8

The "*double curse*" of John Adams,[1] 1798–1800

"John Adams, President of the United States—may we ever respect and esteem him, convinced that while the needle of the American compass is touched by the magnetism of his council; it will ever guide to honor, prosperity, and wealth."[2]

"The Alien and Sedition Laws. May the former purge our country of all intermeddling foreigners, and the latter provide a safe home for such as shall dare blaspheme against the Federal Government, or its administration."[3]

"The Alien and Sedition Acts—may they remain only like monumental marble over the memory of the party that erected them, and let the inscription be 'here continueth to rot!'"[4]

"The Memory of our departed Father and Friend, the late George Washington—may we practice the principle laid down to us in his invaluable precepts, while he is experiencing the reward of—'Well done thou good and faithful servant.'"[5]

Thomas Paine's *Common Sense* called the British colonies an "asylum for mankind." Republicans welcomed freedom-seeking immigrants from Europe and found common cause with the anti–British Irish rebels. Federalists had a different opinion of the Irish, as demonstrated by this toast in the *Porcupine's Gazette*: "May the harbours of America be ever shut against *United Irishmen* and other traitors."[6] The Federalists believed the Irish "posed a distinct threat to the kind of stable and hierarchical society they expected America to become."[7] Federalists believed the bigger fear came from France. The number of French people emigrating to the U.S. was increasing due to the Reign of Terror and the violent slave insurrection in the colony of St. Dominque. French culture and ideas were now everywhere: newspapers, books, songs, philosophy. Federalists were apprehensive about the exposure the immigrants had to "disorderly and Jacobinical ideas."[8]

A liberal naturalization act passed in 1790 had a residency requirement of two years for free white persons before they could become American citizens. The Naturalization Act of 1795 increased the number of years to five.[9] The requirement was raised again to fourteen years after Congress passed the Naturalization Act of June 18, 1798. Aliens from enemy nations were not allowed to become citizens at all. Federalists hoped that the new restrictions would reduce the flow of immigrants. The Alien Act of June 25, 1798, gave the president broad powers concerning aliens, allowing him to expel any foreigner he deemed a threat to national security. A three-year prison sentence would be handed down if a targeted alien refused to leave.[10]

A month later, Congress passed the Sedition Act. Federalist James Lloyd of Maryland argued that treason during peacetime was a reality the government had to face. Seditious measures could be anything "'hostile to the Constitution or the liberties and happiness of the people.'" Opposition to the government's policies appearing in print could now be considered seditious.[11] Reckless press behavior was a cause for Federalist concern. Adams was angry about any opposition to his policies appearing in newspapers.[12] The press was a powerful engine that allowed all people to contribute to the political arena, a fact not lost on Jefferson and James Madison.[13] Federalists saw members of the press as "upstart scandalmongers" who "were destroying the character of the country's political leaders and undermining the entire political order."[14]

Justification for the Sedition Act appeared in a lengthy editorial in the *Albany Centinel* on August 7, 1798, written by "THE AMERICAN. *To the Editor of the COMMERCIAL ADVERTISER.*" The writer defended Adams, who had been insulted in a toast: "*May his written defence of hereditary rank, be the only mark of deficient wisdom the people shall ever receive from him,*" and criticized the following toast to Jefferson: "*May he continue to deserve the reproaches of his enemies, and the respect and admiration of his friends.*" "THE AMERICAN" explained that the United States had been pushed into its present standoff with France, and so there was a need for strong measures against the press:

> A law was also passed at the same session for correcting and restraining the torrents of abuse which, to the dishonor of our country, have long continued to flow from prostituted and venal presses. This is called "attacking the freedom of the press," and the mild tempered judge with his fellow toast makers take the occasion to express their wish, with much decency of expression it must be confessed, that the majority of the members of both houses of Congress were tarred and feathered.[15]

Federalists welcomed the Alien and Sedition Acts. Many writers and editors faced punishment, either fines or incarceration, under the Sedition Act. Federalists saw the law as a necessary restraint to thwart any perceived dangers to the government. One toast given by the Society of the Cincinnati in Connecticut was to "Liberty of speech and of the press; but no treason through either."[16] Supportive toasts for the laws were given throughout Federalist circles:

> May Aliens envying and endeavouring to lessen the dignity of our nation, together with all those who scatter sedition, feel the utmost rigour of the Law.[17]
>
> *The Alien and Sedition Laws*: Like the sword of Eden may they point every way to guard our country against intrigue from without and faction from within.[18]

The Republicans vehemently attacked the new laws. When the residents of Vassalboro, in the District of Maine, hoisted their liberty pole, they burned copies of the Alien and Sedition Acts and toasted freedom of speech, press, and popular sovereignty.[19] Most Republican toasts in the summer of 1798 condemned those in Congress who passed the controversial laws. Senator James Lloyd was "the man, who so far, lost sight of the constitution of the United States, as to propose the sedition bill; may his character and conduct be held up to public view for contempt."[20] Independence Day revelers in Frederick-Town, Pennsylvania, raised their glasses to the hope that Americans would unite against the Sedition Act: "True and genuine federalism.—May its falsely accused garb never screen the rotten carcase of political prostitution or aspiring ambition," "*National Unanimity.*—May its awakened pride spurn from our councils the scandalous opprobrium of *sedition bills.*"[21] Republican toasts were given in the hope that the laws would fail, or to threaten Federalists:

> The Sedition Bill—May it never be known in America; and may the name of its mover ever be remembered with *detestation.*[22]
>
> The Constitution of the United States; may it survive the attacks of *artificial Federalists*; and the deep laid schemes of Aristocracies and Tories.[23]
>
> May the "few deluded and degraded" self stiled federalists, in Morris county, be ornamental with the American coat of mail, and be re-conveyed in safety to Nova Scotia.[24]

James Madison, in "Toasts for an American Dinner," attacked John Adams's personality and praised his own friend and mentor, Thomas Jefferson: "The P. & V.P. may the former never feel the passions J. A. nor the latter be forsaken by the philosophy of T. J." He also criticized Washington: "G. W. the Hero of Liberty. May his enemies have the justice to applaud his virtues, and his friends the candor to acknowledge his errors," and praised the liberties of the Bill of Rights:

8. The "double curse" of John Adams, 1798–1800

> The freedom of speech; May it strike its enemies dumb.
> The freedom of the press, the scourge of guilty, & the support of virtuous Governments.
> The trial by Jury. May its violators be pronounced by the verdict of their Country aliens to justice, & Traitors to liberty.[25]

Vermont congressman Matthew Lyon was the first person to be charged under the Sedition Act, in October 1798. Federalists accused him of having Jacobinic principles, but he was arrested for publishing letters accusing the Adams administration of having pro–British sympathies.[26] He would later be toasted as a hero to the Republicans:

> The first martyr to the detestable sedition bill, and the bold assertor of the rights of the commonality of this country, Matthew Lyon.[27]
> Matthew Lyon: May his virtuous perseverance in the republican cause, be the criterion of imitation of all Republicans, and convince the Aristocrats that their violence merits only to be *smeared* with *Saliva*.[28]

The August 8 issue of the Connecticut paper *Impartial Herald* reprinted a letter that appeared in the *New-York Daily Gazette*, written by "CENSOR MORUM" (translated from Latin as a "censor of morals"). The self-appointed censor took issue with a toast given at a Sunday dinner for Thomas Jefferson in Fredericksburg, Virginia: "'May the press be as free as the circumambient air be [*sic*] breathe.'" The writer had no problem with the toast itself, and in fact applauded the freedom of the press. The issue was the fact that the toast was delivered on a Sunday. Was it necessary for Jefferson to even drink to a toast on that day, the Sabbath? Why not do it the day before, on Saturday? CENSOR MORUM seemed to accuse Jefferson of taking advantage of the freedom of the press to advocate the irreligious attitudes of the new France:

> Was this day chosen in order to shew publicly their disregard of it, that they adopted the principle of the French, and joined them in their impiety? There is to much reason to believe that it was. The sentiments breathed in the toasts are in exact unison with a contempt of the precepts of the Christian religion. There is no more reason to believe that it was the intention, from the known opinion of him for whom the feast was made. And yet one would think a grain of prudence or decency might have taught him that, whatever his speculative notions were, and even if initiated in the society of the Illuminati, his conduct would be censured as unbecoming the office of a Christian nation; that though he regarded not the law of God, yet he ought to regard the law of his country, and enforce it by a good example.[29]

After the XYZ Affair, Federalists accused Republicans of collaborating with France. At the same time, the passage of the Alien and Sedition Acts brought on accusations that the Federalists were in collaboration with Great Britain. People attending a Fourth of July celebration at Jefferson's Village, New Jersey, referred to the Genesis story of Cain and Abel to denigrate all Federalists: "May our *Federalists*, alias gentlemen of the *high order*, have a black mark upon them, as their father Cain had after he slew his righteous brother Abel." Then they drank to the hope that Federalists would be unmasked as monarchists: "May the views of our federalists be unveiled, and may Divine vengeance hurl its red-hot thunder-bolts on their devoted heads, ere they shall succeed in royalizing America, or in causing a war between her and her sister Republic, who has preserved Liberty from the grave assigned for her by the united despots of Europe."[30]

The attacks did not sway the Federalists' conviction that the Sedition Act was necessary. Press freedom was important, but there had to be reasonable limitations: "*The Liberty of the Press*. May it be *preserved* by a timely *correction* of its licentiousness."[31] The law was needed to keep the supporters of France under scrutiny, according to the inhabitants of Frederick County, Maryland, when they toasted "the sedition bill to all friends of France in this country. May they, as a supplement, experience the universal contempt and detestation of their countrymen."[32]

Both Jefferson and Madison started to work secretly against the Alien and Sedition Acts. Since the Supreme Court had not yet exercised its power of judicial review, there was no legal way the acts could be declared unconstitutional and void.[33] Jefferson believed that each state had the right to nullify any federal actions it deemed unconstitutional, and he wrote a resolution to this effect for the Kentucky legislature, while Madison did the same for Virginia.[34] The Kentucky resolution was approved by the state's legislature on November 13, 1798, while the Virginia resolution was passed over a month later, on December 24.[35] Jefferson and Madison made sure their authorship was anonymous to create the perception that the resolutions were the will of the people.[36] Federalists were alarmed that Republicans would be so brazen as to claim that states had the power to nullify federal laws, and possibly even secede from the Union.

No other states supported the resolutions, and Massachusetts declared in a legislative report that only the courts were the arbiters of what was or was not constitutional.[37] The Massachusetts report ended up in a toast given in Freeport, District of Maine, on Washington's birthday: "The Majority of the House of Representatives of this Commonwealth, who voted in favor of the Report respecting the Virginia and Kentucky Resolutions." The next toast was for those who voted against the report, that they "be treated by their constituents with merited contempt."[38] Diners at a Washington's birthday feast in Rutland, Vermont, even refused to include the appropriate number of states in their toasts, excluding both Virginia and Kentucky: "N. B. Majorities in the Legislatures of two of our

8. The "double curse" of John Adams, 1798-1800

sister states, having shown a disposition to secede from the Federal Union, it was thought improper to compliment them on this occasion. Fourteen toasts were accordingly drunk."[39] Toasts given later that summer portrayed the two states as wayward children:

VIRGINIA AND KENTUCKY RESOLUTIONS—"No love between these *two* was lost, / Each was to other kind, / In love they liv'd, in love they died, / And *left no babes behind.*"[40]
Virginia and Kentucky—they are our sisters—may they find a cure for their mischiefs, and a cloak for their shame.[41]

A correspondent wrote to the Connecticut paper *Bee* complaining about a Fourth of July toast very similar to the latter above, given in Norwich, Connecticut. The object of the piece was that "the public should know, they are *not* the genuine sentiments of a majority of the citizens of Norwich." The writer then explained that the toasts were made "to encourage and support that hostile system which is to terminate in a long, bloody, and exterminating war." The correspondent repeated that the feelings expressed in the toasts were only the opinions of "a few infatuated individuals, scorched with the fever of party rage."[42]

Association with France was also a moral threat, as CENSOR MORUM had claimed. The religious issue was used by Federalists to separate themselves from the Republicans. Religious teachers were needed "to repel those atheistical revolutionary principles, which leagued with the Government of *France*, threaten the dissolution of civil society."[43] The Rev. Joseph M'kean offered the following volunteer toast at "*The FEAST of REASON & the FLOW of SOUL*," held in Quincy, Massachusetts: "Church and State. May the virtuous and wise unite in firm opposition, against the wickedness of atheism, and the villainy of Jacobinism."[44] The toasts given by people in Concord, New Hampshire, were more religious in nature: "And we are happy to see among many of those toasts—'*The CLERGY of our Country.*' It is a presage of returning piety, order, and respect for religious institutions—without which, no true Liberty or Government can exist."[45]

Continuing with the religious imagery, Federalists in Charlottesville, Virginia, called the French foreign minister Talleyrand "the forsworn High Priest," and hoped that he and the Directory would "be honored with the society of grim Pluto, ruler of the infernal regions."[46] One toast given in Catskill, New York, at the launching of a ship was to "*M. Talleyrand*—a life of disgrace and an eternity of infamy. When he cries 'Money,' may our guns answer SILENCE!"[47] Bostonians celebrating the October 30 birthday of President Adams portrayed Talleyrand, a former Catholic bishop, as a heretic, warning that he was not trustworthy: "May we be armed against the insidious wiles of the apostate bishop—The sleeping Crocodile, is more dangerous than the roaring Lion—ask Switzerland and Geneva!"[48] This toast prompted a response in New York's *Greenleaf's New York Journal*:

> What an unguarded sentiment this! To be armed against the insidious wiles of *all* our enemies *whoever they are*; good, but I do not understand the latter part of this toaster's meaning, for I will always maintain that the Lion is by far a more dangerous animal than the Crocodile, especially the *British Lyon*, as that race has of late been roaring mad after *Republican flesh*; as to the crocodile, Buonaparte and his army have more to fear from it than the Americans: it is true the *alligators* do now and then beguile a *swine* or two in their pays in the rivers of Carolina and Georgia, but it is treason, yea, more than treason, to compare the good people of Massachusetts, or those of the sister states to the *swinish herd*, who permit themselves to be thus beguiled.[49]

Washington's birthday celebration in 1799 was a patriotic spectacle because of the possibility of war with either Britain or France. Mechanics in Maryland toasted: "May the eagle of America, if insulted, be ready and able to choke the cock, blind the lion, and trample to pieces the chains of tyranny."[50] Bostonians drank to the cause of good government all over the globe, hoping "the annihilating French motto '*Death is an everlasting sleep*,' be soon inscribed upon the tomb, whi'e verified in the fate of Jacobinism."[51] The preparations for war continued with the building up of the navy and army, both of which received many toasts on this holiday:

> Our infant Navy—May it receive in force and discipline, till the thunder of its cannon shall fully protect our Important Commerce, and silence every tributary demand, with which this independent government is or may be insulted.[52]
>
> The army of the United States, as thunder terrifies the voracious fish, may the very voice of her brave guns affright all foes from our coasts. But if that won't do, may we pay full tribute in pure cast metal coin.[53]
>
> The Army of the United States—when called to defend their country from foreign invasion, or to crush domestic faction, may they prove themselves worthy to be commanded by a WASHINGTON.[54]

Washington was given command of the army in June 1798, much to the joy of most Americans. He told Adams that he needed the assistance of his former aide-de-camp and treasury secretary, Alexander Hamilton. Adams, who despised Washington's choice, grudgingly accepted him as the new inspector general.[55] Hamilton's supporters drank to him: "The stimulus of Government—'The Destroying Angel' to *Democracy*."[56] People were confident of his success: "*Alexander Hamilton*—May the future services of this luminary of our western hemisphere be as useful and brilliant as the past."[57]

Republicans meanwhile increased the number of toasts to the Genevan Abraham Alfonse Albert Gallatin, who would later become President

Jefferson's secretary of the treasury. He had been the voice of reason during the Whiskey Rebellion, encouraging farmers to accept the federal government's taxes.[58] Republicans toasted his talents on behalf of the country: "Albert Gallatin—Talents and patriotism are of no country exclusively";[59] "Albert Gallatin the apex of our Constitution: May the heat of his intellectual fire scorch the political *moths* of our Government and its light *discover* the traitor *Sempronius*."[60] The Federalists were wary of his connections to France and Switzerland, and of his criticism of the Washington administration's strong response to the agrarian revolt. One toast given in Vermont on George Washington's birthday was to "Gallatin. May the hand of the hangman imprint Finis to the works of the seditious Genevan, before he can publish a new edition of the whiskey insurrection."[61]

The partisan fighting continued through the summer of 1799. Federalists in Trenton, New Jersey, used their toasts to call for war with France and the banishment of all Jacobins. "Infamy and contempt" were for all who adopted the "French or Jacobinical principles of Atheism and Anarchy."[62] As the Federalists were attacking Jefferson as a French puppet, his followers were already concentrating their efforts on the upcoming presidential election of 1800. This time, they believed their man would defeat Adams and become the next president:

Thomas Jefferson; may his virtues exalt him at the next election for President, to that dignified station.[63]
The Grand Sachem of one of our councils, Thomas Jefferson—may the Great Spirit watch over him, and in mercy to the tribes destine him to be their next Grand Sachem.[64]
Jefferson, the friend of the people—May the Declaration of Independence which he framed, secure him the confidence of his country; and may his honest and patriotic exertions in the cause of universal Liberty meet with success.[65]

Another Connecticut paper, the *Journal of the Times*, printed a list of both Federalist and Republican toasts, side by side in separate columns. The Federalist toasts were given in Litchfield, Connecticut, and the Republican toasts were from Jefferson's Village, New Jersey. The Federalists praised Adams, and the Republicans ordered him to do an "about face." One toast called for the defeat of the French forces in Europe, and literally right next to it was a toast praising the military successes of General Buonaparte. And when the people of Litchfield drank to no one signing a treaty with France, those in Jefferson's Village drank to Britain, "whose monsters, rapines, and abominations, have gone up to the clouds like the smoke of a burning mountain."[66]

The *Albany Centinel* reported on the Litchfield toasts, one of which was "no treaty with France, no league with Pandemonium." A witness proudly commented on the crowd's Federalist ideals: "The unpremeditated and universal shouts of applause with which the political toasts were received, especially the 2d, were demonstrations of the genuine federalism and firmness of the people; and of their being sufficiently aware of the arts of France, and of her perfidious partizans in our country."[67] Another response, written by the *"Non-Exterminator"* in the Connecticut paper *Bee*, was more scathing and sarcastic. The offended writer referred to all the toasts as "mortifying to the friends of liberty, truth and their country." One toast received close attention: *"The people of the United States. May they discern that the man who professes attachment to the constitution and yet clamors against the measures of government is an insidious partizan of France."* After sarcastically detailing "'the dark horrors of Jacobinism,'" the writer continues explaining the British alternative:

> O wonderful, amazingly wonderful! My bowels yearn within me; may hear goes pitty-pat when I *coil* over these sentimental and illuminating toasts. O how I long to be converted from the errors of my whiggism, and to become a *tory*, an *aristocrat*, a jacobite, a passive obedient man, a high-flying churchman, a papistical Jesuitical emigrant, a Muggletonian, or anything but an old whig of '77, or one of the Illuminati. O that I might join this noble and grand coalition of patriots against France; that I might laugh, shout and huzza to these fine, liberal and sentimental toasts. Then how heartily I should love a standing army in time of peace; the navy, the funding system, the British treaty, the 8 per cent loan, a debt of an hundred million of dollars, a land tax, an host of foreign ambassadors and agents, in Europe, Africa, and Asia.[68]

President Adams upset the war hawks of the Federalist Party when he chose a new delegation for another peace mission to France: William Murray, Oliver Ellsworth, and William Davie. Adams had made this decision months earlier, but they finally sailed for Paris in November 1799 after he received assurances from the French that they would be treated with respect.[69] The French government under the Directory crumbled on November 9, 1799, when Napoleon Bonaparte (dropping the Italian name) instituted a coup d'etat and proclaimed himself the First Consul.[70] Although no one knew how negotiations would go with the new French government, people were eager for a peaceful outcome:

> Our new Envoys to France—May they, acting with the same spirit, meet with better success.[71]
>
> Our *Envoys to France*: May they return in safety to their Country, bearing the olive branch of peace, and meet this unanimous applause, *"Well done, good and faithful Patriots."*[72]
>
> Our Envoys in France; may the result of their embassy prove themselves true Americans, and silence every enemy to their appointment.[73]

Adams, confident of peace, saw no need to continue spending additional funds on the army, and he formally disbanded it on June 15, 1800. This

8. The "double curse" of John Adams, 1798–1800

action surely pleased the Republicans. The soldiers were praised for their willingness to go to war to defend the nation:

> The fifteenth of June 1800—May that ever memorable day when an useless and expensive army was disbanded, be recollected with pleasure by Americans.[74]
>
> The 15th of June 1800—may that day's example be followed by every nation on earth—and may those who will not *confide* in the militia, still want the militia's confidence.[75]
>
> Our late disbanded Army—may their patriotism be as much evinced in their return to the plough and the harness, as it was in taking up the sword in defence of American honor.[76]

General Hamilton tried to convince Adams the military had to prepare a strong defense against the French, and consequently Adams's decision infuriated him. Hamilton's chance for military glory was abruptly taken away. He still merited the confidence of most Americans, being toasted as Washington's "confidant."[77] Independence Day celebrants in Portsmouth, New Hampshire, hoped that Hamilton would "ever be ready at his country's call, against foreign or domestic foes, and may his unwearied exertions in her cause, ever be remembered with gratitude by his fellow citizens."[78]

As difficult as it may be to believe, there were some nonpartisan toasts that appeared in newspapers during the latter half of 1799. The New England paper *Spooner's Vermont Journal* offered a rare health to "the Supreme Court of the United States—May they be like a two edged sword to divide asunder those who would divide us."[79] The District of Maine in Massachusetts toasted eventual statehood: "District of Maine: May it soon be a separate state that others as well as ourselves may have the *trimmings* of a *Seventeenth* Toast."[80] And the citizens of Scott County in Kentucky offered toasts to the future success of their own state:

> The prosperity of Kentucky, may she make her advancement in proper gradation, until she aspire to the highest pinnacle.
>
> May the surplus produce of this western world, watered by the river Mississippi, glide unmolested to foreign climes, meet the produce of foreign nations, and commutation without delay.[81]

The most prominent passing of 1799 took place at Mount Vernon on the evening of December 14. Two days earlier, George Washington went out for a routine inspection of his farms, riding for several hours through a rain and snowstorm, and returned drenched from the cold weather. He complained of shortness of breath and a sore throat the next day. Medical experts today speculate that he was suffering from a bacterial infection in his larynx, called epiglottitis. He died after being slowly strangled by his own inflamed throat.[82] Washington's death was an apotheosis, raising him to the level of a civic deity. The Republican and Federalist Independence Day toasts of 1800 appropriately put Washington front and center:

> The memory of the founder of American Independence, the immortal WASHINGTON, beloved by his Country, admired by the World, his name shall live while patriotism glows in the human breast.[83]
> The memory of George Washington—the unrivalled hero, whose firmness in adversity, modesty in victory, and humanity in every stage of fortune, afford perpetual themes for the sublimest eloquence.[84]
> The memory of GEORGE WASHINGTON—who rules his countrymen from his tomb, with a more powerful sway than monarchs their subjects from a throne.[85]
> Washington! Peace to his Manes, Tears to his laurels, Glory to his memory, and Heaven to his Virtues![86]
> WASHINGTON, our late File-leader—May we follow him in slow times to the PERMANENT CANTONMENT; and be all found near his Head Quarters at the FINAL ROLL CALL!!![87]

Acknowledging the change in public sentiment toward Washington, Abigail Adams wrote to her sister Mary Smith Cranch in March and pointed out that "at a late festival in Kentucky, amongst a number of Jacobin toasts is one to the memory of Genll Washington to the Years 1799, and no longer by which they mean to cast a slur upon the whole administration of the Government."[88]

Not all was forgotten or forgiven, however. The New York paper *Daily Advertiser* mentioned the fact that Washington was accused of murder by the Republican paper *Aurora*. Also, only three toasts given on the Fourth of July at one celebration were to Washington's memory, but the memory of Benjamin Franklin Bache received eight.[89] Federalist toasts to President Adams, Alexander Hamilton, and Timothy Pickering "were hollow clarion calls, heard by few and heeded by even fewer."[90] The *New Hampshire Sentinel* pointed out:

> If a foreigner were to judge of the political situation of the U. States, from a majority of the toasts given on the 4th of July, last, he would conclude that Jefferson was President—that rebellion was the order of the day—that the dis-United States were at war with every regular government—and formed and matured the Constitution of the U. States, were either dead, or turned villains, cheats and traitors.[91]

John Adams arrived in the new District of Columbia in the fall of 1800, becoming the first president to reside in the White House. He was probably disappointed when he saw the new capital city. It was a far cry from London, Paris, and Philadelphia because it was filled with empty space: there were no churches or schools, and only a few plain hotels

8. The "double curse" of John Adams, 1798–1800

and boardinghouses were located near the new Capitol building.⁹² George Washington chose the city's location because of the vital economic role the Potomac River played in the region, connecting it to the west via the Ohio River. Toasts were made to both the river and the city's future as the center of government:

> The River Potomac—may the importance of its advantages, engage the early attention and patronage of Congress, and a speedy improvement of its navigation promote the establishment of the shortest communication between the waters of the Ohio and those of the Atlantic.
>
> The city of Washington—May the goddesses of peace and liberty, there establish the seat of their empire.⁹³

Portrait of George Washington by Rembrandt Peale, 1846. George Washington became the most toasted figure during the American Revolution and through the Early Republic, both in life and in death: "The United States, free and Independent—As to the immortal Washington reared our sacred temple, the government of the United States on the pillars of wisdom, strength and beauty, may no unnervating breeze of licentiousness, no whirlwind of anarchy, no tempest of faction, no tornado of despotism, no thunder of tyranny ever shake its foundation" (Toast #1, *Vergennes Gazette and Vermont and New-York Advertiser*, 7-10-1800) (Bequest of Charles Allen Munn, 1924, Metropolitan Museum of Art, New York).

The presidential election of 1800 was the only one in American history with a president and his own vice president running against each other. Toasts to both candidates mirrored each other in emphasizing the talents of Adams and Jefferson. Vice President Jefferson was viewed by many as the man who would bring back the republican values that the Revolution was fought over:

> Thomas Jefferson, the man of the people. May the ensuing elections give the United States, a chief magistrate, and other public functionaries, whose conduct will not require a sedition law to screen it from public inquiry.⁹⁴

> Thomas Jefferson—that grand luminary of America, that friend of the people, whose sun, the traitors, tories aristocrats, and apostate whigs said had set, & retired to that bourne from which no traveller ever yet returned but which has to their central mortification risen again and shines with an additional lustre, to guard the liberties of his country, and to preside over her future councils.[95]

Adams was toasted as "*the Solon of his country, whose administration exemplifies the doctrines and seconds the labours of his Pen, in defence of our excellent Constitution.*"[96] The Society of the Cincinnati in Boston honored Adams as a military hero: "May he turn the Franks of the Enemies, press down their Center, throw their whole line into Confusion, capture their Standards, military Chest and Artillery, and burn their baggage!"[97]

Alexander Hamilton worked hard to deny Adams a second term. Hamilton certainly did not campaign for Jefferson, but his anger toward Adams was so intense over the loss of his army that he was willing to risk a Jefferson presidency. On October 22, 1800, Hamilton published a lengthy diatribe in New York, titled *A Letter from Alexander Hamilton, Concerning the Public Conduct and Character of John Adams, Esq., President of the United States.* Author David McCullogh wrote, "Nothing that Hamilton ever wrote about Jefferson was half so contemptuous."[98] Hamilton attacked how Adams treated his cabinet, fired Federalist officials, and handled the situation with France. *A Letter* completely backfired, deeply affecting Hamilton's reputation. The *Oriental Trumpet* in the District of Maine included a brief description of the atmosphere surrounding Adams's 66th birthday, even after Hamilton's vicious denunciation:

> Impotent have been the attempts to diminish the warm affections and lessen the full confidence of the great body of his countrymen—They feel that he is their friend, and under his administration rest in certain security. Let his opponents console themselves with the fancied merits of Jefferson—his adherents have the proud satisfaction of knowing that his talents and virtues are obvious.
> [Among the toasts given at a public dinner, we notice the following.]
> The Man whose anniversary arrives to place him among the foremost in the Ordre of time; first in the List of Merit, John Adams, the Achyme of the Pyramid: May the weight of his Character, consolidate, by its pressure, all the component parts of the structure.[99]

Federalists celebrating at Boston's Concert Hall wished that Adams himself would heal the party: "May Wounds received by divided Friends, from the Political Tarantula of the Season be headed by the full-toned Chorus of ADAMS & LIBERTY."[100]

William Tudor, Sr., wrote to the president about the birthday celebration at Boston's Concert Hall and rejoiced in the fact that Hamilton's

8. The "double curse" of John Adams, 1798–1800

effort to discredit Adams had failed. Hamilton had gone too far in attacking the leader of his own party, showing that his ego came before the public interest:

> Dear Sir
> The Celebration of the Birth Day of 30 Oct. was more generally & cheerfully enjoyed & rejoiced in than I ever remember. The Company at Concert Hall was more numerous & respectable than I ever before noticed there. Although there was not any of the Faction there. The best Volunteer Toast was "May every Enemy of the President write a Pamphlet." That Book has done much Good. It has justified all that has been charged against the impudent Egotist that wrote it, & satisfied the independent and true Friends of the Country that no Services are a Security against the Attacks of a disappointed Malignant, who at a most critical Period, would risqué the general Interest & Safety to gratify personal Revenge.[101]

True vindication for Adams came in November when news arrived that a treaty with France had been signed on October 3: The Convention of Mortefontaine. The quarrel between the two former allies was over, without resulting in a disastrous war. Adams gambled for peace and won.[102]

The election was on the minds of everyone by November 1800, but Alexander Hamilton was now more concerned with someone other than John Adams: Aaron Burr. Hamilton wrote to Oliver Wolcott, Jr., about Burr's plan to switch parties to gain votes for himself. Hamilton saw this as a vain effort on Burr's part to think that the Federalists would embrace him, based on the toasts Burr had recently drunk:

> What would you think of these toasts and this conversation at his Table within the last three or four weeks 1 The French Republic—2 The Commissioners on both sides who negotiated the Convention—3 Buonaparte—4 la Fayette. What would you think of his having seconded the positions that it was the interest of this country to allow the belligerent powers to bring in and sell their prizes and build and equip ships in our ports? Do you not see in this the scheme of War with Great Britain as the instrument of Power consult them in the object of a War when he thinks it expedient to make one? Can a man who despising democracy has chimed in with all its absurdities be diverted from the plan of Ambition which must have directed this course? They who suppose it must understand little of human nature.[103]

Hamilton later wrote to the Delaware Federalist James Bayard, mentioning the same toasts he brought up with Wolcott, saying that Burr "must have war as the instrument of his Ambition and Cupidity."[104]

Adams lost, but a constitutional crisis occurred because Jefferson and Burr were tied, each receiving an equal number of electoral votes. The House of Representatives had to decide on the winner. After thirty-six ballots, the election was finally declared for Jefferson. Burr became the vice president, but his machinations earned him the enmity of the president-elect.[105] Still, Republican dreams had come true with Jefferson now in the Executive Mansion:

> "The speedy arrival of the Republican Millenium!"
> "In the much desired administration of Mr. Jefferson, *may* ALL our hopes be realized!"[106]

John Adams was very popular because of the XYZ Affair, but his approval of the Alien and Sedition Acts caused an outrage among Republicans. He also angered Federalists because of his decision to avoid going to war with France and trying to negotiate a peaceful resolution to their issues. Alexander Hamilton was especially upset and attacked Adams publicly, a move that backfired. Toasts continued to be given to both Federalists and Republicans, Adams and Jefferson, and the new envoys to France. Most of the toasts by the end of the Adams administration were made to the memory of George Washington, who passed away in 1799. As the American civic deity, he would be remembered with toasts from all factions going into the nineteenth century. Twelve years of Federalist control of the presidency ended in 1800 with the election of Jefferson.

CHAPTER 9

"Thomas Jefferson, the polar star of republicanism,"[1] 1801–1804

"THOMAS JEFFERSON—The exalted and beloved First Magistrate of the United States, firm in the principles of the Revolution, with decision and moderation in his measures, possessed of every social virtue, inspired with an unceasing good will to his fellow citizens, and active only for their good; may his talents and virtues continue to shine with increasing lustre, through the fogs and mists of federal slander and misrepresentation, and may be at the most acceptable reward to a great and virtuous soul, eminently possess the confidence and affections of his fellow citizens, and be universally hailed as the benefactor of his Country."[2]

"Aaron Burr, vice-president of the United States. Democracy can now do without him; therefore let him be *narratived* and *suppressed*."

"Louisiana, the garden of the west—May the wealth flowing from this acquisition convince federalists, that an honourable purchase and peaceable possession are preferable to a bloody war."[3]

The election of Jefferson had not been a certainty. An anonymous pamphlet that tried to persuade voters not to vote for the Virginian appeared in New York City in 1800: *Serious Considerations on the Election of a President: Addressed to the Citizens of the United States.* The unknown author argued that a Jefferson presidency would alienate the United States from other nations since Jefferson would strengthen the alliance with France, and that Jeffersonian principles would have deleterious effects. A supposed atheist, Jefferson would "destroy religion, introduce immorality, and loosen all the bonds of society."[4] Republicans discredited the pamphlet with the following toast: "'Serious Considerations' and its clerical Author—May public odium and bitter disappointment be ever the rewards of such blasphemous prostitution."[5]

The threat to Jefferson's election came in human form: Senator Aaron Burr of New York. The House of Representatives decided the election because the electoral college ended up in a tie between Jefferson and Burr. Alexander Hamilton was unfairly blamed for supposedly creating this confusion: "ALEXANDER HAMILTON—*Depravity* henceforth we name thee *Hamilton*."[6] Jefferson won on the thirty-sixth ballot in February 1801, and the Jeffersonian Society of Orange, New Jersey, celebrated the day: "The 17th of February, 1801—May Americans ever remember the day which, without war, bloodshed or tyranny, completed the triumph of republicanism over monarchy and aristocracy."[7] The prospect of a Jefferson administration elated Republicans from Maine to Georgia, his victory being hailed as "a national revolution, a second Declaration of Independence, and in its aftermath it was described and celebrated in exactly that way, as another Fourth of July."[8] The "respectable" Republicans of Stephen-Town, New York, raised their glasses to the new government and the beginning of a new epoch:

> May the Infant of Monarchy and passive obedience be looked upon as a spurious offspring by every true Republican, and the enemy of the Rights of Man.
> May the Election of this year testify to the world that the cause of Republicanism is just, and must be the Law of the Land.
> The Federal Fever—May its factious contagion and Aristocratic symptoms be evacuated by a Republican Cathartic.[9]

Some historians have claimed that Adams would have won reelection if the Constitution's Three-Fifths Clause did not give the southern states a disproportionate representation in the electoral college. Northerners were bitter about this unfair situation. One year earlier, participants at a feast on Forefathers' Day (December 22) in Boston gave a negative toast to Virginia: "'Our Sister Virginia—when she changes three-fifths of her Ethiopian skin will we respect her as the head of our White family.'"[10] When Jefferson's victory was assured, Republicans quickly "forgave" Adams for the sins of his administration. The "Sage of Quincy" was once again an honorable Revolutionary hero, no longer deluded or led astray by Federalist devils:

> John Adams: may he never be troubled with another office, but retire satisfied with the thanks of a grateful people for all his *worthy actions* during his late administration, while Thomas Jefferson steers the federal ship far from the *rocks* of oppression, the *quicksand* of aristocracy, and the *gulph* of bankruptcy.[11]
> John Adams, thanks for his good ideas, repentance for his evil ones, and an uninterrupted retirement to the dukedom of Braintree.
> John Adams, late President of the United States; may he return to his seat at Braintree by the tune of yankee doodle, and there be permitted to continue

on the stool of repentance, until the United States have recovered from his evil administration.¹²

Abigail Adams later wrote to her son Thomas to tell him about a Federalist feast in New York, upset about the treatment her husband received. Those who supported the policies of the Washington administration "scarcely deign to notice that he had a successor." Washington and John Jay were "justly toasted," and Hamilton was praised. However, "Adams is passed in total neglect."¹³ Connecticut Federalists drank to the hope that their party would eventually return to power: "The DAY—may 'the Sun of Federalism' which sheds a mild and steady radiance in the North, soon revisit the *Moon struck* inhabitants of the South."¹⁴ John Adams continued receiving Federalist toasts, especially in Massachusetts, where he was "a lover of humanity, the promoter of political and religious liberty, a firm friend to our constitution, and a honest man, the noblest work of God,"¹⁵ and his neighbors wished him a long and comfortable life: "May the gratitude of his country follow him in retirement, and Heaven's choicest blessings crown the evening of his *well spent life*."¹⁶

The change in administrations meant the end of the Alien and Sedition Acts. Republican printers were toasted as "of all men the most hated and persecuted, because of all men the most dangerous to tyrants."¹⁷ One student at Hampden Sidney College in Virginia offered a volunteer toast to the freedom of the press, which had been attacked under Adams: "May the ensuing Congress never wish to deprive the American people of the freedom of the press, or, of speech, by a sedition law, and may it have more prudence than to raise a standing army in time of peace."¹⁸ Republicans in Torrington, Connecticut, were ready to do away with all oppressive Federalist policies, such as the "Sedition and Alien laws, standing armies and direct taxes; may the good genius of America say it is enough, henceforth there will be no need of you."¹⁹

Thomas Jefferson was inaugurated on March 4, 1801, which would become an annual day of feasting and banquets. Jefferson's famous inaugural speech was a plea for unification: "We are all Republicans; we are all Federalists." Such high hopes were inspiring, but not very realistic. Although Hamilton did not run as a candidate, his influence was felt within Federalist circles. He was praised by some for his well-known antipathy toward Burr, which they falsely believed swayed the election toward Jefferson. Colonel G. Piper of the Pennsylvania Assembly presided over a celebratory dinner honoring Jefferson. He was supposed to deliver a toast thanking the former treasury secretary, but he was unable to stick to the script:

> The redoubtable Colonel, who may indeed once have been a great scholar, but the treachery of whose mind has almost divested him of the knowledge of the

alphabet, in reading the following toast, which was printed before him—viz. "Alexander Hamilton. Few men have done more to promote the election of Thomas Jefferson—The Devil should have his due,"—delivered it literally in this manner:—Alexander Hamilton—few mens has done more to—p-r-o—(*stammering & spelling!*) p-r-o-m-o-t-e—Yes, I am right, to promote the election of Thomas Jefferson. The Devle shall has us all at last. *Yes, I am right.*[20]

Many Republican printers were relieved that the Sedition Act was in the past. The people of Columbia County in New York praised William Duane, the editor of the *Aurora*: "The Editor of the Aurora, and other republican printers throughout the United States, to whom the people are greatly indebted for their perseverance in promulgating the wicked designs of an unprincipled faction, notwithstanding the Iron Rod which was suspended over their heads—'*The Sedition Law.*'"[21] Such praise of Duane was not shared by everyone:

What a difference do we see between a gentleman and man of sense, and a vulgar upstart incendiary poison bladder. Some of the tho'tless rabble in New-York, and *some people* in Georgetown, toasted Duane, of the virtuous and cleanly *Clonmell*. The Editor of the Aurora gives a pompous account of toasts and proceedings. Mr. Wayne, Editor of the Gazette of the United States, was, on the 4th inst. at Trenton, toasted by the Gentlemen of that place. Mr. Wayne re-publishes the proceedings of the day from the Trenton Federalist, but *omits* the toast given to himself. The man who merits no praise, praises himself: he who merits, would blush at recording encomiums on himself.[22]

The Jeffersonians were the majority now, saluting the Constitution as the "'political bible of Republicans,'" and priding themselves as having saved the government from certain Federalist destruction.[23] The Society of Friends of Philadelphia made the Constitution a sacred relic: "'The Federal Constitution. Like the holy Ark of the ancient Israelites, may it never be considered as the consecrated palladium of our nation's rights.'"[24] The new Congress was toasted as "a striking proof of our political resurrection: If we have wandered from the principle of our revolution, 'in moments of error or alarm, we have hastened to retrace our steps, and to regain the road which alone leads to peace, liberty, and safety.'"[25]

Republicans were eager to institute their own programs and get rid the Adams administration's policies. The dangerous resolutions Jefferson and Madison designed were now viewed as brave actions to save the nation. Kentuckians toasted, "The legislatures of Kentucky and Virginia, whose manly, energetic and well-timed declarations of the rights of the states, gave a check to federal aggression:—May their courage and patriotism always be remembered with gratitude by those who rejoice in the restoration of the principles of '76."[26] Regarding the Alien Act, one Washington, D.C., newspaper called for "a revision of the Law of Naturalization, that the virtuous emigrant may not be a slave in a free economy."[27] The Republicans of Marblehead, Massachusetts, were more concerned with the economy and offered this sentiment: "Public Economy—*May we save our resources, that our resources may save us.*" They considered this to be "*the Republican creed, on the subject of national finances; a text, which we may expect to see ably commented on by the official labours of the new Secretary of the Treasury, who has long been an object of the envy, the admiration and the dread of his political opponents.*"[28] Republicans toasted public credit as "the result of talents assiduously and uprightly exerted," and "preserved with good faith, but employed with great caution."[29] One Republican toast was to "Public Credit. May it never be withered by ill Faith, or impaired by Excessive Use."[30]

The image of Jefferson was created by Albert Newsam and printed in Philadelphia in 1846. The election of Thomas Jefferson in 1800 was sometimes called the "Revolution of 1800," and Americans rejoiced at the prospect of a more democratic republic: "Come cast about the flowing bowl, / Republicans! the day is won; / Let ev'ry honest hearty soul, / Now drink a health to Jefferson. / Huzza! to the constitution! / Huzza! to the Republica! / Huzza! Freedom! Independence! / Huzza! to all America!" (from the song "Independence," *Political Observatory*, 7-14-1804) (Library of Congress).

Republican toasts now included such figures as First Consul Napoleon Bonaparte, William Duane, Elbridge Gerry, and the new secretary of the treasury, Albert Gallatin. The new secretary of state was toasted in Dedham, Massachusetts, on the Fourth of July: "James Madison—his Commercial Warfare more effectual than a navy, and more delightful than the blood of citizens to check the tyrants of the ocean."[31]

Vice President Aaron Burr was honored with an interesting selection of toasts. Some of them suggested that he might not be the most "trustworthy" public official. After all, he had reneged on his promise to allow Jefferson to receive the necessary electoral votes. Burr was first praised for accepting the second-place position of the vice presidency, according to the popular will: "Aaron Burr, Vice-President of the United States; the man who chearfully obeyed the voice of the people by disdaining all competition with Thomas Jefferson—May he be called to succeed him in due time."[32] Some toasts, however, showed that there was a concern about Burr's loyalty to the Republican Party: "*Aaron Burr*, Vice President of the U. States; May he *stick* close to the friends of good Order,"[33] "BURR, may he *stick* to republicanism."[34]

While most toasts during this time were given to political events and figures, Americans also drank to the vital industries they relied on. Massachusetts, for example, had been heavily invested in the fishing industry for many decades, so they toasted its continued success. Agriculture and commerce were not forgotten:

> *The New England Fisheries*—Necessary to the existence of our ancestors and essential to the prosperity of their descendants.[35]
> Agriculture—The chief strength and support of a free people—arts, not arms, our study—no more provisional armies, and no more loans of EIGHT per cent.
> Commerce—May it be extended on peaceable and honourable principles; but never be made a pretext to involve us in dangerous connexions, expensive armaments, or unnecessary wars.[36]

Several toasts during the first year of Jefferson's presidency showed that the public was concerned with an international situation: the Barbary pirates in the Mediterranean. Britain and France found it easier to pay annual tributes to the Barbary States—Morocco, Algiers, Tunis, and Tripoli—to maintain important trade routes. The new United States did not have a navy powerful enough to prevent Barbary pirates from seizing its ships and taking sailors captive.[37] Toasts were given hoping for the eventual release of the Americans held prisoner and an end to their harassment:

> By Lieutenant Edwards, "the squadron bound for the Mediterranean—may it bring the barbarians to a sense of their duty—pay them ten-fold their stripes, and make them crouch to the American Eagle."[38]
> Our Mediterranean fleet—May the tribute it carries to the Barbary powers be punctually paid.[39]
> Our fleet in the Mediterranean—May they, though of a nonpareil size, teach the Barbary Powers, that they have a large font of cannon in store, by which, with well distributed balls, they will maintain our Independence against the "squally looks" of those faithless marauders.[40]

The first anniversary of Jefferson's inauguration became an important occasion for Republicans, since March 4 was "the day that burst the bands of *Anglo Federalism*, and gave a second birth to the freedom of our country" and "the day when God delivered his people out of the fangs of a desperate faction, and placed them under the immediate cure of their favorite Jefferson."⁴¹ The newspaper *Washington Federalist* printed a March 4 toast that reminded readers of the Republican platform: "The six *noes* and a *nothing*, cut and dried in the president's message, *no* army, *no* navy, *no* taxes, *no* money in the treasury, *no* credit, *no* national pride, lest we go to war, therefore may we be cautious to do nothing of which we can be proud."⁴² The euphoria associated with anything "Jefferson" included his native state of Virginia. Republicans in Connecticut gave this anniversary toast: "*Virginia*—May she ever remain the nursery of patriots, philosophers, and statesmen." They later gave a longer toast for the Fourth of July, naming the great figures from the Old Dominion: "*The State of Virginia, our eldest and most virtuous dame*—The nurse of heroes, a Washington, a Jefferson, a Madison, a Mason, a Munroe, a Nicholas, a Giles, and a host of patriots, who took conspicuous parts in that revolutionary torrent which set America free."⁴³

An unusual list of toasts appeared in Connecticut's *Windham Herald* on March 4, although they did not celebrate Jefferson's inauguration. The Philadelphia painter Rembrandt Peale and twelve of his friends had a light lunch while sitting in the interior cavity of a mastodon skeleton. Peale was going to dismantle the skeleton before traveling with it to Europe, so before that the men ate in the skeleton, sitting around a small portable piano, and made several toasts:

> The American People: may they be as pre eminent among the nations of the earth; as the *canopy* we sit beneath surpasses the *fabric* of the mouse.
> The friends of Peace; to all else such *Bones* to *knaw* as, dried by ten thousand moons, may starve their hungry maws.
> All honest men. If they cannot feast in the *breast* of a *Mammoth*, may their own prove large enough.⁴⁴

The editors of the Massachusetts papers *Palladium* and the *Centinel* questioned why toasts to France were not as plentiful as they had once been. The passage of time allowed for new impressions and feelings toward France, "and it is now conceived to be right that there should be no other than a commercial intercourse between the two nations." The Washington and Adams administrations pursued this: "—and is now the opinion of President JEFFERSON."⁴⁵ The *Gazette of the United States* viewed France under the First Consul to be undeserving of any accolades:

> WE cannot deny ourselves the pleasure of presenting to our Democratic *friends* the present condition of their favorite nation, particularly of exhibiting, for their greater entertainment, the present and increasing glory of that champion of *republicanism* who has for years past been the theme of their toasts, their songs and huzzas on the anniversary of our national

independence, while WASHINGTON, who achieved that independence, and those who assisted him in maintaining it, were either passed over in neglectful silence or named only to be calumniated and insulted. Whether Buonaparte will now receive, from our pretended republicans, as loud applauses as while engaged in the murderous work of subjecting the nations of Europe to his control, and endeavoring to add the United States to the number, the ministerial papers, by their accounts of the proceedings of this day, will soon enable us to determine.[46]

It seemed as if Federalists were taking full advantage of the July 4 festivities to increase their assaults on the Jeffersonians. Robert M.S. McDonald, author of *Confounding Father: Thomas Jefferson's Image in His Own Time*, writes that Federalists portrayed the enthusiasm shown at Republican celebrations as examples of the disorder and chaos of democratic rule. He quotes a Connecticut penman: "'—The drunken rabble instinctively follow the standard of Jefferson.'"[47] The Massachusetts *Salem Register* printed several pro-Jefferson toasts that had been given at Salem, and one toast had the effect of an explosive device:

> *The President of the United States—easy in his manners, Republican in his administration, may his philanthropic virtues descend on his successors till man for man shall cease to legislate.*
> This toast roused the ire of a high fed who by *accident* was present, and he heroically gave the following genuine federal toast, *and sualionced* [sic] *it alone.*
> *While numerous encomiums are lavished upon the First Magistrate of our Country, let not its citizens forget he is a* DOWNRIGHT INFIDEL!!!
> Instantly after, by a Republican—
> *Let t'ose who are not please with the present Administration, and with the Man who penned the Declaration of Independence, and who wore the inscription* Rebellion to Tyrants is obedience to GOD, [illegible] *to remote corners, while the People remain happy under his administration.*[48]

Federalists looked to the past for their celebrations. Federalists in Greenfield, Massachusetts, raised their glasses in the hopes that "the 'rising Sun of Federalism' shine resplendent upon the 'Sage of Quincy,' while the Chief of Monticello gropes in the borrowed rays of the Moon of Democracy." They proceeded to belittle Jefferson's famous plea for unity from his first inaugural address: "We are all Wolves, we are all Lambs; we are all Vultures, we are all Doves, We are all Negroes, we are all White Men, 'we are all Wasps, we are all Bees,' 'we are all Republicans, we are all Federalists.'"[49] Federalist toasts to Treasury Secretary Albert Gallatin were not kind:

> *The Treasury of the United States*—May the good Genius of Colombia guard it from the fatal effects of Genevan economy, experienced by that of Louis XVI.[50]

9. "Thomas Jefferson, the polar star...," 1801–1804

> *Monsieur Gallatin, the Genevan financier and whisky insurgent*—May the party which has corrupted the vernacular tongues of our cabinet, find the destruction of Babel, again following the confusion of language.[51]
>
> The Genevan Financier: *May his Fiscal arrangements be equally unsuccessful as his avowed attempts to* "stop de veeles of Government."[52]

Toasts to Vice President Burr revealed a distrustful public. When he appeared unannounced at a Washington's birthday dinner in the national capital in February 1802, he asked permission to give the following toast: "'The union of all honest men.'" Some Republicans took this as Burr's offer to work with fellow Federalists, according to Rufus King.[53] Gouverneur Morris wrote to Hamilton about this toast:

> The apparition and the Toast you heard of are accurately stated. I see little Chance for him as a *Leader* of any Party. Those he is with hate him and tho he as among them a few Adherents they will not follow his Lead just now. He has I think considerable Talents for Government but I do not think the Course which his Situation compels him to pursue will command Respect or excite Confidence. Time and Circumstances do much.[54]

Later toasts to Burr expressed a desire that he would no longer be influenced by political machinations:

> Aaron Burr, Vice-President of the United States—May *Ambition* and *Intrigue* be discarded from public employment.[55]
>
> The Vice-President: It is not only essential to *be* virtuous, but to *appear so*.[56]
>
> The vice-president of the United States—may he give a more *clear proof* of his patriotism, and convince his friends that the *slurs* which have been cast upon him are unfounded.[57]

Celebrants at the Siege of York Tavern in Maryland referred to Hamilton's 1797 effort to clear his reputation when he was accused of financial mismanagement, known as the Reynolds Pamphlet. They hoped that Burr would do the same: "Aaron Burr, vice president—may his OWN narrative, like *Hamilton's defence*, unmask his principles, and shew the world what he really is."[58] The following statement was printed in the *Connecticut Courant* on July 20, 1802, accusing Burr of having no principles at all:

> The Jacobins—who most dearly love a *quibble*—have *hoped* and *prayed*, in their late toasts, that Mr. BURR, would *stick* to the Constitution; would stick to the President, the People, &c. But if one half be true, that DUANE and CHEETHAM, have asserted of him, their prayers and hopes are vain;—for he is a BURR that will *stick at nothing*.

More toasts advocated a separation between the president and his vice president:

> An union among all true republicans; May they never be shaken by the cunning and intrigues of a Burr.[59]

Jefferson and no Burr, except he explains the suppression of the history of Adams to the satisfaction of Republicans.[60]

Aaron Burr, Vice President of the United States—A niche in the temple of Janus for him, and the gates open (a bitter toast).[61]

Jefferson's luster did not diminish because of Burr. The president was the man "whom 20 years incessant efforts of secret malice and public calumny have contributed only to exalt, and endear him to his country."[62] He was especially popular for reforming the federal judiciary. The Federalists were furious that Jefferson repealed the Judiciary Act of 1801 because they believed the court system was immune to reform. He then signed into law the Judiciary Act of 1802, eliminating some of the circuit court appointments made by the previous administration.[63] Republicans in New England cheered the new legislation that summer:

> The Federal Judiciary now restored: constitutionally established to protect the rights of the citizens, may it never be accommodated to the views of a party.[64]

> The Judiciary of the United States—May the Judges HOLD their offices *during good behaviour*, and receive an undiminished *compensation for their service* DURING THEIR CONTINUANCE IN OFFICE *only*.

> The Judiciary of the United States—while wisdom and prudence guide their decisions, may always recollect that *they who can create can destroy*.[65]

A new American figure was toasted during Jefferson's presidency, one who had recently been recalled from his diplomatic duties in Europe: "John Quincy Adams: may the political career, he so gloriously commenced, be *long* continued, with *encreasing splendor*."[66] Jefferson wrote to John Quincy's mother and told her he was unaware that the young man would be dismissed when the state department was expunged of Federalist holdovers. John Quincy, enamored with Jefferson's talents and stature, quickly forgave his father's former friend.[67]

The rivalry between the two political parties made the Union's weaknesses evident. Jefferson's plea for unity from his first inaugural was ignored. Washington had wanted the nation to be an example to the rest of the world. The host of one Washington's birthday celebration in 1803 recalled a toast that Washington himself had handed to him six years earlier in Philadelphia. The toast was reprinted in the *Gazette of the United States* because of its relevance to the political situation in 1803: "'Prosperity to the commerce of Philadelphia, and that of the United States generally—May a spirit of *justice* among nations soon dispel the clouds by which it is at present overcast,—and conducted upon the fair principles of honesty and liberality, may its blessings be diffused through the world.'"[68]

Comparing Jefferson's actions to those of Washington was one way the Republicans fought off attacks. Washington negotiated with the British to avoid war yet prepared for war at the same time. Republicans pointed out that Jefferson acted the same way, but instead of being seen as cautious, he was accused of pusillanimity. Federalists were adept at choosing the virtues of Washington when it was convenient for them:

> Another of the toasts drank by the federalists at Washington was—"freemen when insulted take counsel from their courage"—if this had been drank by a republican while the British were capturing our vessels, impressing our seamen, insulting our coasts, he would have been called a disorganizer, a jacobin; it would have been termed interfering with government, but no such thing now—it was the government of England, that stupendous fabric, which permitted its agents to insult us then, now it is an agent of Spain; how admirably the courage of the federalists comes and goes.[69]

Sarcasm and satire were put to good use by the Federalists when criticizing Republican toasts. When Jeffersonians called March 4 a day to "'be held in lasting remembrance by all genuine republicans,'" Federalists responded by stating, "for the *greatest calamities* ensure the *most lasting remembrance*.'" Federalists countered a Republican toast to the elective franchise with an accusation that Republicans burned ballots and falsified returns.[70] A Republican festival in Hartford, Connecticut, included toasts to both Republican and Federalist states:

> The fourteen Republican states—May they know how to prize the blessing of self-government.
> The three Federal states—May they relinquish the name of republicanism, or deserve the character.[71]

While the political battles raged on, Americans were turning their attention to the lands west of the Appalachians. Commerce was important to them, which was why there had been conflict with the Barbary pirates: "Commerce unchained with Barbarous piracy or unfettered by illiberal policy—May free intercourse among nations, and interchange of their respective productions, convince them that their happiness greatly depends on each other."[72] Farmers needed access to the Spanish-controlled Mississippi River to get their produce and livestock to markets in the east. It was vital for the United States to control the river. Banqueters at a March 4 dinner in Trenton, New Jersey, offered a toast to "the free navigation of the Mississippi: if one minister is insufficient to obtain it, may 80,000 be sent to enforce it." Later, the Hibernian Provident Society gave a St. Patrick's Day toast: "The free navigation of the Mississippi, the outlet of our Western produce—should negociation fail to establish our natural rights, American Bayonets, wielded by a republican youth, will not."[73] The former ambassador to France, James Monroe, was sent back to Europe to negotiate with France and Spain. Americans toasted his success:

James Monroe—His mission will secure the contrivance of peace, or produce an union of exertion that will maintain our national rights.

James Monroe—may his embassy ward off the threatened storms and secure the rights and peace of his country.

James Munroe; the firm republican and enlightened statesman; may pleasant breezes waft him safely over the Atlantic; may his mission be crowned with success and may he happily return to the bosom of his country and his friends.[74]

Since image was so important to the Republicans (indeed, to both parties), toasts appeared that hailed the First Amendment's freedom of religion. More specifically, the toasts were made to the separation of church and state. Federalist newspapers in the northeast included many toasts to the American clergy, possibly as a way of emphasizing Jefferson's supposed atheism. The Republicans responded with toasts to "reason—may she erect her throne in the human breast and bid defiance to every effort of priestcraft, prejudice and delusion."[75] Toasts were also made that defined the danger of government involvement with religion:

> May the meretricious union of Church and State, be known only in the land of abominations, on the other side of the Atlantic.[76]
>
> Church and State—May this conjunction of terms, so heterogeneous in its nature, ever sound discordant to the *tympans* of American ears.[77]
>
> The union of church and state, the poisonous bane of a free government—may its fatal effects never be left in the United States, nor the free born sons of Columbia be forced to submit to the arbitrary laws of an infatuated hierarchy.[78]

Jefferson, an Enlightenment thinker, sought the truths of science and reason, and religious superstition was something he spent his life speaking out against. One toast from Waterville in the District of Maine honored him because he was "owned by Science and Freedom as a favorite Son, and crowned by them with bright laurels of glory, may his country never deny him *merited* honors through the *prejudices* of the bigot, or the *misrepresentations* of the calumniator."[79] The president's close association with Thomas Paine, however, was seen by some as evidence of his ungodliness and hostility to religion: "TOM PAINE—May the wretched calumniator of WASHINGTON, and the reviler of the Christian Religion, meet his just reward from the thankfulness of Nations, 'a halter's price and *leave* to hang himself.'"[80] The Virginia paper *Alexandria Expositor* had a different view of Paine: "*Thomas Paine*—wretched must that government be, that would deny an asylum to him who has contended so strenuously of the rights and privileges of mankind."[81]

Members of the Federalist Party used the national holiday to remind the nation that they still had a voice, which they used to toast John Adams and the accomplishments of his administration. It was important that they "unite and persevere in their attachment to just and patriotic principles, and may the political cloud which for the moment overshadows them, be speedily dispelled like the baseless fabric of a vision."[82] Federalists in Montpelier, Vermont, celebrating the Fourth of July first raised their glasses to the holiday, then Washington, John Adams, and the Constitution. President Jefferson merited fifth place.[83] "A REPUBLICAN" responded to the list of toasts and proceeded to argue about Federalist issues in the toasts: the creation of a navy, the increase in federal spending, and the fact that a foreigner (Hamilton) had been appointed to head the treasury department, just as Jefferson appointed a foreigner (Gallatin) to the same position. The commentary ended with the following statement: "I earnestly wish, that federalists would reflect seriously on the above facts; if they wish well to their country, let them pursue measures to promote the union and happiness of the people, always remembering, that truth is better than falsehood, and reasoning better than reviling."[84]

Aaron Burr was still a favorite target for many toasts, one of which demanded that he be sent to the "gulph of oblivion."[85] Another toast appeared in the form of a poem, suggesting that Burr suffer the same fate as Lot's wife: "Let him stand (says the nation) in public esteem,/ Let him stand as a president,—halt,/ List a while and I'll tell you boys how he should stand,/ He should stand as a pillar of salt."[86] When revelers in Baltimore toasted Burr with "—*Oh! sling away ambition, by that sin fell the angels—*," a Federalist writing as "DECIUS" chided the Republicans for ignoring Burr's service in the American Revolution: "Oh my degraded country! When wilt thou resume the character thou possessed under the administration of WASHINGTON and ADAMS? When wilt thou take the film from thine eyes, and avert the direful calamity that awaits thee?"[87] One of the most controversial toasts concerning Burr was given by the Philadelphia Fusiliers in Newark, New Jersey: "*Aaron Burr and Benedict Arnold. May traitors always meet their due reward.*"[88] The *New York Gazette* responded to this toast with a defense of the vice president, blaming his attack on the supporters of Governor DeWitt Clinton:

> In what condition must that community be, when any men venture thus publicly to abuse the second officer in the government! If government had due spirit and energy, it would arrest such fellows and bring them to condign punishment. What insufferable impudence to traduce the man to whom their fellow-citizens, a short time ago, gave an equal number of votes with him who is now the chief Magistrate; and for whom the electors in New-York gave a cordial and unanimous vote! A man too, to whom those at present in power are more indebted for their exaltation, than to any other! What baseness and ingratitude! What is most to be deprecated, however, is, the tendency to lessen the bonds of society and produce general disorganization.—These are they works, *O Clintonians!*[89]

The New York *Spectator* on July 20, 1803, called the toasts against Burr "indecent, violent, audacious, profane and seditious." The Jeffersonians and *"Clintonians"* were aiming to force an anti-government democracy on all Americans. The fear of democracy, and the violence that might go with it (as in France), was so extreme for the Federalists that toasts praising liberty of the press and freedom of speech in the *Aurora* were *"insolent and abusive."*[90]

Free navigation of the Mississippi River still occupied Americans' attention, especially in the western lands. A new state was added to the Union in 1803: "Our youngest Sister, the state of Ohio—may those blossoms of republicanism, which so highly adorn her first entrance into the union, be expanded by the genial sun of liberty, and produce the glorious fruits of national freedom and prosperity."[91] Since more people were intent on settling the territories beyond the Appalachians, the pressure to control the Mississippi was mounting. One toast given in Lexington, Kentucky, was to "the free and uninterrupted navigation of the Mississippi—The great incentive to industry, by affording a certain prospect of obtaining its merited reward."[92] There were high hopes for James Monroe and Robert Livingston, who were in France negotiating the purchase of New Orleans: "May the successful mission of Mr. Munroe, afford another memorable proof of the wisdom of the Government, which *planned it*, and the diplomatic skill of *him* to whom it was intrusted."[93]

Word reached the United States in July that during the negotiations the previous April, instead of the city of New Orleans, France sold the entire Louisiana Territory for fifteen million dollars. The size of the nation doubled without a shot being fired. Toasts were made to this diplomatic accomplishment, emphasizing the bloodless acquisition, those who procured it, and the invaluable benefits of the Territory to the U.S.:

> The cession of Louisiana, while it reflects credit on the administration, it opens prospects of incalculable advantage to our country.[94]
>
> Louisiana—the more valuable, CEDED TO US by bloodless negociation, than obtained by the carnage of war.[95]
>
> Our western brethren—May the recent convention with France which secures to them the free navigation of the Mississippi, without appealing to arms, convince them of the solicitude and attention of the general government.[96]
>
> JAMES MONROE & ROBERT R. LIVINGSTON—When the present generation, and the next, and those which for ages to come shall have passed away, their names shall be recollected, and repeated with pleasure and applause.[97]

Thomas Jefferson was credited with obtaining the new territory. One Evacuation Day toast given by the Tammany Society of New York City called Louisiana "that bloodless acquisition of whose territory will form a lasting monument to the Wisdom of JEFFERSON."[98] Kentuckians in Lexington drank to Jefferson, asking, "Can he, by whose wise measures we have acquired a New World, continue still to have enemies?" Bostonians celebrating the Festival of the Sons of the Pilgrims were already planning to make use of the new land, now open to white America: "May our *Patriots without a country* occupy what *they* have bought, and leave us to enjoy what *we have inherited.*"[99]

The Louisiana Purchase was immediately accepted by Americans as an essential first step in claiming sovereignty over the entire continent. The American republican experiment was to take over the entire world someday, according to the will of Providence. An oration given at a Fourth of July celebration in Conway, Massachusetts, included this lengthy toast:

> *Our peacefully acquired Brethren of Louisiana*—May their honorable adoption into our American family, animate them to a cordial cooperation in our exertions for the promotion of human happiness; and may our jurisdiction extend, until the whole earth becomes one great republic, and each member of the great political family, peaceably enjoy the fruits of his labor, under the pleasing banner of national liberty.[100]

The euphoria of the summer of 1803 disappeared by February 1804 due to the usual political bickering. The *Washington Federalist* published a list of toasts on February 24 that had been given on Washington's birthday. They were all the typical Federalist fare: the glory of Washington, the army and navy, John Adams, animosity toward Thomas Paine, etc. Volunteer toasts were given by members of Congress and the Supreme Court. Although the toasts were not controversial, they generated several weeks of commentary. William Coleman, the editor of the *New-York Post*, stated that the toasts were all pointed and appropriate. The *Aurora General Advertiser*, calling Coleman "the Hamiltonian organ," quoted the toast for John Adams ("the patriot and statesman will be remembered and admired while virtue and talents are held in estimation") and questioned how Coleman could call the toast appropriate after his idol had published the *Letter from Alexander Hamilton, Concerning the Public Conduct and Character of John Adams, Esq. President of the United States*:

> This is what the tool of Alexander Hamilton declares appropriate—what then are the public to think of the pamphlet published by Mr. Hamilton to prove Mr. Adams was deranged, or that his head was cracked? surely both cannot be appropriate; however, the inconsistency and folly of Coleman in his respect must be accounted for to his protector; it is no longer a matter of great moment whether Mr. Adams or Mr. Hamilton are the greatest fools or knaves, they are both in the back ground, and their mutual exposition has taught the people that it is necessary to keep them alive.[101]

An editorial in the *National Intelligencer* admonished the Federalists for using the memory of Washington for their own political purposes, making it "as powerful an instrument of party malevolence, as his name, while living, was too successfully converted into a cover for many a dangerous design." Whatever party that took such liberties in dragging down the General should be ashamed.[102] The editor of the *Aurora*, William Duane, wrote that it was time to stop using the image of Washington if Federalists were going to continue acting against the country's interests:

> Every one of the remaining toasts is equally a satire on the character of the man by whom it was given, and the toasts altogether are insulting to the memory of the man, whom those friends of order pretend to venerate. It is high time the name of Washington should cease to be the cloak for every assassin of the political persons of the people, and for every enemy of their constitution—let the acts of these men be the test of their virtue and integrity, but let them not be confounded with the real friends of the liberties of the union because they chuse once a year to become intoxicated in honor of Washington; if they really venerate him let them practice what he has recommended, and not endeavor to sever the union which it was his wish to consolidate.[103]

Federalists responded to the Republicans: "Their delicate nerves were exceedingly shocked by the want of decorum in those toasts...," and compared their Washington toasts with the Republican toasts they considered indecorous given in celebration of Louisiana at Petersburgh, Virginia.[104]

One of the Federalists' toasts from the birthday list was given by Supreme Court Associate Justice Samuel Chase, who had been involved with the trial of Republican editor of the *Aurora*, James T. Callender, who was prosecuted under the Sedition Act. Republicans in Manchester, New Hampshire, toasted, "Justice Chase: the times must be bad indeed, when he's a candidate for honest fame."[105] There were, however, grumblings of impeaching Chase, and toasts for such an action were becoming more prevalent:

> The Power of impeachment—but not as a substitute for *"Death or Resignation."*[106]
>
> The power of impeachment. The best means of controlling those who are not restrained by the feelings of honour or the love of virtue.[107]
>
> Impeachments—May we never want men to denounce those officers, who wilfully depart from the line of their duty.[108]

One toast given in Kentucky put Chase in company with some interesting characters: "Beelzebub, Nero, and Judge Chase."[109] Federalists still did not abandon the justice and offered toasts to his continued success in the face of adversity:

9. "Thomas Jefferson, the polar star...," 1801-1804

SAMUEL CHASE, *one of the Associate Justices of the Supreme Court of the United States*:—Violence, intrigue and faction, dash themselves in pieces against him and fall in empty murmers at his feet.[110]

Judge CHASE—Who in the worst of times, when the upright magistrates are no longer respected, an object of foul calumny and disgraceful persecution, dares to render righteous judgement without fear of impeachment.[111]

Foreign affairs were still focused on what was happening in the Mediterranean. Toasts were made for the speedy release of those sailors taken captive by Barbary pirates. The *American Citizen* printed a toast to "our Navy—May they speedily punish the insolence of Tripoli and other Barbary Powers, and compel them to respect our Flag."[112] The taking of the city of Tripoli thrust a naval hero to national prominence: "Lieutenant Decatur and his brave Volunteers, who so nobly supported the Flag of America, and made the Tripolitans tremble under their own Batteries"; "never fading laurels to Capt. Decatur, who lately with 60 American tars, valiantly captured and destroyed a Tripolitan frigate, manned with 340 Barbarians, in the very teeth of their fortresses."[113]

Foreigners who were still receiving toasts included Lafayette and Napoleon, "the first Consul of the French Republic, whose talents in the cabinet and field have become the wonder and administration of the world."[114] Obviously, no one was offering toasts to the English monarch, but the *Alexandria Advertiser* called it a "Horrid Outrage" when London papers relayed an incident when a group of Americans, which included James Monroe, met to celebrate the Fourth of July:

> Among a number of appropriate toasts, we particularly notice, the health of our illustrious sovereign, was echoed with great enthusiasm!! This is one of the most daring offences against genuine republicanism which we have yet remarked; and most surely will meet the merited reprehension of our truly republican administration!![115]

The creation of the American empire began with the Louisiana Purchase. The Tammany Society of New York had a dinner celebrating the new territory and the members raised their glasses to the growth of the nation: "May the extension of the American Empire add new demonstration to the practicability of republican institutions, and eventually convince mankind that maxims drawn from European despotisms apply not on this side of the Atlantic."[116] Republicans were hopeful that the new states created out of the western lands, such as Ohio, Tennessee, and Kentucky, would add to their own electoral strength, and that the nation would continue to grow quickly: "Wonderful, O wonderful, not an aristocrat in the number to administer to the foul fiend of modern federalism the least comfort in the awful hour of its dissolution."[117] Jefferson was even compared to Moses, as "the pacific conqueror, more successful than the legislator of the Hebrews, he has given us the land of promise without crossing the Red Sea."[118]

Some Federalists interpreted the acquisition of Louisiana as a power grab by the Republicans. One group of arch-Federalists from New England was known as the Essex Junto. The Jeffersonians saw them as a "tiny clique of malcontents ... who sought to destroy the Union when they were no longer able to dominate it."[119] The Junto believed that the president was seeking to permanently eradicate the political influence of New England and the Federalist Party.[120] The Philadelphia Republican Blues attacked the Junto at a May celebration for the Louisiana Purchase: "The Essex Junto, who wish the Delaware to be the southern boundary of their empire—May their southern boundary be the river St. Lawrence."[121] Massachusetts Federalist lawyer and future U.S. Senator Christopher Gore hosted a dinner and gave as a toast: "May the dominion of Virginia be limited by the Constitution, or at least by the Delaware."[122] The *Aurora* responded:

> In the first of those toasts we have the exact sentiment, though in an artful phraseology, which was whispered and put about in so many shapes at Washington; Virginia like the mamoth conveys to the Junto nothing but stupendous and overwhelming ideas; the genius and talents produced by Virginia, have eclipsed the gloomy, history and monkish selfishness of the eastern schools—Virginia, alas! wounds them to a point more tender; the Essex Junto had calculated upon a perpetual succession in office, and power, and the distribution of the good things: not content with having by the funding system "transported the palaces of the south to the east," those palaces were to be filled with the nobility—so many holes, for the lords and masters of America.[123]

The Republicans hoped to eventually "convert" the Federalists and toasted, "The honest Federalists of America—Repentance for mistaken zeal; conviction of their error, and a speedy return to better principles," and drank to the possibility of "Massachusetts and Connecticut—the only Federal States in the Union—May their proud walls like Babylon of old bow to the commanding efforts of virtue and Republicanism."[124] A celebration for Louisiana was held in Worcester, Massachusetts, where the toasts seemed to be keeping track of the Republican sentiments of the New England states:

> *Connecticut.*—The Light shineth in Darkness and the Darkness comprehendeth it not.
> *Massachusetts.*—The day has dawned—the mountain tops begin to shine.
> *New-Hampshire.*—It is morning—The bright sun gladdens the hills and the plains.[125]

New Hampshire became a beacon of hope for Republicans in New England when Federalist governor John T. Gilman lost to Republican John

9. "Thomas Jefferson, the polar star...," 1801–1804

Langdon in the governor's race. Independence Day toasts seemed to praise the Granite State as a "prodigal son":

> The State of New-Hampshire; May the SPECK, over the disk of this Republican Sun, be soon dispelled by the brilliant rays of the light of Reason.[126]
> The State of New-Hampshire: may her regeneration to the true faith awaken the penitence, and quicken the conversion of Massachusetts, Connecticut, and Delaware—[127]
> *Newhampshire*—Regenerated, and redeemed from federal error—though she has been astray, we welcome with rapture her return to the virtues of her youth, to the principle of our revolution.[128]

Since 1804 was a presidential election year, Fourth of July toasts were used to solidify support for Jefferson's reelection. New Yorkers wanted the elective franchise to be "preserved violate; and may the result of every election of this state, prove like the last, that the suffrages of its independent yeomanry cannot be influenced by intrigue, bribery and corruption."[129] Bostonians toasted, "The 5th of November, like the 4th of July; let it be a day of joy and triumph to the People, of disappointment to their adversaries."[130] Vice President Burr was not on the Republican ticket, but that did not mean he was safe from being the recipient of more derisive toasts:

> Aaron Burr; he has been weighed in the balance and found wanting.[131]
> Aaron Burr and his satellites, confusion to their councils, and defeat to their supporters—May a cloud of darkness perpetually envelope them.
> The chair of the Vice-Presidency.—May its cushion never be stuffed with *Burrs*, thistles or nettles.[132]

The New England states continued to be outraged about the Constitution's Three-Fifths Clause, which they correctly believed gave the southern slave states an unfair advantage when it came to representation in the federal election. William Ely made a motion to the Massachusetts House of Representatives on June 13, 1804, to instruct that state's senators in Washington, D.C., to propose an amendment to the Constitution eliminating the Clause. Republicans attacked what has been called "Ely's amendment," claiming it resulted "from a factious spirit which would place the country on the verge of civil war to gratify a mistaken and unworthy resentment."[133] Others accused the New England states of fomenting disunion. One toast drank in Keene, New Hampshire, was to "'the constitution of the United States—with Ely's amendment.'" The Republicans responded to this toast: "Without the amendment, the good federalists of Keene, it seems, do not care to retain the constitution!—*Ely's amendment*! the palpable and sole object of which is to *dismember* the Union!"[134]

The Federalists saw Ely's amendment as a way to halt what they perceived as domination by the Virginia-led South. The "Federal Citizens" of Augusta in the District of Maine toasted William Ely "*and the Amendment of the Constitution*: May the Energies of the *Freemen* of New-England be successfully in action against to resist the *audacious domination* of the ancient dominion; and may no man of the *Northern States* be found *degraded* enough to follow any longer the Standard of our Oppressors."[135] One toast from Boston was to "ELY's Amendment!—Let us listen to the prophetic admonitions of WASHINGTON, and 'indignantly frown on this first dawning of an attempt to alienate one portion of our country from the rest.'"[136] Toasts to the amendment continued into the fall: "May the Slaves cease to be represented by freemen and may the Representatives of freemen never act the part of Slaves."[137]

The war with the Barbary States was mentioned in many Independence Day toasts in 1804. Stephen Decatur was "the American Naval Hero," but he was joined by Commodore Edward Preble, "who so ably explains to the Tripolitan pirates the *Cannon Law*."[138] Americans continued to toast the success of the navy and the release of the sailors languishing in captivity in Tripoli. It was important to "convince the barbarians that tribute will only be paid at the mouths of cannon."[139]

To demonstrate the importance of getting the sentiments expressed in toasts correctly, the *New Hampshire Sentinel* ran a series of articles, called "Certificates," that attempted to clarify a set of toasts given on the Fourth of July. Planning of the toasts was taken seriously, and when a sentiment was in question, people reacted. The third toast from this list, delivered by the toastmaster Mr. Griswold, was simple: "*The President of the United States*."[140] "Certificate, No. 1" explains the whole situation, but it reads like a court deposition:

> WE Samuel Grant and Joseph Bellows, jun. two of the committee of arrangements for the 4th of July, and the latter of whom was Marshall of the Day, do certify that the 3d toast was agreed by the committee to be "*The President of the United States*" without any addition; that we never consented to or knew of any agreement to the contrary. We further certify, that no other officers of the day, except the committee of arrangements—were to our knowledge consulted on said toast or any other except that of Louisiana, previous to the time the third toast was about to be drank; at which time we were informed and for the first time, that an addition to said third toast was on the paper in the toast-master's hand. Said Bellows then informed the toast-master that merely "the President of the United States" was to be given; upon which Mr. Griswold, the toast-master turned to Gen. Allen, the president of the day and asked if that was the case, and being informed it was, he then gave "The President of the United States" and that only.—We also certify that immediately after said third toast was agreed on in the first instance, viz. "the President of the United States," Elijah Burroughs began to copy the toasts, and being asked by said Bellows what he was doing, replied he was copying them for his own

amusement, that after Mr. Griswold asserted in his paper that he had said toast in the hand writing of one of the committee, a federalist, we called on said Griswold; and requested to see the paper, which was produced, and found to be in the hand writing of James Campbell, Esq. who was not on the committee and who informed us that the wrote it by request of Mr. Burroughs, and as we suppose on the same paper which said Burroughs was writing for his own amusement.[141]

The controversy regarding what became known simply as the "Third Toast" played out in several issues of the *New Hampshire Sentinel* in August. The September 1 issue of the *Political Observatory* printed a four-column piece that described the many steps taken to get to the bottom of the problem. The opening paragraph showed the exasperation of many over what was getting to be a laughable situation:

> THE disgraceful controversy respecting this toast has occupied already too much attention. We had supposed that an end was effectually put to it in our last publication on the subject, when we produced documents full and expressly in point, amply satisfactory to every candid-mind, and sufficient, one would think, to convince the most obstinate and unyielding. But we were not apprized of the lengths to which men will proceed, when embarked in a desperate undertaking.[142]

As the *New Hampshire Sentinel* picked apart one toast, the District of Maine paper *Gazette* published several commentaries, all titled "STRICTURES ON CERTAIN TOASTS." The articles appeared in ten issues of the paper, from July 23 to October 8, 1804. The writer used these "STRICTURES" to correct grammatical errors found in some toasts, but mainly as a Federalist platform: defining the dangers of Jacobinism, explaining Shays's Rebellion and parts of the Constitution, defending the Jay Treaty and actions of Great Britain, criticizing foreigners holding government posts, and questioning the accomplishments of President Jefferson.

Alexander Hamilton took the national spotlight in the summer of 1804 when he was killed in the famous duel with Vice President Aaron Burr on July 14 at Weehawken, New Jersey. It was almost as if the wind went out of the Federalists' sails. Surprisingly, toasts to Hamilton immediately after his death were almost nonexistent, perhaps because his passing was not an event to celebrate. When a dinner was given to honor Rufus King in Boston in October, the former treasury secretary was remembered: "HAMILTON—May our Country find indemnity for his loss in the value of his Counsels."[143] New Yorkers later toasted, "The memory of our lamented brother, ALEXANDER HAMILTON, the pride of the Thistle and the ornament of the American Eagle."[144]

The November election was a clear victory for the Republican ticket. George Clinton replaced the now-disgraced Burr as vice president.

Jefferson easily defeated the Federalist candidate, Charles Cotesworth Pinckney of South Carolina. Jefferson had navigated the country through the difficulties brought by the "Revolution of 1800," stood up to the Barbary States, and doubled the size of the United States. His second term, however, would not be quite so glorious.

The presidency of Thomas Jefferson was a revolution of sorts. The nation went from one political ideology to another peacefully, and Jefferson was eager to unite the country. Toasts were given in his honor, along with the honor of Aaron Burr and John Adams. Jefferson had to deal with foreign issues, especially the kidnapping of Americans by Barbary pirates. The president was especially praised for the Louisiana Purchase. By the end of his first term, toasts continued to be made to Jefferson, but his vice president had lost favor. New England Federalists were angry about another lost election, blaming it on the Three-Fifths Compromise. Toasts were made to efforts to change the situation. Toasts were also given regarding the impeachment trial of Justice Samuel Chase and the conflict with the Barbary States.

Chapter 10

"The embargo—a deformed bantling of democracy...,"[1] 1805–1808

"THOMAS JEFFERSON, like the great luminary of the Heavens, though his lustre may be eclipsed for a moment, by adverse elements, yet steady and uniform in his course, they only serve to show his majesty in full splendor."[2]

"A non-importation act and sequestration of British property, until ample restitution is made for the insults committed on our flag, and a peace then only on terms congenial to the true laws of nations, not the laws of her own nation."[3]

"Aaron Burr, the man who once received the confidence of a free people—may his treachery to his country exalt him to the scaffold, and hemp be his escort to the republic of dust and ashes."[4]

"*The Embargo*—or national suicide—a philosophical experiment upon the patience of a distressed people."[5]

Toasts offered at the celebration of Forefathers' Day on December 22, 1805, in Plymouth caused a bit of a scandal. They recognized the contributions of the Pilgrims and the "qualities" of New England: agriculture, militia, education, fisheries, and mechanic arts. The fourth through sixth toasts were for the recently departed Federalist heroes, Washington and Hamilton. The ninth toast left no doubt as to the pro–British sentiment of the Federalists: "*The native country of our ancestors* ... having withstood the rage of *democratic France*, may she never be overwhelmed by the tide of *Imperial ambition*."[6]

The reaction from the Republican *Aurora* to the toasts was swift, especially regarding the fact that Hamilton was toasted along with the revered Washington. This fact only served to damage the reputation of the first and second presidents:

The time was when a name gave sanction to the perpetration of every outrage on the civil and religious freedom of the citizens, that time and its troubles are well remembered, and the experience of the imposture put upon an honest people by calling on the shade of a Washington, will prevent a recurrence of such grievances. Washington was unquestionably a great advocate for *union*, and an enemy to the encouragement of state jealousies and prejudices, yet with consummate impudence he is claimed as a member by a faction in New England, who would prefer a division of the states to their exclusion from the administration of the country. It is a proud day, when we can close by saying that the *pilgrims* and their friends are but a *minority* even in *Massachusetts*.[7]

An article in the Maryland *Hornet* considered the celebration and toasts to be "scandalously calculated to abuse and satirize the principles which our ancestors fled to preserve, and suffered to maintain."[8]

Jefferson's second inauguration took place on March 4, 1805. Philadelphians drank to "the President of the United States—uncontaminated by power—uninfluenced by intrigue—unsullied by slanders—first elected in confidence—re-elected by experience—under whose administration our taxes and debt have been diminished and our territory doubled." Revelers in Roxbury, Massachusetts, were grateful that the oppressive laws of the past would remain as nothing more than a bad memory: "Perpetual rest to the Alien and Sedition Laws, the death warrant of the administration which adopted them."[9]

Aaron Burr, whom Jefferson loathed, was no longer vice president. Jefferson's running mate was the Revolutionary War hero, General George Clinton, and Republicans were only too happy to embrace him:

> GEORGE CLINTON—May the principles which warmed his heart and nerved his arm in the Revolution, never be extinguished till the remotest period of time.[10]
>
> General GEORGE CLINTON; Vice-President of the United States, grown old in the service of his country, his correct principles and patriotism are yet in full bloom.[11]
>
> GEORGE CLINTON, the companion of WASHINGTON, the partner of his *toils* and the partaker of his *honors*—may he long live for the good of this country.[12]

Republicans received great election news from New England. New Hampshire and Massachusetts, states that voted for the Federalist candidate in 1800, went with the Republican ticket in 1804. The Democratic Association in Gloucester, New Jersey, wanted Massachusetts to serve as an example for the rest of the nation: "Our sister state, Massachusetts—The strong hold of Federalism heretofore, from whence the sun of Federalism was to illuminate & pervade America—alas how hast thou fallen—May the last election for President and Vice President convince her Sisters that the sacred fire of 1776 is kindled and never can be extinguished, and at the next election may the whole of their Representatives be of the same stamp with their late Electors."[13] Celebrants in Waltham, Massachusetts, blamed Federalists for weakening the region: "'The sleeping Sampsons of New-England,' it was Federal opium that caused their slumbers."[14]

Connecticut, however, joined Delaware in choosing the Federalist candidate Charles Cotesworth Pinckney for president. Toasts to Connecticut either criticized the state or expressed hope that someday its legislature would see the error of its ways:

> *The Constitution of Connecticut*—"Any thing or nothing," the mere creature of the Legislature—May it soon be exchanged for *something* which will secure the rights of the people.[15]
> *Connecticut*—"We have a little Sister, and she hath no" *Constitution*! "what shall we do for our Sister?"[16]
> *Connecticut federalism*—A heap of compost,—fermenting, fumigating, putrifying—a nuisance until dispersed.[17]
> *Connecticut and Delaware*: Like floating islands of ice in a summer's day; how long shall they withstand the melting radiance of truth?[18]

Two years later, the toasts continued to berate the "wayward" states: "Connecticut and Delaware—Two obstinate sisters; they know their errors, but will not retract them. Confinement, in a *dark hole*, is the ready road to repentance."[19]

The effort to weaken the judiciary led to eight articles of impeachment against Justice Samuel Chase, but the trial did not result in Chase's removal. The Senate was unable to achieve the necessary two-thirds majority vote for conviction.[20] A party of gentlemen in Frederick-Town, Maryland, upon hearing of Chase's acquittal, raised their glasses to his success:

> The Hon. Samuel Chase, still a Judge of the Supreme Court of the United States—his official conduct has passed the ordeal and is proved to be pure.
> The managers of the impeachment—the produce of their labors has been weighed in the scales of truth and is found to be wanting.
> The Democratic pack thrown out in the Chase.[21]

The great triumph of Jefferson's first term, the Louisiana Purchase, continued to be a *cause celebre* of Republicans, although Federalists questioned the wisdom of attaining Louisiana at all. Several newspapers printed a Federalist article that criticized some Republican toasts about the Purchase. One toast, for "'the acquisition of the territory of Louisiana—May it compost with our *desired wishes*, and be a lasting monument for future ages,'" met this Federalist response: "What sort of thing are *desired wishes*? That the acquisition of Louisiana will be a lasting monument—*of folly*, no one can doubt."[22]

The Lewis and Clark expedition was still exploring the Louisiana Territory in 1805. A toast was given to the duo in Lexington, Kentucky: "Captains Lewis and Clarke—May their enterprize prove beneficial to the United States, and their services meet the grateful acknowledgements of a generous people."[23] Americans joined Jefferson in thinking that the future of the nation lay in the expansion to the western lands beyond the Ohio River. Opportunities abounded in the west. Celebrants in Youngstown, Ohio, offered several toasts to the taking of the western territories and the defeat of the British forces there:

> The rivers Ohio and Mississippi. As they have once been the seals of war, may they hereafter be the channel of wealth to the western world.
> The Michigan territory. May she be an assylum for the oppressed—as scourge to aristocrats and an honor to the United States.
> Lake Erie—If Great Britain shall ever again, wage unjust war against us, may we have a Hercules strong enough to bear away the whole island, and cast it bottom upward into the lake.[24]

Members of Congress expressed hope that Florida would also be possessed by the United States: "The Floridas—Millions have been appropriated to their purchases should pacific measures fail, may millions be ready for their conquest."[25] Federalists of course objected to what they considered to be a waste of money. The purchase of Louisiana was a "millstone about the neck of the nation." Any money for Florida, they hoped, would be used to get France to actually take the territory from the country: "Two millions—may this little sum be given to France to induce her to compel Spain to sell us the Floriday—and when bought, may they be given to France to induce her to take Louisiana off our hands—and if this will satisfy her, may heaven be praised."[26]

Sometimes Jefferson was on the receiving end of negative sentiments, such as this from Portsmouth, New Hampshire: "Thomas Jefferson—Let the man who attempts to undermine the constitution, reflect, that 'deliberate treachery entails punishment upon the traitor.'"[27] He had to compete for attention with Alexander Hamilton's memory, which was useful for Federalist propaganda. Hamilton was "the true child of Minerva! Inheriting both her wisdom and valor—may his services nor his precepts ever be forgotten."[28] New Londoners in Connecticut toasted, "The memory of HAMILTON—A chilling horror crowds upon the mind, as memory fondly cherishes the recollection of his virtues."[29] Federalists also tried to use the memory of Washington, but they could never "own" it. Republicans focused their toasts on the General's accomplishments during the Revolution:

> "May the tomb of WASHINGTON never be profained with a hypocritical tear!"[30]

10. "The embargo—a deformed bantling...," 1805–1808

> *The memory of* GEORGE WASHINGTON, *the late father and protector of his country*—May his virtues be engraven on our hearts, more durable than a Mausoleum pile, or an Egyptian Pyramid.[31]
>
> *The memory of our beloved Washington and Hamilton*—Hand in hand they established our independence and liberty: May their spirits be the guardian angels of our country.[32]

References to a corrupt land deal from the early 1790s turned up in many toasts in 1805. What has become known as the Yazoo land fraud started when the legislature of Georgia sold off most of the land along the Yazoo River to four land companies. The Creek Nation had been promised the territory by George Washington, but fifteen million acres was sold to speculators in violation of Washington's order. The corrupt Georgia legislatures, who had been bribed by the land companies, were voted out of office by 1796. Unfortunately, by then the land had been resold to third parties.[33] Native Americans once again lost out and more settlers continued moving west. Toasts regarding the scandal disdained the participants:

> *The Yazoo Speculation*—Let it become a political Talisman at the next election for Congress, by which the people may distinguish the *friends* from the *enemies* of their country.[34]
>
> Yazoo men and "constitutional republicans"—synonymous in principle, opportunity alone is wanting to make them anonymous in practice.[35]
>
> Congress of the U. S.—The collective wisdom of the American nation—May their firmness and integrity at their next session defeat the intentions of the Yazoo squad, and raise one more pillar of glory in the sanctuary of American freedom.[36]

Unlike his first term, Jefferson in the beginning of his second term did not have a completely united party. Serious infighting among Pennsylvania and Virginia Republicans threatened his administration. Virginia congressman John Randolph and his followers believed that the president steered the nation too far in a Federalist direction.[37] The radicals who supported Randolph were devotees of the *Aurora*'s editor, William Duane. They wanted a completely Federalist-free government, a judiciary that was answerable to the will of the people, a weakened Senate, and for the president's treaty-making power to be restricted. A new name entered the political lexicon: "Quids," which is from the Latin phrase "*Tertium quid*," meaning a "third thing," or "third something."[38] The Quids constituted a third faction, although they never formed an actual political party. Randolph and the Quids were upset that the impeachment of Samuel Chase "failed." Randolph then started to work against Jefferson's efforts to reach a compromise with the Yazoo land companies, but he was only successful in delaying Congress's actions on it until 1810. Toasts to the Quids accused them of hypocrisy and promoted their failure and demise:

> Third partyism—a new name for an old set of political offenders, or a new modification of selfish policy. May they ever be repelled in their insidious designs.³⁹
>
> *Tertium Quid,* or *third-partyism*—May the mantle of hypocrisy, which at present veils their iniquity, from the public eye, be torn from around them, so that these sons of apostasy may be viewed in their true light; and may the spirit of the great Washington strike the guilty soul of him with terror, who shall endeavor to divide the union by exciting groundless jealousies.⁴⁰
>
> The third party. An union "so checkered as speckled; a piece of joinery so crossly indentured and whimsically dovetailed; a cabinet so variously inlaid; such a piece of diversified mosaic; such a tessellated pavement without cement; here a bit of black stone, and there a bit of white; whigs and tories; treacherous friends and open enemies, that it is indeed a curious show, but utterly unsafe to touch and unsure to stand on."⁴¹

Attacking the Quids in toasts never went out of style. Timothy Matlack, whose penmanship is evident on the parchment of the Declaration of Independence, wrote to Jefferson in February 1807 about a toasting committee that tried to come up with Independence Day toasts. There were Quids and Republicans on the committee, and they could not work together to write the appropriate sentiments:

> A committee of arrangement for the 4th of July, formed of the two Parties met, with the affectation of condescension, perhaps on both sides, to form the toasts for the day &c, when even appearances could not be saved. The coldness of some of the toasts which the Quids wished to be affectionately warm, and the pepper of others which did not suit the republican palate, produced effects which could not, even for the moment, be concealed; and on *the day* when every heart ought to have expanded with benevolence, thee were difficulties in preserving decorum that were not expected.⁴²

Republicans grouped the Quids with the Federalists, although the Quids were former members of both parties. Quiddism was seen as "the spurious progeny of federalism and treachery—from such a connexion, may the deluded and honest be speedily rescued."⁴³ Diners at a Republican festival in Greenbush, New York, celebrated the loss of the Quids' power in the state, warning the Federalists to stay away from the Quids altogether:

> *The Quids of the State of N. York*—Who are they? "*Tag-rag* and *bob-tail*"— *Every thing*—any thing, and *nothing!!!*—May their late downfall in this state be a profitable lesson to apostate republicans in every section of the union.
>
> *Federalists*—While they contend openly as an independent party, we will respect them—Whenever they become the tools of a contemptible faction we will respect them not.⁴⁴

The term "clodhopper" was also in use in 1805. Pennsylvanians who supported the gubernatorial candidacy of German immigrant Simon

10. "The embargo—a deformed bantling…," 1805–1808

Snyder were hoping to completely tear down the state's judicial system and set up a constitutional convention to amend the state's constitution. Governor Thomas McKean, a signer of the Declaration of Independence and former president of the Continental Congress, once in a rage called Snyder's followers "clodhoppers." They adopted the name for themselves and focused their efforts on defeating McKean. More radical than the Quids, the Clodhoppers "defined democracy by its culture, the notion of the common man, rather then the demands of the people, and the sweeping changes to the legal structure needed to achieve them."[45] People drank toasts to Snyder's success in the upcoming election:

> May the election of Simon Snyder and the call of a convention be the result of an honest, and upright republic, and the bellowing, office hunting, and time serving republicans, be held in complete contempt and meet with eternal disappointment.[46]
>
> SIMON SNYDER—the FARMER—the TANNER—the CLODHOPPER—the CLODPOLE—we the people will make him governor if we can.[47]
>
> *The clodhoppers of Pennsylvania.* May their conduct on the 6th of October next, display to the world the spirit and dignity of independent freemen, owing allegiance to no mortal man, and determined never to submit, in silence, to the wanton insults of arbitrary power.[48]

One of the nastiest toasts Pennsylvanians drank to during this political fight was to the governor: "Every dog to his vomit, (witness the feds) who in the year 1799 vomited McKean, and in 1803 returned to their vomit, and voraciously swallowed him up."[49] Fortunately for Jefferson, the radicals were defeated in October and McKean retained his seat.

The commanders of the military and naval forces in the Mediterranean were not forgotten in the toast lists. William Eaton became a hero when he marched with his forces across the Libyan desert and successfully attacked the port city of Derne. A peace treaty was signed with Tripoli in June and the United States no longer had to pay tribute, although it did pay a small ransom for the release of its imprisoned sailors. The treaty, negotiated by Tobias Lear, was declared before Eaton could move against the city of Tripoli itself.[50] He was toasted as "the man who had the abilities to plan, the perseverance to promote, and fortitude to establish the fame of the American character, in a land where it was scarcely known, in defiance of slavery or death."[51] He was even raised to the level of other, more well-known national heroes: "May we never want the prudence of a Washington, the spirit of a Hamilton, nor the enterprize of an Eaton."[52] Both political parties tried to claim him as one of their own:

> Gen. EATON on his way to the North, has received continues marks of distinction. In Fredericksburg a public dinner was given him and a number of toasts drank. Gen. EATON gave the following volunteer—"*The British*

Lyon—if he continues to prowl among our flocks, let us invent measures to starve his WHELPS." If Gen. EATON is a *federalist* (and the party have claimed him as such) we wish all who call themselves *federalists*, were like him; then we should be in the emphatic language of Mr. JEFFERSON, *"all republicans, and all federalists."*[53]

William Duane continued to use his *Aurora* as a mouthpiece for the Republican faction, printing toasts that lauded Dickson and the freedom of the press and cheered the members of Congress who stopped the government's negotiations with the Yazoo speculators. Duane took issue with anyone who offered toasts to the enemy of America, especially after the British frigate *Leander*, while looking for ships off the New Jersey coast involved with illegal commerce, fired a warning shot on an American vessel on April 25, 1806, and killed Seaman John Pierce.[54] Republican toasts made Pierce the latest martyr of British aggression:

> The memory of the murdered Pierce—his blood cries aloud for justice, and nothing short of justice will be the atonement.[55]
> *The murder of Pierce*—The wound in our national dignity is too great to be covered by a proclamation.[56]
> The memory of our fellow citizen John Pierce, murdered near our own shores—May this cruel outrage teach Americans what they ought to expect from the *alliance*, if such is the evidence of British *friendship*.[57]

The nefarious practice of naval impressment, when American sailors were taken off their ships and forced into the Royal Navy, was a major foreign policy issue for the Jefferson administration. Americans were incensed about being bullied once again by the British navy, "plunderers of our fellow citizens and plunderers of our commerce—May their aggressions be duly remembered until full satisfaction is obtained."[58] Patriotic Americans drank to the unfortunate sailors and their eventual release:

> Impressed American seamen on board of British men of war—May our general government soon release them from worse than Algerine slavery.[59]
> Emancipation to our brethren, impressed and confined on board of British ships, and the ships of other sea robbers.[60]
> The impressment of American citizens—by the imprisonment of an equal number of Englishmen as hostages till our citizens are restored.[61]

Another foreign policy issue, as mentioned previously, was the acquisition of the Spanish territory of Florida, important because of its proximity to the port city of New Orleans. James Monroe encouraged Jefferson to simply take the territory, but the president wisely sought to avoid war.[62] Toasts stressed that Spain's glory days were in the past, and that the Spanish colonists should take a lesson from the American Revolution:

10. "The embargo—a deformed bantling...," 1805-1808

Spain—the American Hercules in his cradle, strangled the serpent of British usurpation—in the vigor of his might and manhood, he will find little difficulty in crushing the pigmy of Spanish insolence.[63]

Spain; She will do well to think less of her former glory, and more of her present weakness. The rout of Cortez, of Soto, and of Pizarro, are well-known, and our warriors are on fire to tread in it.[64]

The Inhabitants of Spanish America—May they have virtue to desire, they cannot want power, to attain freedom.[65]

People did not consider Spain to be as severe a threat to the United States as Great Britain was. Americans strove for peace, "yet war is preferable to disgrace."[66]

Former president John Adams, no longer living in anyone's shadow, became the Federalist standard-bearer in 1806 since Hamilton was gone. One volunteer toast from Boston was to "*The Hon.* JOHN ADAMS.—As his morning was unclouded, his meridian full of glory to himself and his country—may the evenings of his days be serene and tranquil.—May his country be just to him and to themselves, by following his advice, and respecting his principles—so will they perpetuate his fame, and their own freedom."[67] When Adams gave his own toast at one celebration, the Republican paper *Boston Chronicle* immediately misconstrued its meaning to portray the ex-president as a monarchist:

The following excellent sentiment was given by the late president ADAMS—"May the trident of Neptune ever protect the Independence of nations, and defend the liberty of mankind."

The Chronicle of yesterday says—"The toast given by Mr. Adams, seems to be, 'Rule Britannia, in prose.'"

We know not what to expect next, for such a compliment to the English nation, we have rarely seen. The Chronicle correspondent says, a wish that the trident of neptune, may ever *protect the independence of nations* and *defend the liberty of mankind*, is the same thing as to say—Rule Britainnia! Bonaparte will not feel himself much complimented by this prompt application.[68]

The idea of the Federalists being monarchists tarnished their image, evidenced by the following toast: "'May we have no monarch—no tyrant—no despot—no emperor—but a good federal *King*: and let his name be—*Rufus*.'" The toast referred to the Federalist senator from New York, Rufus King. The New York *Bee* responded to this toast: "We always thought the federalists wanted a *King*, though we did not suppose they would stand much upon the *name*, if they could be gratified in the substance. What virtue is in the name of *Rufus* more than in *George*? We see no harm in expressing wishes for a monarchy, so long as the sentiment draws upon itself such universal execration."[69]

The successful return of the Lewis and Clark expedition in March, after they reached the Pacific Ocean the previous November, was cause for national pride and celebration. The explorers met "the most sanguine expectations of their countrymen."[70] The pair returned St. Louis in September, and the city's elite turned out to rejoice with a festive dinner and ball. Toasts were made to both men, the Louisiana Territory, and even the memory of the "Admiral of the Open Sea":

> The hardy followers of Captains Lewis and Clark—May they be rewarded by the esteem of their fellow citizens.
> The Territory of Louisiana—Freedom without bloodshed, may her actions duly appreciate the blessing.
> The memory of Christopher Columbus—May those who imitate his hardihood, perseverance and merit, never have, like him, to encounter public ingratitude.[71]

Captain Lewis was toasted at a dinner in Washington, D.C., as being "patriotic, enlightened, and brave; who had the spirit to undertake, and the valor to execute an expedition, which reflects honor on his country." Captain Clark was toasted with everyone else in the expedition: "Their patriotic and manly perseverance entitles them to the approbation of their countrymen."[72]

There were more toasts coming from the western territories. Focused on local affairs, they also had a nationalistic and somewhat defensive tenor: "'The Western Country—Infamy attend the wretch who would separate us from the Union.'"[73] Vermont Federalists were direct in their concern: "The people of the Western territory—May they never be so blinded to their own interest, as to think of a separation from their Atlantic brethren."[74] The fear was that there was a conspiracy regarding the western lands, and there was even speculation of rebellion: "Our Western Brethren—May the rumors of rebellion there prove a *false alarms*."[75] The August 6 issue of Kentucky's *Western World* included a toast to Louisiana that expressed a wish to be free from the source of such conspiracies: "May her virtuous citizens suffer no Burr to grow in her soil—no Factor to preside in their councils—and exercise every legal means to crush usurpation and despotism."

The reason for the concern over the western lands was due to the intrigues of the former vice president. After his duel with Hamilton, Aaron Burr fled New York and ended up on Blennerhassett, an island off the coast of Georgia. In an effort to recoup his political reputation, Burr schemed to either wrest West Florida from Spain, or declare himself emperor of the lands taken from New Spain (Mexico).[76] Still popular to some, western land speculators, such as General Andrew Jackson, offered Burr support. The New York *American Citizen* printed one pro–Burr toast to demonstrate this: "AARON BURR, late Vice-President of the United States—dignified in this chair; prompt in the cabinet; gallant in the field—May his country duly appreciate his talents and his services."[77] The Republican journalist James Cheetham, however, attacked Burr for his plans. When Burr made the toast in 1802, "The union of all honest men," Cheetham explained what Burr most likely meant:

> This toast required no illustration. The uniform tenor of his public life, but especially of that portion of it which immediately precedes the commemoration, will best interpret it. Abstractly considered the sentiment is excellent. Associated with his general and recent conduct, it could not be viewed by the federalists as a modest overture (In the last union, the 'modest overture' proceeded from Mr. De Witt Clinton.) to form an union with them. And it is most probable that Mr. Burr designed the sentiment to be thus expected. He was himself silent as the grave on the subject; not one word escaped him to those at Washington to whom he had been supposed to be politically attached.[78]

In July, a toast given by the Orange Country Republicans at Newburgh, New York, also attacked Burr's toast: "The *'Union of Honest Men'*—We rejoice at their defeat, it is just that conspirators should perish by their own weapons."[79] The Quid label was attached to the former vice president because he was perceived to be a defector from the Republican party. Burr was accused of trying to form a "revolution party" in the west: "Moreover, Quids were defectors from both parties, who aimed to create a hybrid party, and his served to reinforce Burr's earlier reputation (invented by his enemies) as a faux Republican."[80]

Burr was arrested for treason in Alabama on February 19, 1807, after leading a group of well-armed colonists toward New Orleans. He was betrayed by General James Wilkinson and appeared before a circuit court in Richmond, Virginia.[81] His trial eventually ended up in front of Jefferson's cousin and nemesis, the Federalist chief justice of the Supreme Court, John Marshall. Marshall was attacked in the press when he attended a "FEAST OF TREASON," given by one of Burr's defense attorneys, John Wickham: "The judge, who is to preside on the trial of a criminal, joining in a Bacchnalian revelry, and drinking to toasts and sentiments of a traitor!"[82] Burr's supporters and lawyers became targets of particularly venomous Independence Day toasts:

> "*The union of honest men*"—Burr, Dayton, Blannerhassett, and their associates, "choice spirits"!! May their present situation teach those who are above the "*dull pursuits of civil life*," that a republican government possesses *energy* enough to protect the people against machinations of *traitors and apostates*.
> The Burrs of society, may they stick to the skirts of *Tories*.[83]
> Aaron Burr, the treacherous apostate whig—May the portion of eternal infamy be the fate of every traitor to virtue, liberty, and independence.[84]

Burr was often referred to as the "American Catiline" in toasts. Lucius Sergius Catilina, or simply Catiline, attempted to overthrow the Roman Republic. Burr joined him in infamy as an incarnation of treason: "The modern Catiline and his *little band of conspirators*—May they by due course of law get into the hands of a *Marshall* that will see *justice* done to them."[85]

One toast given in Elkton, Maryland, "threatened" one of Burr's lawyers, Luther Martin: "Luther Martin, the ex-attorney general of Maryland, the mutual and highly respected friend of a convicted traitor—May his exertions to preserve the Catiline of America, procure him a humble coat of tar and a plumage of feathers, that will rival in finery all the mummies of Egypt." Martin wrote a lengthy response to the toasts given in Elkton, stating that he wanted to make sure that those who prepared the toasts would be held accountable for their publication:

> To any person of common sense, who possesses one sentiment of candor, one human feeling of the heart, it would be supposed, that none but demons from Hell could on such an occasion, have deliberately prepared and drank the foregoing toasts, unless they had the most perfect knowledge of colonel Burr's guilt. And even in that case he would naturally conclude the persons to be *savages* or *descendants* of savages, who when they kill their prisoner, feast their inhuman souls with every cruelty of torture.
>
> But, Gentlemen, have you any knowledge that colonel Burr is guilty of treason or of any other offense? Doth either of you know of one single fact to prove upon him guilty of any kind? Why have you not come forward and informed your government? And why had I not the pleasure of seeing you as witnesses at Richmond?[86]

Jefferson took a personal interest in the Burr trial. Supposedly more concerned about the security of the nation than any personal animus toward Burr, Jefferson went beyond his authority by gathering information and advising the prosecution.[87] Unfortunately for Jefferson, Chief Justice Marshall made the definition of treason very specific and difficult to prove in this case. Burr was found not guilty, but he fled to Europe afterward because his political future and reputation were irretrievably ruined.[88]

Ironically, the man whose actions were treasonable was General James Wilkinson, who was very much involved in the plots to take western lands. To save himself, he wrote to the authorities about Burr's role. He was complimented for this betrayal in a toast published in the *New-Hampshire Gazette*: "General JAMES WILKINSON, whose patriotism, firmness and vigilance in exposing and defeating the late treasonable projects of Aaron Burr, and thereby saving Louisiana from all the horrors of insurrection, entitle him to the most acceptable reward of a soldier: the approbation and gratitude of his country."[89] During this time, Wilkinson was in the pay of the Spanish government.[90]

10. "The embargo—a deformed bantling...," 1805–1808

The Burr trial added to the usual party rhetoric that was found in the 1807 July Fourth toasts. The *Political Atlas* of Massachusetts stated that the toasts "have swarmed upon us as thick as locusts in ancient Egypt."[91] Federalists focused on the dangers of democracy and Jefferson's downsizing of the military:

> Democracy and Jacobinism—the eternal sleep to them, which they promised to their votaries.
> May the next patent granted by our president be a process for converting fifty gun boats into one ship of the line.[92]

Republicans meanwhile focused on the virtues of their party and the peaceful direction Jefferson was trying to steer the country toward:

> *Republicanism*—May it be like a "marble pin-cushion"—not easily penetrated by foreign or domestic enemies.
> While Burrites, Federalists, and Monarchists foment treason, sedition, faction and war, Republicans will rejoice that the finger of heaven hath not pointed to war since John Adams left the Presidential Chair.[93]

The *True Republican* of Connecticut observed that most Federalist toasts given on the Independence Day holiday had not been published. Whereas Republicans proudly raised their glasses to the Spirit of '76, the Federalists seemed to be avoiding showing any national pride. Did they fear the ideas of democracy and independence?

> Are the *knowing ones* afraid that these toasts are too highly seasoned with their real principles to suit the palates of their honest adherents? 'Tis strange, that men assembled to commemorate one of the most glorious and happy events in the annals of the world, should be ashamed of the sentiments which they uttered on the occasion. Could not the Birth day of the liberty and independence of their country, awaken sentiments worthy of being presented to the public? Could not the present crisis of affairs shield the administration from their attacks? Well may they be ashamed, if the prosperity and rising greatness of their country could not do it. And when every one knows, that this prosperity has been produced by our republican government, now so wisely administered, it should excite indignation or regret that their toasts on this glorious anniversary should be so far hostile to this government and administration, that they should consider the best policy not to make them public.[94]

Such was obviously not true, as there were many Federalist toasts in print for the holiday. They toasted "the Goddess of American Liberty" in the hope that she would return from her pilgrimage, because she had been missing from the scene since 1801.[95] When Federalists appeared at Jefferson's levee, a newspaper reported that they "'mingled with perfect cordiality with their republican brethren.'" They joined in the toast to "'the American People—Ready at a moment's warning to vindicate the rights, and avenge the wrongs of their country.'"[96] Federalist toasts went after the Jefferson administration's weakness when it came to foreign affairs. Jefferson had gutted the navy and decreased military expenditures, leaving the nation in a state of unpreparedness. The August 8 issue of the *Virginia Argus* printed several Federalist toasts that were given in New England:

> *Our national administration*—a system without nerves, a body without spirit.
> *Our navy and army*—the first sold or rotten, the second headed by Wilkinson.
> *The American eagle*—bleeding and fluttering beneath the paws of the British lion, her wings clipped by the shears of economy.

Problems with Great Britain were becoming much more serious and violent. The seizure and impressment of American sailors forced Jefferson to finally act in 1806 when he recommended that Congress pass a mild Non-Importation Act.[97] The two opposing parties viewed the Act separately. Republicans were hopeful that it would work and economically harm the British people: "A general non-importation law, that we may convince the government and people of Great Britain, that they have not a loom nor an anvil, but what is stamped with the United States of America."[98] Diners in Paterson, New Jersey, considered the Act to be a way for American industries to prosper: "The non-importation act: May it be put into immediate and efficient force, to give a rise to the too much neglected manufactories of our country."[99] Federalists, on the other hand, believed the Act was futile and would not change Britain's behavior: "The Non-Importation Act—on a philosophical experiment to *stifle fire* with a dry straw."[100]

Americans were outraged when the British frigate HMS *Leopard* stopped the USS *Chesapeake* on June 22, 1807, to search for deserters. The captain of the *Chesapeake*, James Barron, refused to allow the British to board his vessel, and so the *Leopard* fired its guns, killing four sailors and wounding seventeen. The British then boarded the ship and hauled off the four deserters.[101] Public condemnation was fierce:

> The British outrage committed on the U.S. Frigate Chesapeake—If Americans want feeling to celebrate this day, let them have recurrence to this dastardly attack of the Leopard.[102]
> The memory of JOHN PIERCE, and the rest of our murdered brethren, and every tory who defends her horrid deeds—If we have to draw swords, let it be first against them:—And may the American, who does not feel for the innocent, feel the banquet of the merciless.[103]
> Our brethren who were wounded and slaughtered on board of the Chesapeak—Their blood cries for vengeance, and when our government directs, vengeance it shall have, till then we can only mourn their loss and sympathize in their sufferings.[104]

Americans were united, as they had been during the XYZ Affair, and demanded vengeance. One patriotic toast was given to "'the American People—Ready at a moment's warning to vindicate the rights, and avenge the wrongs of their country.'"[105] The Non-Importation Act was seen as a way to harm Britain:

> Sequestration and non-intercourse—British agents and British property as hostages, and starvation is the best care for British outrage, rapine and murder.[106]
>
> A non-importation act and sequestration of British property, until ample restitution is made for the insults committed on our flag, and a peace then only on terms congenial to the true laws of nations, not the laws of her own nation.[107]

The Spirit of '76 returned, along with reminders of the crimes of the former enemy:

> The Jersey prison ships, in which 1800 Americans perished, and the ships which are the prisons of 4000 American citizens—may the late of the former never be forgotten, nor the wrongs of the latter be ever sacrificed to British tyranny.[108]
>
> *Great Britain*: "The voice of our brother's blood crieth from the ground"—May that powerful appeal to justice and vengeance not be disregarded by any true American, and we shall again teach those robbers (like their countrymen Burgoyne and Cornwallis) to march to the tune of "Yankee Doodle."[109]
>
> May they who destroyed the Tea, and they who floated the Kegs, and they who knocked out the Hogshead Heads, be ever esteemed by their countrymen.[110]

Federalists gathering for the Fourth in Northampton, Massachusetts, caused an uproar with a very pro-British toast: "Great Britain—a splendid Constellation of genius and learning! May she hold Europe balanced in scales, and cause nor suffer domination."[111] Federalists all over the country had been painted with the same brush and were viewed as traitors to America. They seemed to bring the outrage upon themselves by giving Britain any respectable sentiments. Republicans in Boston drank to such traitors suffering the same fate as the loyalists who survived the Revolution: "May all those traitors in our country, whether of American or British extraction, who encourage British insults against our government and nation, be confined to the shattered mansions of Port Rosaway, now the residence of bats and owls, till a potatoe and a lobster shall sell for as many pieces of silver as an ass's head and a cub of doves' dung ever did in the streets of Samaria."[112] The *Democratic Press* of Pennsylvania printed commentary on the toast under the title "LOOK OUT FOR TRAITORS." The Northampton toast took on special meaning since it was given on a day when patriotism was supposed to swell in each American's chest:

Such men, though they may walk on American ground, must have their affections in Great-Britain. Though they may effect the zeal of Patriots, they must have the hearts of Traitors: and in the event of the war to which we seem to be wantonly provoked, they ought to be severely looked to. We have the charity to believe, that such sentiments will meet the pointed reprobation of the better sort of Federalists through the country; while they tend to prove, what has often been suggested, that they Northampton Brethren were so deeply sunk in prejudice and ignorance, that they groped along at least half a century behind their neighbours in point of principle and civility.[113]

One "Jeffersonian editor" in Norfolk, Virginia, demanded that no toasts be made to the former enemy, and he objected to the "moderate" terms Federalists sometimes used when drinking to Britain:

> In the name of all that is holy, powerful, manly or just, are we to FEED THEM for KILLING US? Are we to suffer them to send a BOAT-LOAD OF MURDERED CITIZENS ashore and take a LOAD OF PROVISIONS in return?—Are we to pay them, to hire them with the luxuries of our land to cut our throats? Away with such words as *coolness* and *moderation*: they are the *cloak*, the *coverings* of *treachery*, and we have heard too much, seen too much and *know whence* this moderation proceeds—from people who would tie our hands and bend our heads to the butcher! Let them beware—let us have no more of this—no MODERATION now! The storm is up, and at the least varying of the wind it will overwhelm domestic treason in its course.[114]

Republican toasts to France continued without the same amount of controversy, which is not to say that were no objections to toasting the French. On August 16, which was the day of St. Napoleon in France, toasts were drank on board the ship *Patriot*, anchored in the Patuxent River, Maryland. Napoleon was toasted as "the great, emperor of the French and king of Italy," and his Grand Army was "the conquerors of Italy of Egypt and Prussia—May they enter France under the triumphal arch, and repose themselves under that glory which is attached to their invincible courage."[115] Criticism appeared in papers concerning the third toast: "The President of the United States and the people of America—May they never forget the French as their ancient and true friends, and that they may always count upon them." It was made clear that the British were not the only ones harassing American ships:

> (Say you so? we wish we could *count* upon them for eighteen or twenty millions of dollars of American property, taken from the citizens of the United States; and we wish we *could* count upon their desisting from the daily practice of taking our vessels; one instance of which, out of many before us, we shall publish in our next, by way of commentary on the text contained in this toast).[116]

Napoleon issued the Milan Decree in December 1807, forbidding trade with Great Britain and authorizing French ships to capture neutral ships sailing from any British port. The French emperor then issued the Bayonne Decree in April 1808, which treated all American vessels arriving in Europe as if they came from British ports. The British had already been targeting American vessels and impressing sailors, but in November 1807, they forbade neutral nations from trading with France with the "Order in Council." Americans were not ready to go up against both Britain and France, but standing up to the European powers was vital to maintain respectability:

> France; peace with her if a fair and honorable peace she wishes, she need not hope we are dazzled, or panic-struck with the splendor of her arms.
> Great Britain; her habitual violations of the rights of nations have impoverished her resources and will accelerate her downfall; in our youth we contended with her cannon, in our manhood its thunder does not alarm us.
> The French Decrees and British Orders of Council—Base and disgraceful violations of the laws of nations; the want of our commerce shall inflict upon them a punishment for their insolence.[117]

Jefferson signed the Embargo Act into law on December 22, 1807, and the Second Embargo Act almost a month later. The Embargo Act was twofold: avoid war with foreign belligerents and strengthen domestic industries. The Mutual Assistant Society of Hair Dressers and Surgeon Barbers of Philadelphia was concerned about the new legislation: "May the cause which gave rise to the embargo, be soon removed, so that the vessels of our useful and enterprising Merchants may be wafted to their destined ports."[118] The Albion Benevolent Society of New York City welcomed the Act: "When the Albions meet to be merry and civil,/ May they lay an Embargo on all that is evil."[119] Republicans supported the embargo as a necessary action, and the difficulties that Americans might suffer were a small price to pay. Toasts given in favor of the embargo seemed to demonstrate that the entire nation was behind it. The *New York Aurora* printed the following observation of the July Fourth toasts of 1808:

> If the toasts and songs, at the different entertainments throughout the U. States given in honor of the 4th of July, are considered as indicative of public opinion—and, we believe, they may be fairly so considered—it is evident, that the late measures of the administration are upheld by a weight of popularity at least equal to that which has attended any administration in this country. The Embargo, particularly, seems to be approved, even with enthusiasm; not, from an insensibility to the privations we endure under it; but from a sincere conviction that those privations are ascribable to a higher source, and that they would have existed with ten-fold aggravation for it.[120]

Examples of pro-embargo toasts were overly patriotic, making the argument that the Embargo was a national endeavor:

The *embargo*—May our citizens prove themselves worthy of their country and their freedom, by submitting with fortitude, to some temporary inconveniences, to secure to themselves and posterity their important natural rights, by the only means in the power of government without the effusion of human blood.[121]

The Embargo—The wise measure of a prudent administration—the patriotic pride and boast of all real republicans—the stumbling block of the enemies of our government—more powerful against the tyrants of the ocean than a hundred ships of the line, and far less expensive than ten frigates; May it be continued until haughty John Bull and arrogant Napoleon shall learn to fight their enemies without plundering their friends.

The embargo, adopted by our government for the preservation of peace, of our independence, and national rights. May its violators be considered "the most worthless of society," and be rewarded with "permanent" contempt and disgrace.[122]

The EMBARGO: he that will not patiently submit to temporary privations when his country's interests and independence require them, deserves not the name of an American citizen.[123]

The strengthening of domestic industries was the silver lining to the Embargo's pains. Celebrants in the counties of Middlesex and Essex, Massachusetts, drank to "DOMESTIC MANUFACTURIES: now is the day for their promotion; all true friends to their country: independence will lend their aid."[124] Ohioans in the township of Fairfield toasted, "May the embargo law have its desired effect and be productive of the greatest degree of improvement in the manufactures of our country."[125]

Federalists were outraged, for they saw the Embargo Act as a repressive law that was worse than the Alien and Sedition Acts. New Englanders were especially angry because so much of their economy was based on overseas trade. To them, the embargo was wasteful and "deadly":

The embargo—Deliver us from putrid stagnant waters—they cause *death*.[126]
The EMBARGO—a good thing!—So was *Haman's Gallows!*[127]
The Fisheries—"Something is *rotten* in the State of Denmark."[128]
The principle of '76. Equal laws, equal rights for them we fought. Bills shutting our ports, denials and unnecessary suspensions of the writ of Habeas Corpus, transportation of our citizens beyond sea for trial. Oppressive revenue Laws, opposed to the spirit and the laws of the land: Against those we fought and conquered.[129]
Commerce—Though dead and buried, may its departed spirit haunt the halls of Congress, and write upon the Presidential palace the prophetic denunciation, "Mene mene tekel upharsin."
The Embargo—A tragedy in five "acts"—followed by an afterpiece called flour licenses—may the actors be hissed from the stage, and the authors consigned to infamy.[130]

Republicans were disgusted by the Federalists' pro-British position: "*Federalism*—While it can stigmatize the most salutary acts of the general government, it can sign for his crumbs of Monarchy. O, shame, where is thy blush!"[131] Federalist toasts were either defensive or focused on how the Embargo Act was hurting trade:

> Commerce of the U. States; Sad dilemma! thy handmaid is sick, and thou art on thy death bed.
> Federal Republicanism; Equally removed from British influence & French Jacobinism.[132]
> The Fourth of March, 1809—Let us hail it as the era of emancipation from the dreams of philosophy, the intrigues of ambition, and the thraldom of foreign influence.[133]

Two individuals stood out in the Fourth of July toasts in 1808. The first was Secretary of State James Madison, who had to deal with both the French and the British during the embargo crisis. He was more enthusiastic for drastic measures than Jefferson was.[134] Supporters of the embargo drank to Madison and his abilities as a statesman, while his detractors blamed him for the consequences of the embargo and for favoring France over Britain:

> James Madison—as a statesman, few equal, none superior, who with a single breath *withered* the *British rose*, and exposed to the view of the civilized world the *thorn* of imposition.[135]
> James Madison, the present secretary of state—may the firm and

9. The inflexible patriot Gen: George Clinton, Vice-President of the United States.
10. May the virtues of the brave never be forgotten.
11. The Congress of the United States; wisdom to their councils and energy to their measures.
12. The Militia and Navy of the United States.
13. Every
   M-oderate
   B-rave
   A-merican that
   R-espects
   G-ood
   O-rder.
14. The spirit which our Government breaths; peace on earth, good will towards men.
15. May the love of Liberty and Independence bind us so inseparably in unanimity that the bow of party spirit may be bent in vain, and its poisoned dart completely blunted in attempting to divide us.
16. May the support we bear our Government, demonstrate our wisdom; our unity proclaim our strength; and every part of our conduct exhibit a firm determination to maintain the rights of man unblemished.
17. The American Fair.
   VOLUNTEER.
   Colonel Robert M'Kelvey of the 30th Regiment.

The Third Company of the lower District of Christ Church Parish in Charleston, South Carolina, offered several toasts on the Fourth of July, saving the thirteenth toast for the Embargo Act (Toast #13, *Carolina Gazette*, 7-22-1808).

independent principles which has always characterized his conduct, be predominant in his breast as our next president.[136]

James Madison—May the people of the United States duly estimate the man who had the memories to declare, "THAT FRANCE WANTED MONEY, AND WE MUST GIVE."[137]

Madison would continue to receive toasts through the rest of 1808. There was a presidential election that year, and Madison ran on the Republican ticket. The citizens of Washington County met at Wakefield, Maryland, and toasted Madison as Jefferson's successor: "James Madison—may the president elect so preside, that duty and expectancy be coincident to the wishes of the people."[138] The Federalist candidate was once again South Carolina's Charles Cotesworth Pinckney. New Hampshire Federalists drank to "PINCKNEY—who never polluted his lips by saying, 'France wants money, and we must give it.'"[139]

The second figure to receive many notable Independence Day toasts was John Quincy Adams. The brilliant son of the former president, he disappointed many by supporting Jefferson and the embargo. Federalists felt betrayed, but Republicans honored him for putting principles above party politics:

Hon. J.Q. Adams—Federalism knew his integrity and disclaimed him; republican justice will honor his patriotism and revere his wisdom and virtue.[140]

John Quincy Adams—The foe of political iniquity, the all-powerful advocate of his country's honor and interests; patriotism, political honor and honesty are his characteristics. The admiration and affections of his countrymen and their posterity will be the reward of his virtues.[141]

John Quincy Adams, the patriot who preferred the interests of his country to the triumphs of faction, and consulted his conscience rather than his party.[142]

Federalist toasts made him out to be a scoundrel:

John Quincy Adams,/ Alas! poor Johnny has mistook/ The road to fame and glory:/ He set out well, but made a *crook*, / When late he turned a Tory.

John Q. Adams "can frame his face to all occasions, play the orator as well as Nestor, deceive more slily than Ulysses, change shape with Proteus for advantages, and set aspiring Cataline to school"—and shall be made president![143]

J. Q. Adams—MEASURES—NOT MEN—"Think not revolted spirit, thy shape the same,/ Or undiminished brightness, to be known/ As when thou stod'st in leaven upright and pure:/ That glory then, when thou no more wast good,/ Departed from thee, and thou resemblest now/ Thy sin and place of doom secure and foul."[144]

Toasts were also given to other famous figures, such as Aaron Burr, Timothy Pickering, John Marshall, and even Citizen Genet. When

10. "The embargo—a deformed bantling...," 1805–1808

Republicans in Hartford, Connecticut, drank to "*Choice Spirits—Pickering, Marshall* and *Burr—if raised* above the '*dull pursuits of civil life*' may it be done by impartially administering to them the justice due from their country," Federalists responded angrily because of the association of any Federalists with the American Catiline:

> The meaning of this toast is too obvious to need explanation. Who else but a true disciple of *Bonaparte* would have the affrontery and malice to couple the two venerable patriots *Pickering* and *Marshall* with the murderer *Burr*? And what but the most infernal malice of a blood-thirsty jacobin could induce a wish so diabolical!![145]

Special recognition must be given to the unique toasts of the Ugly Club in Annapolis, Maryland. Ugly Clubs originated in England; the first one was established in Liverpool in 1743. The Clubs satirized deformities and ugliness through debates, but by the time they reached the United States, they had become a fraternal organization whose merchant-class members met in taverns to drink and sing songs.[146] When the Ugly Club of Annapolis met on the Fourth of July, their toasts began with a justification of the Club itself:

> This Club is of several years standing, and has rather increased than decreased in number, being composed of sixteen as ugly men as have lived since the days of Thersites. A man of little soul is apt to be ashamed of any defects which may appear in his person, but the present members conscious that they are fit subjects for such an institution, wish to prove that they are above an idle affectation of beauty. Happy in being the first to participate in the mirth which they themselves create.[147]

The Club's toasts were all patriotic, but each one stressed the value of "ugliness":

> The day we celebrate, dear to the heart of every American patriot—may our sour looks and ugly faces made when we were declared free, never be changed into smiles and pleasant phizes at seeing us again subjected to any nation.
> The Club—harmonized by the discord of ugliness, may they learn to perform on the harp of love, the armorial motto of Maryland "*crescite et multiplicanimi.*"
> The Arms of the Club—a Gorgon's head and a Serpent's tail—may the one turn our enemies into stone, the other sting them unto death.
> Our Brethren throughout the world—may all the curiosities of nature be ardently sought after.[148]

Thomas Jefferson happily left for Monticello at the conclusion of his second term. The president-elect, James Madison, inherited a fractured political system, an economy teetering on the brink of collapse, and the prospect of war with either Britain or France. One toast to Madison from

Petersburgh, Virginia, expressed confidence that his stature alone would get the country through the coming dark days: *"James Madison*—The light of the Sun is not obscured by the atoms that pass over its surface."[149]

The second term of the third president started on a euphoric high, especially since the nation had doubled in size with the Louisiana Purchase. Toasts praised the Republicans, but some took a dark turn when Aaron Burr was put on trial for treason. Toasts were also made to John Adams, the defeat of the Barbary pirates, the memory of Washington, the impeachment of Samuel Chase, the Yazoo land fiasco, and the proponents of a third party ("Quids"). Jefferson's popularity sank due to foreign entanglements when he had to restrict American commerce and trade in an effort to force both France and Great Britain to treat the United States with respect. The Embargo Act was praised in some toasts and vilified in others. At the end of Jefferson's second term, toasts to James Madison were made because he seemed to be the best choice to succeed Jefferson.

CHAPTER 11

"James Madison— 'tho last, not least'...,"[1] 1809–1811

"*James Madison, President of the United States.*—Well done thou good and faithful servant—Our country was naked, and ye clothed her—sick and in prison, and ye visited her—and hungered, and ye gave her meat—a thirst, and ye gave her drink—Come then, and behold the joy of the people, that ye may persevere in the good work, even unto the end."[2]

"Our fellow Citizens, prisoners on board British ships of war—whilst Congress are wasting days in debating on modes of relief for those captured in Miranda's illegal expedition—why are the thousands impressed and unslaved by Britain, totally forgotten."[3]

"Here's a health to our Countrymen, imprisoned in the floating dungeons of Great Britain and prisons of France; cut off from those dear privileges which this day sheds upon their country; let us remember them now, that our swords may avenge their wrongs hereafter."[4]

Republicans continued to support Jefferson's embargo policies, but the nation was suffering economically. New England, the shipbuilding center of the nation, saw a 75 percent drop in its exports. Thousands of sailors were out of work and merchants faced bankruptcy.[5] Critics in Northampton, Massachusetts, angrily toasted on Independence Day 1809: "The Jefferson Administration—A prostrate judiciary, ruined credit, an exhausted treasury, commerce annihilated, the rights of the citizen invaded, individual distress and national calamity, disunion as at home and contempt abroad—These are its fruits—the execrations of an injured and indignant people and of posterity will be its reward."[6] Volunteer toasts given in Boston by a "Gentleman of Hampshire County" included one that defended "*The* RIGHTS *of* NEW ENGLAND:—The *Rights* they will never surrender—The *Right* to walk the *Earth*—the *Right* to breathe the *Air*—and the *Rights* to NAVIGATE THE OCEAN."[7] Blame for the embargo went in one direction:

> The Administratsion of Jefferson—The reign of popular delusion and state juggling—A substitution of professions for arguments—of appearance for realities—the people taught to fancy the ROD over their heads, a SCEPTRE in their hands. But the genius of federalism has broken the spell, and truth, justice and public spirit resume their influence.
>
> Thomas Jefferson's saving administration—Like a farmer burning his fence round his wheat to save his fire-wood.[8]
>
> Non-importation, non-intercourse and embargo laws, with their train of additions, supplements and enforcements, farewell—a long farewell to all their mischiefs![9]

One toast given in Portland referred to the turtle made famous by the 1807 political cartoon known as "Ograbme," which is "embargo" spelled backward: "*The Times*.... A speedy change of the 'terrapin policy' of the present administration."[10] Diners at a feast in Bedford, Pennsylvania, drank to "the Terrapin System—Conceived in the brain of a crazed Philosopher, born in folly, nurtured in Jacobinism—It has died through too much care of the nurse."[11]

The purpose of the embargo laws was to hit back at France and Great Britain, whose actions on the high seas interrupted American commerce. Toasts for or against Great Britain and France depended on the political leanings of the gathering. Republicans drank to France and against Great Britain, while Federalists drank to Great Britain and against France. Toasts given by members of the Tammany Society in New York City pointed out the differences between the two belligerents:

> Our differences with the English, when by *actions* they shall have evinced their sincerity for an amicable adjustment of them, our doubts will be removed, but until then we must continue to *doubt*.
>
> Our differences with France: as it is our interest to be at peace with all the world, may the emperor of that country be convinced, that it is his interest to be at peace with us.[12]

Napoleon's 1808 invasion of the Iberian Peninsula, known as the Peninsula War, prompted a wave of popular resistance to French occupation in both Spain and Portugal.[13] Toasts to the resistance fighters mirrored those given years earlier to freedom fighters in Corsica and Ireland:

> May advocates for French usurpation over Spain and Portugal, be forever embargoed from the enjoyment of the exhilarating juice of their grapes, and be condemned to a perpetual non-intercourse, with their rich fruits and precious commodities.[14]

11. "James Madison—'tho last, not least'...," 1809-1811

Political cartoon in 1807 that attacked the Embargo Act, personifying it as a turtle: "The Terrapin System—Conceived in the brain of a crazed Philosopher, born in folly, nurtured in Jacobinism—It has died through too much care of the nurse" (Toast #14, *True American and Commercial Daily Advertiser*, 7-13-1809) (Wikimedia Commons).

> The Patriots of Spain—May they establish such liberty as will make government just; and such a government as will make liberty immortal.
>
> The nation that discovered our country. As they were the first that openly favoured our independence, may we not be the last openly to favour theirs.[15]

The Spanish Catholic Church and its leaders were included in some toasts, such as this one given by a Boston clergyman: "The Spanish Clergy, now militant, may they soon be triumphant." It seemed shocking that American religious leaders from Massachusetts, where the Puritan culture still influenced every aspect of culture, would dare sing the praises of any Roman Catholic institution:

> The clergymen of Boston have long had the character of being extremely liberal; but we did not expect to hear them toast the holy fathers of the Inquisition. The wall of partition between papists and protestants being now broken down by clerical hands, we expect at the next ordination to have a volunteer for the Pope. When we compare this liberality with their late prayers against Pagan superstition, Mahometan delusion, and popish idolatry; and when we read of the hanging witches, quakers and baptists for non-conformity, by the ancestors of these same Boston clergymen, we are astonished at that rapid

progress of catholicism which musts soon embrace the whole world in one communion, Protestants, Papists, Bramins, Jews, Mahometans, and pagans of all descriptions. What wonderful times we live in! New-England clergymen toasting the Inquisition![16]

The presidential election of 1808 provided an opportunity for the escalation of tensions between the Republicans and the Federalists. James Madison easily defeated Federalist candidate Charles C. Pinckney, who carried only the four New England states and Delaware. The embargo had obviously taken its toll on the Republicans, but Madison prevailed in other parts of the country with enough electoral votes to win: 122 to Pinckney's 47 and George Clinton's 6.[17] Republicans were angry about the fact that Massachusetts, which had voted for Jefferson in 1804, returned to the Federalist ticket. One Republican toast was to "our infatuated brethren of Massachusetts—we pity their weakness, we deplore their want of patriotism and we abhor their disorganizing projects."[18] Federalists, of course, celebrated the election results of New England:

> *The New England States.*—They rubbed the scales from the nation's eyes.
> *Massachusetts, New-Hampshire, and Rhode-Island.*—May their return to Federalism be as lasting as it is joyful.[19]
> Connecticut—The land of correct and steady habits—The head quarters of good principles—The tribe of Benjamin in our political Israel, whose sons, tho few in number, are chosen men, that know how to wield the *sling* of *truth* against error to a hair's breadth—may she remain as she is.[20]

To Republicans, Timothy Pickering seemed to embody the "duplicity" of Massachusetts: "*Timothy Pickering*—The British apologist, and leader of the Essex Junto—We envy no party the possession of a statesman whose public conduct tends to the disgrace of his own government by exalting that of Great Britain."[21] Pickering's association with the Essex Junto and his criticism of the embargo made him a threat to Republican government: "Timothy Pickering, the Essex Junto, and all those who have attempted to thwart the measures of government. May their schemes wither within them, and may the conviction of their own conscience be their punishment. Go to the Devil and shake yourself."[22] Federalists instead held him in high regard: "TIMOTHY PICKERING—His luminous mind penetrated the unhallowed recesses of the Cabinet; the minions of a wicked administration writhed under the last of truth, and corruption trembled as she spoke."[23]

Many of the Independence Day toasts of 1809 praised Madison, who was a highly respected diplomat and a defender of natural rights. People were confident that he would be able to steer the nation through both domestic and international problems:

The President of the United States—A great and necessary work is before him, nor will it be difficult "to re-unite the American people," broken into feuds and factions by the contemptible passions, follies and persecution of his predecessor: a magnanimous and real comprehension of the virtues and talents of the nation can alone, but it will, inspire confidence and rank him by the side of Washington.[24]

James Madison—"tho last, not least"—may his lucid mind never be obscured; and when he has done his work, may we be enabled by a continuance of his wise conduct, in good health and good wine, to say and drink, "well done, thou good and faithful servant, may you long enjoy the delights of private citizenship, in a prosperous, happy country."[25]

The American Republican Society in Philadelphia gave a lengthy toast to Madison that listed all of his previous accomplishments, associations, and talents:

James Madison, president of the U. S.—He was a zealous advocate, in the general convention for framing the present constitution of the U.S. He facilitated, by his arguments and eloquence, its adoption in the convention of Virginia: He, in conjunction with those well tried and honorable patriots, John Jay and Alexander Hamilton, organized the departments of government, and with them timely wrote the able and meritorious numbers under signature of FEDERALIST—He promptly for the honor and interest of United America, accepted the overture of Great Britain for a settlement of our differences with her, the only nation on earth that can materially injure us. His private character is fair and upright: Let us hope then, that in his public career at the head of the national government, he will "correct the procedure of his predecessor," Thomas Jefferson; that by his justice and independence, party distinctions may thereby subside; and the whole community of our country become one undivided people, feeling just cause to say: *Madison*, you sir like our departed *Washington*, as president of the U. States, deserved well of your country.[26]

Expectations were high for a resolution to the problems with Great Britain. People toasted a successful negotiation in the hopes that a treaty would result, and "that embargoes and non-intercourse will no more ever cloud our prosperity."[27] Federalists were more concerned with France and wanted negotiations to decrease French power: "Peace with Great-Britain—The PEOPLE have secured it, French influence in their cabinet and over their presses notwithstanding; let the people maintain it on the federal principles of Washington by good faith and national spirit."[28]

One of the lasting effects of the embargo was the reliance on domestic manufactures. Commerce, agriculture, fishing, and industry were regularly included in toast lists. Supporting these enterprises was patriotic and essential for the growing nations. Sheep-shearing festivals became popular opportunities for people to gather and celebrate industrial success. Merino wool was used more often in textiles, and so it was deserving of the following toast: "May Merino wool be soon as abundant among the northern farmers as cotton is among the southern planters, and may they prove two main pillars of American independence."[29] The sixth anniversary of the Arlington Sheep Shearing event in Alexandria, Virginia, was a jubilee, and a Mr. Custis volunteered a toast to agriculture, commerce, and manufactures: "Agriculture, the basis of our strength; Commerce, the patron of our labor, and Manufactures the resource for our wants. May these important interests ever be united with generous sympathy, in support of the wealth industry and independence of the republic."[30] Other toasts emphasized the superiority of American products and the need to lessen the reliance on foreign goods:

> MANUFACTURES—May the people of America be no longer blinded by foreign artifices, and may they discover in time, that the encouragement of home industry is a more sure source of national riches, and more secure bond for peace and independence, than the carrying trade of the whole earth and seas.[31]
>
> Home manufactures—essential to the independence of a country—may the patriotism of our citizens, by making homespun fashionable, atone for the neglect of their representatives.[32]
>
> The spinning wheel and the loom—When our soil shall feed us, and our manufactures and artizans clothe us, then, and not till then, shall we be independent indeed, as we are now only in name.[33]
>
> *Fisheries*—May the hardy and industrious Fishermen find a *Bank* with an inexhaustible *Capital*, which *discount* without an endorser.[34]
>
> Domestic Manufactures—the pride of a growing people, may every American feel it his interest to encourage industry at home rather than depend on the superfluities of European toy-shops.[35]

One particular Washington's birthday toast referred to an individual who was as much of a concern to Madison as Citizen Genet had been to Washington: "Whatever disposition Great Britain might feel towards this country, we wish to be peaceable; at the same time, whatever she may think of the skill of her *Ministers*, *Subjects* or *Sons*, in riding her Political *Horse*, still we condemn the conduct of a *Jackson*."[36] The reference was to the British ambassador to the United States, Francis James Jackson. Just as Genet tried to intimidate Washington, Jackson's only purpose seemed to be manipulating the new president into doing Britain's bidding. Jackson's popularity was extremely limited. He was sometimes referred to as the "Copenhagen bully" because of his 1807 ultimatum to the prince regent of Denmark to surrender the Danish fleet to the British. The prince refused and Copenhagen was brutally shelled.[37] Jackson attended a dinner of the anti–Hibernian Society on St. Patrick's Day in New York City and offered toasts against both his host country and Ireland. The writer who described the event in the New York paper *Columbia* was furious:

11. "James Madison—'tho last, not least'...," 1809-1811

They complimented him with *loyal* songs and malignant toasts. One toast was pointed at our secretary, Mr. Smith, and compared him insidiously and basely to a pettifogging attorney. The emissary could not himself stifle his contempt for his entertainers. Other guests, who went from good nature or curiosity, were so disgusted that they never again will be seen in such orgies. Every thing that could hurt the feelings of an honorable American, or patriotic Irishman, was cheered with the cry of keep it up, full bumpers and clamorous shouts for the health of the miserable king of England, whose crown surmounts the Irish harp, and was displayed upon their table as in triumph. They toasted the bloody union of Ireland with England. The revival of commerce, and a full treasury, was addressed as a compliment to the Copenhagen bully, in order to persuade him that the financial security of this nation depended upon his negociations.[38]

Jackson's toast at another gathering, this time in Boston in June, prompted an angry reaction in the *Baltimore Evening Post*: "'Perpetual harmony between the United States and Great Britain. May the swords of the ancient and honorable artillery be drawn against those who would interrupt it.'" The sentiment expressed bitter acknowledgment of Jackson's purpose: "*Jackson knew were* [sic] *he was*—for had the desire of his toast been *literally* and *justly* fulfilled, *he would have found himself in an ugly predicament*, having, with unparalled impudence, done all he could to destroy that harmony he hypocritically desires may be preserved." When another toast wished that the "'*prejudices* against the British nation'" would vanish, the *Post* pointed out, "These '*prejudices*,' are *Chesapeake, murder, robbery, impressment*—and IMPUDENCE."[39] The governor of Massachusetts, as a result, refused to be introduced to Jackson.[40] Vitriol against Jackson was widespread:

Francis J. Jackson, the willing instrument of perfidy and corruption—may the treatment he received near the United States, be a memorable lesson to his master in selecting a minister to free government.[41]

Copenhagen Jackson—May he be haunted like Richard the third, with the ghosts of the poor innocent children whom he has the occasion of being butchered by the merciless blood hounds of his majesty George the third.[42]

Francis James Jackson, the insolent British intriguer, there is too much liberality in our government to do justice to such a wretch.[43]

People who dared drink to the health of Ambassador Jackson risked their own reputation, evidenced by this Philadelphia toast: "The old tories and young men of Boston, who feasted Copenhagen Jackson—May they be permitted to retire with him their much admired friend—with the execrations and contempt of every true friend to the honor and dignity of the United States."[44]

Many Americans also saw France as a dangerous threat. One toast from Ballston Spa, New York, described all the French "crimes" recently committed against the nation:

> A Picture for our Great men to look on.—136 American vessels loaded with millions of wealth confiscated by our friendly sister France in one corner;—in another, French prisons, crowded with American seamen starving; in another, French armed vessels, filled with other American seamen forced on board to prey on their countrymen; in another, French privateers, fed clothed and sheltered, in an American harbour. The middle space crowded with Americans, compelled by French spoilation to beg their bread.[45]

Napoleon Bonaparte was perceived as nothing more than a warmonger and a dictator and was subject to bitter toasts:

> THE OMNIPOTENT NAPOLEON!—After he has packed off his old wife to the nunnery and consummated his burnt and peace offerings, with his dear bride before the altars of Hymen and Bacchus—May he in the plenitude of his royal goodness, invite her to take a peep through the grates, to see how Americans fair in prison on bread and water![46]

Jefferson and Napoleon were to blame, according to some, for the bad economy and maritime conflicts: "*Tom Jefferson & Bonaparte*, the fell destroyers of American commerce: May the Devil be their escort to the shades of oblivion!"[47]

The American minister to France, John Armstrong (author of the Newburgh Address in 1783[48]), was recalled by Madison in 1810. The *Federal Republican* printed a frustrated toast given in Boston on Independence Day: "Hopeless Diplomacy.—American rights against Gallic power. *Armstrong* may be a good negociator, but a *strong arm* would be better."[49] The *Baltimore Evening Post* sarcastically commented on Armstrong's role in government policy supposedly leaning toward France: "'French Influence.' At almost every meeting of the republicans on the 4th of July, general ARMSTRONG was toasted with marked applause, because he manfully repelled and spiritedly resisted the pretentions and practices of the *French* government in regard to the United States. This fact, most assuredly, shews the republicans are willing to *submit* to *France*, being under 'French Influence.'"[50]

The brilliant son of John Adams was attacked in some toasts because of his earlier support for Jefferson's embargo policies. In Salem, he was toasted as "*the modern Iscariot.*—He has received his thirty pieces of silver; let him now go hang himself."[51] John Quincy believed that Jefferson was entirely in the right when American commerce was shut down in the effort to injure England and France economically. As a result, some questioned John Quincy's ability to be the minister to Russia.

Republicans held John Quincy Adams in high regard. His mother wrote to him after the Fourth of July holiday in 1810 to tell him that "the Republicans did you the honour to Toast you in various places. the Federalists did not this year abuse you—they only past you by in Silence."[52] The eighth volunteer toast given in Cambridge recognized him as "our minister at the court of St. Petersburg, who has proved himself to be the son of John Adams, the sage of Quincy."[53] The District of Maine's *American Advocate* printed a more detailed toast praising Adams for his efforts in Russia: "JOHN Q. ADAMS, our minister in Russia. The early merit of his diplomatic services, his rich contributions to the science of this country, this able defence of the principles of the American people, and the active part he has taken in the government of the nation, with the present glory which surrounds him, are the greatest claims he can have upon the grateful recollections of his countrymen. It is honorable to our country that it has not been insensible of his high obligations."[54]

The colonial independence movements against Spain in Latin America were widely recognized in toast lists by 1810. While Napoleon's troops were occupying Spain, a Mexican-born Spanish priest named Manuel Hidalgo y Costilla inspired his parishioners in the Mexican town of Dolores to rise up in arms against the Spaniards who had been exploiting Mexico's wealth for three centuries. This event has become known as the "*Grito de Dolores*" ("Shout of Dolores"),[55] and it was the beginning of Mexican independence. John K. Worrell volunteered the following toast in Frankford, Pennsylvania, directly associating the fight of the Spanish colonies with the American Revolution: "The inhabitants of Spanish America—Animated by the example of their brethren in the United States, they have learned that liberty is the natural right of man; and like them have already declared this glorious sentiment—may their noble exertions to emancipate their country from the shackles of *despotism* and *separation*, be crowned with complete success."[56] Toasts to the Spanish colonies confirmed the American Revolution's legacy:

> *The People of South America*—Embarked in the cause of liberty for the support of which, like the Congress of '76, they have pledged their lives, their fortunes and sacred honor: may we shortly hail them a republic, free sovereign and independent.
> *The Independence of Southern America*—May its consummation lay another great foundation for the freedom, the friendship, the peace, and the prosperity of the new world.[57]
> *Spanish America*—May its Declaration of Independence be supported with that bravery in the field and wisdom in its measures, as was that of North America, and bring it to the dignity of a Republic.[58]

The battles between the two political factions continued through the years preceding the War of 1812. The Republicans were the majority party in Congress, giving them license to occasionally attack and belittle the Federalist minority. A toast appeared in the *Reporter* newspaper of Kentucky, given in "honor" of this minority, saying, "if they do not repent of their shameful and nefarious conduct, may they be troubled with a guilty conscience and be at liberty to remove from the United States, and to have the company of the Essex junto, all old tories, British agents, Timothy Pickering, Quincy, &c. &c. &c."[59] The Republicans, still angry about the Jay Treaty, sought to limit British influence. One institution that had concerned them was the Bank of the United States. Toasts clearly showed their worries of British influence:

> The independent members of both houses of Congress, who *put down* that hydra of *toryism*, the *Anglo United-States Bank*—They all deserve well of the Republic, especially the venerable patriot and veteran who, when it hung in awful suspense, gave the *finishing blow* which consigned the monster to oblivion.[60]
>
> May the views of our pretended Federalists be unveiled, and may Divine Vengeance hurl its red hot thunder bolts on their devoted heads, ere they shall succeed in Royalizing America.
>
> The non-renewal of the Charter of the United States Bank—We hail it as a grand step towards the downfall of British influence.[61]

"A Native American" (not an Indian) wrote of his anger at Republicans' use of Washington's name and memory in toasts. When the Baltimore Union Greens published the following toast, "'The memory of Washington, his name is abused as a cloak for *tories*; but revered only by Democrats,'" the writer called it "Barefaced Hypocrisy!" and then reminded readers of the former Republican position regarding the first president, as it was printed in the *Aurora*:

> When a retrospect is taken of the WASHINGTON administration for eight years, it is subject of the greatest astonishment that *a single individual could have cankered the principles of republicanism in an enlightened people, and should have carried his designs against public liberty so far as to have put in jeopardy its very existence.* Such, however, are the facts, and with these staring us in the face, *this day ought to be a day of Jubilee in the United States.*

"A Native American" finished with Federalist praise of Washington and a defense of the party's own claim to him: "This, Mr. Editor was the shameful denunciation of the democrats at that day against the father of his country, the best and greatest of men, WASHINGTON—they now have the effrontery to tell us that 'his name is revered only by Democrats'!"[62]

The popular fourth president never had the devotion from Republicans that they had always shown for Jefferson. The Rhode Island paper

Newport Mercury printed an article titled "*Alas! POOR MADISON!*" which claimed that Madison's fall from popularity was demonstrated in the lack of praise in toasts. He was often toasted simply as "The President," while revelers would drink much more elaborate toasts to Jefferson and certain military leaders. Madison's reputation seemed to be "in a galloping consumption, and he, poor partial man, is rapidly descending into the sewer of contempt and oblivion." Regarding toasts to Madison, "in most places he has been wholly passed by; in others, damned with faint praise; and in others, his conduct has been openly and unequivocally condemned. How are the might fallen!!"[63]

Madison did not have a figure like Burr in his administration to cause him grief, but he did have problems with his choice for secretary of state, Robert Smith, who was a divisive cabinet official who worked to undermine both Treasury Secretary Albert Gallatin and Madison himself.[64] After Madison asked him to resign in April 1811, Smith struck back by publishing a defense of his behavior to further damage Madison. In *An Address to the People of the United States*, Smith explained, "In this undertaking, I have an eye to the storm that I will have to buffet;—a storm that will be excited by the parasites of power: but I, at the same time, enjoy the consolation of having in my view the American axiom, 'Measures and not Men'; the distinguishing characteristic of the independent people of a representative Republic."[65] Toasts appeared that praised Smith for "exposing" Madison's duplicity:

> Robert Smith, late secretary of state—"Can self defence be sin?" Le the galled jade wine, his withers are unwrung.
> Robert Smith—Late secretary of state—the steady friend of his country—Guided by "MEASURES, *not men*," he has become a dread to apostate whigs.[66]
> Robert Smith's precious confession—May the man who would barter his country's independence for French promises receive his reward and then go hang himself.[67]
> *The SMITH who has unlocked the Cabinet*—May no French *Lock-Smith* be able to close it.[68]

By 1811, Republicans remained united on what they considered to be "minor subjects": disapprobation of Smith, approbation for those who opposed renewing the Bank's charter, disgust with Timothy Pickering, and undiminished confidence in Madison. "On the whole, the toasts exhibit the public sentiment on every important point correct and united; and are highly gratifying to every friend of his country and government."[69] Special recognition should go to the following piece from Virginia's *Alexandria Gazette*'s July 19 issue, for it showed that all toasts on the holiday were not solemn, celebratory, or dignified:

> The Toasts on the Fourth of July are not always to be regarded as a fair index of Public Sentiment. Some of them are silly in the extreme. The last Enquirer contains several of this description. Take the following examples:
> May all British factions within the U. States be sent into the *floating Hells* of Britain, there to share the *same fate* of his Majesty's Little Belt.
> This rivals the old song, "some says the Devil's dead, and *gone into Jamaica*, &c. the last accounts left the Little Belt at Halifax. It is but justice to mention, that the above was the *sixteenth* Toast.—Again:
> George III and Napoleon Bonaparte—A speedy meeting to them, and their corrupt minions, in the *Council Chamber* of Neptune. 4 cheers.
> There is something so *deep* in this toast, that it must have originated in the *Council Chamber* of Bacchus. It is a pity that a few glasses of wine should give rise to such unintelligible rhapsodies; and a greater pity still, that they should be uttered on so august a day as our national anniversary.

Chief Justice John Marshall received a fair number of toasts. His tenure on the bench had already strengthened the Supreme Court with such decisions as *Marbury v. Madison* (1803). The judicial branch received a supportive Washington's birthday toast from the *Philadelphia Gazette*: "Our Judiciary—bold, upright and enlightened—equally invulnerable to the assaults of powerful vice and party rage. In their exaltation, they will reign like Aurelius, and should they fall, it will be to 'bleed like Socrates.'"[70] Federalists often drank to Marshall's talents and abilities:

> The Honourable John Marshall, Chief Justice of the United States—An able and upright expounder of the law, and who will not be intimidated by the *man of the people.*
> The Chief Justice of the United States—Equally to be admired for his energy and simplicity, as for his wisdom and purity.[71]
> John Marshall, Chief Justice of the U. States—While he continues to preside in a Court of Justice, we shall have no Star Chamber decisions.[72]

Virtually every toast list between 1819 and 1812 contained a reference to the ongoing problem of British impressment. Denver Brunsman, author of *The Evil Necessity: British Naval Impressment in the Eighteenth Century*, explained that the practice "was a fundamental component of Britain's early imperial success." The skilled Atlantic seafarers in British society were the ones the press gangs sought.[73] The Napoleonic threat to the British navy forced the British to look toward impressing American seamen to replenish its numbers. John Quincy Adams called the practice exactly what it was: "'an authorized system of kidnapping upon the ocean.'"[74] How were the British able to justify the practice? To Great Britain, this was an existential life-or-death struggle that accepted no compromises or negotiations. Americans were humiliated by their being treated once again as colonial subjects:

11. "James Madison—'tho last, not least'...," 1809–1811

The British never claimed the right to impress American citizens, but since British and American sailors looked and sounded so much alike, aggressive British naval officers often made mistakes that might take years to correct. Although the United States did not employ press gangs to supply seamen for its navy, it never denied the right of the Royal Navy to impress British sailors on American ships in British ports. It did, however, deny Britain's authority to board American ships to impress men on the high seas. For their part, the British never admitted the right of the United States to do to them what they did to the United States; they never conceded the right of American naval officers to board British ships to impress American deserters—not that there were many of them. This discrepancy is what made impressment seem to the Americans to be an act of British neo-colonialism.[75]

Republicans especially took issue with impressment. The possibility of war with America's former enemy was welcomed by some as the only way to stop the illegal seizures and to show strength before a bully:

> War with England, and banishment to all her partizans, until the releasement of our unfortunate seamen, and immediate freedom of the seas.[76]
>
> Our Brethren who are impressed on board British ships of War—May the God of our fathers send them relief. If the voice of justice cannot be heard by the tyrants of the ocean, may they be awakened by the American thunder.[77]
>
> Impressment of American Seamen, "piracy by the law of nations and of England." We hope to see the time when the American flag will be a sufficient protection for every man who sails under it.[78]

"American thunder" would become a wish granted within almost a year's time.

President James Madison had to deal with the negativity caused by the economically damaging Embargo Act of his predecessor. New England toasts especially criticized the administration. Massachusetts returned to the Federalist fold in 1808, but the loss of favorite son John Quincy Adams, toasted as a traitor, was hard to bear. While New England suffered, other states focused on domestic manufacturing. Toasts continued to be given in Washington's memory, and figures such as Napoleon, Francis Jackson, John Armstrong, Robert Smith, and John Marshall were included in many celebrations. The issue of impressment became a major foreign policy issue, and toasts called for war with Great Britain.

Chapter 12

"...War.—The offspring of an *adulterous* intercourse...,"[1] 1812–1815

> "War"—"*The last resort of injured nations.*" "Tis with a view to peace we have taken up arms"—"With UNION the contest will be short; its success, certain."[2]
>
> "Our Army—They are ready to march either to Florida, Canada, or the Western woods, and fully adequate to the expulsion of malicious Spaniards, perfidious British, or cruel Savages."[3]
>
> "Our navy—the gallant tars of Columbia have marched the trident from the haughty foe; they have humbled the British flag and tarnished the naval glory of England."[4]
>
> "Major-General Andrew Jackson, the Leonidas of America—he has exalted our national character, and by a touch of his wand, has dissolved the magic spell of British invincibility."[5]

Historian Gordon S. Wood referred to the War of 1812 as "the strangest war in American history." The fact that the result of the conflict was a return to prewar conditions leads one to dismiss any military accomplishments or acquisitions. Wood points out in his book *Empire of Liberty*:

> The United States told the world in 1812 that it declared war against Great Britain solely because of the British impressment of American sailors and the British violations of America's maritime rights. Yet on the face of it, these grievances scarcely seemed to be sufficient justifications for a war, especially a war for which the United States was singularly unprepared. In 1812 the U.S. Army consisted of fewer than seven thousand regular troops. The navy comprised only sixteen vessels, not counting the dozens of gunboats. With this

meager force the United States confronted an enemy that possessed a regular army of nearly a quarter of a million men and the most powerful navy in the world, with a thousand warships on the rolls and over six hundred of them in active service.[6]

Americans were dismayed about the impressment of American seamen, and this was probably the most legitimate rationale for going to war. A strong navy was needed, but the Republican administrations of Jefferson and Madison scaled back the navy's strength. John Adams, referred to as the "Father of the Navy," undoubtedly smiled as more people demanded a stronger naval force. He wrote to Benjamin Rush in January 1812: "I have toasted The Wooden Walls, the Floating Castles the floating Batteries and the floating Citidels of The United States for Six and thirty years: and I now rejoice to find that many Persons now begin to drink my Toast with Huzzas."[7]

While impressment was an important reason for going to war, there were others who wanted an excuse to claim Canada. The Ohio paper *Liberty Hall* printed a toast on Washington's birthday that laid out the argument for taking Canada: "The Canadas—we have no security against the great pirate of the ocean, on our sea coast, nor against the savages on our frontiers, while the haughty Briton holds a foot of territory on this continent."[8] The territory of Florida was also seen as a possible American possession: "The Patriots of Florida, like our revolutionary forefathers, they have asserted those rights so dear and invaluable to mankind—May success crown their struggle for freedom."[9]

Federalist New England was hardly excited about any conflict with Britain. Revelers in Salem, Massachusetts, drank to the conquest of Canada as an unnecessary alarm: "'Fire! fire! All out, all out—'twas *only a chimney.*'"[10] While many Americans were hoping for a unified response to the approaching hostilities, New England, especially Massachusetts, was considered a danger to the rest of the nation. A letter written to the New Jersey paper *Centinel of Freedom* sought to separate the figure of Washington from the Federalist party:

> The effects have been too obvious to need enumeration. Witness the course pursued by the federal legislature of Massachusetts, and the threats made to divide the union, the celebration of the King's birthday, and the scandalous toasts drank by the federalists. *Oh, Washington*, if you had remained amongst us until the present time, would you have owned such men for your disciples?[11]

As the Madison administration prepared for war, it suffered a major loss. Vice President George Clinton died of a heart attack on April 20, and the Independence Day toasts praised the elder Revolutionary War hero and statesman:

> Our late venerable vice President, George Clinton—Although his sun is set, its retiring rays still enlighten our councils.[12]

> The memory of gen. Clinton, late vice president of the U.S. the soldier and the statesman, the friend of virtue and of mankind, the smiles of heaven his compensation.[13]
>
> *The memory of the Venerable George Clinton, late Vice-President of the United States*—his morn of life bespoke fair day; his noon was splendid, like the mid-day Sun darting his fiery beams o'er all the earth; his evening, mild, tranquil and glorious.[14]

Clinton's death did not prevent Madison from asking Congress for a declaration of war on June 1, 1812, and the Senate followed the House in approving Madison's declaration on June 17. He signed it the next day, turning June 18 into a "second" Independence Day:

> The 18th of June, 1812—The day the United States determined by an appeal to arms, to support the liberty and independence bequeathed to them by the blood and treasure of the heroes of 1776.
>
> The eighteenth day of June, 1812—may the Declaration of War on that day, result in the establishment of the neutral and national rights of these United States as effectually as the declaration on the day we now celebrate, established our freedom, sovereignty, and independence.[15]
>
> *The* 18*th of June* 1812—The memorable day on which war was declared to maintain that independence. The British lion will find us *now*, a goodly number, animated by the same spirit, truly—begotten sons of his old pursuers.[16]

The president's supporters offered toasts to his firmness and patriotism, emphasizing that Madison, a peaceful man, "prefers war to dishonour."[17] The Republicans of Dover, Delaware, drank to "our virtuous & beloved JAMES MADISON, President of the United States—His wise and inflexible conduct will be joyfully remembered, and the plaudits of a grateful people will attend him through life."[18] The majority of states that supported war were from regions of the country, such as the West and South, that were furthest from the maritime commerce that would be strongly affected by any war with Great Britain.[19] Kentucky representative Henry Clay, one of the most vocal and effective of the "War Hawks," was included in many toasts. Ohio's *Liberty Hall* printed a toast given in Lexington, Kentucky, saying of Clay, "In supporting the declaration of war—he was indeed our representative."[20] B. Warfield gave a volunteer toast in Mount Sterling, Kentucky, on July 4 to Clay, "our worthy representative in Congress; he is not to be intimidated by the British lion's peals of thunder, though the earth quakes, but stands firm and undaunted, and speaks the sentiments of his constituents."[21]

General and former Secretary of War Henry Dearborn was in command of the American army, which was not ready for a war against Great Britain. Republicans still toasted both the army and Dearborn: "*The American Army*—When a DEARBORN commands American Soldiers

12. "...War.—The offspring of an adulterous...," 1812–1815

are *permitted to wield the sword*, in defence of their Rights and Liberties, our foreign enemies may tremble, and domestick foes hide their guilty heads."[22] Conquering Canada, a goal that was never achieved in the Revolution, was now a possibility: "The Army of the United States—May they speedily march to the walls of Quebec; by their courage and fortitude overcome every obstacle; Our enemies return to their reason, & acknowledge the Americans worthy to be repeated as a free and independent nation."[23] Redemption of the failed expedition to Canada, led by Benedict Arnold and Richard Montgomery, was at hand. One toast from the tiny Massachusetts town of Hardwick claimed that "the feats of Don Quixote shall no longer excite laughter, nor his character want a parallel."[24] The Canadian beaver would soon be rescued by the American eagle:

> Quebec—May the bones of our gallant countrymen now mouldering on the plains of Abraham, soon have a splendid monument erected to receive them by the hands of Americans within this proud and haughty metropolis.[25]
>
> May the Canadian Beaver, soon liberated by the warlike genius of the Republican Eagle, prove the precursor of freedom, to the chained wolf dog of Ireland.[26]
>
> The Canadas—May they see the perfidy and oppression of their old mother whore, and with disdain flee from her ranks to the standard of the American arms, and lean to feel the glow and animating spirit of nationalism.[27]

Most of the 1812 Independence Day celebrations included toasts to the navy, under the command of Commodore John Rodgers:

> Commodore Rodgers, the gallant commander of who silenced the blistering of the insolent *Bingham*, by shattering his *Little Belt*—he merits and will receive the plaudits of his countrymen.[28]
>
> The Navy of the Union—While the gallant Rogers commands, and heroic Tars obey, its flag bids defiance to the freebooters of Europe.[29]
>
> Our Navy—*Small* yet *brave*—Let it be *increased*—and soon be able to pay *down* for depredations committed on the watry element—in "*handy change*" from the *mouths* of their *cannon*.[30]

During the summer of 1812, some toasts targeted an embarrassing situation that President Madison and Secretary of State James Monroe had found themselves in the preceding March. The episode is known as the "Henry Plot," named after an Irish-born American named John Henry. Henry was supposedly employed by the governor of British North America, Sir James Craig, to foment disunion in Federalist New England. Feeling guilty for his actions, Henry offered to sell his correspondence with Craig to the administration. Madison and Monroe jumped at the chance to portray the Federalists as disloyal, and so paid Henry the unbelievable sum of $50,000 for the documents. The letters, however, only demonstrated what crimes the New England Federalists had not committed against the nation.[31] Toasts castigated the actions of Henry and his supporters, while others made fun of Madison and the exorbitant price he paid:

> The confederates of *Henry*, who are driving with such furious zeal to the dissolution of the union—May they pause and reflect before they raise the standard of rebellion and civil war.[32]
>
> *The "Henry Plot"*—The man who squanders "fifty thousand dollars" of the nation's money to prove the folly of himself and his Coadjutors, must be a promising candidate for a mad house.[33]
>
> James Madison—The man who paid Fifty Thousand Dollars to the Spy Henry to prove that Federalists are true to their country—Let French partizans blush at the word Tory.[34]

Washington Benevolent Societies, set up by Federalists as political clubs to electioneer for votes, were highly critical of the war. Republicans viewed these societies as pro-British, with one toast calling it "a society which has mystery for its basis, is a league of robbers against a republican government." Another toast included the Societies as part of *"Federalism's last hope.*—Submission to England, the British Navy, John Henry, and the Washington Benevolent Society."[35] When the following toast was made in Portsmouth, New Hampshire, against the Society, "'The Washington Benevolent Societies—Conceived in sun and brought forth in iniquity, let them beware of kindling the flame of discord, lest they perish in the conflagration,'" angry commentary appeared in the *Portsmouth Oracle*:

> Here is another among the innumerable proofs of the bitterness of democratic gall against every thing, which bears the name or principles of Washington. The disciples of Washington are not however to be intimidated by any men or set of men; let them remember the vile slander and calumny heaped on their great political father by the same party, which is now constantly reviling them.[36]

New Englanders were upset that Massachusetts native Elbridge Gerry, a signer of the Declaration of Independence and a staunch Republican, was being considered as Madison's next vice president. Toasts were given in support of Gerry because of his past patriotism, but others were critical of his manipulation of election districts that gave Republicans an unfair advantage in Federalist Massachusetts (hence the creation of a new political term "gerrymander"):

> Elbridge Gerry—A political star in the east, emitting rays of light and truth, which has attracted the public eye as the next Vice President.[37]
>
> Elbridge Gerry—The patriot and statesman who regardless of factious clamor, never deviated from correct principles—may the voice of the nation reward his virtues.[38]

12. "...War.—The offspring of an adulterous...," 1812–1815

Gerrymander Senate.—May the monster, after having bitten its own tail off, have its head quashed by the whole weight of public indignation.[39]

Violence over the war erupted in Baltimore in June and July. The Federalist newspaper *Federal Republican* condemned Madison's declaration of war, and Republican crowds, made up of German, Irish and French immigrants, destroyed the office of publisher Alexander Cotee Hanson. Hanson refused to allow his freedom of speech and the press to be curtailed by a mob, so the *Federal Republican* reappeared. The mob attacked the paper's new offices, and a rioter was shot by the paper's defenders, who included General "Lighthorse" Harry Lee. The defenders relocated to the city jail, but the mob attacked them there. James M. Lingan, a Revolutionary War general, was stabbed to death, and Lee and Hanson were brutally beaten.[40] General Lingan became a martyr to the advocates a free press, but the Baltimore mob was seen as being in the service of Republicans, and by proxy of France:

> Freedom of Speech and of the Press—We will enjoy them, not withstanding the threats of the despicable slaves of France.[41]
> Mr. Madison's Mob at Baltimore—When Governments resort to mobs, they exhibit at once the badness of their cause, and the weakness of their means.
> *The Liberty of Speech, and of the Press*—We fear not a law that forbids lying, and allows the truth to be given in evidence, although the Jeffersonians complained that it *gagg'd them*.[42]
> The memory of Gen. LINGAN, the revolutionary hero and patriot, at whose death Liberty weeps, and at the manner of which, his country blushes—He has fallen in defence of the liberties of his country.[43]

Defenders of the administration accused war dissenters as being worse than Benedict Arnold because they "would relinquish the rights of the whole nation to the same foe." It was hoped that those in opposition of the war would "speedily remove to Ireland, where they can undergo the pleasures of British shackles without obliging their fellow citizens to endure such ignominy and disgrace."[44] Members of the Tammany Society in New York drank to "the Federal hypocrites of Massachusetts and Connecticut, who under pretence of adhering to the constitution, violate its plainest principles—'O! generation of vipers! how can ye escape.'"[45] Republicans surely tasted blood when the former British minister to the United States, Francis James Jackson, attended a dinner in Glasgow, Scotland, and offered toasts that were "COMPLIMENTARY TO OUR FRIENDS THE FEDERALISTS IN AMERICA." The *Carlisle Gazette* of Pennsylvania was dismayed, asking, "Does this not prove that *the British consider the Federalists* as their friends—that they *count upon their friendship* in the present contest—and that *this encourages their Government* to pursue that '*firm policy,*' which Mr. JACKSON recommends, and which consists in refusing our just claims and rejecting our pacific overtures?"[46] The Massachusetts *Democrat* issued a warning regarding this incident:

> We know these Scottish merchants and Mr. Jackson have mistaken their friends; we know however well disposed some individuals in the party are to them, that the federal party generally do not prefer the interests and honor of Britain, to those of their own country; but we are induced to publish this as a warning to them of the interpretation put upon their conduct, when they condescend to fraternize with the known enemies of their country.[47]

When it came to the actual war, Americans were not the inferior naval force that their opponents had assumed. The USS *Constitution* defeated the HMS *Guerriere* on August 19, 1812, earning the famous nickname "Old Ironsides," and then was victorious against the HMS *Java* on December 29. That date was toasted at a naval dinner in Boston as "the *day star* of *American glory* then first beamed in the Southern *hemisphere—* May its *lustre* increase through the successive periods of time, and in all the divisions of the Globe."[48] The America sailor, or "tar," was honored as the frontline defender of the nation in many toast lists:

> THE MEMORY OF THOSE BRAVE TARS WHO HAVE NOBLY FALLEN IN ACQUIRING GLORY TO THE AMERICAN NAVY.[49]
>
> The Brave Tars of our Country—The victories they have gained for us on the ocean prove them worthy of protection:—Gold must be that heart which would surrender to our enemy, the Heroes who have humbled his pride.[50]
>
> *The American Tars*—Nobly contending in defence of "*Sailors Rights and Free Trade.*" When their expiring breath heaves forth the exhortation "*don't give up the ship*" who can doubt their courage; who can withhold them the best wishes o'success.[51]

The fact that all the toasts to the navy omitted former President John Adams was not lost on his supporters. Abigail Adams received a letter from her brother William Stephens Smith early in 1813, in which he pointed out the slight:

> I noticed as you did, in the late celebrations of our Naval victories that no notice was taken, in the toasts given of the original Patron and founder of our navy, that the name of Adams was not even mentioned springs from the contaminating breath of the essex Junto—but "no might nor greatness in Mortality can censure 'scape: back wounding calumny the whitest Virtue strikes, what man so strong, can tie the gall up in the slanderous tongue?"[52]

One of the most violent episodes of the war took place in Frenchtown in the Michigan territory in January 1813. The engagement is known as both the Battle of the River Raisin and the River Raisin Massacre. Brigadier General James Winchester and his Kentuckian soldiers were captured by British forces under Commander Henry Proctor. Some of the prisoners were marched to Canada, but about thirty wounded soldiers remained. Left unattended, Indians later attacked them, scalping many and burning others in their cabins.[53] Americans cried "Remember the Raisin!" in battle, and toasts were given to honor the slain. The Kentucky paper *Union* printed the following volunteer toast later in 1814: "The *massacre of the wounded American prisoners, at the River Raisin*—It was a *hellish tragedy*, written with the *best*, the *indelible* blood of our country—*a crime recorded in Heaven, which the tears of Angels cannot wash out*."[54] A retaliatory toast was given by some of the prisoners taken at the River Raisin. British officer Captain Shaw made the following toasts to the prisoners: "'*Success to King George and to all his Allies*'" and "'May we always have such successes as this.'" American captive Captain John M'Kinsay responded bitterly:

> Here's wishing Capt. Shaw well for his good treatment to us prisoners, and success to all good Republicans, and especially, to all *true-hearted* Kentuckians; wishing that we may shortly obtain the *SKIN of King George for drum heads*, and the *Shin Bones* of all d—d *Tories for Drum Sticks*, to beat the Kentuckians to arms, to revenge their country's wrongs for all *this*. (pointing round to all his fellow prisoners as Capt. Shaw had done.)[55]

New England, especially Massachusetts, sought peace and an end to war. The nation was not unified, and many Americans laid the blame on New England. Opponents of the war were grouped together and labeled as the pro–British and anti–American "Peace Party." Toasts to the "Party" were damning:

> *The self-styled Peace Party*—The advocates of British politics. "Crying *peace, peace,* when there is no peace."[56]
> *The Peace Party*—Precisely what the British Government would form in all countries but England.[57]

When Oliver Wolcott gave the following toast on December 22, 1812, "'*The Seamen of the United States*:—Whose perseverance, fidelity and patriotism entitle them to the confidence and protection of all just and honorable men—May their personal rights be defended while our country enjoys any rights worth defending,'" the *American Advocate* in the District of Maine published a telling response:

> The above toast, given on a great public occasion, and by a gentleman who is a federalist, and has heretofore been looked up to as one of the first of his party, sufficiently indicates with what detestation and abhorrence he views the faction in this state, who disturb and jeopardise the best interests of our country; who have assumed the name of "peace party," without any regard to our country, its just rights and honor.[58]

Massachusetts's heavy reliance on overseas trade made it an anti-war leader. Independence Day celebrants in Northfield, Massachusetts, toasted President Madison, associating him with Jefferson, as "greatly to be pitied; having run into great troubles by treading in the steps of the great man, who eat the greatest cheese, and swallowed the greatest insults and abuses, from the greatest, the most ambitious, and vicious Tyrant upon Earth." They called the war "the joint production of French Corruption and Madisonian Quixotism; may it not end in Gallic Freedom."[59] War Hawks saved their most venomous toasts for what they once considered to be the "Cradle of Liberty" and its governor, Caleb Strong:

> *The Political Bedlam of Massachusetts, the state Legislature*—May their delirium be succeeded by a just sense of duty to their country and their consciences.[60]
> *The Legislature of Massachusetts*—A set of moonstruck maniacs, who employ the public lime in cutting political gambols for the diversion of their country's enemies and the ridicule of its friends.[61]
> The Federalists in the Senate of Massachusetts—an undisguised band, whose principles and language fully accord, (they have merited a toast from the Prince Regent, on his birth day) to all appearance the bulwark of religion, their idol, Governor Strong, the high priest, the wooden walls of Britain the altar, and America's liberties the sacrifice.[62]

A tragic event in Virginia was mentioned several times throughout the summer of 1813, stoking the flame of anti–British hatred. On June 25, a British force of over 2,000 attacked the coastal town of Hampton, easily overrunning the small American force. For ten days the British Independent Companies ravaged the town. What damage they actually did is still questionable, but the American propaganda machine relayed incidents of violent brutality.[63] Admiral George Cockburn's forces plundered the town: "So villainous was the trial of plunder, homicide and sexual assault left largely by the French soldiers who made up Cockburn's command that one incensed Virginian offered a reward of $1,000 for the admiral's head and $500 for each of his ears." "Remember Hampton!" became a popular battle cry.[64] Toasts regarding the attack included details of the crimes committed:

> The suffering people of Hampton—a beacon to warn Americans of the necessity of preparations even onto death.[65]
> HAMPTON.—The bravery of its defenders, and the brutality of its assailants will never be forgotten.[66]
> May the American soldiery avenge the cause of female innocence and virtue immolated at Hampton by savage British barbarity.[67]

The sacking of Havre de Grace, Maryland, earlier in May was also remembered: "Havre-de-Grace in flames.—This is the conflagration that will light the deluded portion of our countrymen, to a knowledge of the savage and remorseless character of our enemy."[68]

New Englanders advocated separation from the union, but southern products were still necessary for their survival: "The voice of New-England in 1812, '*Dissolve the union,*' in 1813, 'Give us bread from the South, or we perish.'"[69] One Newark toast was hopeful for a change of heart from New England, but it also carried a warning: "Our Eastern Brethren of the Union—They rocked the cradle of independence;—conversion to those who have *erred*—punishment to those who are *criminals*."[70] The western states, the scene of some of the fiercest fighting in the war, were enthusiastically praised:

> *Our Western Brethren*—They have bravely fought and freely bled, daring the uplifted tomahawk and reeking scalping knife of British savages, in defence of commercial rights, and for the liberation of impressed Americans;—Americans, whom Eastern Avarice & party animosity would wickedly abandon, at the moment they are rioting in the Millions heaped on them by the toils, tears, and the groans of the enslaved.[71]
>
> *Our Soldiers on the Frontiers*—While the British scalping knife in the hands of their Savage Allies is bathed in the blood of the Prisoner and spare not even "innocent women and children"—the American Soldier conquers only by honorable means, and always protects "the fallen foe."[72]
>
> The States of Kentucky and Ohio—may their brave sons triumph over cruel Britons & their savage allies, and take ample vengeance for the massacre at French Town, on the River Raisin.[73]

General William Henry Harrison was recognized as the "Washington of the West" who would avenge "the barbarities of Tecumseh."[74] War heroes who were killed received toasts that made them martyrs to the American cause. Zebulon Pike was killed in an explosion in York (Toronto) the previous April, and Captain James Lawrence, known for his dying words, "Don't give up the ship,"[75] was killed when the USS *Chesapeake* was taken by the British ship *Shannon*:

> *Zebulon Montgomery Pike*—may the memory of thy worth, stimulate thy former Companions in arms to noble and valorous deeds.[76]
>
> *Gen. Pike*—He fell bravely and successfully asserting his country's rights in the midst of a glorious victory.
>
> *Captain Lawrence*—He fell gallantly in the defence of "Free trade and sailor's rights." Though fortune refused a continuance of her smiles, the laurels he gained will never fade.[77]
>
> JAMES LAWRENCE—The Brave, the Wise, the Good—May his last words be signal of victory to the U. States commanders—"Don't give up the Ship."[78]

Russia took an interest in the American–British dispute when Czar Alexander I offered to mediate a peace. He approached the American minister to Russia, John Quincy Adams, earning the czar a toast as *"the hopeful instrument, in the hand of Providence for the deliverance of Nations."*[79] Federalists saw the Russians as like-minded patriots since Napoleon and the Grand Army were turned back from Moscow in 1812. Toasts given at a Boston festival praised the Russian emperor, who "weeps not for the conquest of a *new* world, bur rejoices in the salvation of the *old*," and the Russian armies as "too brave for the arms, and too loyal for the arts of France—May their virtue be as readily imitated as admired." The anti-French sentiments of Massachusetts led to a toast comparing the state with Russia: *"The Commonwealth of Massachusetts*—May the fire of its patriotism, like the flames of Moscow, expel what is French, and burn Southward and Westward, until it consumes all but native influence."[80] Most important, Russia could bring about an end to the war and a commerce-friendly peace: "Peace—Our most ardent wish; peace with land of our ancestors; peace with our natural friends; an end to this war of passion and *infatuation*—to this war without *object* and without hope."[81]

The Russian mediation team included Adams, Albert Gallatin, and James Bayard. Bayard and Gallatin left for St. Petersburg on the *Neptune* in early May. Americans raised their glasses to the success of the mission, if the peace was honorable: *"Our embassy to Russia*—Let not the paw of the Northern Bear awe to the abandonment of a single right belonging to a free and independent nation.—peace on honorable terms—if not, war of extermination from the continent of America, the British—their agents—and their barbarous allies."[82] Not everyone was confident that Russia could settle the dispute with a peace that would favor Americans: "The Russian Mediation—Our rights are too sacred to be decided by a foreign despot; no treaty that will not secure indemnification for past injuries and security for the future."[83]

The anniversary dinner of the Boston Independent Cadets in October caused a controversy due to the "pointed and insidious" toasts given. The *Baltimore Patriot* printed commentary on the toasts on October 28 under the heading "IDLE AND INSOLENT VAUNTING," offering them "to the contempt and detestation of our readers." The toasts were as follows:

> 3. *Massachusetts*—When the eloquence of her orators shall fail to secure the rights she has acquired, the thunder of her cannon shall enforce them.
> 7. *The Militia of Massachusetts*—Equally determined to resent the injuries of domestic oppression, as to resist the assaults of foreign foes.
> 11. *The patriots of Massachusetts*—Traduced, but not debased; they have still the spirit to rouse the people in defence of their assaulted liberties.

The concern that New England would separate from the union by force was clear. The *Patriot*, in another commentary titled "SEDITIOUS ORGIES,"

12. "...War.—The offspring of an adulterous...," 1812–1815

asked, "Now, who are 'the thunder of her cannon' to be directed against? Not against the *enemies* of our country, they say. Dare these *Shaysites* turn then upon our government?" Later, the Boston Cadets were accused of "such rank toryism, such cowardly sedition, such gross attachment to the enemy," that "if they should dare to act as they insinuate, Nova Scotia or the British shipping would be their abode in a month."[84]

The toasts given through the remainder of 1813 focused primarily on military and naval victories, including the defeat of the HMS *Boxer* by the USS *Enterprise*: "American ENTERPRISE—May it instruct British and French *Boxers*, that the Ocean is the great common of *all nations*."[85] Toasts were given in the hope that Canada would be defeated and taken by the country, along with Florida:

> Canada, once conquered, no consideration should induce us to surrender it to the enemy.
> Upper Canada, purchased with the blood of the west, may it never be sacrificed to the prejudices of the East.[86]
> Florida and the Canadas—Necessarily ours by conquest or purchase.[87]

Commodore Perry was the hero of Lake Erie "and the pride of Columbia,"[88] whose "name shines like another sun in the galaxy of naval glory. The Nelson of the Nile in all his dazzling splendor, is eclipsed by the blaze of victory, that bears on its embrace, as it mounts to the skies."[89]

1840 Campaign picture of Indiana governor William Henry Harrison, created by Peter S. Duval and printed in Philadelphia. William Henry Harrison, the "Washington of the West," became a popular military hero on the western frontier, fighting against Tecumseh's Confederation and the British: "Governor Harrison, with all out brethren on the frontier settlements, who exposed to the evils which arise from savage cruelty, may they be speedily succoured with troops sufficient to suppress the merciless foe, and may those who excite these untutored savages to murder our frontier settlements, meet the just reward of their deeds" (Toast #15, *Pittsburgh Gazette*, 7-24-1812) (Library of Congress).

President Madison left himself open to attacks because the war was continuing without a definite victorious path ahead. The anti-war faction in Massachusetts was especially vocal about its animosity toward the president, who was toasted in Taneytown, Massachusetts, as *"James Madison, President*—'Tis mortifying to think what he was—'Tis infamy to see what he now is, the tool of a bloody tyrant, the author of a wicked and wasteful war, conducted with extreme folly, and ending in extreme disgrace."[90] The *Baltimore Patriot* again went after the Massachusetts "tories" and responded: "See how the manners as well as the morals of those, who suck sedition and scurrility out of the '*Common Sewer,*' are deteriorated and corrupted!"[91]

The state of Connecticut was singled out in certain toasts because of its supposed interference with an American naval action. Stephen Decatur, after capturing the British ship *Macedonian*, found himself hiding in the Thames River in New London. On December 12, 1813, he tried to make a break for the Atlantic, hoping to avoid the four British blockaders that were eager to take him. As he was about to begin his attempt, he heard that the British ships had allegedly been warned by signals of blue lights from the shore. His opportunity to escape was lost.[92] The Hibernian Provident Society of New York called for *"Kentucky Hemp.*—A patent extinguisher for Connecticut blue lights."[93] Even some in Connecticut were alarmed by what they thought was a treasonous act. The Columbian Society of New Haven drank to *"Blue Lights*—Connecticut is not yet rid of her Arnolds."[94] When Madison signed a more restrictive embargo act, one New Jersey toast saw it as "summary justice on the 'Blue Lights' that would attempt to violate it."[95]

Napoleon's armies had been driven back in several places and Holland and Switzerland were liberated by 1814. Bitter sentiment was thrown Napoleon's way in Kinderhook, New York: "Napoleon Bonaparte—The dreadful gorgon of the world, 'conquered by the inclemencies of a frightful climate'—May the groans of the dead, whom he has murdered; the curses of the living, whom he has oppressed; be a lullaby for his repose, and a requiem to his departing spirit."[96] One of Napoleon's greatest defeats was the destruction of his Grand Army during its retreat from Moscow in 1812. The city, torched by the Muscovites to deny Napoleon a true victory, became a symbol of anti-French sentiment: "Moscow—From her burning ruins has arisen a spirit which pointed to the freedom of the world; which appalled the proud heart, and disappointed the ambitious projects of a bloody and unrelenting despot."[97] Czar Alexander became "the friend of America—he has nobly testified to the justice of our cause: may we soon behold him reviving the just and rational principles of the armed neutrality, and firmly vindicating the freedom of the seas."[98] The New York paper *Columbian* expressed a certain dismay that the czar was not getting enough due respect in toasts:

> *Alexander the mediator*, a character to be respected and admired in the United States, has not been so regarded in any of the toasts of the late federal celebrations. They applaud him as the *conqueror* of Bonaparte [for England] but not as the *mediator* for the United States [*against* England]. We hope he will compel every enemy to this *mediatorial* office to acknowledge his decisive and effectual services to us in that noble and benevolent capacity.[99]

With Napoleon's abdication and the return of the Bourbon dynasty to France in April, Russia and the German Allied Armies were told to "rest from your labors—Europe is delivered by your valor, and the world applauds your deeds."[100] The excesses of the republican experiment in France almost turned many Americans into monarchists. They certainly did not want to return to the days of living under the heel of a despot, but sympathy associated with the order of autocratic rule was strong: "*Louis, king of France, and the French Nation*—The United States recollect with interest the family of the Bourbons, in aid of our revolution."[101] Diners at a July Fourth banquet in Waterville in the District of Maine tried to make sense of the evolving situation overseas:

> *The astonishing events in Europe, and the downfall of Bonaparte*—While they shew the instability of all human greatness, may they remind assuming faction, aiming at supremacy, that however organized and intrenched in self created power, its importance must, when its views shall be fully developed, and the national will expressed, suddenly vanish like the Napoleon Dynasty, and be as unreal "as the baseless fabric of a vision."[102]

Madison's preference for Gallic culture was not acceptable to many Americans. The president and his administration were blamed for the military defeats, the economic ailments, and the alienation of the Northeast. Negative toasts continued to associate him with both Jefferson and Napoleon:

> James Madison.—His sheet anchor (Napoleon) lost—the cables of his ship democracy fouled—timbers rotten and no longer sea-worthy.[103]
>
> James Madison, the administrator, *de bonis non*, upon Bonaparte's continental estate: May the people of the U.S. soon call him, and Thomas Jefferson, his surety, into the great court of probate, to account for a wanton *devastavit*.[104]
>
> *President Madison's Administration*—Loans, internal taxes, double duties, non-intercourse, embargoes and war—ruinous to ourselves, harmless to our enemies.[105]

Some anti-war toasts were deemed to be treasonous. The Washington Benevolent Society of Winchendon, Massachusetts, drank to Washington and Alexander I as "deliverers of America and Europe," and then referred to Madison as "*James I of America*. In imitation of his prototype may he soon be compelled by the voice of the people to *abdicate* in favor of a *rightful heir*."[106] Perhaps even worse was what happened at a Society gathering in Fryeburg, Ohio. According to the paper *Spirit of the West*, when the fourth toast was made to the president, it was "[Drunken, in profound silence, with water.]"[107] The president's supporters were not idle. They came up with their own toasts to battle the Society, considered to be "'an abominable abomination of all abominations.' The name of the immaculate hero, statesman and patriot, is employed to serene treason, corruption and party intrigue, beneath the garb of benevolence."[108] Pro-British toasts made at Dorchester, Massachusetts, angered many because they were considered to be "bitter and malignant thrusts at democracy." One toast attacked the very concept of democracy: "The illegitimate brat, Democracy—It was conceived, in the womb of Sedition—Ambition was its father—Disorganization was the midwife—love of office was its wet nurse—and Thomas and James were its god fathers." One writer, in an article titled "CANDIDATES FOR NOVA SCOTIA," asked, "Is it uncharitable to wish them a same and speedy passage to the land of aristocracy and monarch, to which so many of their brethren in sentiment were conveyed at the close of the revolutionary war?"[109]

Not all New Englanders were against the war. The *Salem Gazette* reminded its readers that the issue of impressment had been a major cause of the war. Should there not be more toasts for the poor sailors who were kidnapped at sea? It was estimated that 40,000 sailors "were groaning in cruel bondage in 'British H—lls.'" One toast given at Zanesville, Ohio, stood out "for its sympathy as for its brief, terse, pungent, and epigrammatic qualities":

> *Our* impressed *seafaring* citizens—For 20 years they have been enslaved on board British ships of war—they have been loaded with chains in their *poisonous* holds—their flesh has been torn in pieces from their bodies at the gangway—they have been subjected to every contumely and reproach—their projections have been torn to atoms and cast *into* their teeth—they have been compelled to fight against their *beloved* country—and they have been stigmatized as "*Yankee Rebels against his Majesty*"—And yet, O shame! the federalists call not this a cause for war! when all their crime was claiming the rights of American citizens.[110]

The land campaign in the eastern region was turning into a disaster in 1814. After the British victory at Bladensburg, Maryland, on August 24, there was nothing to stop their forces from marching on Washington, D.C., and setting it to the torch. It is no surprise that there were very few American toasts mentioning the tragedy. A simple one showed up in the Pennsylvania paper *Weekly Aurora*: "May the incendiary blaze of the

12. "...War.—The offspring of an adulterous...," 1812–1815

capital, kindle the flame of patriotism to the extremities of the union."[111] The *Daily National Intelligencer* attacked the British as nothing more than vandals: "The Capitol of the US—the flames that twisted round its Corinthian pillars, have not blazed in vain, they have reflected the true character of the Vandals who lighted them."[112] Not surprisingly, a toast from Gloucester, Massachusetts, made fun of Madison, who escaped from the British on horseback as they entered the capital city: "James Madison—the prince of jockies, who distanced his followers at the Bladensburg races, may he speed his course to political obscurity with additional velocity."[113]

Meanwhile, the naval war on the Great Lakes and Lake Champlain was going well and was a cause for celebration. Commodore Thomas MacDonough defeated the British on September 11 at the Battle of Lake Champlain, and so glasses were raised:

> Our Naval Officers and brave Tars on Lake Champlain—They have added to the bright lustre of our Naval renown; the Heroes of Erie and of the Ocean shall own them brothers with pleasure and with pride.
> COMMODORE MACDONOUGH, *The Hero of Lake Champlain*—The brilliant and important Victory achieved by him over the British Squadron of Superior force, entitle him to the warmest expressions of National gratitude.[114]
> *The Battles near Niagara.*—Fame, in proclaiming the glorious deeds of those actions, shall mingle the not of her trumpet, with the thunders of the cataract, and be heard till times is not more.[115]

As the fighting continued both on land and water, a peace delegation met in the Belgian city of Ghent between August and December 1814. Henry Clay and Jonathan Russell, the American minister to Sweden, joined the other three delegates who had already been in Europe: John Quincy Adams, Albert Gallatin, and James Bayard.[116] It was important to most Americans that the peace treaty being negotiated would be based on honorable terms:

> Our ministers at Ghent—firm in vindication of just rights, may their labors prove honourable to their country and themselves.[117]
> The Negotiation at Ghent—May it soon terminate in a treaty of peace, honorable to both belligerents, and may the nations of the two worlds return to the emulation only, of commerce, industry, and friendly pursuits.[118]

The negotiated treaty was signed in Ghent on December 24, 1814. The peace commissioners were recognized for their efforts:

> The American Commissioners at Ghent—May the Peace which they have so ably and honorably negotiated, be as lasting as time, and productive of equally *durable* happiness.[119]
> Our Commissioners at Ghent—They have ably maintained the interests of their country, and will receive their reward in its honors and its gratitude.[120]

> *The American Commissioners at Ghent*—A constellation of talents and patriotism which has eclipsed the splendor of British diplomacy—called forth the administration of Europe, and commanded the applause even of federal partisans in America.[121]

Neither nation claimed a victory, and things as they were before the war were reestablished. New Yorkers drank to "the *status post bellum*—We have character, peace, commerce, wealth, liberty and independence."[122] The treaty itself was described as "an honorable result of a necessary war—May its blessings be perpetuated to the latest generations."[123] Americans were eager to finally drink to peace. A volunteer toast from Watertown, Massachusetts, was given: "Peace with Britain, permanent and lasting—May it never be disturbed or interrupted by a philosophical, theocratical, *hypocritical*, deistical, *illuminatical*, Bonapartian, 'one God or twenty God' President."[124] President Madison's legacy was strengthened with the end of the war, and he deserved to be toasted: "*JAMES MADISON, President of the United States*—under whose administration was war declared, and during whose administration an honorable peace was made; justice his guide, his country's good his object."[125]

As the news of the peace treaty was making its way across the ocean from Europe, Americans were basking in the martial glory the Battle of New Orleans on January 8, 1815, a date deserving of praise: "May it be a Sabbath in the Calendar of Freedom, and a Jubilee throughout the United States."[126] General Andrew Jackson was the most popular man in the country, easily eclipsing Madison. Compared to both Washington and Leonidas, his victory over the British seemed so sound that it must have been divinely arranged:

> *General Jackson*—Steel of the true polish, whose prowess flashed conviction on his foe, what Americans dare and can achieve.[127]
> *General Jackson's Victory*—13 to 2600—astonishing the odds—it is unmatched in the warlike annals of the world—it stands a miracle—*it pleased the Almighty*.[128]
> *Major General Jackson and his brave coadjutors*—The shield of the Almighty has covered them in the day of battle.—Let the munificence and gratitude of their country reward their exertions.[129]

The casualties did not end with the Battle of New Orleans, however. Many Americans captured during the conflict were taken to Britain's Dartmoor Prison in Devonshire. Over 250 men had already died there of smallpox and pneumonia when news of the peace arrived. The prisoners could not be repatriated until the Treaty of Ghent was ratified. On April 6, 1815, the prison commander panicked when the prisoners got into an altercation with the sentries over a ball game, and he ordered the soldiers to fire their weapons, killing seven prisoners.[130] Toasts given in memory of the victims put the outrage Americans felt toward Great Britain on display once again:

> *Massacre of prisoners at Dartmoor prison.*—May every American be fired with patriotic indignation, until the retributive hand of justice shall overtake those worse than savage perpetrators.[131]
>
> *The Prison at Dartmoor*—Another mournful evidence that humanity and honor have no longer a residence on the shores of Great Britain.[132]
>
> The Dartmoor Massacre. In barbarity unequalled:— The laws of God cry aloud for the punishment of the perpetrator; may our government tear away the veil that shall attempt to conceal the crime.[133]

National outrage was not just directed at the former enemy. The New England states were targets of odium and disgrace. Governor Caleb Strong and the Massachusetts legislature had always considered

General Andrew Jackson half-portrait, between 1810 and 1825. General Andrew Jackson was celebrated throughout the United States because of his brilliant victory over the British at the Battle of New Orleans in 1815. His fame would later propel him to the presidency: "The magnanimous Jackson, whose splendid achievements in reducing the savage foes—and his unparalleled victory (over chosen veterans) on the plains of New Orleans will shine in the annals of the world—a memento of his valor and his country's rising fame. 'Sure form'd thee of superior dust, / As Caesar generous, and as Cato just'" (Toast #13, *American Watchman*, 3-8-1815) (Library of Congress).

the war to be unjust and withheld men and supplies that the government needed. Madison retaliated by withholding necessary military appropriations for Massachusetts for the defense of the New England coastline.[134] Twenty-six delegates from New England met in a convention at Hartford from December 15, 1814, to January 5, 1815, to discuss the situation. Some toasts made after the Hartford Convention considered New England to be acting out of patriotic sentiment. The Washington Benevolent Society gave a toast in Wallingford, Connecticut, that extolled the Convention's integrity: "The Members of the New England Convention, lately assembled at Hartford—Firm, prudent and discreet, 'they have dared to be honest in the worst of times.'"[135]

The Convention's final report was sent with some delegates to Washington, D.C. Some of the report's proposals included abolishing the Three-Fifths Compromise, limiting all embargoes to sixty days, and requiring a two-thirds vote in the Senate to declare war.[136] There was an implied threat that New England might break off from the Union. News of Jackson's New Orleans victory reached the capital around the same time the Convention delegates did, dashing their hopes. After an embarrassing and brief audience with Madison, they shirked back to New England.[137] The Hartford Convention was not seen in any positive light by most Americans, especially after Jackson's successful campaign. Shame was especially heaped on Massachusetts: "Massachusetts—She has shown by melancholy example how degraded a brave people may appear, when guided by weak and infatuated rulers."[138] One toast from a celebration in Rutland, Vermont, was to the Constitution, which "survived the rude attempts of a *Hartford Convention* to subvert its most important provisions."[139] There seemed to be no forgiveness toward New England any time soon:

> *The Hartford Convention*—The future historian will blush while he records their deeds, and our children will declare them worthy the exaltation of Mordecai.[140]
>
> *The Hartford Convention*—The contempt of the enemy they would have served, the pity of the country they would have destroyed.[141]
>
> The Hartford convention—the first born of disappointed ambition; a treasonable conspiracy to rend the Union—may the instruments of that rebellion, give evidence of political repentance and reformation that they may obtain National forgiveness.[142]

The Massachusetts District of Maine had already made several attempts to break off from the Bay State by 1815: "*District of Maine*—Of full age; may she soon manage her own affairs, and be no more under the control of an idolatrous parent, who has so long worshipped the 'Bulwark.'"[143] There was no District representation at the Hartford Convention, an event seen by a Hallowell toast as "the mongrel offspring of a combination of luckless knaves." Another toast made at the same event emphasized the fact that Maine was absolved of any guilt regarding the Convention: "*The District of Maine*—Let her separate from pollution; she is guiltless of the crimes and madness of her consort."[144]

The toasts given during the War of 1812 both supported the Madison administration and criticized its decision. Madison and war commanders on the ground and sea were commended in toasts for standing

12. "...War.—The offspring of an adulterous...," 1812–1815

up to Britain. Toasts given by the Republicans against the Federalists, and vice versa, continued unabated. The new American heroes were Generals Andrew Jackson and William Henry Harrison. Alexander I of Russia offered to negotiate a peace, and he was toasted along with John Quincy Adams and other ministers, who later made a peace treaty with Great Britain in Ghent, Belgium. The New England states worked against the progress of the war and sent delegates to Hartford to debate how to "force" the federal government to end the war. Jackson's brilliant victory at New Orleans came while the Hartford Convention was submitting its report. Jackson was toasted with adoration, but the toasts about the Convention saw it as an act of treason.

Chapter 13

"The American Fair—May every Mother give a WASHINGTON to her Country,"[1] 1760–1815

"The Daughters of America—May they, by their patriotism and Industry, be as indefatigable to preserve, as they were to rear, a new empire."[2]

"The daughters of Columbia—May their smiles reward virtuous men; and may they teach their children, that morality and respect for the laws, are the sure foundations of civil society."[3]

"The fair daughters of America—May they ever cherish in their bosoms, that industry, economy, prudence and the promotion of domestic happiness, will ever be the distinguishing traits of an amiable woman; that on them depends the refinement of manners and the happiness of society."[4]

Toast lists in newspapers printed between 1760 and 1815 almost always included one to the "American Fair." These toasts were reliably full of emotional sentiments. Occasionally newspapers included toasts given by women, but this was rare since the toasting ritual was exclusively for men. It was socially unacceptable for women to even witness the tradition, and they were expected to leave the scene before men began their endless rounds of toasts. A woman who was inebriated was scandalous, and she certainly should never be around a group of besotted men who might be using vulgar language in her presence.[5] Women of the higher classes might make a toast at dinner, but decorum demanded that they refrain from indulging in the repetitive drinking associated with toasts.[6]

J. Roach, the editor of 1793's collection of British toasts, *The Royal Toast Master*, lamented the exclusion of women because their participation would only enhance the festivity:

Nor can we see any reason why they should be excluded from society in those joyful moments, when the soul, freed from the shackles of corroding cares, gives herself up to all her feelings; as their participation would certainly enhance our mirth, and add to the exquisite satisfaction that then possesses us. We do not, by any means, pretend to insinuate, that they should enter deeper into these scenes of conviviality than is consistent with that modesty which so eminently distinguishes our British fair. But cannot they, over their tea and chocolate, take part in our conversations, and in rotation give their toasts without offering decorum.[7]

Toasting was targeted by women's temperance societies because many believed that it caused excessive drinking.[8] Women drank in private since they were not "welcome" in taverns. Entering one was a risk to a woman's reputation. While women were banned from public drinking, they drank in communal settings, with other women.[9] Women's participation was expected for certain celebrations, such as militia presentations. Women led processions, instigated, and organized these events, and sometimes initiated toasts themselves.[10] They still had to be careful of how they behaved at these public festivities.

Since toasting was a tradition that displayed one's sentiments and values, women had to be aware of what they said in toasts avoid any social awkwardness. Take the case of Margaret Moncriefe. She was staying at the headquarters of General George Washington on Broadway in New York City while waiting for the opportunity to be allowed to cross over British lines so that she could be reunited with her father, a British officer. Maintaining her loyalty to the British, Moncriefe refused to raise her glass during dinner to the Continental Army. Washington glared at her and coldly said, "Miss Moncriefe, you don't drink your wine." She responded, "General Howe is the toast." Washington diplomatically told her, "Well, Miss, I will overlook your indiscretion, on condition that you drink to my health, or General Putnam's, the first time you dine at Sir William Howe's table, on the other side of the water." Moncriefe later complied with this request.[11]

The young Margaret Moncriefe was attuned to the political situation, aware that her bold refusal to toast Washington was a clear statement. In fact, women were politically active and participated in the events that brought on the Revolution. Their role as the main household consumers made their use of the boycott much more effective. Some women even refused to marry if their prospective husbands purchased a marriage license printed on stamped paper.[12] The literary contributions of Mercy Otis Warren and Phyllis Wheatley were effective propaganda. Abigail Adams was instrumental as the chief advisor to her husband John, both during the Revolution and in his later presidency. Women ran and defended their farms while their husbands were on the battlefield or in the halls of Congress. They worked as spies and fundraisers, and they proved themselves indispensable in the Continental Army camps. All the while, they continued to bear and raise children.[13] Two toasts appeared in the *New Hampshire Gazette* on March 2, 1770, that recognized women's efforts prior to the Revolution:

> The patriotic Ladies of Virginia, who have nobly distinguished themselves by appearing in the Manufactures of America, as may those of the Massachusetts be laudably ambitious of not being outdone even by Virginians.
> The wise and virtuous Part of the fair Sex in Boston and other Towns, who being at length sensible that by the Consumption of Tea, they are supporting the Commissioners and other—famous Tools of Power, have voluntarily agreed, not to give or receive any further Entertainments of that kind, until those Creatures, together with the Boston Standing Army, are removed, and the Revenue Acts are repealed.

Although women were expected to be patriots, a group in North Carolina shocked many throughout the colonies by signing a petition to boycott British goods. Known to history as the Edenton Tea Party, it was a response to the Intolerable Acts in 1774. Colonists were taken aback by the Edenton women's foray into the world of politics, a role reserved for men. The violation of social mores opened the women up to ridicule and derision.[14] A political cartoon satirizing the Tea Party was circulated throughout the colonies showing the women as promiscuous and unfit mothers and drinking to excess.[15] The Revolution did lessen these social norms slightly. After the war, "a respectable number of ladies" in Northampton, Massachusetts, gave their own toasts at a celebration for the proclamation of peace because they felt that the gentlemen present did not fully recognize the efforts made by women. Toasts were made to Martha Washington, the thirteen states, and to their husbands, in the hope that they might reform themselves.[16]

Women received more attention for their contributions to American civilization in the early nineteenth century. Queen Isabella of Spain, who was responsible for Columbus's first voyage, was toasted because Americans realized that "it was a *woman* who first patronized the plan for discovering the New World."[17] On the Forefathers' Day holiday in Plymouth, Massachusetts, a toast was made to "*the memory of Lady Arabella Johnson, and all the primitive Dames of New England*, who cheered the toils of the *Pilgrims*, and participated in the hardships of their *arduous enterprise*."[18] A remarkable toast was given by the Speaker of the House of Representatives in 1804: "'The *real* sovereigns of the United States—the American Fair.'" A writer who was amazed at this toast responded in the New York paper *Commercial Advertiser*:

We have long heard of the "sovereign people," but were not till now informed that we were ruled by women. It cannot be believed, because the government then, would have been more wise, just, and mild, than what has been experienced under the iron rod of democracy. Perhaps the toast is to be considered only as the ebullition of wit in the Speaker; or he may be *over head and ears* in love.[19]

The Independence Day holiday was the perfect setting for women to demonstrate their patriotism. They participated in parades, feasts, balls, fireworks, and bonfires. Orators acknowledged the sacrifices that women had made to the "Glorious Cause." These events were inclusive, so men and women toasted together.[20] By commemorating the war, women were putting themselves at the center of the political discourse. Although they were "not" as deserving of gratitude as war veterans, women were crucial in helping the nation demonstrate that gratitude to those very veterans.[21] The active part that women were allowed to play later made them useful tools for future political parties. Republicans recognized the efforts of Mary Dickson, the wife of William Dickson, the editor of the Republican paper *Intelligencer Journal*. When he was jailed for libel by a Federalist judge,[22] Mary ran the newspaper during his confinement. Republicans toasted her for her active role in spreading their

A society of patriotic ladies, at Edenton in North Carolina. Drawing by Philip Dawe; published by Robert Sayer and John Bennett in March 1775. A satirical jab at the idea of women involving themselves in the male-dominated world of politics. The women agree to boycott English tea in response to the Continental Congress's resolution to boycott British goods in 1774. Participating in politics, according to the illustration, has caused women to ignore their children and to drink to excess (Library of Congress).

ideals: "Mrs. DICKSON—the female patriot, who submitted to the confinement of, and separation from husband of her bosom for three months, rather than ask his liberation from the hands of a tyrant."[23]

The major emphasis of toasts to women was not political. The absence of women from the ritual was done, according to men, to protect them from men behaving badly. Why was this so important? The answer concerns the image of women. Rosemarie Zagarri, in *Revolutionary Backlash: Women and Politics in the Early American Republic* (2007), explains how the portrayal of women was related to how the nation was to be seen:

> The depiction of females, both visually and through words, has a long history. Women as a symbol, a labile construction capable of being manipulated and appropriated in many ways. Women could symbolize Eve, the temptress, but she could also be Mary, the chaste mother of God. She could be used as a symbol of vice and excess or the representative of innocence and simplicity. During the American Revolution, printers often produced images of America as a bare-breasted woman with a Native American appearance, evoking both the ferocity and the militancy of the American cause. Over time the iconography shifted. The new nation was represented in the female form of the Goddess Columbia, in an attempt to link the country with the classical heritage of ancient Greece or Rome.[24]

Associating liberty with the female form was captured in an antebellum toast from Dorchester, Massachusetts: "May that chaste matron, fair LIBERTY, never want any of her Race in America, to curb the Insolence of Despots, and open the Eyes of her Sons, that they may see the Artifice of those who strive to enslave them."[25] The picture of a chaste, nurturing female representing republicanism was apparent in most toasts. Toasts to the fair stressed purity, chastity, and virtue: "*The Fair of America.—* May they reward with their smiles the mind which respects and the arm which protects their important station in society."[26] The image also supposedly helped men monitor their behavior when they drank bumper after bumper. According to Margaret Visser's book *The Rituals of Dinner: The Origins, Evolution, Eccentricities, and Meanings of Table Manners* (2001), "The ideal claimed by Americans in the nineteenth century, when the custom of the ladies leaving the men after dinner was found distasteful, was in fact a sign that grown men were ready to think it normal to behave decently even when there were no women present."[27] Toasts to women brought virtue itself to men:

> Toasts gave voice to men's attempts to affect the contest between traditional apprehensions of women as shallow, supercilious daughters of Eve and the assertive, morally superior image that women wanted to project. Toasts that cast women as "Life's first endearment—The best friends of our heroes and patriots"; pledges that hoped for "the Fair of America, in the arms of those

who best deserve them," placed virtue (as symbolized by women) within men's grasp.[28]

The Society of the Cincinnati was second to none in staging commemorative events, and their toasts to women were made in gratitude for their service during the war. Domestic life, however, was still relegated to them:

> May the Honor of the Brave protect the Virtue of the Fair.[29]
> The patriotic fair of America—May all the sweets of domestic life recompense their zeal in behalf of their country.[30]
> Those ladies who have ever countenanced and encouraged the supporters of American Independence.[31]

There was a perception that the patriotism of women was below that of men. Women supported their husbands' patriotism, remaining passive actors. They were still recognized for their efforts, just so long as they stayed in their assigned gender roles. The only rights they had included choosing a husband, instructing children, keeping the family neat and clean, and promoting such values as frugality, industry, and economy.[32] If women exercised these rights, men had a duty to protect them.

Passengers on board the ship *Polly Packet*, toasting Virginia's ratification of the federal constitution, made it clear that what women were praised for was completely different from men: "May the Daughters of America ever be as celebrated for Virtue, Merit and Beauty, as her Sons have been for Skill and Courage in Battle."[33] A gentleman in Luzerne County, Pennsylvania, wrote to his friend in Philadelphia about the idea of beauty, but he equated it with the virtue of industry. If women wished to be beautiful, then they also had to be industrious. The "lower creation," as he put it, would be deemed truly beautiful if women were "rightly and industriously employed":

> Beauty without virtue is contemptible. Merit only gains the heart. Idleness is disgraceful. Industry is the ornament of wealth, the support and consolation of poverty. We hope soon to see the time, when the fair daughters of America will be cloathed in the manufactures of their own hands. Happy are we that some have already set the example.[34]

The division in Washington's cabinet, due to the French Revolution, led to two political factions that were concerned with image, so toasts by and about women needed to reflect the sentiments of each party. Each one claimed that the women of America were on their side, and if women participated in party festivities, it was a validation of the party's values.[35] Invoking women's influence was seen as a path back to the republicanism of the American Revolution.[36]

The Republicans supported the radical changes in France. The Tammany Society of New York City chose to honor the women of France on July 14, Bastille Day, "a day in which twenty-five millions of people were emancipated from the shackles of despotism, and on which the genius of freedom triumphed over the abject spirit of slavery": "The patriotic fair of France, may the Guardian of their honor and Liberty be inspired with double souls whenever tyranny dare invade it."[37] Supporters of an extreme democratic viewpoint, either in France or the United States, were referred to as sansculottes, and it was hoped that women would choose to favor them: "The Fair Daughters of America—May they ever smile on a patriotic Sans Culotte—but ever frown on an aristocratic sop."[38] One toast from New Jersey wished that women would choose to be single rather than live under a Federalist government: "The fair daughters of America—*may they rather prefer dying old maids than give their hands in wedlock to slaves of autocratic principles.*"[39] The Republican Citizens of Frederick-Town determined that women would be better off living simply with Republicans as opposed to living in style with Federalists: "*The Fair Daughters of Columbia*—May they prefer an union with a republican in a cottage, to an aristocrat in a palace."[40]

Federalists were horrified by the violent turn of events in France, and so they saw themselves as representing constitutionality and law and order. Support of the federal government in the 1790s "demanded" wide participation in civic celebrations, such as Independence Day and Washington's birthday. The presence of women at these festivities was announced in Federalist newspapers.[41] Women in York, Pennsylvania, organized their own July Fourth event in 1794 and made the proper Federalist toasts to the day itself, Washington, and "'the Constituted Authorities.'" A toast to "'The Rights of Women,'" however, went too far:

> It was their desperate attempt to retain sovereignty over the Fourth that encouraged the Federalists to fashion the day into a public show of civic unity in support of a duly elected republican government. In those kinds of Independence Day festivities the Federalists were far more likely than their opponents to encourage and even celebrate the participation of women, who as fairly passive spectators, as guests at celebratory balls, or even as the organizers of their own rites made public show of the support of their section of the body politic for the duly constituted governing authorities. The toast of "a Number of Ladies" in York, Pennsylvania, to "The Rights of Women" suggests that some of these women made use of this opportunity to express a level of political self awareness and a consciousness of the possible extension of the rights that inhered within republican rhetoric. In acknowledging the political existence of subordinate members of the polity, the Federalists risked admitting women's agency and even their independence.[42]

Federalists associated a woman's happiness with the choice of federalism, but they feared that women might support the other side. July Fourth revelers in Boston in 1796 offered a toast to "'the American Fair: May the serpent of faction never lurk in the paradise of beauty.'"[43] The fact that Massachusetts was a Federalist stronghold meant that most of the state's women were sympathetic to the Federalist point of view. "A party of ladies" celebrating Washington's birthday in Newburyport toasted the president and Mrs. Washington, "the respected consort of our illustrious chief." Then they drank to Charlotte Corday, the French woman who stabbed the radical revolutionary writer Jean Paul Marat to death in his bathtub: "Maria Charlotte Corde, may each Columbian daughter, like her, be ready to sacrifice their life to liberty."[44] In a toast list titled *"FIRE OF FEMALE FEDS.,"* a group of women in Deerfield made the following toasts on Independence Day, 1798:

> Mrs. Adams—May her love of her country not be exceeded by the illustrious man of her heart.
> Mrs. Washington—May she long continue to enjoy in retirement the sweets of independence and her George.
> Should Gallic perfidy, force Columbia's Sons to the Field—Let it be the study and delight of her Daughters to furnish *Balm* for their *Wounds*, and *Laurels* for their *Brows*.
> May each Columbian Sister perceive and pursue the infallible system of extinguishing Jacobinism.[45]
> *The American Fair*: May they be able to distinguish between the *fungous* and phlegmonic phiz of Jacobinic intemperance, and the lovely suffution on the cheeck of Federal soberness.[46]

Abigail Adams received many toasts from both men and women during her husband's presidency, especially when John's popularity rose during the XYZ Affair. Martha Washington had always been a favorite person to toast. Toasts were very supportive of her after the death of "His Excellency":

> A speedy restoration of health to that ornament of her sex, the LADY of the PRESIDENT. May the strength of her constitution, equal the energies of her mind.[47]
> Mrs. President—May she always bias the chief magistrate the *right way*.[48]
> Lady Washington—may the fruit of her husband's labor seen in the felicities and prospects of the nation, afford to her declining years, the consolation of many sons and daughters.[49]
> *The American Fair*—May they copy the manners, and imitate the virtuous of the deceased MARTHA, consort of our beloved WASHINGTON.[50]

Women did not question the roles they were meant to play. Equality meant that everyone had an equal right to be free. Women in Newburyport,

Massachusetts, drank "to their hope that 'the fair patriots of America never fail their independence which nature equally dispenses.'"[51] A list of toasts in New York's *American Citizen* made by women celebrating the Fourth in 1800 confirmed what everyone understood: that women's husbands, brothers, and fathers had secured the rights of both sexes, and it was hoped that the sons would follow their fathers' example. The other toasts included one to the republican women of France: "The Graces—May the fair sex never be without them," a free and "chaste" press, the memory of Washington, and the "infant manufactures of our country, and may they ever preclude the necessity of foreign importations."[52] The twenty-second toast was to women who refused to marry, that they "never experience the sweets of love." The twenty-fourth toast was to "the rights of women—May they never be curtailed." These rights were not the ones that the suffragists would later pursue, but the rights of citizenship, which for women was to be an America free from foreign tyranny. An 1801 explanation addressed to the "Republican Ladies of Lancaster" made it clear that men had successfully defended the rights and status of women, and promised that they would never be challenged. The address also solidified the expectations of women's roles in American society:

Abigail Adams portrait by Gilbert Stuart, between 1830 and 1860. She was unusual in that she was very well read and politically aware. A true equal to her husband John, Abigail constantly wrote to her "dearest friend" and kept him informed of the many toasts he received. She also wrote frequently to her son John Quincy and related similar details (Library of Congress).

LADIES—It is the brightest honor of those who have matured society in America, and who have secured its blessings by our happy constitutions, that they have banished those oppressions of your amiable sex, which have disgraced the practice and institutions of other countries. We freely engage, that the rights of our female relatives and friends shall never be diminished or impaired by us.—

We foresee with joy, that the virtue of mankind will render to your sex more and more of those advantages which you claim by the high title of divine justice. The rising generation must always acknowledge with heart-felt gratitude, the preserving care of our matrons and our sisters in all the stages of infancy and youth, and in seasons of infirmity, pain, and sickness. Nor can they ever cease to remember the lessons of purity and knowledge—infused by their female relations into their opening minds.[53]

Those who defended the "'Rights of Man'" would "protect the 'Rights of Women.'"[54] A toast made in Bridgewater, Massachusetts, probably referred to the 1792 publication of Mary Wollstonecraft's *A Vindication of the Rights of Woman* and cautioned American women about it: "The American fair;—may they never lose their rights by asserting the 'Rights of Women.'"[55] An interesting toast from Virginia associated Wollstonecraft with the Roman woman who was raped by Sextus Tarquinias: "The American Fair—With the *talents* of a WOLLSTONECRAFT, may they ever display the bland and fixed *qualities* of a Lucretia."[56] The same newspaper a month later printed a toast from Chillicothe, Ohio, referring to the real rights of women as being "Innocence, Modesty and Prudence; may she rest satisfied with these without investigating any others."[57]

The focus of toasts to women continued to be about the idealized image that men had. Motherhood, purity, chastity, frugality, industry, and beauty were extolled above other qualities and values. The overwhelmingly Protestant Christian population accepted the Genesis story of Adam and Eve, and that Eve was created for Adam. She existed to ornament his life, and so that was how American men saw "their" women:

> The Fair of America—Woman was formed to ornament creation—herself made fair to share that self with man. Be theirs the only chains which freemen wear.[58]
> Women: Without her ameliorating influence, man would be savage, and life would be dreary. Let us be thankful to Heaven, for this its first and best gift.[59]
> The Fair Sex—Formed by a second moulding in the hands of the Deity, as if on purpose to embellish creation and give the finishing touches of perfection to the works of God.[60]

The Tammany Society usually used Native American imagery in its toasts. Women were squaws, children were wrapped in papooses, states were tribes or fires, and the nation was led by the Grand Sachem. The imagery still underlined the expectations of women: "Our squaws and papooses—may they sit secure in their Wigwams, while we are hunting the deer, planting our cornfields, or conquering the enemies of our country."[61] Martha Washington was honored in one such toast: "The Squaw of our Grand Sachem, the squaw of our town, and all the squaws who inhabit our land."[62]

Virtue appeared to be the most important quality that women were expected to have in abundance, and beauty was secondary: "*The Fair Daughters of Columbia*—May they be esteemed more for their virtues than admired for their beauty."[63] Residents in Pittsburgh, Pennsylvania, raised their glasses to the women of their city, hoping that "their beauty be heightened by virtue not by affectation, a greater enemy to handsome faces than the small pox."[64] Independence Day toasts given by the "Matrons and Misses" of Otsego, New York, listed the many qualities that all women were expected to have:

> *Modesty*, the loadstone which attracts—*Virtue*, the charm which binds—May they both predominate while time shall endure.
> *Female Independence*—May it never be infringed by a masculine arm, or forfeited by feminine frailty.
> *Female Weapons*—Frowns, disapprobations, and censures.
> *Female Attractions*—Cheerfulness, kindness, affection and chastity.
> *Feminine Arguments*—Truth, candor, and innocence.
> *Feminine Superiority*—Sympathy, tenderness, and gentleness.
> *Female Heroism*—Inflexible chastity, and invulnerable modesty.[65]

Toasts cherished the institution of motherhood. Children were embraced as the future of the nation, so it was crucial that women educate them properly, and they were to honor their mothers, to "rise up and call them blessed."[66] A Fourth of July toast from Huntingdon Springs, Pennsylvania, was to women because only they could bear more women, who would in turn bear more children: "Female Americans, and the production of female Americans—may they turn out virtuous Wives, able statesmen, and brave Soldiers."[67] The image of matriarchy was clear in a toast in 1808 to the Mississippi Territory, which was seen as "the fairest daughter of Columbia holding out to her maternity, the steady and dutiful hand of plenty and prosperity."[68] A comment was made in the *American Mercury* in 1804 regarding the placing of the toast to the Fair at the end of the list, where it was commonly put:

> IN our celebrations, it is common to Toast 1st,—*The 4th of July* 1776;—our national birthday—2d, *The 4th of March* 1801;—the birth day of republicanism, and to toast all other natal days, except our own—then to close off with "*The American Fair.*" The rejoicers should remember that *they were born*, before they began to make toasts, and that if every thing is to be in its own order, the Ladies are entitled to the first compliment.[69]

A great deal of toasts to women contained references to either Greek and Roman figures or literary characters. The Fair Sex should be "virtuous, generous, and patriotic," like the women who saved Rome from Coriolanus.[70] The Fair in South Carolina were as patriotic as Spartan women,[71] and the "Matrons and Maids of New Jersey" were as prudent and chaste as the historical examples set by the women of Greece and Rome.[72] The Fair were to "be as beautiful as Venus and chaste as Diana," which would, with "the wisdom of Minerva, dignify and distinguish the daughters of Columbia, from those of all the world beside!"[73] Honoring the work of Cervantes's *Don Quixote*, one toast hoped that old bachelors would find "*Dulcineas* to lend warmth the their cold hearts, give animation to their enervated frames, and balm to their wounded consciences."[74]

Women were expected to take on a more political role again during the embargo crises of the Jefferson and Madison administrations. One toast from the Falls of Schuylkill had a double meaning regarding one of the legislative acts in 1807: "The American fair—May they rigidly adhere to a non-intercourse with the enemies of their country."[75] Men at an Independence Day banquet in York, in the District of Maine, drank to their "fair countrywomen—without whom POLITICS would be but a dull and dreary subject. We would submit to any other non-intercourse rather than have a non-intercourse with them. We deprecate, as the greatest political evil, that anti-commercial spirit which actuates so many bachelors at the present day."[76]

During the embargo crisis of Jefferson's second term, women were encouraged to "lay aside foreign gew-gaws, and clothe themselves, their husbands, and children, in the emblems of patriotism, the works of their own fair hands."[77] The Fair were "never handsomer" than when they were sewing and spinning. It was hoped that their talents in such activities would be an impediment to British commerce: "The American fair—may their wheels, shuttles and needles be employed, their hands to clothe our soldiers, thus stab the British in their most vital parts."[78] The Bunker Hill Association in Charlestown, Massachusetts, recognized that women were crucial in the economic war: "*The American Fair*—Industrious and partial to their own works, they can guide the spindle, direct the loom, and make us independent of every influence, but their own."[79]

When the Virginia paper *Alexandria Gazette* printed the following Fourth of July toast: "'The *fair* sex. How much *fairer* would they appear in homespun dresses,'" a humorous anecdote was included:

> A patriotic son of St. Patrick, who is a great *economist*, on reading this toast, said he could provide a dress for the *fair* sex, which should be much *cheaper* than even homespun. They would appear *much fairer*, said he, if they were dressed in no clothes *at all, at all*. Some of our fashionable ladies seem to have adopted the Hibernian idea.[80]

People who did not support the war were not tolerated, including women. When a young woman burned a Liberty Pole in Norwalk, Connecticut, a toast about the incident included a warning: "The American Fair—May the girls who attempt to burn the Liberty poles die old maids."[81]

With the War of 1812 on the horizon, men looked to women to continue their political activism: "The American Fair—May they on all occasions like the present, manifest the same political zeal with their fathers, husbands and brothers—may they ever distinguish the man of merit and the true patriot from the *fawning sycophant and the grouching office-seeker*—may they reward the first with their smiles and spurn the latter from their presence."[82] Women were to give comfort and relief to the sick and wounded, as their mothers had done, and copy "the hardier sex to the discharge of their duties to their country."[83] They were to use their various talents to put others in their place:

> The American Fair—May they bestow a Judas-like kiss to the enemies of their country.[84]
> The fair sex—May their charms be reserved for those alone who dare courageously brave every danger attending their country's service—and may those possessing frowns deal them liberally around the pusillanimous wretches who shrink from the arduous task.[85]
> The American fair, modest, virtuous and lovely; may their smiles be reserved for the patriot and hero: but their frown of contempt the traitor's and coward's reward.[86]

There were civilian casualties during the War of 1812, but what happened in the town of Hampton, Virginia, in June 1813 was egregious. Anti-British propaganda easily stoked hatred against the British invaders and their Indian allies. Women who were attacked at Hampton became a centerpiece of political toasts that cried out for vengeance:

> The Female Sufferers at Hampton—Respect for their misfortunes, sympathy in their sufferings, and vengeance for their wrongs.[87]
> May the American Soldiery avenge the cause of Female innocence and virtue immolated at Hampton by savage British barbarity.[88]
> The Rights of Women—The right of avenging the outrages at Hampton by withholding their affection for apologists of Britain.[89]

Native Americans received plenty of vitriol because they allied themselves with the British during the war. Both were grouped together as "savages": "*The Savages of England who was with the helpless underprotected*—The day of retribution must come."[90] It was imperative to protect the country's valuable partners from the merciless Indians, as many toasts made clear: "The American fair—may they be always protected from the savages who made the spoils of their beauty their incitement for fighting."[91]

The coast of the District of Maine was open to possible invasion all throughout the war. The attack on the town of Falmouth (Portland) during the Revolution was not forgotten. When the militia gathered at Wiscasset to defend the community, the women of Hallowell provided them with tents, along with patriotic mottos to inspire the men. When the Hallowell Artillery gathered to celebrate their anniversary, they concluded their toasts with one that was set to poetic verse for the women who aided the Wiscasset militia:

> *The Fair of Hallowell.—*
> When fond employments we to duty yield,
> And change our firesides for the martial field,
> How smiles the soldier when to him is sent
> The grateful present of a welcome TENT,
> Each cheerful motto he with pleasure reads
> That speak the noblest of Columbia's deeds.
> And when from toils his ample cabin sought,
> Will bless the hands that his fond shelter wrought.[92]

Toasts to the American Fair were, for the most part, ornamental. Women's existence was for the betterment of men. Women were recognized in many toasts for their contributions to the war effort, such as participating in boycotts, caring for the sick and the wounded, and bearing children who would continue the republican traditions. It was socially unacceptable for women to participate in drinking toasts themselves, but there were some occasions when women did raise glasses at patriotic events. The political parties did their part to get the American Fair on their side, which validated their values. The women who were toasted in the Early Republic included Martha Washington, Abigail Adams, Dolley Madison, Josephine Bonaparte, and the classical figures of Diana, Minerva, and the Muses. The female virtues that were advocated in many toasts to the Fair were chastity, economy, frugality, and motherhood.

Chapter 14

Red Savages and Our National Curse, 1760–1815

"Peace with our brethren, the brave aborigines of America."[1]

"May the western wilderness, become the garden of innocence, and its savage inhabitants the pruners of the olive branch of peace."[2]

"The Aboriginal tribes of America; civilized and happy under the protection of the United States."[3]

"May the time soon arrive when men shall be ashamed to make their fellow creatures an article of commerce."[4]

"The hardy Yeomanry of New England:—May the fair tree of liberty, which their fathers planted, never be bruised by the black cattle of Virginia."[5]

"African slavery our national curse: may reason and humanity work its overthrow, and not steel."[6]

Women were prevalent in toast lists, as evidenced by the preceding chapter. They were rarely participants in the ritual, but they were recognized in virtually every list. Two groups of people, whose presence in the Early Republic was certainly unique, seemed to be "invisible" in the toast lists. They were rarely mentioned, so toasts about or to them stand out. These groups are the original inhabitants of the Americas and the enslaved people from Africa.

Toasting was never an Indian custom. If they did participate, it was out of deference to English traditions. When Indians and whites gathered to drink, it was often at treaty negotiations. People drank to what they hoped would be a favorable treaty, and then they drank to its conclusion. When negotiations for the Treaty of Lancaster opened in Pennsylvania in June 1744, Governor George Thomas and the commissioners from

Maryland and Virginia welcomed a delegation from the Iroquois League. The colonists offered toasts to the Indians' health, which the Indians reciprocated. Then the colonists raised their glasses to their king's health. Again, the Indians joined in, but they were taken aback by the English giving several loud "Huzzas." After the Iroquois drank several rounds of toasts, they ended up signing a deed that released their land claims in Maryland.[7] In July 1773, the *Newport Mercury* of Rhode Island printed some "sundry toasts usually drank by the Sachems at the different treaties of peace made with the English, viz.":

> *Conceachampktooonelize*; in English, *Our good friend and brother the English King.*
> *Conceachakongettgoomoobuttbatte*; in English, *My good friend the Governor I bury the hatchet.*
> *Gonquahannettupott*; in English, *Englishmen my brother are all one we.*
> *Woookenttunmenattickawarndtoondoo*; in English, *Me fight for my brothers the English when war.*[8]

Individual Indians were recognized in early toasts. New Englanders honored the Pilgrims by celebrating Forefathers' Day every December 22, and they drank to the Wampanoag sachem who was instrumental in the survival of Plymouth colony: "To the memory of *Sachem Massasoit*, our first and best friend and ally."[9] Even early in the nineteenth century, the "venerable sachem" Massasoit was praised because he "revered the altar of his God, and respected the rights of his friend."[10] Massasoit was a "good" Indian who welcomed the English settlers, and toasts were made in the hope that all Indians would follow Massasoit's example: "The memory of our Ancestors.—May our ardour inspire and their success encourage their descendants to maintain their birthright and may all enemies be converted like MASSASOIT, or suffer like PHILLIP."[11] Massasoit's son Philip was another story.

King Philip's War almost destroyed the English settlements in Massachusetts in the 1670s. According to James Loewen's classic work, *Lies My Teacher Told Me: Everything Your American History Textbook Got Wrong* (1995), it was the bloodiest conflict in American history, in proportion to population.[12] The label of "savage" was attached to all native peoples partially because of the catastrophe. Frustrated with Parliament, celebrants in Roxbury, Massachusetts, in August 1768 referred to all Indians as savages, but claimed that they would rather deal with them than greedy government officials: "*Scalping Savages* let loose in *Tribes*, rather than *Legions* of *Placemen, Pensioneers* and *Walkerizing Dragoons!*"[13] The Declaration of Independence's only racist comment reinforced this prejudice. George III allied his armies with the Indians, whose tactics were too horrific for

Americans to accept: "He has excited domestic insurrections amongst us, and has endeavoured to bring on the inhabitants of our frontiers, the merciless Indian Savages, whose known rule of warfare, is an undistinguished destruction of all ages, sexes and conditions."

During the Revolutionary War, Indians fought on both sides, but most favored the British. The Iroquois League was shattered by the conflict, and George Washington targeted the Mohawk Valley for destruction. He sent General John Sullivan on an expedition in the fall of 1779 to "burn out the Iroquois." Sullivan succeeded in setting fire to forty towns, destroying crops, cutting down orchards, and leaving the land bare.[14] Before the expedition, Sullivan's officers drank a toast that promised "'civilization or death to all American savages.'"[15] One Iroquois leader, the Seneca chief Ki-on-twog-ky, also known as Cornplanter, tried to pursue a policy of cooperation with the new United States after the war. He was recognized for his efforts by the Society of St. Tammany in Philadelphia. Using Indian imagery, members of the Society drank to "our Brother Iontonkque, of the Cornplant—may we ever remember that he visited our wigwam, and spoke a good talk from our great grandfather."[16] The St. Tammany Society of New York used similar terms in a toast for peace: "May the war hatchet be buried, and the pipe of peace be smoked, till time shall be no more."[17] Americans' bitter memories lasted into the nineteenth century, however. The following overview appeared in Baltimore in 1813:

Engraving by Augustus Robin between 1870 and 1900. Massasoit was considered to be a "good Indian" because of his behavior toward the first English settlers in Massachusetts. He was often toasted on Forefathers' Day: "The memory of the *ancient Sachems* of our Country, the *faithful* friend of the *Pilgrims*" (*Columbian Centinel*, 12-29-1802) (Library of Congress).

14. Red Savages and Our National Curse, 1760-1815

During the revolutionary war, all the six nations of Iroquois, except the Oneidas, joined the enemy. The behaviour of the Mohawks, Onondagos, Seneckas, Cayugas, and Tuscarorras, was so murderous and destructive, that the famous expedition against them under general Sullivan was made. But their savage cruelty against the peaceful farmers and their families at Wyoming, Cherry Valley, and along the Mohawk River, will be long remembered.[18]

Alexander McGillivray of the Creek Nation in the southeastern section of the country journeyed to New York City to negotiate with the Washington administration for a treaty that protected Creek territory. People toasted "'the Creek Washington'" as he traveled north.[19] On August 5, 1790, he was feted along with members of his delegation and joined in drinking the following toasts:

> Washington: the beloved Sachem of the 13 Fires.
> May the injured ever have spirit to claim, and power to secure their rights.
> May justice indite the treaty that shall bind us and the Creek nations in perpetual peace and amity.
> Universal peace and happiness, or the Tammanical Chain, extend through the Creek nations and round the whole earth.[20]

The Treaty of New York, 1790, negotiated by Secretary of War Henry Knox and the Creek delegation, gave some security to Creek sovereignty in exchange for land. The people of Georgia, however, resented what they considered to be an infringement of their rights. When the Combined Society met to discuss the treaty in Washington, Georgia, after-dinner toasts clearly showed unwillingness to accept the treaty:

> May Georgia possess virtue and firmness to assert her constitutional rights against all attempts to infringe them.
> May every freeman prefer an honorary death rather than be tributary to, or commanded by the Red Hero.
> May every sister state condole with Georgia in the loss of her darling territory, and each reflect it may be her turn next.
> May the friends of the treaty with the Creeks either retract, or suffer the most ignominious annihilation.[21]

President Washington tried to implement an evenhanded approach in dealing with the Indians.[22] The main threat to American expansion was north of the Ohio River. Washington considered members of the Shawnee, Cherokee, and Wabash nations to be "'bad Indians.'"[23] Major General Arthur St. Clair led an expedition to put down all Indian resistance in the Ohio River Valley. On November 4, 1791, over a thousand Indians pounced on the American army camp on the Wabash River in a surprise attack, routing St. Clair's men and destroying half of the expedition force.[24] It was the greatest military defeat of the U.S. Army. Toasts in 1792 honored the slain soldiers and promoted either peace with or a campaign of vengeance against the Indians:

> The memory of the unfortunate heroes who fell at "the flight" of St. Clair; rest to their souls.[25]
> May the measures pursuing against the hostile Indians, prove honourable to us, and profitable to them.[26]
> May the proffered benevolence of the nation correct the errors of our savage enemy, and incline their hearts to peace.[27]

In response to St. Clair's defeat, a new force, called the Legion of the United States, was to be led by Revolutionary War veteran "Mad" Anthony Wayne. People were thirsty for vengeance:

> May St. Clair's defeat be revenged on the heads of their murderers.[28]
> May our meeting with the Savages produce conviction in the world, that the American Legions are the only troops proper to oppose them.[29]
> "May the Enemies of America be metamoph'd into pack-horses, and sent on a Western Expedition against the Indians."[30]

Although the calls for Indian blood were loud, Washington and Knox still wanted to hold out for a negotiated peace.[31] People raised their glasses to that possibility:

> May our negotiations with the Indian tribes terminate the necessity and calamities of war; or, may the valour of our army procure for their country that peace which her justice and levity shall be unable to obtain.[32]
> A speedy and permanent peace with our red brethren, the aborigines of America.[33]
> The Western Army—may they be instrumental in effecting an honorable and lasting peace with our Indian neighbors.[34]

Other toasts served as a warning to the Indians of the Western Confederacy: "Humanity, or total destruction to the barbarous and savage nations."[35] Once the Indians were defeated, white America was intent on "civilizing" them:

> May the hatchet, now raised to the destruction of our western brethren, be buried in the dust, and the Savage be called from a precarious course of existence, to taste the sweets of civil society.[36]
> The Indian tribes; may the great spirit soften their ferocious minds, and to dispose them to a sacred observance of treaties.[37]

The end of the Western Confederacy came on August 20, 1794, at the Battle of Fallen Timbers. Wayne and a force of over 3,000 soldiers delivered a stunning defeat to Indian nations, breaking Indian power and the influence of the British.[38] The Treaty of Greenville, 1795, ceded most of Ohio to the United States, and also promised the Indians a lasting boundary

14. Red Savages and Our National Curse, 1760–1815

between their lands and American territory.[39] Expansionist-minded Republicans did not support the treaty:

> The President of the United States—may he comply with the unanimous wishes of every true friend of his country, by preventing Grenville's late treaty from becoming the supreme law of the land.[40]
> May the late defeat of the Indians and their white allies, the British, by Gen. Wayne's army, be a prelude to nobler achievements.[41]
> The Savages of the western wilds—May they bury the Hatchet of Blood, and smoke the Calumet of Peace around the great council fire of Columbia.[42]
> ANTHONY WAYNE, and his successful negociations with the Indian Tribes—May Peace dwell on our frontiers, and the Wilderness, late the field of Carnage, now blossom like the Rose.[43]

After Wayne died in 1796, he was toasted as "the hero of the Western country, who first taught the Savages of America the important lesson that the Stroke of the Tomahawk must give way to the Push of the Bayonet, and that no retreat is inaccessible to the Armies of the United States."[44]

Since the United States was overwhelmingly Protestant, conversion of the Indians was a high priority. Bringing the Indians over to Christianity was necessary to "civilize" them. Republican duties included the education of children, the abolition of slavery, and the civilization of Indians.[45] Once they were civilized, they could learn to farm, being easier to control. Toasts about Indians, who were understood to be "savages," expressed a desire that eventually they would become true Americans:

> May the Light of CHRISTIAN CIVILIZATION soon reach the abode of the Aboriginals of our country, and may their Wigwams be converted into mansions of Peace, Knowledge, Virtue and Happiness.[46]
> The civilization of the Indians—may they learn from us industry, and become useful members of society.[47]
> Education, the parent of liberty—May she so diffuse her nourishing rays that the Indian may rejoice under the happy influence of mild civilization and rational independence.[48]

More optimistic toasts referred to Indians as "'our red brethren,'" and although "nature is their guide, may it be more improved by the arts and sciences."[49] White Americans raised their glasses to Indians burying their tomahawks and settling down to a civilized peace: "Our red brethren, the aborigines of this land; instead of savage warfare and unjustifiable cruelties, may they improve the advantages they now enjoy in the cultivation of useful arts, and the prospect of undisturbed tranquility.—*To Jefferson the change they owe.*"[50] Thomas Jefferson had a softer touch when it came to his Indian policies. He still wanted the country to expand onto their lands, but he was no "*Conotocarious*," or "Town Destroyer," as Washington was referred to by the Iroquois. Jefferson wanted to win over the Indians by stressing agriculture and conversion to Christianity: "The aborigines of this land—They are greatly indebted to the wise and pacific policy of Thomas Jefferson, for the change from deeds of savage barbarity to undisturbed tranquility, and an advantageous cultivation of their soil."[51]

One of the reasons members of Congress wanted to go to war with Britain in 1812 was to end the Indian threat in the Indiana Territory. The Treaty of Greenville was ignored and more settlers took Indian land. The Shawnee leader Tecumseh was defeated by forces led by the governor of the Indiana Territory, William Henry Harrison, at the Battle of Tippecanoe in November 1811, and so the day was cause for banquets and toasts: "The seventh of Nov. 1811—On this ever memorable day, American bravery proved victorious, when suddenly attacked at all points, by a numerous band of savages, shielded by the impenetrable darkness of the night."[52] Harrison was feted as the "Washington of the West," and western toasts heaped praise on him:

> *Governor Harrison.*—The brave and consummate general—He deserves not only the praises, but the benedictions of his countrymen.
> General William Henry Harrison, and his brave officers and soldiers who fought the glorious battle on the 7th of November, at Tippecanoe.[53]
> Governor Harrison—The battle of Tippecanoe, is a pledge to his country that they will find in him an able and patriotic defender.[54]

Tecumseh had allied his Indian confederacy with Great Britain, "that nation which has proved the curse of the civilized world,"[55] to stem the tide of American expansion.[56] The rhetoric of Americans toward the Indians was now much more threatening. Pledges of genocide were included in many toasts, along with the hopes that the armies of the west would properly "carry retribution for Indian barbarity, until they reach the hearts of British instigators."[57] Celebrants at a festival near Cynthiana, Kentucky, promised that if the Indians "perfidiously reject our offers of peace, and prefer an alliance with Great Britain, we are ready to wage a war of extermination."[58] One toast from Nicholas County, Kentucky, proclaimed that the sword would never be sheathed until "the red men of Columbia ... are taught a lesson of extermination."[59] There seemed to be no separation to Americans between the British enemy and the Indians. Both were viewed as being savage:

> *The Indians*—As they have extinguished the calumet of peace, and dug up the hatchet of war; may it never again be buried until they are forever separated from the British, their abettors, and taught to feel and respect the authority of the United States.[60]
> The martyred heroes of Tippecanoe—their blood cries for vengeance on the *British* Savage.[61]
> May the British government make better use of their bounty than to bestow

it on the savage tribes, for the scalps of our defenceless frontier inhabitants, men, women and infant children.[62]

British outrage and murder, at Wyoming, Paoli and Hampton—they have forfeited the title of civilization, let us treat them like savages.[63]

Tecumseh was a target in many toasts during the war. In one South Carolina toast, he was compared to Royal Navy Commander Sir George Cockburn. They were allies, or in Latin, "'*par nobile fratrum*'—The one on the frontiers, the other on the sea coast—they have mutually agreed to 'save neither sex, age or condition.'"[64] In another, Tecumseh and "his more savage allies, the British" would be civilized before they were finished off.[65]

An unusual toast from Buffalo, New York, called for forgiveness toward the Indians: "Our red brethren of the west—Their sins have been great—but we are men and christians, let us forgive and forget them."[66] The Pennsylvania Society of the Cincinnati drank to a return to Washington's Indian policy, "practised for *their happiness, and the honor of the United States.*"[67] Other toasts advocated education, so "that the Indian may rejoice under the happy influence of mild civilization and rational independence."[68] Not all toasts denigrated the Indians. One volunteer toast given in Nashville, Tennessee, was to the Cherokees who fought with the United States soldiers: "may their services be duly appreciated by government."[69] Unfortunately, the end of the war did not bring education, civilization, or appreciation. Tecumseh's confederation died with him in 1813. The Creeks were then defeated by Andrew Jackson at the Battle of Horseshoe Bend in 1814. The Indian confederacies that had tried to stop American expansion ended with the War of 1812.[70]

Indians did not usually participate in the European/English toasting ritual unless it was at a celebration of the negotiation of a treaty. Some individual Indians were mentioned by name in early American toasts, but the most constant image was that of the Indian "savage." Toasts were made for those who suffered defeats at the hands of the Indians, pledging revenge. And when victories against the Indians were celebrated, the toasts praised the victors and continued to portray the Indians as wild savages, intent on the white man's destruction. Kinder toasts to the Indians pledged support for their religious conversion and civilization under white control.

African Americans witnessed many toasting events, but usually as servers, not drinkers. They were excluded from such celebrations, although there are a few instances of African Americans gathering at feasts and giving toasts. Those who recorded the history of the Revolution ignored the contributions of Black soldiers. If Black people were mentioned at all, it was to criticize those who ran away to British lines in the hopes of achieving their freedom.[71]

One of the reasons for the absence of African Americans from Independence Day festivities was the understanding that the holiday was meant for whites only. This therefore denied the Declaration of Independence's promise of equality to Black people.[72] Len Travers, in *Celebrating the Fourth* (1997), recounts a Black citizen's clear understanding of the paradox: "'Is it not wonderful that the day set apart for the festival of liberty, should be abused by the advocates of freedom, in endeavoring the sully what they profess to adore?'"[73] Southerners especially never saw the hypocrisy of celebrating freedom and equality while maintaining a slave society. Bostonian Edward Hooker was traveling through South Carolina in 1806 and joined revelers at a Fourth of July dinner. He was shocked by this after-dinner toast: "'The silken fetters of love—the only signs of American slavery.'" Hooker was also aghast at the exclusion of enslaved people from the idea of independence, all the while filling the glasses for their white masters. Enslaved people set the table and poured the wine, and their enslavers drank to the ideals of freedom.[74] When Hooker returned to see his friends a year later, he was tasked with writing the formal after-dinner toasts. Once again, he was made aware of the social and cultural differences between North and South regarding the enslaved:

> He proposed (innocently he insisted) a toast that ran: "the principles of rational liberty—May the blissful period ere long arrive when they shall prevail throughout the inhabitants of the globe!" Congressman John Taylor, also on the committee, "took it up and looking it over a little at first seemed to find no fault, but all at once spoke out, 'O this will never do! Why 'twill include our cursed black ones,' or words to that effect." Somewhat taken aback, Hooker protested that he had not intended to be that specific, but that he "suppose[ed] there is none of us but would wish it to extend event to them at some period or other." There was an uncomfortable pause, and then another committeeman, the state surveyor general, said, almost as in a prayer, "I hope it may not be till we are gone." Hooker tried feebly to recover the initiative by offering to strike the words "ere long" from the text, but it was too late: "Taylor said the toast would not be an acceptable one at the Table, so we concluded to drop it."[75]

Toasts that did mention slavery were usually not about Black chattel slavery. They referred to the British government treating the colonists as enslaved people: "May an Abhorrence of Slavery still and ever remain the best Criterion of a true British Subject."[76] There were few toasts during the Revolutionary War that were about African American enslaved people. One printed in Philadelphia was made in Amsterdam on July 4, 1779: "May the Lilies of France, and the Stripes of America, correct the slaves, and delight the free inhabitants of all the earth,"[77] and a simple one was made on Washington's birthday in Milton, Massachusetts, at the close of the war: "Freedom to the slave."[78]

14. Red Savages and Our National Curse, 1760–1815

The republican virtues of the American Revolution were taken seriously by African Americans. A group of free Black people in Providence, Rhode Island, met on the Fourth of July, "pleased with the Prospect of a Stop being put to the Trade to Africa in our Fellow-Creatures, by the adoption of the Federal Constitution." They clearly understood the meaning of the American Revolution and the potential of the Constitution:

> May the natives of Africa enjoy their natural Privileges unobstructed.
> May the Freedom of our unfortunate Countrymen (who are wearing the Chains of Bondage in different Parts of the World) be restored to them.[79]

Not all the toasts were specifically about ending Black slavery. Northerners were more willing to directly attack the peculiar institution of the South. They toasted the efforts of the British government and William Wilberforce, "the defender of the rights of the unfortunate Africans,"[80] to end slavery, especially the slave trade. The Windsor Light Infantry in Vermont drank to "the British Nation—May their Philanthropy in the abolition of the Slave Trade, be imitated by all Nations."[81]

While many antislavery toasts were reserved for the American seamen being held captive in Algeria in the 1790s, such as "Relief to our citizens in Algerine slavery. May humanity, or the sword, soon conquer their cruel oppression,"[82] toasts calling for the end of Black chattel slavery were becoming more prevalent. One toast given by the Washington Juvenile Society in Washington, D.C., made it clear that if Americans were concerned about Algerine slavery, then they should be just as concerned about African slavery in America: "May the sufferings of our fellow citizens in Tripoli teach their country-men an early lesson of humanity, and to emancipate the unfortunate sons of Africa."[83]

The values associated with freedom and liberty were on the minds of many because of the events in France. The French Revolution affected virtually every aspect of American society, and the idealism of liberty, equality, and fraternity was embraced by many. Slavery was a jarring contradiction to those values:

> May the fetters of slavery never be imposed on those who have the courage to assert their rights.[84]
> A total abolition of Slavery. May disappointment, loss and disgrace attend its abettors.[85]
> Both Houses of the Legislature of the United States—may their wisdom point out, and their hearts approve a speedy plan for the prohibition of the slave trade, and the general emancipation of all the unhappy Africans, and thereby make this country, truly the seat of Freedom and Happiness.[86]

Virginia, the largest of the slave states, received special attention:

> May Virginia slave drivers cease to theorize on the "Rights of Man," till they cease to tyrannize over their sable brethren.[87]
>
> The Virginia—Although attempting to break the line, may she escape a Mutiny from her crew of Blacks.[88]

Federalists, angry about another slave-owning Virginia planter in the presidency, pointed out the obvious disconnect the Republicans exhibited when it came to the meaning of freedom. Republicans were upset with the abuse and enslavement of Americans by the Barbary States, but they seemed to be blind to the situation in their own country. The following commentary appeared in the *Connecticut Centinel* in 1804:

> What an ungrateful set of being the Democrats are, ha, in perusing the last TRUE REPUBLICAN, we find it crammed with Toasts (drank in this and the neighboring towns on the 4th int. by some of our genuine *Equality* men,) among the number "*Our enslaved Brethren in Tripoli, &c. &c.*" frequently occurs; but not a syllable not a lisp mentioned about their *enslaved Brethren in Virginia!* as black as those slaves are they must blush at this base ingratitude of the sect. Do Mr. *True* Republican let us here a little more about your *Liberty* your *Equality* and *Oppressed Humanity*, &c. as we find those terms so *nearly* correspond with your late proceedings as almost to convince us that you assumed title "*Republican*" is no *sham!*[89]

The grief that many northern states had regarding slavery concerned the Three-Fifths Compromise, which allowed slave states to count three-fifths of their slaves for the purpose of congressional representation, giving them a disproportionate voice in Congress. Many historians believe that John Adams would have won reelection if it had not been for the Three-Fifths Compromise. One Forefathers' Day toast from Plymouth in 1802 was to "Our Sister Virginia—When she changes the three-fifths of her Ethiopian Skin, we will respect her as the head of our *white* family."[90] The contention over the Compromise continued after the end of the War of 1812: "Slave Representation—That 5 Virginia negroes should have the same political weight with three Pennsylvania farmers, is neither consistent with Liberty nor Justice."[91]

South Carolinians were always concerned about the fact that Black people outnumbered white people. Festivals that honored freedom, liberty, and equality were completely closed off to Blacks because of the fear of slave insurrections. Only the whites in Charleston celebrated the Fourth, but they were uneasy about Black people realizing their numerical superiority. The overwhelming fear of slave insurrection led to brutal laws meant to completely subjugate the Black population. Laws were also passed in the state to protect the slave trade. As far as treatment of enslaved people went, South Carolina was much more repressive than Virginia:

14. Red Savages and Our National Curse, 1760–1815

> The legislature of South Carolina—May the genius of American liberty frown on them with indignation, until they repeal their dangerous and infamous slave act.[92]
>
> The State of South Carolina—A speedy abrogation of those laws which disgrace human nature—Let not man (and best of all a freeman) enslave his fellow man.[93]
>
> South Carolina—may the expression of public indignation from every part of the union, compel her to renounce for ever a traffic which is a disgrace to humanity.[94]

When a Dr. Ramsay gave an oration on the acquisition of the Louisiana Territory, one of the toasts given on the occasion by the Republicans of Charleston was to *"the Governor and State of South-Carolina.—Mild laws, executed in mercy, mark the happy state of society, and the benevolent disposition of our chief magistrate."* A vitriolic rebuke was printed in the *Connecticut Courant*, listing the many evils of *"man stealing."* The commentary concluded with an exposure of the toast's hypocrisy: "While people, calling themselves republicans, and professing a warm attachment to the equal rights of man, do thus permit the existence of a statute, the operations and effects of which must necessarily bring inexpressible misery upon a portion of the human race, it fairly does not become them to boast of their *'mild laws, executed in mercy.'"*[95]

South Carolina, and indeed all the slave-holding states, were increasingly concerned about events in the Caribbean. The ideals of the French Revolution were embraced by the enslaved people of France's most profitable colonial possession, the island of Saint-Dominque (St. Domingo). They rebelled in 1791, and by 1793 the rebellion became a bloody race war. The rebel leader, Francois Dominque Toussaint L'Ouverture, was hailed as a hero and freedom fighter, but enslavers in the United States were terrified by his influence, even after his death in 1803. Most southern states refused to allow any enslaved people or free Blacks to escape the rebellion through their borders. Any hopes that enlightened southern planters, such as Washington and Jefferson, had about eventual emancipation evaporated.[96] Washington joined South American liberator Simon Bolivar and Toussaint L'Ouverture in toasts given by free Black people. The Haitian rebellion was viewed by Black people as a part of the revolutionary abolition movement.[97] Glasses raised to the Caribbean rebellion served as a warning to the slave states:

> May the island of St. Domingo, and the Republics of Europe, ere long be liberated from the Tyranny of the many headed monster of France.[98]
>
> *The inhabitants of Hayti*—May they continue to afford the convincing proof, that the human heart, when it has once tasted liberty is invincible.[99]
>
> May the state of South Carolina learn wisdom from no other experience than reading the history of St. Domingo.[100]

> *The memory of the unfortunate* TOUSSAINT, *the Chiefs, the Heroes and Freemen of St. Domingo*—They have gloriously rescued their country form the grasp of despotism.¹⁰¹

The mention of enslaved people, the slave trade, and slavery itself in toasts prior to the War of 1812 displayed the evils of human bondage and how the existence of the institution was counter to the ideals of 1776. The infamous Gag Rule, which slave states used in Congress to prevent the discussion of antislavery measures and petitions, was a subject in a Washington's birthday toast in 1810: "The Gag-Rule—A Representative who would abridge the freedom of Debate in Congress cannot be a friend to the freedom of his Constituents."¹⁰² Antislavery toasts criticized the Constitution, grieved the loss of republican values, and called for universal emancipation:

> The Slave Trade—disgraceful to the country that permits it—May the foul stain be wiped from our country.¹⁰³
> A complete check to negro traffic; and no RICKETY compromises in the cause of humanity.¹⁰⁴
> Universal Emancipation—May despotism and oppression forever cease—May the poor enslaved Africans be reinstated in their former joys, and may all, all find protection under the fostering wing of liberty. *What pleasing things before me ran.*¹⁰⁵

Boston was more cosmopolitan than most American cities, and free Black people were a part of the economic structure. They did take part in patriotic celebrations, although they were frequently ignored in the press. In a rare instance, the toasts of a group of free Black people celebrating the abolition of the slave trade were printed. They drank to whoever helped alleviate the sufferings of all Black people:

> *Mr. Wilberforce*, and other members who advocated the abolition of the slave trade in the British Parliament.
> The memory of *Hancock, Franklin*, and *Sullivan*; and all who have advocated the cause of the Africans.
> Liberty to our African brethren in St. Domingo, and elsewhere.¹⁰⁶

Antislavery toasts did not eliminate racism. The Tammany Society printed a set of toasts that were written colloquially, portraying all African Americans as speaking an ignorant version of English. The language would make a modern reader cringe:

> *Old Massa Tammany himself*—his spirits no be ashamed to be wid us at de council fire which be lighted to day—petter be here wid a porr honest negur African, den way out younder wid de deblish demicat.
> *Our Broder Tom, de last grand Sachem of dis nation*—We be all red men—all white men—and lib together in peace and unicorn; but de dam fellow desert Missa, so de people desert him.

De 4th of July—Wish he came half a dozen times a year; de sons of Tammany, free to-day, do he work like hell to-morrow. We don't hab a *talk* but we hab dam good toasts.[107]

The language in the above toasts was printed in newspaper broadsides in Boston celebrating "BOBOLITION" Day by the African Society, which was July 14, 1808, when the Constitution's stipulation that the slave trade would end after twenty years went into effect. Or rather, in the degrading language that David Waldstreicher calls "literary blackface": "GRAND SELEBRASHUM BY DE AFICUM SHOCIETEE!!!!"[108] The Bobolition Day broadsides did not respect free men who were celebrating on their own; they were meant to speak for the Black people, who were not expected to speak for themselves. Broadsides served the purpose of putting words in the mouths of all Black people, and so obviously people came away with an impression that they were ignorant and unsophisticated. As intended, Black people lacked social equality and cultural independence.[109] The following toasts appeared in 1810:

Massa Presidamp Monroe—May he lib foreber, and one day arter.
De Nited Tate—De land of Liberty, sept he keep slave in de Sout.
De African School—Bress dare little souls, how fass de do larn Mattymattacks and Combomblifications.
De Tate of New England—He be no more like Africa dan my old gun like a beer barrel, or tumble in a mud puddle and got out again.[110]

Some Americans were still optimistic for a future of freedom for everyone. The term "slavery" meant how the colonists were treated by the British, the American seamen taken by the Barbary States, and the abducted Africans who were brought by the hundreds of thousands. The Fourth of July was always the most recognized occasion to drink to the idea of freedom: "*The day which we celebrate*—The bright era of our emancipation from the shackles of slavery—a day that will ever be held sacred by freemen."[111]

Toasts regarding slavery during the Early Republic were usually not in reference to African slavery, but instead to Britain's treatment of the colonists as enslaved people or the captured American sailors languishing in the Barbary States. Toasts to the end of African slavery were few and far between, but when they did appear, they were in northern newspapers. Some people were aware of the contradiction of the promise of American freedom and the reality of African slavery. Toasts given by free Black people were few. The celebration of Bobolition Day in Boston presented an opportunity to satirize Black language by printing toasts in broadsides.

Conclusion

John Adams's physician later told the president that when town leaders had asked his father on June 30th for a Fourth of July toast, he had declared "Independence forever!" Asked if he would like to add something more, he replied, "Not a word."[1]

The former president went back to the Revolution less than a month before he died on the Fourth of July in 1826, and his son, President John Quincy Adams, must have been comforted that his father seemed at peace with his role in the nation's founding. He was still the revolutionary from '76. John Adams held his friend and former foe in great esteem when he died, saying, "Thomas Jefferson lives," which were the last words he supposedly uttered. Sadly, Adams had no idea that Jefferson passed away earlier that same day.[2]

The deaths of Adams and Jefferson coincided with the final years of the period known as the Early Republic. Adams's final toast was an affirmation of that important American ideal: independence. The toast was quick and brief, not unlike the toasts given to the British king and his family, which were all short but plentiful. Some foreigners and temperance-minded colonists found the toasting ritual to be either ridiculous and savage or socially dangerous. By 1815, there were not as many short toasts given at events, but they stood out as meaningful works of literature. Toasts were convenient propaganda, and the newspapers effectively spread these sentiments through the new nation.

George Washington replaced George III at the top of toast lists during the American Revolution. Toasts lauded the military heroes and vilified the enemies of the nation. Joseph Warren, members of the Second Continental Congress, Lafayette and the French alliance, Benjamin Franklin, Thomas Jefferson, and John Adams were all toasted. After the war, toasts showed that unity among the states was an important goal. The Confederation Congress led to the Constitutional Convention of 1787, and the toasts kept track of the ratification process. Washington maintained his position on toast lists, this time as the nation's first president.

The political division of the United States was evident in toasts during Washington's first term. The French Revolution was at first an event that was filled with possibilities of liberty and equality, and the toasts to the Revolution were euphoric. But then its violence split the presidential cabinet into two factions, and for the remainder of Washington's presidency and the entire Adams presidency, the toasts of the Federalists and the Republicans were used to spread vitriol against each other. While toasts praised the Neutrality Proclamation, the Farewell Address, and how Adams handled the XYZ Affair, other toasts viciously attacked the Jay Treaty and the Alien and Sedition Acts. Glasses were optimistically raised to the election of Thomas Jefferson and his achievements, such as the Louisiana Purchase and the war against the Barbary States. Toasts were split regarding the Embargo Act, but they unified national feeling against Aaron Burr.

James Madison had to contend with a precarious situation by trying to stay neutral between Britain and France. Toasts sympathized with the cause of the American sailors impressed into the British navy, and they called for war. The War of 1812 provided another opportunity for displays of patriotism. Toasts praised the naval victories and the two new national heroes: William Henry Harrison and Andrew Jackson. Toasts from Federalist New England demanded an end to the war. New Englanders drank to the possibility of leaving the union, but all other Americans were toasting the brilliant success of Jackson at New Orleans and the Treaty of Ghent.

The toasts of three specific groups of Americans were rare. Women were not allowed to participate in the toasting ritual, but they were everpresent in many toast lists as the "American Fair." Toasts to them were always ornamental and advocated what men considered to be feminine virtues. Indian culture did not include the giving of toasts. They did join in at times and drank toasts at treaty negotiations. Toasts almost always referred to them negatively as "savages." African slaves and free Black people did not participate in the giving or receiving of toasts because independence had been denied them. Toasts promoting an end to slavery were rare during the Early National Period. "Bobalition" toasts were printed on newspaper broadsides, satirizing the speech of free Black people.

Toasts continued well into the nineteenth and early twentieth centuries, and many of them were political. The "golden age" of toasting was between 1786 and 1920.[3] Patriotic toasts were an important part of the nation's centennial celebrations. The Eighteenth Amendment brought Prohibition in 1920, but it did not prevent people from drinking. Toasting lists did not appear in the newspapers during this time. Although the tradition returned after Prohibition ended in 1933, the use of the toast as a political tool had waned. The wedding toast became the most popular among most Americans. Gone were the days when one could drink to the enemies of America having cobweb breeches and porcupine saddles.

It is only proper to end this book on toasts with a toast given to you: May you continue to read in comfort and always have a savory beverage by your side. And may we part as friends with the hope of seeing each other in the future.

Chapter Notes

Introduction

1. *American Herald of Liberty,* 7-22-1794.
2. *Boston News-Letter,* 8-21-1766.
3. *Massachusetts Mercury,* 7-5-1793.
4. Waldstreicher, *In the Midst of Perpetual Fetes: The Making of American Nationalism, 1776–1820* (Chapel Hill: University of North Carolina Press, 1997), p. 110.

Chapter 1

1. Saxon term meaning "Be Healthy," attributed to King Vortigen in 450. Rebecca Rupp, "Cheers: Celebration Drinking Is an Ancient Tradition," https://www.nationalgeographic.com/culture/article/drinking-alcohol-culture. 7-12-2022.
2. Falstaff in William Shakespeare's *The Merry Wives of Windsor,* III, v, line 1749 (1602).
3. "The Opera," *Seinfeld,* season 4, episode 9.
4. *Reporter,* 5-26-1804.
5. Waldstreicher, p. 115.
6. Paul Dickson, *Toasts: The Complete Book of the Best Toasts, Sentiments, Blessings, Curses, and Graces* (New York: Delacorte Press, 1981), p. 1.
7. Mark Urban, *Fusiliers: The Saga of a British Redcoat Regiment in the American Revolution* (New York: Walker & Company, 2007, Kindle edition), loc. 208–222 of 7543.
8. Rebecca Rupp, "The (Often Manly) History of Toasting," https://www.artofmanliness.com/character/advice/often-manly-history-toasting-bring-back/. 7-12-2022.
9. Peter Thompson, "'The Friendly Glass': Drink and Gentility in Colonial Philadelphia," *Pennsylvania Magazine of History and Biography,* Vol. 113, No. 4 (October 1989), 549–573; p. 564.
10. *Ibid.,* p. 560.
11. Richard J. Hooker, "The American Revolution Seen Through a Wine Glass," *The William and Mary Quarterly,* Vol. 11, No. 1 (January 1954), 52–57; p. 54.
12. *Ibid.,* p. 66.
13. Waldstreicher, p. 17.
14. J. Roach, *The Royal Toast Master: Containing Many Thousands of the Best Toasts Old and New, to Give Brilliancy to Mirth and Make the Joys of the Glass Supremely Agreeable: Also The Seaman's Bottle Companion, Being a Selection of Exquisite Modern Sea Songs* (London: 1793), Preface, i.
15. Adrian Covert, *Taverns of the American Revolution* (San Rafael, CA: Insight Edition, 2016), p. 134.
16. Jeffrey L. Pasley, "The Cheese and the Words: Popular Culture and Participatory Democracy in the Early American Republic," in Jeffrey L. Pasley, et. al., *Beyond the Founders: New Approaches to the Political History of the Early American Republic* (Chapel Hill: University of North Carolina Press, 2004), p. 40.
17. Remy Duthille, "Political Toasting in the Age of Revolutions: Britain, America and France, 1765–1800," in Gordon Pentland, et al., *Liberty, Property and Popular Politics: England and Scotland, 1688–1815. Essays in Honour of H.T. Dickinson* (Edinburgh: Edinburgh University Press, 2016, pp. 73–76), p. 74.
18. Hooker, p. 52.
19. *Ibid.,* p. 64.

20. Rupp, "The (Often Manly) History of Toasting."
21. Ibid.
22. Dickson, p. 5.
23. Luis J. Orozco, II, "The History and Ritual of 'The Toast,'" Paper submitted to the Britannia Council No. 303, Allied Masonic Degrees (Los Altos, CA: 1994), p. 10.
24. Dickson, p. 5.
25. Edward Gibbons, *The Decline and Fall of the Roman Empire* (Kindle edition), loc. 40649.
26. Margaret Visser, *The Rituals of Dinner: The Origins, Evolution, Eccentricities and Meaning of Table Manners* (New York: Grove Weidenfeld, 1991), p. 255.
27. Dickson, pp. 8–9.
28. Rupp, "The (Often Manly) History of Toasting."
29. Rebecca Rupp, "Cheers: Celebration Drinking Is an Ancient Tradition"; Dickson, pp. 8–9.
30. Visser, pp. 255–257.
31. Dickson, p. 10.
32. Workplace Depot, "A 'Bumper' Blog," https://www.theworkplacedepot.co.uk/news/2013/10/10/bumper-blog/.
33. W.J. Rorabaugh, *The Alcoholic Republic: An American Tradition* (New York: Oxford University Press, 1979), pp. 20–21.
34. https://sites.suffolk.edu/franklin/2016/03/29/beer-is-proof-that-god-loves-us-and-wants-us-to-be-happy-2/ Accessed 8-30-2020.
35. Merril D. Smith, ed., *The World of the American Revolution: A Daily Life Encyclopedia. Volume I* (Santa Barbara, CA: ABC-CLIO, 2015), p. 389.
36. Reverend Richard Valpy French, *The History of Toasting, or Drinking Healths in England* (London: National Temperance Publication Depot, 1881), p. 69.
37. Peter Thompson, *Rum, Punch and Revolution: Taverngoing and Public Life in Eighteenth-Century Philadelphia* (Philadelphia: University of Pennsylvania Press, 1999), p. 99.
38. Christine Sismondo, *America Walks Into a Bar: A Spirited History of Taverns and Saloons, Speakeasies and Grog Shops* (New York: Oxford University Press, 2014), pp. 25–26.
39. Ibid., pp. 23–24.
40. David Conroy, *In Public Houses: Drink and the Revolution of Authority in Colonial Massachusetts* (Chapel Hill: University of North Carolina Press, 1995), p. 13.
41. Paul Dickson, "A Brief History of Raised Glasses," http://www.toastsbook.com/History, p. 7.
42. Conroy, pp. 29–30.
43. *New York Chronicle*, 7-13-1769.
44. Michelle Orihel, "Just Add Sparkling Grape Juice: Toasting and the Historical Imagination in the Early Republican Classroom," in *Common Place: The Journal of Early American Life* (Issue 16.2, Winter 2016), p. 2.
45. Dickson, *Toasts*, pp. 25–28.
46. Simon P. Newman, *Parades and the Politics of the Street: Festive Culture in the Early American Republic* (Philadelphia: University of Pennsylvania Press, 1997), p. 29.
47. Alice Morse Earle, *Customs and Fashions in Old New England* (Williamstown, MA: Corner House Publishers, 1974), p. 231.
48. Edward L. Pierce, *The Diary of John Rowe: A Boston Merchant, 1764–1779. A Paper Read by Edward L. Pierce Before the Massachusetts Historical Society, March 14, 1894* (Cambridge, MA: John Wilson and Son, University Press, 1895), p. 45.
49. Sarah J. Purcell, *Sealed With Blood: War, Sacrifice, and Memory in Revolutionary America* (Philadelphia: University of Pennsylvania Press, 2010), p. 39.
50. Hooker, p. 55.
51. *Rutland Herald*, 8-16-1806. Spelling errors are in the text.
52. Purcell, p. 7.
53. Mary P. Ryan, *Civic Wars: Democracy and Public Life in the American City during the Nineteenth Century* (Oakland: University of California Press, 1998), p. 15.
54. Michal Jan Rozbicki, *Culture and Liberty in the Age of the American Revolution* (Charlottesville: University of Virginia Press, 2011), p. 107.
55. Johann N. Neem, "The Elusive Common Good: Religion and Civil Society in Massachusetts, 1780–1833," in *Journal of the Early Republic* 24, No. 3 (Autumn 2004), p. 382.
56. Thompson, *Rum, Punch and Revolution*, p. 99.
57. Ibid., p. 160.

58. French, p. 86.
59. Benjamin H. Irvin, "Tar, Feathers, and the Enemies of American Liberties, 1768–1776," in *New England Quarterly* Vol. 76, No. 2 (June 2003), 197–238, p. 216.
60. David Head, *A Crisis of Peace: George Washington, the Newburgh Conspiracy, and the Fate of the American Revolution* (New York: Pegasus Books, 2019), p. 197.
61. "To John Adams from Benjamin Rush, 21 July 1789," *Founders Online*, National Archives, https://founders.archives.gov/documents/Adams/06-20-02-0064.
62. Eric Jay Dolin, *Rebels at Sea: Privateering in the American Revolution* (New York: Liveright Publishing Corporation, 2022), p. 115.
63. *Chronicle, or, Harrisburgh Visitor*, 12-26-1814.
64. *True American and Commercial Daily Advertiser*, 6-18-1805.
65. Thompson, "The Friendly Glass," pp. 557–558.
66. H.W. Brands, *Heirs of the Founders: The Epic Rivalry of Henry Clay, John Calhoun and Daniel Webster, the Second Generation of American Giants* (New York: Doubleday, 2018), pp. 179–180.
67. Newman, p. 5.
68. Waldstreicher, p. 38.
69. Len Travers, *Celebrating the Fourth: Independence Day and the Rights of Nationalism in the Early Republic* (Amherst: University of Massachusetts Press, 1997), pp. 51–52.
70. *Balance*, 7-2-1801.
71. "Abigail Adams 2d to John Quincy Adams, 4 July 1785–11 August 1785," *Founders Online*, National Archives, https://founders.archives.gov/documents/Adams/04-06-02-0072.
72. *Daily Advertiser*, 8-11-1788.
73. Lindsay M. Chervinsky, *The Cabinet: George Washington and the Creation of an American Institution* (Cambridge, MA: Belknap Press of Harvard University Press, 2020), p. 45.
74. Covert, p. 134.
75. Thompson, *Rum, Punch and Revolution*, pp. 192–193.
76. Travers, p. 50.
77. Philip Thomas Tucker, *Alexander Hamilton's Revolution: His Vital Role as Washington's Chief of Staff* (New York: Skyhorse Publishing, 2017), Kindle edition, loc. 4790.
78. Mark Edward Lender and James Kirby Martin, editors, *Drinking In America: A History* (New York: The Free Press, 1982), p. 12.
79. Louis Booker Wright, *The Cultural Life of the American Colonies 1607–1783* (New York: Harper & Brothers, 1957), p. 248.
80. Thompson, *Rum, Punch and Revolution*, p. 75.
81. Victoria Bissell Brown and Timothy J. Shannon, "Toasting Rebellion," in *Going to the Source* (New York: Bedford/St. Martin's, 2012), p. 92.
82. Conroy, p. 199.
83. Steven Grasse, *Colonial Spirits: A Toast to Our Drunken History* (New York: Abrams Image, 2016), p. 14.
84. Mehmet Samuk, "Taverns in Early Massachusetts" (St. Mary's University Media, 12-6-2016), https://stmuscholars.org/taverns-in-early-massachusetts/.
85. Covert, pp. 18–19.
86. *Federal Gazette*, 7-9-1798.
87. Arthur M. Schlesinger, *Prelude to Independence: The Newspaper War on Britain, 1764–1776* (New York: Alfred A. Knopf, 1957), pp. 97–98.
88. Purcell, pp. 39–40.
89. Simon, pp. 29–30.
90. Philip Davidson, *Propaganda and the American Revolution: 1763–1783* (Chapel Hill: University of North Carolina Press), p. 209.
91. Purcell, p. 1.
92. Waldstreicher, pp. 33–34.
93. Pasley, p. 41.
94. *Federal Gazette*, 9-3-1791.
95. Newman, p. 3.
96. Duthille, p. 10.
97. Jeffrey L. Pasley, *"The Tyranny of Printers": Newspaper Politics in the Early American Republic* (Charlottesville, VA: University Press of Virginia, 2001), pp. 6–7.
98. *Petersburgh Intelligencer*, 7-1-1808.
99. *Farmer's Library*, 1-27-1794.
100. Brown and Shannon, pp. 96–97.

Chapter 2

1. Toast #1, *Connecticut Gazette*, 7-29-1768.

2. *Virginia Gazette*, 6-6-1766.
3. Toast #13, *New York Journal*, 11-2-1769.
4. Toast #14, *New-York Gazette and Weekly Mercury*, 9-26-1774.
5. Richard L. Bushman, *King and People in Provincial Massachusetts* (Chapel Hill: University of North Carolina Press, 1985), p. 16.
6. Travers, p. 16.
7. *Newport Mercury*, 8-22-1763.
8. Andrew Roberts, *The Last King of America: The Misunderstood Reign of George III* (United States: Viking Press, 2021), p. 346.
9. A.J. Languth, *Patriots: The Men Who Started the American Revolution* (New York: Simon & Schuster, 1988), pp. 52–53.
10. Toast #14, *Boston News-Letter*, 8-21-1766.
11. Toasts #4–5, *Newport Mercury*, 1-20-1766.
12. Toasts #4–5, *New-York Mercury*, 4-21-1766.
13. Toast #2, *New-Hampshire Gazette*, 5-30-1766.
14. Toast #6, *New-York Mercury*, 6-9-1766.
15. Toast #17, given by the General Assembly in Philadelphia, *Pennsylvania Gazette*, 6-12-1766.
16. Toasts #9, 11, *Boston Gazette* (Supplement), 8-11-1766.
17. Alan Axelrod, *The Complete Idiot's Guide to the American Revolution* (Indianapolis: Alpha Books, 2000), p. 72.
18. Toast #14, *Newport Mercury*, 8-24-1767.
19. Toast #6, *Pennsylvania Chronicle*, 8-31-1767.
20. Axelrod, p. 74.
21. *Ibid.*, p. 73.
22. Richard Archer, *As If an Enemy's Country: The British Occupation of Boston and the Origins of Revolution* (New York: Oxford University Press, 2010), pp. 97–98.
23. Hooker, p. 61.
24. "Committee of the Boston Sons of Liberty to John Wilkes, 5 October 1768," *Founders Online*, National Archives, https://founders.archives.gov/documents/Adams/06-01-02-0072.
25. Jane Kamensky, *A Revolution In Color: The World of John Singleton Copley* (New York: W.W. Norton & Company, 2016), p. 130.
26. Toasts #5, 8, 13, *Connecticut Gazette*, 7-29-1768.
27. Toast #44, *New-York Journal*, 9-8-1768.
28. Bob Ruppert, "Paoli: Hero of the Sons of Liberty," *Journal of the American Revolution*, 5-11-2016, https://allthingsliberty.com/2016/05/paoli-hero-of-the-sons-of-liberty/.
29. Toast #10, *Boston Gazette*, 3-21-1768; Toast #8, *New Hampshire Gazette*, 8-26-1768.
30. Toasts #9, 12, 17, *Pennsylvania Chronicle*, 4-17-1769.
31. Toast #13, *New-York Journal*, 3-23-1769.
32. Toast #28, *New-York Journal*, 3-30-1769.
33. Sean Murphy, "Remembering Dr Charles Lucas, 1713–71," in *History Ireland*, Vol. 21, No. 6 (November/December 2013), http://www.historyireland.com/volume-21/remembering-dr-charles-Lucas-1713-71.
34. *Boston Evening Post*, 6-19-1769, from "JOURNAL OF THE TIMES"; 4-17-1769.
35. "Virginia Nonimportation Resolutions, 17 May 1769," *Founders Online*, National Archives, https://founders.archives.gov/documents/Jefferson/01-01-02-0019.
36. Stacy Schiff, *The Revolutionary: Samuel Adams* (New York: Little, Brown and Company, 2022), p. 163; Toast #45, *Boston Evening Post*, 8-21-1769.
37. Pauline Maier, *From Resistance to Revolution: Colonial Radicals and the Development of American Opposition to Britain* (New York: Alfred A. Knopf, Inc., 1972), Kindle edition, loc. 3823–3840.
38. Toasts #12, 25, *New York Journal*, 11-2-1769.
39. *Boston Gazette*, 4-2-1770.
40. Toast #16, *New Hampshire Gazette*, 6-8-1770.
41. Toast #29, *New-York Journal*, 3-22-1770.
42. John R. Alden, *A History of the American Revolution 1775–1783* (New York: Harper & Row, Publishers, 1954), p. 141.
43. Christian Di Spigna, *Founding Martyr: The Life and Death of Dr. Joseph Warren, the American Revolution's Lost Hero* (New York: Crown Publishing House, 2018), p. 137.

44. Axelrod, p. 94.
45. *Essex Journal*, 10-26-1774.
46. Toast #16, *Norwich Packet*, 9-29-1774.
47. Eric Hinderaker, *Boston's Massacre* (Cambridge, MA: Belknap Press of Harvard University Press, 2017), p. 243.
48. William M. Fowler, Jr., *The Baron of Beacon Hill: A Biography of John Hancock* (Boston: Houghton Mifflin, 1979), p. 173.
49. Alan Taylor, *American Revolutions: A Continental History, 1750-1804* (New York: W.W. Norton & Company, 2017), Kindle edition, loc. 3343.
50. James H. Stark, *The Loyalists of Massachusetts and the Other Side of the American Revolution* (Boston: W.B. Clarke Company, 1907), Kindle edition, loc. 8477–8483.
51. "[September 1774]," *Founders Online*, National Archives, https://founders.archives.gov/documents/Adams/01-02-02-0004-0006. [Original source: *The Adams Papers*, Diary and Autobiography of John Adams, vol. 2, *1771–1781*, ed. L.H. Butterfield. Cambridge, MA: Harvard University Press, 1961, pp. 118–146.] The toast was made in September 1774. The Thomas Paine referred to was not the famous writer.
52. "[September 1774]," *Founders Online*, National Archives, https://founders.archives.gov/documents/Adams/01-02-02-0004-0006.
53. Toast #10, *Pennsylvania Packet*, 9-19-1774.
54. Toasts #9, 14, *New-York Gazette and Weekly Mercury*, 9-26-1774.
55. Toasts #10–11, 18, *Essex Journal*, 10-26-1774.

Chapter 3

1. Toast #2, *Connecticut Courant*, 12-23-1783.
2. Toast #14, *Massachusetts Spy*, 7-24-1776.
3. Toast #4, *Independent Ledger*, 7-9-1781.
4. Toast #10, *Providence Gazette*, 5-3-1783.
5. Purcell, pp. 13–15.
6. William Sterns Randall, *Benedict Arnold: Patriot and Traitor* (New York: Dorset Press, 2001), Kindle edition, loc. 1717.
7. "To Benjamin Franklin from Jonathan Shipley, [June 1775]," *Founders Online*, National Archives, https://founders.archives.gov/documents/Franklin/01-22-02-0050.
8. *Connecticut Gazette*, 10-13-1775.
9. Waldstreicher, p. 30.
10. Hooker, p. 77.
11. Toasts #1, 4, *Virginia Gazette*, 1-13-1776.
12. Thomas Paine, *Common Sense* (New York: Barnes and Noble, 1995), pp. 14–15.
13. *Massachusetts Spy*, 4-12-1776.
14. Toasts #1–2, *Connecticut Gazette*, 6-7-1776.
15. Ric Atkinson, *The British are Coming: The War for America, Lexington to Princeton, 1775-1777* (New York: Henry Holt and Company, 2019), p. 309.
16. Toast #13, *The Massachusetts Spy*, 7-24-1776.
17. Silverman, pp. 371–372.
18. Dickson, p. 19.
19. David Waldstreicher, "The Invention of the Fourth of July," p. 3. http://hnn.us/roundup/entries/12527.html.
20. Toasts #10, 13, *New York Journal*, 8-8-1776.
21. Covert, p. 134.
22. *Pennsylvania Evening Post*, 8-17-1776.
23. "To Benjamin Franklin from Elizabeth Wright, 13 February 1777," *Founders Online*, National Archives, https://founders.archives.gov/documents/Franklin/01-23-02-0204.
24. Samuel Johnson, "Taxation No Tyranny: An Answer to the Resolutions and Address of the American Congress," www.samueljohnson.com/tnt.html.
25. James Boswell, *Life of Johnson* (New York: Oxford University Press, 1961), p. 876.
26. Travers, p. 24.
27. *Norwich Packet*, 7-21-1777.
28. *Virginia Gazette*, 8-15-1777.
29. "John Adams to Abigail Adams, 2 September 1777," *Founders Online*, National Archives, https://founders.archives.gov/documents/Adams/04-02-02-0271.
30. John Ferling, *Almost a Miracle: The American Victory in the War of Independence* (New York: Oxford University Press, 2007), Kindle edition, loc. 4383.
31. Toast #1, *Massachusetts Spy*, 10-30-1777.

32. Thomas Fleming, *Washington's Secret War: The Hidden History of Valley Forge* (New World City, 2016), Kindle edition, loc. 3585.
33. John Ferling, *The Ascent of George Washington: The Hidden Political Genius of an American Icon* (Bloomsbury Press, 2009), Kindle edition, loc. 3260.
34. Fleming, loc. 5596.
35. Toasts #3, 11, *New-York Gazette and Weekly Mercury*, 1-3-1780.
36. *Freeman's Journal*, 4-28-1778.
37. Toasts #3–5, *New Jersey Gazette*, 2-17-1779.
38. Toast #7, *Providence Gazette*, 2-9-1782.
39. Toasts #11–13, *Continental Journal*, 3-4-1779.
40. "Toasts at an Independence Day Banquet, [5 July 1779]," *Founders Online*, National Archives, https://founders.archives.gov/documents/Franklin/01-30-02-0032.
41. Toast #12, *American Journal*, 3-17-1781; Toast #9, 7-11-1781.
42. Toasts #11, 9, *Independent Ledger*, 7-9-1781.
43. Toast #8, *Massachusetts Spy*, 11-22-1781.
44. Eutaw Springs was the last battle fought in the Carolinas, on 9-8-1781. Toast #9, *New-Jersey Gazette*, 10-31-1781.
45. Toast #11, *New-Jersey Gazette*, 11-7-1781.
46. Toast #4, *Massachusetts Spy*, 11-8-1781.
47. Robert Middlekauff, *The Glorious Cause: The American Revolution, 1763–1784* (New York: Oxford University Press, 1982, 2005), Kindle edition, loc. 10217.
48. T. Cole Jones, *Captives of Liberty: Prisoners of War and the Politics of Vengeance in the American Revolution* (Philadelphia: University of Pennsylvania Press, 2020), p. 236.
49. Waldstreicher, *In the Midst*, p. 65.
50. Toast #2, given in Worcester, *Salem Gazette*, 5-29-1783.
51. Brett Palfreyman, "Toasting," https://www.mountvernon.org/library/digitalhistory/digital-encyclopedia/article/toasting/.
52. Toasts #2, 4, 11, *Continental Journal*, 2-13-1783.
53. Dickson, p. 19.
54. Toast #10, *Independent Gazetteer*, 3-4-1783.
55. Toast #9, *New-Jersey Gazette*, 4-16-1783.
56. Toast #8, given in Brunswick, New Jersey; Toast #7, Snyder's tavern, *New-Jersey Gazette*, 4-30-1783.
57. Toast #11, *Salem Gazette*, 5-1-1783.
58. Toast #9, *Independent Gazetteer*, 5-3-1783.
59. Head, p. 47.
60. Toast #10, *Providence Gazette*, 6-10-1783.
61. Toast #13, *Independent Gazette*, 7-12-1783.
62. Toasts #7, 9, *Connecticut Journal*, 7-9-1783.
63. Toast #8, *Vermont Gazette*, 12-11-1783.
64. Toast #11, *New-Jersey Gazette*, 12-16-1783.
65. Joseph J. Ellis, *His Excellency: George Washington* (New York: Alfred A. Knopf, 2004), p. 158.
66. Purcell, p. 86.
67. Cotlar, p. 72.
68. Seth Cotlar, *Tom Paine's America* (Charlottesville: University of Virginia Press, 2011), p. 72.
69. Jill Lepore. *These Truths: A History of the United States* (New York: W.W. Norton & Company, 2018), p. 108.
70. Head, p. 215.
71. Bob Drury and Tom Clavin, *Valley Forge* (New York: Simon & Schuster, 2018), p. 353.
72. Toast #11, *Political Intelligencer*, 12-9-1783.

Chapter 4

1. Toast #8, *Massachusetts Centinel*, 7-7-1787.
2. Toast #2, *Providence Gazette*, 5-29-1784.
3. Toast #13, *New-York Journal*, 5-15-1788.
4. Toast #3, *United States Chronicle*, 7-17-1788.
5. Purcell, p. 58.
6. Axelrod, p. 343.
7. David M. Kennedy, et al., *The Brief American Pageant: A History of the Republic* (Boston: Cengage Learning, 2016), p. 127.

8. Edward Larson, *The Return of George Washington: Uniting the States, 1783–1789* (NY: HarperCollins, 2014), Kindle edition.
9. Travers, pp. 6–7.
10. Travers, p. 50.
11. Waldstreicher, *In the Midst*, pp. 68–69.
12. *Ibid.*, p. 70.
13. *Ibid.*, p. 71.
14. Gordon S. Wood, *The Radicalism of the American Revolution* (New York: Alfred A. Knopf, 1991), pp. 222–223.
15. Forman, p. 122.
16. Toasts #2, 4–5, *Litchfield Monitor*, 2-8-1785.
17. Toasts #2, 4, 13, *Daily Advertiser*, 1-5-1787.
18. Toast #13, *American Mercury*, 7-12-1784.
19. Toast #11, *Providence Gazette*, 5-29-1784.
20. Toast #13, *New-Jersey Gazette*, 9-6-1784.
21. *Salem Gazette*, 11-9-1784.
22. John C. Miller, *Sam Adams: Pioneer in Propaganda* (Stanford, CA: Stanford University Press, 1936), p. 346.
23. Toast #13, *Pennsylvania Packet*, 1-1-1784.
24. Toasts 1, 9–10, *Independent Gazetteer*, 3-1-1787.
25. *New-Hampshire Gazette*, 6-19-1784.
26. *South-Carolina Weekly Gazette*, 7-21-1784.
27. *South-Carolina and General Advertiser*, 7-6-1784.
28. *South Carolina Weekly Gazette*, 11-15-1785.
29. *New-York Packet*, 5-27-1784.
30. Toast #13, *Independent Journal*, 2-5-1785.
31. Toasts #8–9, *State Gazette of South Carolina*, 7-14-1785.
32. Waldstreicher, pp. 87–88.
33. Toasts #10, 12, *Providence Gazette*, 7-8-1786.
34. Toast #7, *Charleston Morning Post*, 11-15-1786.
35. Leonard L. Richards, *Shays's Rebellion: The American Revolution's Final Battle* (Philadelphia: University of Pennsylvania Press, 2002), p. 26.
36. Walstreicher, p. 64.
37. Richards, p. 2.
38. Toast #11, *Massachusetts Centinel*, 7-7-1787.
39. Toast #7, *Salem Mercury*, 7-10-1787.
40. Toast #5, *Massachusetts Centinel*, 7-14-1787.
41. *Providence Gazette*, 8-4-1787.
42. *Daily Advertiser*, 2-14-1788.
43. Toast #9, *Maryland Journal*, 10-19-1787.
44. Toast #4, *Connecticut Courant*, 12-31-1787.
45. *Independent Gazetteer*, 12-21-1787.
46. Toasts #2–7, 10, *Independent Chronicle*, 2-21-1788.
47. Toast #13, *New-Hampshire Gazette*, 5-15-1788.
48. Toast #10, *Independent Chronicle*, 6-12-1788.
49. Toast #4, *New-Hampshire Spy*, 7-1-1788.
50. Toasts #9, 13, *Impartial Gazetteer and Saturday's Evening Post*, 7-5-1788.
51. Waldstreicher, pp. 99–100.
52. Toast #13, *New-Hampshire Recorder*, 7-1-1788.
53. Toast #10, *Independent Gazetteer*, 7-19-1788.
54. Toasts #2, 4, *Newport Herald*, 7-17-1788.
55. Toast #10, *Carlisle Gazette*, 8-6-1788.
56. *New-Hampshire Spy*, 9-20-1788.
57. Toast #11, *Independent Chronicle*, 6-12-1788.

Chapter 5

1. Toast #10, *Daily Advertiser*, 7-6-1792.
2. Volunteer, *New-Hampshire Spy*, 6-1-1791.
3. Toast #5, *Daily Advertiser*, 7-6-1792.
4. Toast #2, *Concord Herald*, 7-11-1792.
5. Matthew R. Costello, *The Property of the Nation: George Washington's Tomb, Mount Vernon, and the Memory of the First President* (Lawrence: University of Kansas Press, 2019), p. 6.
6. Toast #2, *New-York Daily Gazette*, 5-14-1789.
7. Toast #2, *New-York Packet*, 3-10-1789.
8. Toast #1, *New-Hampshire Gazette*, 7-9-1789.
9. Toast #8, *Massachusetts Centinel*, 6-3-1789.
10. Editors of *Horizon Magazine*, *The French Revolution* (New York: American

Heritage Publishing Company, 1965), pp. 37–39.

11. Matthew Rainbow Hale, "On their Tiptoes: Political Time and Newspapers during the Advent of the Radicalized French Revolution, circa 1792–1793," in *Journal of the Early Republic*, Vol. 29, No. 2 (Summer 2009), 191–218; p. 194.

12. Stanley Elkins and Eric McKitrick, *The Age of Federalism: The Early American Republic, 1788–1800* (New York: Oxford University Press, 1993), p. 309.

13. Gordon S. Wood, *Empire of Liberty: A History of the Early Republic, 1789–1815* (New York: Oxford University Press, 2009), pp. 174–175.

14. Toast #2, *New-Hampshire Gazette*, 11-5-1789.

15. Toast #7, *Freeman's Journal*, 12-30-1789.

16. Toasts #9–10, *New-Hampshire Gazette*, 7-8-1790.

17. *New York Gazette*, 12-8-1790.

18. *Cumberland Gazette*, 2-22-1790.

19. Toasts #6–7, *Newport Herald*, 3-26-1789.

20. Toast #7, *Federal Gazette*, 7-15-1790.

21. Toast #12, *New-York Journal*, 7-16-1790.

22. Toasts #6–8, *Newport Herald*, 8-19-1790.

23. *Daily Advertiser*, 8-26-1790.

24. Volunteer 1, *New-York Daily Gazette*, 2-25-1791.

25. Toasts #6–8, *Vermont Gazette*, 3-21-1791.

26. Toast #6, *Herald of Vermont*, 6-25-1792.

27. *Columbian Herald*, 6-23-1791.

28. Toast #1, *Dunlap's American Daily Advertiser*, 7-4-1791.

29. *Spooner's Vermont Journal*, 5-24-1791.

30. Toast #5, *City Gazette*, 6-6-1791.

31. *Gazette of the United States*, 9-21-1791.

32. Toast #14, *Massachusetts Spy*, 6-14-1792.

33. Toasts #10, 14, *City Gazette*, 5-14-1791.

34. Toast #6, *Weekly Museum*, 5-14-1791.

35. Toast #6, *City Gazette*, 5-27-1791.

36. Toast #14, *Independent Gazette*, 6-4-1791.

37. Toast #6, *City Gazette*, 6-6-1791.

38. *Gazette of the United States*, 7-16-1791.

39. Elkins and McKitrick, pp. 237–238.

40. Toasts #6, 11, *Independent Chronicle*, 7-17-1791.

41. Toast #8, *Daily Advertiser*, 12-29-1792.

42. Toast #7, *New-York Daily Gazette*, 7-17-1792.

43. Cotlar, p. 80.

44. Travers, pp. 90–91.

45. *Argus*, 9-20-1791.

46. Toast #5, *Vermont Gazette*, 9-5-1791.

47. Waldstreicher, p. 126.

48. "From John Adams to Thomas Brand Hollis, 19 February 1792," *Founders Online*, National Archives, https://founders.archives.gov/documents/Adams/99-02-02-1315.

49. *Federal Gazette*, 7-28-1792.

50. Waldstreicher, p. 128; *National Gazette*, 7-7-1792.

51. Toast #3, *Newport Mercury*, 7-30-1792.

52. Ron Chernow, *Alexander Hamilton* (New York: Penguin Books, 2004), p. 432.

53. Duthille, pp. 7–8.

54. A. Young, *The Shoemaker and the Tea Party: Memory and the American Revolution* (Boston: Beacon Press, 1999), p. 111; Rosemarie Zagarri, *Revolutionary Backlash: Women and Politics in the Early American Republic* (Philadelphia: University of Pennsylvania Press, 2007), p. 85.

55. Toasts #12, 14, *Baltimore Evening Post*, 7-24-1792.

56. Toasts #16–17, *National Gazette*, 8-1-1792.

57. "An American No. I [4 August 1792]," *Founders Online*, National Archives, https://founders.archives.gov/documents/Hamilton/01-12-02-0126.

58. Toasts #1, 4, 7, *Federal Gazette*, 6-25-1792.

59. Toasts #5, 7, *Daily Advertiser*, 7-6-1792.

60. Toasts #4, 7, 9, *Diary*, 7-4-1792.

61. Toast #11, *City Gazette*, 7-6-1792.

62. Suzanne M. Desan, *Living the French Revolution and the Age of Napoleon: Course Guidebook* (Chantilly, VA: Teaching Company, 2013), pp. 139–140.

63. Toasts #9–10, *City Gazette*, 10-30-1792.

64. Toast #3, *Diary*, 1-5-1793.

65. From Ulster, *Catskill Packet*, 3-4-1793.
66. Toast #4, *Dunlap's American Daily Advertiser*, 2-7-1793.
67. Toast #11, *Dunlap's American Daily Advertiser*, 2-26-1793.
68. Toast #12, *Daily Advertiser*, 12-25-1793.
69. Toast #16, *Greenleaf's New-York Journal*, 7-22-1796.

Chapter 6

1. Toast #13, *Washington Spy*, 7-14-1795.
2. Toast #8, *Aurora General Advertiser*, 11-29-1794.
3. Toast #2, *Greenleaf's New York Journal*, 8-5-1795.
4. Volunteer toast #3, *Washington Spy*, 7-14-1796.
5. Ellis, p. 220.
6. *General Advertiser*, 3-15-1793.
7. Philip S. Foner, ed, *The Democratic-Republican Societies, 1790–1800* (Westport, CT: Greenwood Press, 1976), p. 23.
8. Ibid., p. 429.
9. Toast #9, *State Gazette of South Carolina*, 2-13-1793.
10. Toast #6, *Mail*, 12-26-1792.
11. Toast #16, *Federal Gazette*, 7-29-1793.
12. Jeremy D. Popkin, *A New World Begins: The History of the French Revolution* (New York: Basic Books, 2019), p. 172.
13. Toast #7, *Columbian Centinel*, 2-23-1793.
14. Toast #10, *Independent Chronicle*, 2-14-1793.
15. Toast #9, *Salem Gazette*, 2-26-1793.
16. Toast #9, *Gazette of the United States*, 7-20-1793.
17. *Columbian Herald*, 9-19-1793.
18. Jay Winik, *The Great Upheaval: America and the Birth of the Modern World, 1788–1800* (New York: Harper Perennial, 2007), pp. 465–466; Chernow, p. 437.
19. Harlow Giles Unger, *"Mr. President": George Washington and the Making of the Nation's Highest Office* (Boston: Da Capo Books, 2013), p. 163.
20. Thompson, *Rum, Punch and Revolution*, pp. 199–200.
21. Toasts #4, 6–7, *Diary*, 6-5-1793.
22. *United States Chronicle*, 6-20-1793.
23. David McCullough, *John Adams* (New York: Simon & Schuster, 2001), pp. 443–444.
24. *State Gazette of South Carolina*, 8-14-1793.
25. Toast #7, *Herald of the United States*, 10-5-1793.
26. Toasts #7–9, *Gazette of the United States*, 6-8-1793.
27. *National Gazette*, 6-12-1793.
28. *Virginia Chronicle*, 6-29-1793.
29. McDonald, *Confounding Father: Thomas Jefferson's Image in His Own Time* (Charlottesville: University of VA Press, 2016), p. 39.
30. Newman, p. 63.
31. Toasts #7, 11, *Massachusetts Mercury*, 7-5-1793.
32. Toast #14, *Albany Register*, 7-29-1793.
33. *National Gazette*, 7-17-1793.
34. Newman, p. 141.
35. *Diary*, 2-11-1794.
36. *Gazette of the United States*, 2-8-1794.
37. Toasts #3, 8, 10–11, *Daily Advertiser*, 2-26-1794.
38. Volunteer toasts #1–2, *Daily Advertiser*, 3-3-1794.
39. Toasts #7, *Connecticut Courant*, 3-17-1794.
40. *Independent Gazetteer*, 3-8-1794.
41. *New Jersey Journal*, 4-30-1794.
42. Toasts #12–13, *Baltimore Daily Intelligencer*, 5-8-1794.
43. Toasts #4, 6, 9, *Greenleaf's New York Journal*, 6-28-1794.
44. Newman, p. 93.
45. Toast #13, *United States Chronicle*, 7-10-1794.
46. Toast #2, *Dunlap's American Daily Advertiser*, 7-17-1794.
47. *United States Chronicle*, 7-31-1794.
48. Toast #12, *Virginia Chronicle*, 2-22-1794.
49. Toast #7, *Dunlap's American Daily Advertiser*, 3-17-1794.
50. Toast #9, *Newport Mercury*, 7-8-1794.
51. Toast #3, *Diary*, 7-5-1794.
52. Toast #8, *Baltimore Daily Advertiser*, 7-17-1794.
53. Toast #9, *American Herald of Liberty*, 7-22-1794.
54. Toast #9. *Aurora General Advertiser*, 2-25-1795.

55. Ellis, p. 224.
56. Toast #15, *Daily Advertiser*, 9-24-1794.
57. Toast #15, *Gazette of the United States*, 11-5-1794.
58. Toast #12, *Gazette of the United States*, 2-18-1795.
59. Purcell, pp. 92–93.
60. Toast #8, 2-25-1795, *New-Jersey Journal*.
61. Toast #8, 7-15-1795, *New-Jersey Journal*.
62. Toast #6, *Medley or Newbedford Marine Journal*, 2-13-1795.
63. Toast #9, *Imperial Herald*, 7-7-1795.
64. *Federal Intelligencer*, 3-12-1795.
65. "To George Washington from John Jay, 6 March 1795," Founders Online, National Archives, https://founders.archives.gov/documents/Washington/05-17-02-0419.
66. *City Gazette*, 4-18-1795.
67. Ellis, p. 227.
68. Unger, p. 210.
69. Toast #10, *Impartial Herald*, 7-11-1795.
70. Toast #1, *Western Star*, 7-28-1795.
71. Toast #3, *Eagle*, 5-16-1796.
72. Ellis, p. 227.
73. Nancy Eisenberg, *Fallen Founder: The Life of Aaron Burr* (New York: Penguin Books, 2007), Kindle edition.
74. Newman, p. 148.
75. David O. Stewart, *George Washington: The Political Rise of America's Founding Father* (New York: Dutton, Penguin Random House, 2021), p. 388.
76. *Courier*, 7-18-1795.
77. Toasts drunk by the Tammany Society, *Newport Mercury*, 7-14-1795.
78. Toast #13, *Washington Spy*, 7-14-1795; "via juncta in uno" is translated as "three joined in one."
79. Toast #9, *New-Jersey Journal*, 7-15-1795.
80. Given by the Cincinnati of Newcastle, Delaware, *Greenleaf's New York Journal*, 7-15-1795.
81. *Guardian of Freedom*, 8-20-1795.
82. Toast #10, *Vermont Gazette*, 9-11-1795.
83. Toast #13, *Daily Advertiser*, 1-3-1795.
84. Toast #8, *Daily Advertiser*, 11-13-1795.
85. Toast #15, *Argus*, 11-27-1795.
86. Toast #11, *Greenleaf's New York Journal*, 5-20-1796.
87. Toast #5, *Federal Gazette*, 1-22-1796.
88. *Independent Gazette*, 7-20-1796.
89. Toasts #2, 5, *Spooner's Vermont Journal*, 11-4-1796.
90. Toast #11, *Washington Spy*, 3-10-1796.
91. Newman, p. 64.
92. Costello, p. 21.
93. *Wood's Newark Gazette*, 2-24-1796.
94. *Columbian Centinel*, 3-9-1796.
95. "Abigail Adams to John Adams, [28] February 1796," Founders Online, National Archives, https://founders.archives.gov/documents/Adams/04-11-02-0096.
96. Toast #3, *Columbian Centinel*, 2-24-1796.
97. "Abigail Adams to John Adams, [28] February 1796," Founders Online, National Archives, https://founders.archives.gov/documents/Adams/04-11-02-0096.
98. Toast #12, *Herald*, 7-16-1796.
99. Toast #5, *Gazette of the United States*, 7-14-1796.
100. McDonald, p. 51.
101. *Claypoole's American Daily Advertiser*, 7-22-1796.
102. Travers, *Celebrating the Fourth*, pp. 99–101.
103. Toast #1, *Herald of the United States*, 10-15-1796.
104. Toasts #3–4, 13, *Federal Gazette*, 12-7-1796.
105. Toast #4, *Eastern Herald*, 10-24-1796.

Chapter 7

1. Toast #2, *Philadelphia Gazette*, 7-10-1798.
2. Toast #3, *Albany Gazette*, 8-4-1797.
3. Toast #2, *Genius of Liberty*, 11-8-1798.
4. Toast #8, *Daily Advertiser*, 9-24-1798.
5. Toast #8, *Columbian Centinel*, 3-4-1797.
6. Given in Salem, Massachusetts, *Porcupine's Gazette*, 3-8-1797.
7. Toast #9, *Gazette of the United States*, 3-7-1797.
8. Toast #1, *Porcupine's Gazette*, 3-8-1797.
9. Cotlar, pp. 97–98.

Notes—Chapter 7

10. Purcell, p. 139.
11. "To George Washington from Francis Peyton, Jr., 20 March 1797," *Founders Online*, National Archives, https://founders.archives.gov/documents/Washington/06-01-02-0030.
12. Ellis, pp. 239–240.
13. *Ibid.*, p. 222.
14. Toast #4, *Centinel of Freedom*, 1-25-1797.
15. Toast #8, *Claypoole's American Daily Advertiser*, 1-31-1797.
16. Toast #7, *Diary*, 2-7-1797.
17. Robert Kelley, "Ideology and Political Culture from Jefferson to Nixon," in *The American Historical Review*, Volume 82, No. 3 (June 1977), 531–562; p. 539.
18. Travers, p. 89.
19. *Porcupine's Gazette*, 8-4-1798.
20. Rozbicki, p. 108.
21. Newman, p. 111.
22. Toast #7, *Centinel of Freedom*, 2-8-1797.
23. Purcell, p. 107.
24. Toasts #2, 5, 9, 13, *Diary*, 2-25-1797.
25. Joseph J. Ellis, *First Family: Abigail and John Adams* (New York: Alfred A. Knopf, 2010), p. 176.
26. McDonald, p. 64.
27. Toasts #2–3, *Impartial Herald*, 2-24-1797.
28. *Porcupine's Gazette*, 4-15-1797.
29. Toast #12, *Columbian Mirror*, 7-6-1797.
30. Toast #8, *Albany Centinel*, 7-11-1797.
31. Toast #2, *Carey's Daily Advertiser a Literary, Political and Commercial Evening Gazette*, 7-19-1797.
32. Toast #3, *Albany Gazette*, 8-4-1797.
33. Toast #14, *Daily Advertiser*, 7-6-1797.
34. Toast #12, *Daily Advertiser*, 7-7-1797.
35. Toast #15, *Carlisle Gazette*, 7-5-1797.
36. Toast #16, *Connecticut Courant*, 7-10-1797.
37. *Porcupine's Gazette*, 7-13-1797.
38. Toast #10, *Newport Mercury*, 8-29-1797.
39. Toast #14, *Diary*, 8-24-1797.
40. Toasts #9–11, *American Mercury*, 10-30-1797.
41. Toast #10, *Porcupine's Gazette*, 11-3-1797.
42. *Bee*, 11-1-1797.
43. Toast #7, *Federal Gazette*, 2-19-1798.
44. Toast #8, *Herald of Liberty*, 2-26-1798.
45. "William Cranch to John Quincy Adams, 5 March 1798," *Founders Online*, National Archives, https://founders.archives.gov/documents/Adams/04-12-02-0233.
46. *Gazette of the United States*, 5-4-1798.
47. "From Alexander Hamilton to George Washington, 19 May 1798," *Founders Online*, National Archives, https://founders.archives.gov/documents/Hamilton/01-21-02-0258.
48. Wood, *Empire of Liberty*, p. 241.
49. Chernow, p. 549.
50. Wood, pp. 241–242.
51. Chernow, p. 549.
52. McCullough, p. 497.
53. Winik, p. 525.
54. McCullough, p. 498.
55. Chernow, pp. 550–551.
56. Toast #2, *Philadelphia Gazette*, 7-10-1798.
57. Toast #16, *Amherst Village Messenger*, 7-21-1798.
58. Toast #4, *Maryland Herald and Hager's-Town Weekly Advertiser*, 7-12-1798.
59. Deerfield, Massachusetts, *Mirrour*, 7-24-1798.
60. McCullough, p. 499.
61. Toast #2, *Virginia Herald*, 8-7-1798.
62. Toast #1, *Daily Advertiser*, 8-27-1798.
63. "Abigail Adams to John Quincy Adams, 20 July 1798," *Founders Online*, National Archives, https://founders.archives.gov/documents/Adams/04-13-02-0089.
64. McCullough, p. 499.
65. Toast #7, *Alexandria Times*, 6-29-1798.
66. Toast #13, *Amherst Village Messenger*, 7-7-1798.
67. Toast #7, *Portland Gazette*, 7-9-1798.
68. Toast #12, *Northern Centinel*, 7-23-1798.
69. Toast #13, *Federal Gazette*, 7-11-1798.
70. Toast #11, *Gazette Portland*, 7-9-1798.

71. Toast #7, *Massachusetts Spy*, 7-11-1798.
72. Toast #13, *Litchfield Monitor*, 11-14-1798.
73. Toast #6, *Gazette of the United States*, 11-5-1798.
74. Toast #16, *Commercial Advertiser*, 4-26-1798.
75. Toast #5, *Federal Gazette*, 8-1-1798.
76. Volunteer toast, *Russel's Echo*, 7-11-1798.
77. Toast #5, *Bee*, 7-8-1798.
78. Toasts #5–6, *United States Chronicle*, 7-12-1798.
79. Toasts #1, 5, *Federal Galaxy*, 7-17-1798.
80. Toast #14, *Russel's Echo*, 7-11-1798.
81. Toast #19, *Amherst Village Messenger*, 7-21-1798.
82. *Federal Gazette*, 7-9-1798.
83. *Federal Gazette*, 7-19-1798.
84. Toast #16, *Gazette of the United States*, 8-6-1798.
85. *Gazette of the United States*, 8-9-1798.
86. *Farmer's Weekly Museum*, 7-17-1798.
87. Toast #3, *Western Star*, 9-4-1798.
88. Waldstreicher, p. 165.
89. Toast #15, *Federal Gazette*, 9-19-1798.
90. Toast #9, *Albany Centinel*, 7-3-1798.
91. Toast #9, *Maryland Herald and Hagers-Town Weekly Advertiser*, 7-12-1798.
92. Toast #10, *Gazette of the United States*, 7-14-1798.

Chapter 8

1. Toast #11, *New-Jersey Journal*, 7-9-1799.
2. Toast #3, *Connecticut Gazette*, 7-10-1799.
3. Toast #9, *Farmer's Weekly Museum*, 7-22-1798.
4. Toast #10, *Centinel of Liberty*, 7-11-1800.
5. Toast #16, *Albany Gazette*, 7-7-1799.
6. Toast #10, *Porcupine's Gazette*, 8-4-1798.
7. Wood, *Empire of Liberty*, p. 247.
8. McCullough, p. 249.
9. Wood, p. 248.
10. *Ibid.*, pp. 249–250; Elkins & McKitrick, p. 591.
11. Elkins & McKitrick, p. 592.
12. Thomas E. Ricks, *First Principles: What America's Founders Learned From the Greeks and Romans and How That Shaped Our Country* (New York: Harper-Collins, 2020), p. 240.
13. Chernow, p. 570.
14. Wood, p. 258.
15. *Albany Centinel*, 8-7-1798.
16. Toast #10, *Weekly Oracle*, 7-14-1798.
17. Toast #9, *Newport Mercury*, 8-13-1799.
18. Toast #12, *American Mercury*, 7-11-1799.
19. Newman, p. 175.
20. Toast #7, *Daily Advertiser*, 7-19-1798.
21. Toasts #7, 11, *Carey's United States Recorder*, 7-17-1798.
22. Toast #1, *Aurora General Advertiser*, 7-20-1798.
23. Toast #2, *Greanleaf's New York Journal*, 7-7-1798.
24. Toast #2, *New-Jersey Journal*, 7-17-1798.
25. Toasts #4, 9–12, "Toasts for an American Dinner, [4 July] 1798," Founders Online, National Archives, https://founders.archives.gov/documents/Madison/01-17-02-0109.
26. Caryn E. Neumann, "Matthew Lyon," https://www.mtsu.edu/first-amendment/article/1442/matthew-lyon.
27. Volunteer toast #2, *New-Jersey Journal*, 7-9-1799.
28. Toast #5, *Carlisle Gazette*, 7-10-1799.
29. *Impartial Herald*, 8-7-1798.
30. Toasts # 3, 5, *Aurora General Advertiser*, 7-26-1798.
31. Toast #9, *Massachusetts Mercury*, 9-17-1798.
32. Toast #8, *Rights of Man*, 9-5-1798.
33. Fawn M. Brodie, *Thomas Jefferson: An Intimate History* (New York: W.W. Norton & Company, 1974), p. 311.
34. McCullough, pp. 520–521.
35. McKitrick & Elkins, pp. 719–720.
36. Chernow, pp. 573–574.
37. See this article for a precise explanation of the legislation: http://www.u-s-history.com/pages/h466.html.
38. Toasts #13–14, *Gazette*, 3-4-1799.
39. *Philadelphia Gazette*, 3-19-1799.
40. Toast #16, *Connecticut Journal*, 7-31-1799.

Notes—Chapter 8

41. Toast #6, *Oracle of Dauphin*, 7-24-1799.
42. *Bee*, 7-31-1799.
43. Toast #8, *Massachusetts Mercury*, 9-7-1798.
44. Toast #7, *Massachusetts Mercury*, 9-18-1798.
45. *Courier of New Hampshire*, 7-27-1799.
46. Toast #12, *Daily Advertiser*, 9-13-1798.
47. Toast #5, *Genius of Liberty*, 11-8-1798.
48. Toast #19, *Philadelphia Gazette*, 11-7-1798.
49. *Greenleaf's New York Journal*, 11-14-1798.
50. Toast #13, *Telegraphe and Daily Advertiser*, 2-26-1799.
51. Toast #16, *Massachusetts Mercury*, 2-26-1799.
52. Toast #8, *Massachusetts Mercury*, 2-26-1799.
53. Toast #7, *Carlisle Gazette*, 2-27-1799.
54. Toast #6, *New-Hampshire Gazette*, 2-27-1799.
55. Chernow, p. 560.
56. *Massachusetts Mercury*, 12-28-1798.
57. Toast #19, *Berkshire Gazette*, 1-2-1799.
58. Jane Clark, "Gallatin: A Voice of Moderation During the Whiskey Rebellion," https://www.nps.gov/frhi/learn/historyculture/gallatin-a-voice-of-moderation-during-the-whiskey-rebellion.htm.
59. Toast #6, *Aurora General Advertiser*, 2-2-1799.
60. Toast #4, *Carlisle Gazette*, 7-10-1799; "Sempronius" refers to a character in Joseph Addison's play *Cato*.
61. Toast #5, *Vergennes Gazette and Vermont and New-York Advertiser*, 3-7-1799.
62. Toast #8, *Gazette of the United States*, 7-10-1799.
63. Toast #2, *Aurora General Advertiser*, 5-6-1799.
64. Toast #4, *Aurora General Advertiser*, 5-13-1799.
65. Toast #3, *Greenleaf's New York Journal*, 7-6-1799.
66. *Journal of the Times*, 7-23-1799.
67. *Albany Centinel*, 7-19-1799.
68. *Bee*, 7-31-1799.
69. Wood, pp. 272–273.
70. McCullough, p. 534.
71. Toast #5, *Carolina Gazette*, 7-10-1799.
72. York, ME, Toast #14, *United States Oracle*, 7-12-1800.
73. Toast #5, *Oriental Trumpet*, 7-9-1800.
74. Toast #2, *Maryland Herald and Hager's-Town Weekly Advertiser*, 7-17-1800.
75. Toast #11, *American Mercury*, 7-17-1800.
76. Toast #10, *New-Hampshire Gazette*, 7-8-1800.
77. Toast #6, *Oriental Trumpet*, 7-9-1800.
78. Toast #9, *New Hampshire Gazette*, 7-8-1800.
79. Toast #8, *Spooner's Vermont Journal*, 7-9-1799.
80. *Kennebunk Gazette*, 7-15-1799.
81. Toasts #2, 9, *Maryland Herald and Hager's-Town Weekly Advertiser*, 8-22-1799.
82. Ellis, pp. 268–269.
83. Toast #7, *Daily Advertiser*, 7-7-1800.
84. Toast #5, *Columbian Museum*, 7-8-1800.
85. Toast #3, *Providence Gazette*, 7-12-1800.
86. Toast #3, *Gazette of the United States*, 7-16-1800.
87. Volunteer, *Genius of Liberty*, 7-17-1800.
88. "Abigail Adams to Mary Smith Cranch, 15 March 1800," *Founders Online*, National Archives, https://founders.archives.gov/documents/Adams/04-14-02-0097.
89. *Daily Advertiser*, 7-12-1800.
90. Newman, p. 113.
91. *New Hampshire Sentinel*, 7-26-1800.
92. McCullough, p. 541.
93. Toast #15, *Maryland Herald and Hager's-Town Weekly Advertiser*, 7-10-1800; Toast #13, *Carolina Gazette*, 7-24-1800.
94. Toast #7, *American Citizen*, 7-7-1800.
95. Toast #8, *Vermont Gazette*, 8-11-1800.
96. Toast #3, *Eastern Herald*, 7-14-1800.
97. Toast #4, *Gazette of the United States*, 7-11-1800.
98. McCullough, p. 549.
99. *Oriental Trumpet*, 11-5-1800.

100. Toast #14, *Gazette of the United States*, 11-7-1800.
101. "To John Adams from William Tudor, Sr., 5 November 1800," *Founders Online*, National Archives, https://founders.archives.gov/documents/Adams/99-02-02-4672.
102. McCullough, p. 552.
103. "From Alexander Hamilton to Oliver Wolcott, Junior, [December 1800]," *Founders Online*, National Archives, https://founders.archives.gov/documents/Hamilton/01-25-02-0151.
104. "From Alexander Hamilton to James A. Bayard, 27 December 1800," *Founders Online*, National Archives, https://founders.archives.gov/documents/Hamilton/01-25-02-0146.
105. Chernow, p. 638.
106. *Philadelphia Gazette*, 11-4-1800.

Chapter 9

1. Toast #2, *American Citizen*, 7-9-1801.
2. *Salem Register*, 7-21-1803.
3. Toast #1, *Alexandria Expositor for the Country*, 8-1-1804.
4. *Serious Considerations on the Election of a President: Addressed to the Citizens of the United States*. New York: Printed by John Furnam, 1800, p. 24.
5. Toast #11, *American Citizen*, 3-6-1801.
6. Toast #8, *Guardian of Liberty*, 3-7-1801.
7. Toast #1, *Centinel of Freedom*, 3-24-1801.
8. Waldstreicher, p. 190.
9. Toasts # 6, 8, 11, *American Citizen*, 2-9-1801.
10. Waldstreicher, p. 253.
11. Toast #5, *Centinel of Freedom*, 3-17-1801.
12. Toasts #4, 15, *Centinel of Freedom*, 3-24-1801.
13. "From Abigail Smith Adams to Thomas Boylston Adams, 22 April 1801," *Founders Online*, National Archives, https://founders.archives.gov/documents/Adams/99-03-02-0949.
14. Toast #16, *Rural Gazette*, 7-13-1801.
15. Toast #10, *Hampshire Gazette*, 7-8-1801.
16. Toast #4, *Newburyport Herald*, 7-14-1801.
17. Toast #8, *Bee*, 3-25-1801.
18. Volunteer toast by Samuel Jones, *Virginia Argus*, 4-14-1801.
19. Toast #7, *American Mercury*, 3-19-1801.
20. *Philadelphia Gazette*, 5-11-1801.
21. Toast #6, *Hudson Gazette*, 6-2-1801.
22. *Washington Federalist*, 7-13-1801.
23. Newman, p. 116.
24. Toast #1, *Washington Federalist*, 7-1-1801.
25. Toast #8, *Impartial Observer*, 7-18-1801.
26. Toast #10, *Stewart Kentucky Herald*, 7-14-1801.
27. Toast #16, *National Intelligencer and Washington Advertiser*, 7-17-1801.
28. *Alexandria Times*, 8-20-1801.
29. Both toasts appeared in different issues of the *National Intelligencer*: #13, 2-6-1801; #14, 7-10-1801, Francis's Hotel, Philadelphia.
30. Toast #11, *Washington Federalist*, 2-24-1801.
31. Toast #2, *Daily Advertiser*, 7-15-1801.
32. Toast #3, *Carolina Gazette*, 4-30-1801.
33. Toast #3, *Middlesex Gazette*, 4-11-1801.
34. *American and Commercial Daily Advertiser*, 11-21-1801.
35. Toast #7, *Evening Post*, 12-31-1801.
36. Toasts #11–12, *National Intelligencer*, 2-6-1801.
37. Wood, *Empire of Liberty*, p. 634.
38. Volunteer toast #3, *Gazette of the United States*, 6-26-1801.
39. Toast #13, *Fincastle Weekly Advertiser*, 7-10-1801.
40. Toast #9, *New Hampshire Sentinel*, 7-25-1801.
41. *New-Hampshire Gazette*: Toast #2, 7-20-1802; Toast #4, 7-27-1802.
42. Toast #16, *Messenger*, 3-23-1802.
43. *American Mercury*: Toast #11, 4-1-1802; Toast #9, 7-15-1802.
44. Toasts #2, 7–8, *Windham Herald*, 3-4-1802.
45. *American Mercury*, 7-22-1802.
46. *United States Chronicle*, 7-15-1802.
47. McDonald, p. 121.
48. *Salem Register*, 7-15-1802.
49. Toasts #3, 11, *Commercial Advertiser*, 7-19-1802.
50. Toast # 5, *New-York Herald*, 7-12-1802.

51. Toast # 4, 9-1-1802.
52. Toast #7, *Salem Register*, 8-23-1802.
53. Rufus King, *The life and correspondence of Rufus King, comprising his letters, private and official, his public documents, and his speeches* (New York: G.P. Putnam's Sons, 184–1900), IV, 103.
54. "To Alexander Hamilton from Gouverneur Morris, 11 March 1802," *Founders Online*, National Archives, https://founders.archives.gov/documents/Hamilton/01-25-02-0301.
55. Toast #4, *American Citizen*, 7-12-1802.
56. Toast #5, *American Citizen*, 7-13-1802.
57. Toast #4, *Virginia Argus*, 7-17-1802.
58. Toast #6, *Telegraphe and Daily Advertiser*, 7-9-1802.
59. Volunteer 1, *American Citizen*, 7-13-1802.
60. Toast #3, *Carlisle, Gazette*, 7-14-1802.
61. Given by the Philadelphia Blues, *Evening Post*, 7-17-1802; opening the door of the Temple of Janus is a call to war.
62. "From the Aurora"; Volunteer 2, *American Citizen*, 10-25-1802.
63. Jon Meacham, *Thomas Jefferson: The Art of Power* (New York: Random House, 2012), p. 374.
64. Toast #11, *Providence Phoenix*, 7-13-1802.
65. Toasts #7–8, *Rhode-Island Republican*, 8-21-1802.
66. Toast #10, Volunteer 2, *Columbian Centinel*, 12-29-1802.
67. Brodie, p. 340.
68. *Gazette of the United States*, 2-23-1803.
69. *Farmer's Register*, 3-22-1803.
70. *Albany Centinel*, 3-111803.
71. Toasts #6–7, *Albany Register*, 3-22-1803.
72. Toast #8, *Evening Post*, 6-27-1803.
73. *American Citizen*: Toast #6, 3-9-1803; Toast #7, 3-22-1803.
74. *American Citizen*: Toast #9, 14, 3-15-1803; Toast #12, 3-17-1803.
75. Toast #11, *American Citizen*, 7-26-1803.
76. Toast #10, *Albany Register*, 4-1-1803.
77. Toast #1, *Genius of Liberty*, 7-16-1803.
78. Toast #5, *American Citizen*, 7-26-1803.
79. Toast #2, *Kennebec Gazette*, 7-14-1803.

80. Toast #12, *New-England Palladium*, 7-12-1803.
81. Toast #18, *Alexandria Expositor*, 7-22-1803.
82. Volunteer 3, *Albany Gazette*, 7-7-1803.
83. *Weekly Wanderer*, 7-23-1803.
84. *Weekly Wanderer*, 8-13-1803.
85. Toast #14, *American Citizen*, 7-26-1803.
86. Toast #12, *Alexandria Expositor*, 7-22-1803.
87. *Spectator*, 7-13-1803.
88. Toast #13, *Centinel Of Freedom*, 7-6-1803.
89. *Albany Centinel*, 7-22-1803.
90. *Balance*, 7-26-1803.
91. Toast #12, *Mirror of the Times and General Advertiser*, 7-13-1803.
92. Toast #14, *Guardian of Liberty*, 8-24-1803.
93. Toast #5, *Carlisle Gazette*, 7-6-1803.
94. Toast #10, *Morning Chronicle*, 7-8-1803.
95. Toast #17, *Albany Register*, 7-12-1803.
96. Toast #16, *Alexandria Expositor*, 7-13-1803.
97. Toast #3, *Guardian of Freedom*, 8-24-1803.
98. Toast #5, *Weekly Eastern Argus*, 12-23-1803.
99. Toast #12, *Albany Gazette*, 12-29-1803.
100. Josiah Goddard, *Oration, Delivered on the Anniversary of Independence, at Conway* (Northampton, MA: Printed by Andrew Wright, 1804), 2.
101. *Aurora General Advertiser*, 3-7-1804.
102. *Republican Watch-Tower*, 3-7-1804.
103. *Republican Star*, 3-13-1804.
104. *Washington Federalist*, 3-16-1804.
105. Toast #16, *Virginia Argus*, 3-7-1804.
106. Volunteer 7, *Albany Centinel*, 3-9-1804.
107. Toast #9, *National Intelligencer and Washington Advertiser*, 3-28-1804.
108. Toast #16, *Albany Register*, 5-22-1804.
109. Toast #7, *Guardian Of Freedom*, 5-26-1804.
110. Toast #9, *Kennebec Gazette*, 7-5-1804.
111. Toast #14, *Portsmouth Oracle*, 7-28-1804.

112. Toast #14, *American Citizen*, 6-27-1804.
113. *Carolina Gazette*: Toast #14, 7-13-1804; Toast #4, 7-6-1804.
114. Toast #5, *Albany Gazette*, 5-10-1804.
115. *Alexandria Advertiser*, 9-24-1804.
116. Toast #8, *Republican Watch-Tower*, 5-16-1804.
117. Toast #4, *Guardian Of Freedom*, 5-26-1804.
118. Philadelphia, Toast #3, *Bee*, 6-5-1804.
119. David Hackett Fischer, "The Myth of the Essex Junto," *William and Mary Quarterly*, Vol. 21, No. 2 (April 1964), p. 1991.
120. Kevin M. Gannon, "Escaping 'Mr. Jefferson's Plan of Destruction': New England Federalists and the Idea of a Northern Confederacy, 1803–1804," *Journal of the Early Republic*, Vol. 21, No. 3 (Autumn 2001), p. 415.
121. Toast #12, *Vermont Gazette*, 6-5-1804.
122. Toast #14, *Albany Centinel*, 5-8-1804.
123. *Farmer's Gazette*, 6-9-1804.
124. Toasts #6, 8, *Political Observatory*, 6-2-1804.
125. Toasts #14–16, *Political Observatory*, 6-16-1804.
126. Toast #12, *Democrat*, 7-7-1804.
127. Toast #7, *American Citizen*, 7-10-1804.
128. Toast #12, *Political Observatory*, 7-28-1804.
129. Toast #9, *American Citizen*, 7-16-1804.
130. Toast #12, *Centinel of Freedom*, 7-17-1804.
131. Toast #12, *Vermont Gazette*, 7-10-1804.
132. *American Citizen*: Toast #4, 7-10-1804; Toast #4, 7-16-1804.
133. *Aurora General Advertiser*, 11-30-1804.
134. *Political Observatory*, 7-11-1804.
135. Toast #10, *Kennebec Gazette*, 7-5-1804.
136. Toast #15, *American Citizen*, 7-10-1804.
137. Toast #12, *Commercial Advertiser*, 10-25-1804.
138. Toast #12, *Republican Watch-Tower*, 7-14-1804; Toast #11, *New-Hampshire Gazette*, 7-17-1804.
139. Toast #10, *True Republican*, 7-11-1804.
140. *New Hampshire Sentinel*, 8-25-1804.
141. *Ibid.*
142. *Political Observatory*, 9-1-1804.
143. *Commercial Advertiser*, 10-25-1804.
144. Toast #4, *Albany Gazette*, 12-6-1804.

Chapter 10

1. Toast #9, *Political and Commercial Register*, 7-16-1808.
2. Toast #20, *American and Commercial Daily Advertiser*, 3-2-1805.
3. Toast #12, *Democratic Press*, 7-7-1807.
4. Toast #9, *Aurora General Advertiser*, 7-11-1807.
5. Toast #4, *Federal Republican*, 7-20-1808.
6. Toast #9, *New York Herald*, 1-5-1805.
7. *Aurora General Advertiser*, 1-5-1805.
8. *Hornet*, 1-22-1805.
9. Toast #1, Philadelphia; Toast #3, Roxbury, *Weekly Eastern Argus*, 3-22-1805.
10. Toast #2, Dorchester, *Weekly Eastern Argus*, 3-22-1805.
11. Toast #3, *Albany Register*, Roxbury, Massachusetts, 3-22-1805.
12. Toast #1, Norwich, Connecticut, 4-2-1805.
13. Toast #7, *True American*, 3-25-1805.
14. Toast #5, *Weekly Eastern Argus*, 3-22-1805.
15. Toast #14, *True Republican*, 3-13-1805.
16. Toast #4, Worcester, *Weekly Eastern Argus*, 3-22-1805.
17. Toast #13, *American Mercury*, 4-4-1805.
18. Toast #6, *Centinel Of Freedom*, 7-16-1805.
19. Toast #9, *Aurora General Advertiser*, 7-14-1807.
20. Wood, *Empire of Liberty*, pp. 422–424.
21. Toasts #1, 5, Volunteer 1, *Post-Boy*, 4-23-1805.
22. *Litchfield Monitor*, 4-17-1805.
23. Toast #14, *Republican Watch-Tower*, 6-6-1805.
24. Toasts #13–14, 16, *Aurora General Advertiser*, 7-19-1805.

25. Toast #9, *Aurora General Advertiser*, 5-13-1806.
26. Toasts #11–12, *New Hampshire Sentinel*, 7-26-1806.
27. Toast #7, *Portsmouth Oracle*, 7-6-1805.
28. Toast #5, *Gazette*, 7-9-1805.
29. Toast #9, *Connecticut Gazette*, 7-10-1805.
30. *New Hampshire Sentinel*, 7-20-1805.
31. Toast #6, *Farmer's Register*, 7-9-1805.
32. Toast #2, *Post-Boy*, 7-23-1805.
33. Editors of Encyclopedia Britannica. "Yazoo land fraud." https://www.britannica.com/topic/Yazoo-land-fraud; Wood, *Empire of Liberty*, pp. 128–129.
34. Toast #8, *Enquirer*, 3-5-1805.
35. Toast #12, *American Citizen*, 7-11-1805.
36. Toast #6, *Aurora General Advertiser*, 7-8-1805.
37. Meacham, p. 416.
38. *Ibid.*; Joyce Appleby, *Thomas Jefferson: The American President Series. The 3rd President* (New York: Henry Holt and Company, 2003), p. 123.
39. Toast #16, *Aurora General Advertiser*, 7-16-1805.
40. Toast #4, *Vermont Gazette*, 7-22-1805.
41. Toast #12, *Aurora General Advertiser*, 7-10-1805.
42. "To Thomas Jefferson from Timothy Matlack, 25 February 1807," Founders Online, National Archives, https://founders.archives.gov/documents/Jefferson/99-01-02-5160.
43. Toast #13, *Democratic Press*, 4-22-1807.
44. Toasts 15–16, *Democratic Press*, 6-22-1807.
45. M.C. Johnson, "Malcontents, Quids and Clodhoppers," https://www.mathewcarey.info/life-legacy/carey-the-nationalist-1796-1819/malcontents-quids-and-clodhoppers/.
46. Toast #9, *Aurora General Advertiser*, 7-22-1805.
47. Toast #12, *Carlisle Gazette*, 8-9-1805.
48. Toast #10, *Aurora General Advertiser*, 7-10-1805.
49. Toast #11, *Aurora General Advertiser*, 8-8-1806.
50. Wood, pp. 638–639.
51. Toast #9, *American and Commercial Daily Advertiser*, 9-27-1805.

52. Volunteer 7, *Commercial Advertiser*, 12-4-1805.
53. *Providence Phoenix*, 12-7-1805.
54. Brian Gandy, "John Pierce's Death." http://dchblog.net/2018/07/13/john-pierces-death/.
55. Toast #14, *Aurora General Advertiser*, 5-15-1806.
56. Toast #2, *Connecticut Gazette*, 7-16-1806.
57. Toast #13, *Enquirer*, 7-22-1806.
58. Toast #11, *Centinel Of Freedom*, 7-8-1806.
59. Toast #13, *True American*, 3-24-1806.
60. Toast #15, *Aurora General Advertiser*, 7-18-1806.
61. Volunteer 11, *National Intelligencer and Washington Advertiser*, 11-21-1806.
62. Wood, pp. 374–375.
63. Toast #5, *Commonwealth*, 4-2-1806.
64. Toast #14, *Enquirer*, 7-11-1806.
65. Toast #6, *City Gazette*, 7-9-1806.
66. Toast #11, *Western World*, 7-19-1806.
67. *Troy Gazette*, 7-29-1806.
68. *True American and Commercial Daily Advertiser*, 7-14-1806.
69. *Bee*, 7-15-1806.
70. Toast #14, *Western World*, 7-7-1806.
71. Toasts #4, 6–7, *Western World*, 10-11-1806.
72. *Virginia Argus*, 1-23-1807.
73. Waldstreicher, p. 277.
74. Toast #17, *Political Observatory*, 8-10-1807.
75. Toast #14, *Portsmouth Oracle*, 2-28-1807.
76. Wood, p. 384.
77. Toast #3, *American Citizen*, 2-20-1806.
78. *Morning Chronicle*, 3-15-1806.
79. Toast #14, *Morning Chronicle*, 7-14-1806.
80. Eisenberg, p. 299/ loc. 5767–5784.
81. "Aaron Burr arrested for alleged treason," http//:www.history.com/this-day-in-history/aaron-burr-arrested-for-treason.
82. *Democratic Press*, 4-22-1807.
83. Toast #14, Volunteer 1, *National Intelligencer and Washington Advertiser*, 7-31-1807.
84. Toast #10, *Democratic Press*, 7-22-1807.
85. Toast #11, *Commonwealth*, 7-22-1807.
86. *Poulson's American Daily Advertiser*, 7-31-1807.

87. Meacham, pp. 421–422.
88. Wood, pp. 384–385.
89. Toast #16, *New-Hampshire Gazette*, 7-21-1807.
90. Wood, p. 420.
91. *Political Atlas*, 8-15-1807.
92. *Public Advertiser*, 7-22-1807.
93. Toasts #12, 14, *American Mercury*, 7-23-1807.
94. *True Republican*, 7-29-1807.
95. Toast #4, *Newburyport Herald*, 7-9-1807.
96. Meacham, p. 426.
97. Appleby, p. 125.
98. Volunteer by Mr. Thackata, *Aurora General Advertiser*, 7-7-1807.
99. Toast #8, *Centinel Of Freedom*, 7-21-1807.
100. Toast #16, *Salem Gazette*, 2-24-1807.
101. Meacham, p. 425; Appleby, p. 125.
102. Toast #11, *Democrat*, 7-8-1807.
103. Toast #11, *Democratic Press*, 7-13-1807.
104. Toast #13, *National Intelligencer*, 7-31-1807.
105. Meacham, p. 426.
106. Toast #2, *National Intelligencer*, 7-13-1807.
107. Toast #12, *Democratic Press*, 7-7-1807.
108. Toast #9, *Aurora General Advertiser*, 7-9-1807.
109. Toast #7, *New-Hampshire Gazette*, 7-21-1807.
110. Toast #2, *Public Intelligencer*, 7-22-1807.
111. Thorp Lanier Wolford, "Democratic-Republican Reaction in Massachusetts to the Embargo of 1807," *New England Quarterly*, Vol. 15, No. 1 (March 1942).
112. Volunteer 1, *Newbury Herald*, 7-10-1807. Port Rosaway was a loyalist enclave in Nova Scotia.
113. *Democratic Press*, 7-31-1807.
114. *Balance*, 8-4-1807.
115. Toasts #1, 3, *Public Advertiser*, 8-29-1807.
116. *Norfolk Gazette and Publick Ledger*, 8-31-1807.
117. Toasts #8–9, 12, *Enquirer*, 7-22-1808.
118. Toast #16, *Democratic Press*, 1-20-1808.
119. Toast #12, *American Citizen*, 2-12-1808.
120. *New York Aurora*, 7-20-1808.

121. Toast #5, *Sciotto Gazette*, 7-19-1808.
122. Selected Toasts, Sag Harbor and Elkton (Maryland) *Bee*, 7-26-1808.
123. Toast #6, *Centinel Of Freedom*, 7-12-1808.
124. Toast #7, *Centinel Of Freedom*, 7-12-1808.
125. Toast #14, *Liberty Hall*, 7-16-1808.
126. Toast #1, *Federal Republican*, 7-20-1808.
127. Toast #15, *Massachusetts Spy*, 7-13-1808.
128. Toast #5, *Gazette*, 7-11-1808.
129. Toast #8, *North American and Mercantile Daily Advertiser*, 12-27-1808.
130. Toasts #2, 6, *Gazette*, 7-11-1808 (*Mene mene tekel upharsin* is Aramaic for "You've been weighed in the balance and found wanting").
131. Toast #14, *Political Observatory*, 7-11-1808.
132. Toasts #10–11, *Political and Commercial Advertiser*, 7-12-1808.
133. Toast #5, *True American and Commercial Daily Advertiser*, 7-14-1808.
134. Wood, pp. 651–652.
135. Toast #3, *Public Advertiser*, 7-21-1808.
136. Toast #5, *Liberty Hall*, 7-30-1808.
137. Toast #4, *Columbian Centinel*, 7-16-1808.
138. Toast #6, *American and Commercial Daily Advertiser*, 8-15-1808.
139. Toast #7, *Charleston Courier*, 8-3-1808.
140. Toast #14, *Freeman's Friend*, 7-9-1808.
141. Toast #14, *Savannah Republican*, 7-5-1808.
142. Toast #5, *Bee*, 7-19-1808.
143. Toasts 3–4, *Federal Republican*, 7-20-1808.
144. Federal toasts at Greenbush, last volunteer, *American Mercury*, 8-25-1808.
145. *Bridgeport Advertiser*, 7-21-1808.
146. Gretchen E. Henderson (contributor), "Ugly Clubs," http://nineteenthcenturydisability.org/items/show/48.
147. *Freemen's Friend*, 8-6-1808.
148. Toasts #1, 5 (*crescite et multiplieanimi* is Latin for "increase and multiply"), 12–13, *Savannah Republican*, 7-30-1808.
149. Toast #8, *Columbian Phoenix*, 3-26-1808.

Chapter 11

1. "James Madison—the man who can truly distinguish between the praises of the wise and the good, and the shouts of a mob. May he persevere in well doing, unawed by Faction."
2. Toast #3, *Independent American*, 7-11-1809.
3. Toast #16, *Reporter*, 7-8-1809.
4. Toast #4, *Freemen's Press*, 7-26-1810.
5. A.J. Languth, *Union 1812: The Americans Who Fought the Second War of Independence* (New York: Simon & Schuster, 2006), pp. 134–135.
6. Toast #3, *Philadelphia Gazette*, 7-19-1809.
7. Volunteer 5, *Repertory*, 1-31-1809.
8. Toast #4; Volunteer 3, *Gazette*, 5-29-1809.
9. Toast #2, *Alexandria Gazette*, 5-20-1809.
10. Toast #2, *Freeman's Friend*, 1-7-1809.
11. Toast #14, *True American and Commercial Daily Advertiser*, 7-13-1809.
12. Toasts #4–5, *Green Mountain Farmer*, 7-31-1809.
13. "The French Invasion and the War of Independence." http://www.britannica.com/place/Spain/The-French-invasion-and-the-War-of-Independence-1808-14.
14. Toast #12, *Spirit of 'Seventy-Six*, 1-3-1809.
15. Toasts #1, 9, *Carolina Federal Republican*, 2-23-1809.
16. *Suffolk Gazette*, 3-25-1809.
17. Lynne Cheney, *James Madison: A Life Reconsidered* (New York: Viking, 2014), p. 360.
18. Toast #12, *National Intelligencer*, 3-17-1809.
19. Toasts #8–9, *Connecticut Gazette*, 7-12-1809.
20. Volunteer toast #9, *Political and Commercial Register*, 7-15-1809.
21. Toast #9, *Albany Register*, 5-26-1809.
22. Toast #17, *Savannah Republican*, 7-8-1809.
23. Toast #9, *New Bedford Mercury*, 7-7-1809.
24. Toast #3, *Trenton Federalist*, 7-10-1809.
25. Toast #16, *Savannah Republican*, 7-11-1809.
26. *Alexandria Gazette*, 7-17-1809.
27. Volunteer toast #4, *Alexandria Gazette*, 7-12-1809.
28. Toast #9, *Trenton Federalist*, 7-10-1809.
29. Volunteer 3, *Carthage Gazette*, 7-20-1810.
30. Toast #1, *Virginia Patriot*, 5-11-1810.
31. Toast #7, *Carolina Gazette*, 4-21-1809.
32. Toast #21, *National Intelligencer*, 7-14-1809.
33. Toast #8, *Suffolk Gazette*, 3-18-1809.
34. Toast #4, *New-Hampshire Gazette*, 10-17-1809.
35. Toast #14, *New-York Journal*, 7-8-1809.
36. Toast #14, *Carolina Gazette*, 3-9-1810.
37. Cheney, p. 360.
38. *Columbia*, 3-20-1810.
39. *New-York Journal*, 6-16-1810.
40. *Centinel of Freedom*, 6-19-1810.
41. Toast #13, *Carthage Gazette*, 7-6-1810.
42. Toast #10, *New-York Journal*, 7-14-1810.
43. Toast #15, *Bee*, 7-13-1810.
44. Toast #3 from Philadelphia, *Liberty Hall*, 8-1-1810.
45. Toast #13, *Independent American*, 7-10-1810.
46. Volunteer toast #2, *Concord Gazette*, 7-10-1810.
47. Drank at Salem, *Green Mountain Farmer*, 7-16-1810.
48. Katie Hill, "John Armstrong, Jr.," http://mountvernon.org/library/digitalhistory/digitalencyclopedia/article/john-armstrong-jr/.
49. Toast #14, *Federal Republican*, 7-11-1810.
50. *Columbian*, 7-14-1810.
51. Toast #1, *Evening Post*, 7-12-1809.
52. "From Abigail Smith Adams to John Quincy Adams, 25 July 1810," Founders Online, National Archives, https://founders.archives.gov/documents/Adams/99-03-02-1836.
53. *New-York Journal*, 7-14-1810.
54. *American Advocate*, 7-26-1810.
55. Enrique Krauze, *Mexico: Biography of Power—A History of Modern Mexico, 1810–1996* (New York: HarperCollins, 1997), pp. 11–12.
56. Volunteer toast #8, *Weekly Aurora*, 7-17-1810.

57. Volunteer toast #1, Tammany Society in New York City; Toast #3, Norwalk, Connecticut, *American Watchman*, 7-14-1810.
58. Toast #12, *Augusta Chronicle*, 7-21-1810.
59. *Reporter*, 4-6-1811.
60. Toast #3, *American Watchman*, 3-30-1811.
61. Toasts #13–14, *New-York Journal*, 4-6-1811.
62. *Alexandria Gazette*, 7-15-1811.
63. *Newport Mercury*, 7-20-1811.
64. Cheney, pp. 368–369.
65. Robert Smith, *An Address to the People of the United States* (London: J. Hatchard, Bookseller, 1811), pp. 5–6.
66. *Weekly Aurora*, Toast #9, 7-9-1811; Toast #6, 7-16-1811.
67. Toast #1, *Eagle*, 7-16-1811.
68. Toast #11, *Newburyport Herald*, 7-19-1811.
69. *American Watchman*, 7-24-1811.
70. Toast #15, *Philadelphia Gazette*, 2-25-1811.
71. *Philadelphia Gazette*, toast #9, 7-11-1811; Toast #7, 8-10-1811.
72. Toast #2, *Star*, 7-26-1811.
73. Denver Brunsman, *The Evil Necessity: British Naval Impressment in the Eighteenth Century* (Charlottesville: University of Virginia Press, 2013), Kindle edition, loc. 187 of 8581.
74. Wood, p. 641.
75. Ibid., p. 642.
76. Toast #14, *Enquirer*, 7-13-1810.
77. Volunteer toast #1, *American Advocate*, 7-17-1811.
78. Toast #7, *Public Advertiser*, 7-30-1811.

Chapter 12

1. Toast #11, Blandford, *Hampden Federalist*, 7-14-1814.
2. Toast #8, *American Mercury*, 7-8-1812.
3. Toast #14, *Palladium of Liberty*, 7-9-1812.
4. Toast #9, *Democratic Press*, 7-19-1813.
5. Toast #4, *City Gazette*, 4-6-1815.
6. Wood, *Empire of Liberty*, p. 659.
7. "From John Adams to Benjamin Rush, 27 January 1812," Founders Online, National Archives, https://founders.archives.gov/documents/Adams/99-02-02-5747.
8. Toast #14, *Liberty Hall*, 2-26-1812.
9. Toast #16, *Republican Star*, 5-19-1812.
10. Toast #13, *Connecticut Herald*, 3-24-1812.
11. *Centinel of Freedom*, 5-19-1812.
12. Toast #17, *Liberty Hall*, 7-7-1812.
13. Toast #6, *Carthage Gazette*, 7-8-1812.
14. Volunteer 9, *City Gazette*, 7-1-1812.
15. Toast #9, Volunteer 1, *Savannah Republican*, 7-7-1812.
16. Harrodsburg, Kentucky, Toast #2, *Liberty Hall*, 7-14-1812.
17. Lexington, Kentucky, Toast #3, *Reporter*, 7-18-1812.
18. Toast #4, *American Watchmen*, 7-15-1812.
19. Wood, p. 660.
20. Toast #4, *Liberty Hall*, 7-14-1812.
21. Volunteer 2, *Reporter*, 7-18-1812.
22. Toast #6, *National Aegis*, 7-15-1812.
23. Toast #11, *New-Jersey Journal*, 7-21-1812.
24. Toast #11, *Thomas's Massachusetts Spy, or Worcester Gazette*, 7-22-1812.
25. Toast #14, *True American*, 7-20-1812.
26. Toast #5, *Weekly Aurora*, 7-21-1812.
27. Toast #3, *Liberty Hall*, 7-11-1812.
28. Toast #16, *American Watchmen*, 7-15-1812.
29. Toast #16, *Columbian Phenix*, 7-11-1812.
30. Putney, Vermont, Toast #10, *Washingtonian*, 7-20-1812.
31. Jon Latimer, *1812: War with America* (Cambridge, MA: Belknap Press, 2007), p. 32; Samuel Eliot Morison, "The Henry-Crillon Affair of 1812," *Proceedings of the MA Historical Society*, October 1947-May 1950, 3d Series, Vol. 69, pp. 207–231.
32. Volunteer 8, *New-Bedford Gazette*, 7-17-1812.
33. Toast #3, *Gazette*, 7-20-1812.
34. Volunteer 1, *Commercial Advertiser*, 7-16-1812.
35. Toasts #3, 6, *Democrat*, 7-21-1812.
36. *Portsmouth Oracle*, 8-15-1812.
37. Toast #8, *American and Commercial Daily Advertiser*, 7-17-1812.
38. Toast #9, *American Advocate*, 7-23-1812.
39. Toast #1, *Franklin Herald*, 7-28-1812.
40. "Baltimore residents riot against antiwar dissenters," www.nps.gov/articles/baltimore-riots.htm; Languth, pp. 200–201.
41. Toast #7, *Berkshire Star*, 7-18-1812.

Notes—Chapter 12

42. Toasts #8–9, *Boston Commercial Gazette*, 7-13-1812.
43. Toast #5, *Poulson's American Daily Advertiser*, 8-21-1812.
44. Toasts #7–8, *New-Jersey Journal*, 8-25-1812.
45. Toast #15, *Public Advertiser*, 11-27-1812.
46. *Carlisle Gazette*, 12-25-1812.
47. *Democrat*, 12-15-1812.
48. Toast #4, *Constitutionalist*, 3-16-1813.
49. Toast #7, *Carolina Federal Republican*, 1-16-1813.
50. Toast #2, *American Watchman*, 7-21-1813.
51. Toast #13, *Weekly Eastern Argus*, 7-15-1813.
52. "From William Stephens Smith to Abigail Smith Adams, 25 January 1813," *Founders Online*, National Archives, https://founders.archives.gov/documents/Adams/99-03-02-2240.
53. Languth, pp. 239–241.
54. *Union*, 5-24-1814.
55. *Western Citizen*, 8-6-1814.
56. Toast #10, *American Mercury*, 1-13-1813.
57. Toast #4, *Democrats*, 3-23-1813.
58. *American Advocate*, 1-28-1813.
59. Toasts #2–3, *Franklin Herald*, 7-20-1813.
60. Toast #6, *Liberty Hall*, 7-20-1813.
61. Toast #2, Pittsfield, *American Watchman*, 7-21-1813.
62. Toast #12, *True American*, 7-26-1813.
63. Latimer, pp. 171–172.
64. Mark St. John Erickson, "War of 1812: British Raiders Pillage Hampton." https://www.dailypress.com/2013/06/22/war-of-1812-british-raiders-pillage-hampton-2/.
65. Toast #5, Washington, *American Watchman*, 7-14-1813.
66. Toast #6, Richmond, *American Watchman*, 7-17-1813.
67. Toast #15, *Albany Argus*, 7-20-1813.
68. Toast #7, *Democratic Press*, 6-21-1813.
69. Toast #17, *Albany Argus*, 7-20-1813.
70. Toast #14, *Centinel Of Freedom*, 7-13-1813.
71. Toast #10, *American Mercury*, 7-13-1813.
72. Toast #12, *City Gazette*, 7-8-1813.
73. Toast #5, *Carlisle Gazette*, 7-23-1813.
74. Toast #13, *Democratic Press*, 7-7-1813.
75. Latimer, p. 166.
76. Toast #17, *New-Jersey Journal*, 7-20-1813.
77. Toasts #8–9, *Chronicle*, 7-19-1813.
78. Toast #5, *Centinel of Freedom*, 7-13-1813.
79. Toast #12, *Repertory*, 7-17-1813.
80. Toasts #1, 4, 13, *Bennington News-Letter*, 4-14-1813.
81. Toast #16, *New-Hampshire Sentinel*, 4-3-1813.
82. Toast #10, *Pennsylvania Correspondent and Farmer's Advertiser*, 7-19-1813.
83. Toast #13, *Reporter*, 7-10-1813.
84. *Baltimore Patriot*, 10-28-1813.
85. Toast #8, *Gazette*, 9-20-1813.
86. Toast #19, Volunteer 5, *Reporter*, 11-13-1813.
87. Toast #10, *Columbia*, 11-27-1813.
88. Toast #4, *Weekly Eastern Argus*, 11-11-1813.
89. Toast #11, *Democratic Press*, 11-1-1813.
90. Toast #17, *Boston Daily Advertiser*, 2-4-1814.
91. *Allegany Freeman*, 2-12-1814.
92. "Summer 1813: Mysterious 'blue lights' appear on the Connecticut coast": https://www.nps.gov/articles/blue-lights.htm.
93. Volunteer 11, *National Advocate for the Country*, 3-22-1814.
94. Toast #16, *Columbian Register*, 7-12-1814.
95. Toast #16, *Palladium of Liberty*, 3-17-1814.
96. Toast #3, *Connecticut Herald*, 3-8-1814.
97. Toast #7, *Northern Whig*, 3-8-1814.
98. Volunteer 6, *Columbia*, 3-9-1814.
99. *Columbian*, 3-3-1814.
100. Toast #10, *Palladium of Liberty*, 6-16-1814.
101. Toast #15, *Pennsylvania Correspondent, and Farmer's Advertiser*, 7-18-1814.
102. Toast #14, *American Advocate*, 7-16-1814.
103. Toast #10, *Gleaner*, 7-8-1814.
104. *Non de bonis* is Latin for "of goods not delivered"; *devastavit* is Latin for wasteful mismanagement; Toast #1, *Dartmouth Gazette*, 7-20-1814.

105. Toast #3, Hampshire County; Hampden Federalist, 7-14-1814.
106. *Columbian*, 7-26-1814.
107. Toast #4, *Spirit of the West*, 8-9-1814.
108. Toast #4, *American Watchman*, 7-27-1814.
109. *Western American*, 8-5-1814.
110. *Salem Gazette*, 8-2-1814.
111. Toast #8, *Weekly Aurora*, 9-27-1814.
112. Toast #4, *Daily National Intelligencer*, 12-14-1814.
113. Toast #7, *Columbian Centinel*, 7-8-1815.
114. Toast #14, Volunteer 1, *Albany Gazette*, 10-10-1814.
115. Toast #10, *Newburyport Herald*, 11-30-1815.
116. Wood, p. 695.
117. Toast #12, *New-England Palladium*, 9-23-1814.
118. Volunteer 4, *Columbia*, 12-16-1814.
119. Toast #14, *City Gazette*, 3-22-1815.
120. Toast #12, *Columbian Patriot*, 3-29-1815.
121. Toast #3, *Vermont Republican*, 3-6-1815.
122. Toast #7, *Pennsylvania Correspondent and Farmers' Advertiser*, 9-18-1815.
123. Toast #9, *Vermont Republican*, 3-6-1815.
124. Volunteer 2, *Connecticut Herald*, 3-21-1815.
125. Toast #2, *Rhode-Island Republican*, 3-1-1815.
126. Toast #10, *Enquirer*, 11-15-1815.
127. Toast #15, *Rhode-Island American*, 3-3-1815.
128. Toast #5, *Reporter*, 4-5-1815.
129. Toast #5, *Vermont Republican*, 3-6-1815.
130. Languth, pp. 397–398.
131. Toast #11, *Burlington Gazette*, 7-21-1815.
132. Toast #10, *American Friend*, 7-7-1815.
133. Toast #7, *Rutland Herald*, 8-2-1815.
134. Languth, pp. 338–339.
135. Toast #4, *Connecticut Herald*, 3-7-1815.
136. "The Hartford Convention: Hints of Secession," http://sageamericanhistory.net/jeffersonian/documents/Hartford Conv.htm.
137. Languth, p. 374.
138. Toast #14, *Columbian Register*, 7-8-1815.
139. Toast #4, *Rutland Herald*, 7-12-1815.
140. Volunteer toast #2, *American Friend*, 7-7-1815.
141. Toast #5, *City Gazette*, 7-8-1815.
142. Toast #13, *Carlisle Gazette*, 8-9-1815.
143. Toast #10, *American Advocate*, 7-15-1815.
144. Toasts #16, 15, *American Advocate*, 7-8-1815.

Chapter 13

1. Toast #7, *Genius of Liberty*, 7-23-1802.
2. Toast #10, *Salem Mercury*, 7-10-1787.
3. Toast #15, *Philadelphia Gazette*, 7-5-1797.
4. Toast #17, *Centinel of Freedom*, 4-1-1806.
5. Rebecca Rupp, "The Often (Manly) History of Toasting," https://www.artofmanliness.com/character/advice/often-manly-history-toasting-bring-back/.
6. Brown and Shannon, p. 92.
7. J. Roach, The Royal Toast Master, pp. ii–iii.
8. Rupp, p. 3.
9. Mallory O'Meara, *Girly Drinks: A World History of Women and Alcohol* (Toronto: Hanover Square Press, 2021), pp. 113, 115.
10. Susan Branson, *These Fiery Frenchified Dames: Women and Political Culture in Early National Philadelphia* (Philadelphia: University of Pennsylvania Press, 2001), p. 85.
11. Quotations are taken from Mary Coughlan's *Memoirs of Mrs. Coughlan, Daughter of the Late Major Moncriefe, Written by Herself and Dedicated to the British Nation* (London, 1794); Russell Shorto, *Revolution Song: A Story of American Freedom* (New York: W.W. Norton & Company, 2018), p. 262.
12. Lecture by Carol Berkin, "Women in the Decade of Protest," Gilder Lehrman Institution self-paced course, *Women in the American Revolution*.
13. Cokie Roberts, *Founding Mothers: The Women Who Raised Our Nation* (New York: William Morrow, 2004), p. xix.

Notes—Chapter 13

14. Maggie Hartly Mitchell, "Treasonous Tea: The Edenton Tea Party of 1774," in *North Carolina's Revolutionary Founders*, edited by Jeff Broadwater and Troy L. Kicker (Chapel Hill: University of North Carolina Press, 2019), pp. 30, 35.
15. Ibid., pp. 35–36.
16. *Massachusetts Gazette*, 5-16-1783.
17. Toast #1, *American Citizen*, 7-24-1804.
18. Toast #16, *New York Herald*, 1-5-1805.
19. *Commercial Advertiser*, 3-4-1804.
20. Zagarri, pp. 70–71.
21. Purcell, p. 84.
22. Lee J. Stoltzfus, "The Black Art: A History of Printing in Lancaster County, PA," https://pennblog.typead.com/printers/m_william_and_roberty_dickson/index.html.
23. Volunteer 3, *Commonwealth*, 3-19-1806.
24. Zagarri, p. 102.
25. Toast #13, *Boston Gazette, and Country Journal*, 8-17-1772.
26. Toast #14, *Herald*, 7-7-1794.
27. Visser, p. 283.
28. Travers, p. 140.
29. Toast #12, *Providence Gazette*, 10-30-1784.
30. Toast #8, *Independent Journal*, 7-12-1786.
31. Toast #11, *Pennsylvania Mercury*, 7-14-1786.
32. Zagarri, pp. 159, 176–177.
33. Toast #9, *United States Chronicle*, 7-17-1788.
34. *New York Packet*, 8-15-1788.
35. Zagarri, p. 85.
36. Waldstreicher, p. 235.
37. Toast #14, *Newport Mercury*, 7-30-1792.
38. Toast #13, *Dunlap's American Daily Advertiser*, 7-17-1794.
39. Toast #8, *Wood's Newark Gazette*, 3-26-1794.
40. Toast #16, *Maryland Herald and Hager's Town Weekly Advertiser*, 11-8-1798.
41. Newman, p. 95.
42. Ibid., pp. 102.
43. Waldstreicher, p. 169.
44. Toasts #2, 4, *Rutland Herald*, 3-28-1796.
45. Toasts #2–6, *Massachusetts Mercury*, 7-17-1798.
46. Toast #17, *Kennebec Gazette*, 7-14-1803.
47. Volunteer 3, *Massachusetts Mercury*, 9-18-1798.
48. Toast #11, *Columbian Museum*, 8-15-1800.
49. Toast #16, *Washington Federalist*, 7-24-1801.
50. Toast #17, *Patriot*, 7-11-1803.
51. Newman, p. 68.
52. Toasts #9, 17, *American Citizen*, 7-10-1800.
53. *Guardian of Liberty*, 7-18-1801.
54. Toast #16, *American Citizen*, 7-7-1802.
55. Toast #17, *Connecticut Centinel*, 7-13-1802.
56. Toast #4, *Alexandria Expositor for the Country*, 7-18-1804.
57. Toast #4, *Alexandria Expositor for the Country*, 8-4-1804.
58. Toast #17, *Savannah Republican*, 7-11-1807.
59. Toast #17, *Vermont Centinel*, 7-9-1806.
60. Toast #17, *Weekly Eastern Argus*, 7-30-1812.
61. Toast #15, *Public Advertiser*, 5-30-1805.
62. Toast #8, *City Gazette*, 5-27-1791.
63. Toast #17, *Sun*, 7-18-1807.
64. Toast #17, *Commonwealth*, 7-15-1807.
65. Toasts #5–6, 8–11, 17, *Otsego Herald*, 7-11-1805.
66. Toast #16, *American Mercury*, 8-5-1802.
67. Toast #11, *Carlisle, Gazette*, 7-14-1802.
68. Toast #4, *American and Commercial Daily Advertiser*, 8-15-1808.
69. *American Mercury*, 9-6-1804.
70. Toast #16, *National Intelligencer*, 7-16-1804.
71. Toast #10, *Carolina Gazette*, 7-6-1804.
72. Toast #16, *American and Commercial Advertiser*, 11-21-1801.
73. Toast #2, *Providence Phenix*, 3-10-1804; Toast #7, *Democratic Press*, 8-3-1807.
74. Toast #12, *Connecticut Gazette*, 7-10-1805.
75. Toast #17, *Aurora General Advertiser*, 7-7-1807.
76. Toast #16, *Boston Patriot*, 7-14-1810.

77. Toast #9, *Democratic Press*, 7-19-1808.
78. Toasts #17, Volunteer 2, *Carlisle Gazette*, 8-20-1813.
79. Toast #6, *Columbian Phenix*, 7-15-1809.
80. *Alexandria Gazette*, 8-4-1808.
81. Toast #17, *Republican Farmer*, 3-22-1809.
82. Volunteer 3, *Northern Post*, 7-12-1810.
83. Toast #17, *True American*, 7-13-1812.
84. Toast #17, *Palladium of Liberty*, 7-30-1812.
85. Toast #13, *Commonwealth*, 7-28-1812.
86. Toast #12, *Pennsylvania Correspondent and Farmer's Advertiser*, 8-2-1813.
87. Toast #6, *American Watchman*, 7-17-1813.
88. Volunteer 1, *American Watchman*, 7-7-1813.
89. Toast #18, *Columbia*, 8-2-1815.
90. Toast #9, *American and Commercial Daily Advertiser*, 7-9-1813.
91. Toast #18, *Weekly Aurora*, 2-28-1815.
92. *Hallowell Gazette*, 6-7-1815.

Chapter 14

1. Toast #11, *State Gazette of South Carolina*, 2-13-1793.
2. Toast #12, *Gazette of the United States*, 7-18-1792.
3. Toast #14, *Albany Gazette*, 3-10-1813.
4. Toast #11, *American Minerva*, 7-8-1795.
5. Toast #7, *Connecticut Centinel*, 7-13-1802.
6. Toast #5, *Pennsylvania Correspondent*, 7-18-1804.
7. Colin G. Calloway, "The Chiefs Now in This City": Indians and the Urban Frontier in Early America (New York: Oxford University Press, 2021), pp. 127–128.
8. *Newport Mercury*, 7-19-1773.
9. Toast #5, *Essex Gazette*, 1-30-1770.
10. Toast #3, *Albany Gazette*, 1-21-1805.
11. Toast #7, *Columbian Centinel*, 12-28-1799.
12. James Loewen, *Lies My Teacher Told Me: Everything Your American History Textbook Got Wrong* (New York: New Press, 1995, 2007), Kindle edition, loc. 2457 of 10025.
13. Toast #36, *Boston Post-Boy*, 8-22-1768.
14. Colin G. Calloway, *First Peoples: A Documentary Survey of American Indian History* (Boston: Bedford/St. Martin's, 2016), p. 207.
15. Colin G. Calloway, *The Indian World of George Washington: The First President, the First Americans, and the Birth of the Nation* (New York: Oxford University Press, 2018), p. 250.
16. Toast #7, *Columbian Herald*, 5-25-1786.
17. Toast #9, *Daily Advertiser*, 5-4-1787.
18. "TEXTS FOR VOTERS...No. V. - SCALPING.," *Baltimore Patriot & Evening Advertiser*, 8-28-1813.
19. Calloway, *The Indian World*, p. 366.
20. *New-Jersey Journal*, 8-11-1790.
21. Toasts #2–3, 5, 12, *City Gazette*, 10-7-1790.
22. Chernow, p. 666.
23. Calloway, *The Indian World*, p. 378.
24. Chernow, p. 666–667.
25. Toast #6, *Federal Gazette*, 2-23-1792.
26. Toast #12, *Concord Herald*, 7-11-1792.
27. Toast #12, *Herald of Vermont*, 6-25-1792.
28. Toast #7, *Wood's Newark Gazette*, 7-17-1793.
29. Toast #1, *Gazette of the United States*, 3-20-1793.
30. Philip Thomas Tucker, *How the Irish Won the American Revolution: A New Look at the Forgotten Heroes of America's War of Independence* (New York: Skyhorse Publishing, 2015), Kindle edition, loc. 3992.
31. Alvin M. Josephy, Jr., *500 Nations: An Illustrated History of North American Indians* (New York: Alfred A. Knopf, 1994), p. 296.
32. Toast #8, *Gazette of the United States*, 7-20-1793.
33. Toast #4, *General Advertiser*, 7-30-1793.
34. Toast #10, *Diary*, 11-26-1793.
35. Toast #13, *The Farmer's Library: Or, Vermont Political & Historical Register*, 2-3-1794.
36. Toast #4, *Greenleaf's New York Journal*, 7-12-1794.
37. Toast #6, *Gazette of the United States*, 7-26-1794.
38. Chernow, p. 717.

39. Calloway, *First Peoples*, p. 220.
40. Toast #1, *Newport Mercury*, 7-14-1795.
41. Toast #12, *Gazette of the United States*, 7-26-1794.
42. Toast #10, *United States Chronicle*, 6-18-1795.
43. Toast #10, *Eagle*, 5-16-1796.
44. Volunteer toast #4, *Claypoole's American Daily Advertiser*, 7-14-1798.
45. Toast #10, *Aurora General Advertiser*, 3-8-1805.
46. Toast #11, *Greenleaf's New York Journal*, 5-17-1797.
47. Toast #6, *Western Telegraphe*, 7-11-1797.
48. Toast #13, *Aurora General Advertiser*, 7-6-1805.
49. Toast #12, *Democratic Press*, 5-15-1807.
50. Toast #11, *Monitor*, 5-18-1809.
51. Toast #15, *National Intelligencer*, 5-23-1811.
52. Toast #6, *Hagers-town Gazette*, 3-3-1812.
53. Toast #3, Volunteer 1, *Reporter*, 1-11-1812.
54. Toast #9, *Reporter*, 2-8-1812.
55. Toast #8, *Commonwealth*, 5-18-1808.
56. Calloway, *First Peoples*, p. 260.
57. Toast #17, *Savannah Republican*, 5-2-1812.
58. Toast #16, *Reporter*, 6-13-1812.
59. Toast #6, *Reporter*, 8-15-1812.
60. Toast #7, *City Gazette*, 7-14-1812.
61. Volunteer 4, *Virginia Patriot*, 7-10-1812.
62. Volunteer 5, *True American*, 8-17-1812.
63. Toast #14, *Democratic Press*, 7-7-1814.
64. Toast #10, *Carolina Gazette*, 7-10-1813.
65. Toast #12, *Chronicle, or, Harrisburgh Visitor*, 7-13-1813.
66. Toast #16, *America and Commercial Daily Advertiser*, 11-24-1813.
67. Toast #17, *Poulson's American Daily Advertiser*, 7-6-1814.
68. Toast #9, *American and Commercial Daily Advertiser*, 7-10-1814.
69. Volunteer 10, *Nashville Examiner*, 5-25-1814.
70. Calloway, *First Peoples*, p. 260.
71. Purcell, pp. 23-24.
72. Travers, p. 145.
73. *Ibid.*, p. 143.
74. *Ibid.*, p. 145.
75. *Ibid.*, p. 151.
76. Toast #6, *Boston Evening Post*, 8-17-1767.
77. Toast #1, *Connecticut Courant*, 9-28-1779.
78. Toast #11, *Continental Journal*, 2-13-1783.
79. Toasts #2-3, *United States Chronicle*, 7-17-1788.
80. Toast #13, *General Advertiser*, 7-28-1792.
81. Toast #8, *Morning Ray, or, Impartial Oracle*, 7-10-1792.
82. Toast #3, *Massachusetts Spy*, 1-16-1799.
83. Toast #7, *National Intelligencer*, 7-8-1805.
84. Toast #9, *City Gazette*, 7-18-1793.
85. Toast #14, *General Advertiser*, 2-12-1793.
86. Toast #11, *New-York Daily Gazette*, 7-8-1794.
87. Toast #13, *Vergennes Gazette and Vermont and New York Advertiser*, 3-7-1799.
88. Toast #12, *Connecticut Courant*, 5-5-1800.
89. *Connecticut Centinel*, 7-17-1804.
90. Toast #14, *Massachusetts Mercury*, 12-24-1802.
91. Toast #14, *Philadelphia Gazette*, 7-12-1815.
92. Toast #12, *Aurora General Advertiser*, 7-6-1804.
93. Toast #12, *Republican Gazette and General Advertiser*, 7-13-1804.
94. Toast #5, *Alexandria Expositor for the Country*, 7-13-1804.
95. *Connecticut Courant*, 8-15-1804.
96. Gordon Wood, *Empire of Liberty*, pp. 533-534.
97. Manisha Sinha, *The Slave's Cause: A History of Abolition* (New Haven, CT: Yale University Press, 2016), p. 63.
98. Toast #7, Smithfield, North Carolina, *Gazette of the United States*, 7-30-1799.
99. Toast #9, *Hive*, 7-10-1804.
100. Toast #5, *Mirror of the Times, and General Advertiser*, 7-18-1804.
101. Toast #14, *New-Hampshire Gazette*, 3-20-1804.
102. Toast #7, *Star*, 3-8-1810.
103. Toast #10, *Centinel of Freedom*, 3-12-1805.

104. Toast #9, *Enquirer*, 3-17-1807.
105. Volunteer 4, *Farmer's Register*, 6-27-1809.
106. Toasts #2, 5, 8, *Columbian Centinel*, 7-18-1810.
107. Toasts #2–3, 6, *Rhode-Island American*, 10-24-1809.
108. Waldstreicher, p. 337.
109. *Ibid.*, p. 337.
110. "Bobolition of Slavery!!!!" https://www.masshist.org/database/viewer.php?item_id=3201&img_step=1&pid=3&ft=Object%20of%20the%20Month&nodesc=1&mode=transcript.
111. Toast #1, *American Advocate*, 7-16-1814.

Conclusion

1. Stephen Puleo, audiobook *American Treasures: The Secret Efforts to Save the Declaration of Independence, the Constitution and the Gettysburg Address*, 8:17:10, 72%.
2. McCullough, *John Adams*, p. 626.
3. Dickson, *Toasts*, pp. 20–22.

Bibliography

Books

Alden, John R. *A History of the American Revolution 1775–1783*. New York: Harper & Row, Publishers, 1954.

Appleby, Joyce. *Thomas Jefferson: The American Presidents Series: The 3rd President, 1801–1809*. New York: Henry Holt and Company, 2003.

Archer, Richard. *As If an Enemy's Country: The British Occupation of Boston and the Origins of Revolution*. New York: Oxford University Press, 2010.

Atkinson, Rick. *The British Are Coming: The War for America, Lexington to Princeton, 1775–1777*. New York: Henry Holt and Company, 2019.

Axelrod, Alan. *The Complete Idiot's Guide to the American Revolution*. Indianapolis: Alpha Books, 2000.

Boswell, James. *Life of Johnson*. New York: Oxford University Press, 1961.

Brands, H.W. *Heirs of the Founders: The Epic Rivalry of Henry Clay, John Calhoun and Daniel Webster, the Second Generation of American Giants*. New York: Doubleday, 2018.

Branson, Susan. *These Fiery Frenchified Dames: Women and Political Culture in Early National Philadelphia*. Philadelphia: University of Pennsylvania Press, 2001.

Broadwater, Jeff, and Troy L. Kickler, eds. *North Carolina's Revolutionary Founders*. Chapel Hill: University of North Carolina Press, 2019.

Brodie, Fawn M. *Thomas Jefferson: An Intimate History*. New York: W.W. Norton & Company, 1974.

Brown, Victoria Bissell, and Timothy J. Shannon, eds. *Going to the Source*. New York: Bedford/St. Martin's, 2012.

Brunsman, Denver. *The Evil Necessity: British Naval Impressment in the Eighteenth-Century Atlantic World*. Charlottesville: University of Virginia Press, 2013.

Bushman, Richard L. *King and People in Provincial Massachusetts*. Chapel Hill: University of North Carolina Press, 1985.

Calloway, Colin. *"The Chiefs Now In this City": Indians and the Urban Frontier in Early America*. New York: Oxford University Press, 2021.

Calloway, Colin. *First Peoples: A Documentary Survey of American Indian History*. Boston: Bedford/St. Martin's, 2016.

Calloway, Colin. *The Indian World of George Washington: The First President, the First Americans, and the Birth of the Nation*. New York: Oxford University Press, 2018.

Cheney, Lynne V. *James Madison: A Life Reconsidered*. New York: Viking Press, 2014.

Chernow, Ron. *Alexander Hamilton*. New York: Penguin Books, 2004.

Chervinsky, Linda M. *The Cabinet: George Washington and the Creation of an American Institution*. Cambridge, MA: Belknap Press of Harvard University Press, 2020.

Conroy, David. *In Public Houses: Drink and the Revolution of Authority in Colonial Massachusetts*. Chapel Hill: University of North Carolina Press, 1995.

Costello, Matthew. *The Property of the Nation: George Washington's Tomb, Mount Vernon, and the Memory of the First President*. Lawrence: University of Kansas Press, 2019.

Cotlar, Seth. *Tom Paine's America*.

Charlottesville: University of Virginia Press, 2011.

Covert, Adrian. *Taverns of the American Revolution*. San Rafael, CA: Insight Edition, 2016.

Davidson, Philip. *Propaganda and the American Revolution: 1763-1783*. Chapel Hill: University of North Carolina Press, 1941.

Desan, Suzanne M. *Living the French Revolution and the Age of Napoleon: Course Guidebook*. Chantilly, VA: Teaching Company, 2013.

Dickson, Paul. *Toasts: The Complete Book of the Best Toasts, Sentiments, Blessings, Curses, and Graces*. New York: Delacorte Press, 1981.

Di Spigna, Christian. *Founding Martyr: The Life and Death of Dr. Joseph Warren, the American Revolution's Lost Hero*. New York: Crown Publishing House, 2018.

Dolin, Eric Jay. *Rebels at Sea: Privateering in the American Revolution*. New York: Liveright Publishing Corporation, 2022.

Drury, Bob, and Tom Clavin. *Valley Forge*. New York: Simon & Schuster, 2018.

Earle, Alice Morse. *Customs and Fashions in Old New England*. Williamstown, MA: Corner House Publishers, 1974.

Eisenberg, Nancy. *Fallen Founder: The Life of Aaron Burr*. New York: Penguin Books, 2007.

Elkins, Stanley, and Eric McKitrick. *The Age of Federalism: The Early American Republic, 1788-1800*. New York: Oxford University Press, 1993.

Ellis, Joseph J. *First Family: Abigail and John Adams*. New York: Alfred A. Knopf, 2010.

Ellis, Joseph J. *His Excellency: George Washington*. New York: Alfred A. Knopf, 2004.

Ferling, John. *Almost a Miracle: The American Victory in the War of Independence*. New York: Oxford University Press, 2007.

Ferling, John. *The Ascent of George Washington: The Hidden Political Genius of an American Icon*. Bloomsbury Press, 2009.

Fleming, Thomas. *Washington's Secret War: The Hidden History of Valley Forge*. New Word City, 2016.

Foner, Samuel S. *The Democratic-Republican Societies, 1780-1800*. Westport, CT: Greenwood Press, 1976.

Forman, Samuel A. *Dr. Joseph Warren: The Boston Tea Party, Bunker Hill, and the Birth of American Liberty*. Gretna, LA: Pelican Publishing Company, 2012.

Fowler, William M., Jr. *The Baron of Beacon Hill: A Biography of John Hancock*. Boston: Houghton Mifflin, 1979.

French, the Reverend Richard Valpy. *The History of Toasting, or Drinking of Healths in England*. London: National Temperance Publication Depot, 1881.

Gibbons, Edward. *The Decline and Fall of the Roman Empire*. Kindle version. ISBN 978-80-7583-628-1.

Gildrie, Richard P. *The Profane, the Civil, and the Godly: The Reformation of Manners in Orthodox New England, 1679-1749*. University Park: Pennsylvania State University Press, 1994.

Grasse, Steven. *Colonial Spirits: A Toast to Our Drunken History*. New York: Abrams Image, 2016.

Head, David. *A Crisis of Peace: George Washington, the Newburgh Conspiracy, and the Fate of the American Revolution*. New York: Pegasus Books, 2019.

Hinderaker, Eric. *Boston's Massacre*. Cambridge, MA: Belknap Press of Harvard University Press, 2017.

Horizon Magazine editors. *The French Revolution*. New York: American Heritage Publishing Company, 1965.

Jones, T. Cole. *Captives of Liberty: Prisoners of War and the Politics of Vengeance in the American Revolution*. Philadelphia: University of Pennsylvania Press, 2020.

Josephy, Alvin M., Jr. *500 Nations: An Illustrated History of North American Indians*. New York: Alfred A. Knopf, 1994.

Kamensky, Jane. *A Revolution in Color: The World of John Singleton Copley*. New York: W.W. Norton & Company, 2016.

Kennedy, David M., Lizabeth Cohen, and Mel Piehl, eds. *The Brief American Pageant: A History of the Republic*. Boston: Cengage Learning, 1999.

King, Rufus. *The life and correspondence of Rufus King: comprising his letters, private and official, his public documents, and his speeches*. New York: G.P. Putnam's Sons, 1894-1900.

Krauze, Enrique. *Mexico: Biography of Power: A History of Modern Mexico, 1810-1996*. New York: HarperCollins Publishers, 1997.

Languth, A.J. *Patriots: The Men Who Started the American Revolution*. New York: Simon & Schuster, 1988.

Languth, A.J. *Union 1812: The Americans Who Fought the Second War of Independence*. New York: Simon & Schuster, 2006.

Larson, Edward J. *The Return of George Washington: Uniting the States, 1783–1789*. New York: William Morrow, 2014.

Latimer, Jon. *1812: War with America*. Cambridge, MA: Belknap Press of Harvard University Press, 2007.

Lender, Mark Edward, and James Kirby Martin. *Drinking in America: A History*. New York: Free Press, 1982.

Lepore, Jill. *These Truths: A History of the United States*. New York: W.W. Norton & Company, 2018.

Loewen, James. *Lies My Teacher Told Me: Everything Your American History Textbook Got Wrong*. New York: New Press, 1995, 2007.

Maier, Pauline. *From Resistance to Revolution: Colonial Radicals and the Development of American Opposition to Britain 1765–76*. New York: Alfred A. Knopf, 1972.

McCullough, David. *John Adams*. New York: Simon & Schuster, 2001.

McDonald, Robert M.S. *Confounding Father: Thomas Jefferson's Image in His Own Time*. Charlottesville: University of Virginia Press, 2016.

Meacham, Jon. *Thomas Jefferson: The Art of Power*. New York: Random House, 2012.

Middlekauff, Robert. *The Glorious Cause: The American Revolution, 1763–1789*. New York: Oxford University Press, 1982, 2005.

Miller, John C. *Sam Adams: Pioneer in Propaganda*. Stanford, CA: Stanford University Press, 1936.

Mulford, Carla, and David Shields, eds. *Finding Colonial Americas: Essays Honoring J.A. Leo Lemay*. Newark: University of Delaware Press, 2001.

Newman, Simon P. *Parades and the Politics of the Street: Festive Culture in the Early American Republic*. Philadelphia: University of Pennsylvania Press, 1997.

O'Meara, Mallory. *Girly Drinks: A World History of Women and Alcohol*. Toronto, Canada: Hanover Square Press, 2021.

Paine, Thomas. *Common Sense*. New York: Barnes & Noble, 1995.

Pasley, Jeffrey L. *"The Tyranny of Printers": Newspaper Politics in the Early American Republic*. Charlottesville: University of Virginia Press, 2001.

Pasley, Jeffrey L., Andrew W. Robertson, and David Waldstreicher, eds. *Beyond the Founders: New Approaches to the Political History of the Early American Republic*. Chapel Hill: University of North Carolina Press, 2004.

Pentland, Gordon, and Michael T. David, eds. *Liberty, Property and Popular Politics: England and Scotland, 1688–1815*. Edinburgh: Edinburgh University Press, 2016.

Pierce, Edward L. *The Diary of John Rowe, a Boston Merchant, 1764–1779: A Paper Read by Edward L. Pierce Before the Massachusetts Historical Society, March 14, 1895*. Cambridge, MA: John Wilson and Son, University Press, 1895.

Popkin, Jeremy D. *A New World Begins: The History of the French Revolution*. New York: Basic Books, 2019.

Purcell, Sarah J. *Sealed with Blood: War, Sacrifice, and Memory in Revolutionary America*. Philadelphia: University of Pennsylvania Press, 2010.

Randall, William Sterns. *Benedict Arnold: Patriot and Traitor*. New York: Dorset Press, 2001.

Richards, Leonard L. *Shays's Rebellion: The American Revolution's Final Battle*. Philadelphia: University of Pennsylvania Press, 2002.

Ricks, Thomas E. *First Principles: What America's Founders Learned from the Greeks and Romans and How that Shaped Our Country*. New York: Harper Collins, 2020.

Roach, J. *The Royal Toast Master: Containing Many Thousands of the Best Toasts Old and New, to Give Brilliancy to Mirth and Make the Joys of the Glass Supremely Agreeable: Also The Seaman's Bottle Companion, Being a Selection of Exquisite Modern Sea Songs*. Printed in London, 1793.

Roberts, Andrew. *The Last King of America: The Misunderstood Reign of George III*. New York: Viking Press, 2021.

Roberts, Cokie. *Founding Mothers: The Women Who Raised Our Nation*. New York: William Morrow, 2004.

Rorabaugh, W.J. *The Alcoholic Republic: An American Tradition*. New York: Oxford University Press, 1979.

Rozbicki, Michal Jan. *Culture and Liberty in the Age of the American Revolution*. Charlottesville: University of Virginia Press, 2011.

Ryan, Mary P. *Civic Wars: Democracy and Public Life in the American City during the Nineteenth Century*. Oakland: University of California Press, 1998.

Schiff, Stacy. *The Revolutionary: Samuel Adams*. New York: Little, Brown and Company, 2022.

Schlesinger, Arthur M. *Prelude to Independence: The Newspaper War on Britain, 1764–1776*. New York: Alfred A. Knopf, 1957.

Shorto, Russell. *Revolution Song: A Story of American Freedom*. New York: W.W. Norton & Company, 2018.

Silverman, Kenneth. *A Cultural History of the American Revolution: Painting, Music, Literature, and the Theatre in the Colonies and the United States from the Treaty of Paris to the Inauguration of George Washington, 1763–1789*. New York: Thomas Y. Crowell Company, 1976.

Sismondo, Christine. *America Walks Into a Bar: A Spirited History of Taverns and Saloons, Speakeasies and Grog Shops*. New York: Oxford University Press, 2014.

Smith, Merril D., ed. *The World of the American Revolution: A Daily Life Encyclopedia. Volume I*. Santa Barbara, CA: ABC-CLIO, 2015.

Smith, Robert. *Robert Smith's Address to the People of the United States [concerning his removal from the office of Secretary of State]*. The British Library, 1811.

Stark, James H. *The Loyalists of Massachusetts and the Other Side of the American Revolution*. Boston: W.B. Clarke, 1907.

Stewart, David O. *George Washington: The Political Rise of America's Founding Father*. New York: Dutton, Penguin Random House, 2021.

Taylor, Alan. *American Revolutions: A Continental History, 1750–1804*. New York: W.W. Norton & Company, 2017.

Thompson, Peter. *Rum, Punch and Revolution: Taverngoing and Public Life in Eighteenth-Century Philadelphia*. Philadelphia: University of Pennsylvania Press, 1999.

Travers, Len. *Celebrating the Fourth: Independence Day and the Rights of Nationalism in the Early Republic*. Amherst: University of Massachusetts Press, 1997.

Tucker, Philip Thomas. *Alexander Hamilton's Revolution: His Vital Role as Washington's Chief of Staff*. New York: Skyhorse Publishing, 2017.

Unger, Harlow Giles. *"Mr. President": George Washington and the Making of the Nation's Highest Office*. Boston: Da Capo Press, 2013.

Urban, Mark. *Fusiliers: The Saga of a British Redcoat Regiment in the American Revolution*. New York: Walker & Company, 2007.

Visser, Margaret. *The Rituals of Dinner: The Origins, Evolution, Eccentricities and Meaning of Table Manners*. New York: Grove Weidenfeld, 1991.

Waldstreicher, David. *In the Midst of Perpetual Fetes: The Making of American Nationalism, 1776–1820*. Chapel Hill: University of North Carolina Press, 1997.

Winik, Jay. *The Great Upheaval: America and the Birth of the Modern World, 1788–1800*. New York: Harper Perennial, 2007.

Wood, Gordon S. *Empire of Liberty: A History of the Early Republic, 1789–1815*. New York: Oxford University Press, 2009.

Wood, Gordon S. *The Radicalism of the American Revolution*. New York: Alfred A. Knopf, 1991.

Wright, Louise Booker. *The Cultural Life of the American Colonies 1607–1783*. New York: Harper & Brothers, 1957.

Young, Alfred F. *The Shoemaker and the Tea Party: Memory and the American Revolution*. Boston: Beacon Press, 1999.

Zagarri, Rosemarie. *Revolutionary Backlash: Women and Politics in the Early American Republic*. Philadelphia: University of Pennsylvania Press, 2007.

Articles

Brown, Richard D. "The Emergence of Urban Society in Rural Massachusetts, 1760–1820." *The Journal of American History*, Vol. 61, No. 1 (June 1974), 29–51.

A 'Bumper' Blog." https://www.theworkplacedepot.co.uk/news/2013/10/10/bumper-blog/.

Clark, Jane. "Gallatin: A Voice of Moderation During the Whiskey Rebellion."

https://www.nps.gov/frhi/learn/history culture/gallatin-a-voice-of-moderation-during-the-whiskey-rebellion.htm.

Dickson, Paul. "A Brief History of Raised Glasses." http://www.toastsbook.com/History.

Editors of Encyclopedia Britannica. "The French Invasion and the War of Independence." http://www.britannica.com/place/Spain/The-French-invasion-and-the-War-of-Independence-1808-14.

Editors of Encyclopedia Britannica. "Yazoo land fraud." https://www.britannica.com/topic/Yazoo-land-fraud.

Fischer, David Hackett. "The Myth of the Essex Junto." *William and Mary Quarterly*, Vol. 21, No. 2 (April 1964), 191–235.

Gandy, Brian. "John Pierce's Death." http://dchblog.net/2018/07/13/john-pierces-death/.

Gannon, Kevin M. "Escaping 'Mr. Jefferson's Plan of Destruction': New England Federalists and the Idea of a Northern Confederacy, 1803–1804." *Journal of the Early Republic*, Vol. 21, No. 3 (Autumn 2001), 413–443.

Hale, Matthew Rainbow. "On their Tiptoes: Political Time and Newspapers during the Advent of the Radicalized French Revolution, circa 1792–1793." *Journal of the Early Republic*, Vol. 29, No. 2 (Summer 2009), 191–218.

Henderson, Gretchen E. "Ugly Clubs." http://nineteenthcenturydisability.org/items/show/48.

Hill, Katie. "John Armstrong, Jr." https://www.mountvernon.org/library/digitalhistory/digital-encyclopedia/article/john-armstrong-jr/.

Hooker, Richard J. "The American Revolution Seen Through a Wine Glass." *The William and Mary Quarterly*, Vol. 11, No. 1 (January 1954), 52–57.

Irvin, Benjamin H. "Tar, Feathers, and the Enemies of American Liberties, 1768–1776." *New England Quarterly*, Vol. 76, No. 2 (June 2003), 197–238.

Johnson, M.C. "Malcontents, Quids and Clodhoppers." https://www.mathewcarey.info/life-legacy/carey-the-nationalist-1796-1819/malcontents-quids-and-clodhoppers/.

Kelley, Robert. "Ideology and Political Culture from Jefferson to Nixon." *The American Historical Review*, Volume 82, No. 3 (June 1977), 531–562.

Leonard, Thomas C. "News for a Revolution: The Expose in America, 1768–1773." *The Journal of American History*, Vol. 67, No. 1 (June 1980), 26–40.

Mann, Stephanie A. "Smithfield on July 30, 1540: Catholics and Zwinglians." http://supremacyandsurvival.blogspot.com/2014/07/smithfield-on-july-30-1540-catholics.html.

Murphy, Sean. "Remembering Dr Charles Lucas, 1713–71." *History Ireland*, Vol. 21, No. 6 (November/December 2013). http://www.historyireland.com/volume-21/remembering-dr-charles-Lucas-1713-71.

National Park Service. "Baltimore residents riot against antiwar dissenters." www.nps.gov/articles/baltimore-riots.htm.

National Park Service. "Summer 1813: Mysterious 'blue lights' appear on the Connecticut coast." https://www.nps.gov/articles/blue-lights.htm.

Neem, Johann N. "The Elusive Common Good: Religion and Civil Society in Massachusetts, 1780–1833." *Journal of the Early Republic* 24, No. 3 (Autumn 2004), 381–417.

Neumann, Caryn E. "Matthew Lyon." https://www.mtsu.edu/first-amendment/article/1442/matthew-lyon.

Orihel, Michelle. "Just Add Sparkling Grape Juice: Toasting and the Historical Imagination in the Early Republican Classroom." *Common Place: The Journal of Early American Life* (Issue 16.2, Winter 2016).

Orozco, II, Luis J. "The History and Ritual of 'The Toast.'" Paper submitted to the Britannia Council No. 303, Allied Masonic Degrees (Los Altos, CA: 1994).

Palfreyman, Brett. "Toasting": https://www.mountvernon.org/library/digitalhistory/digital-encyclopedia/article/toasting/.

Rupp, Rebecca. "Cheers: Celebration Drinking Is an Ancient Tradition," *National Geographic*. http://theplate.nationalgeographic.com/2014/12/26/drinking-alcohol-culture/.

Rupp, Rebecca. "The (Often Manly) History of Toasting": https://www.artofmanliness.com/character/advice/often-manly-history-toasting-bring-back/.

Ruppert, Bob. "Paoli: Hero of the Sons of Liberty." https://allthingsliberty.com/

2016/05/paoli-hero-of-the-sons-of-liberty/.
Sage American History. "The Hartford Convention: Hints of Secession." http://sageamericanhistory.net/jeffersonian/documents/HartfordConv.htm.
St. John Erickson, Mark. "War of 1812: British Raiders Pillage Hampton." https://www.dailypress.com/2013/06/22/war-of-1812-british-raiders-pillage-hampton-2/.
Samuk, Mehmet. "Taverns in Early Massachusetts." (St. Mary's University Media, 12-6-2016): https://stmuscholars.org/taverns-in-early-massachusetts/.
Stoltzfus, Lee J. "The Black Art: A History of Printing in Lancaster County, PA." http://pennblog.typepad.com/printers/m_william_and_roberty_dickson/index.html.
Thompson, Peter. "'The Friendly Glass': Drink and Gentility in Colonial Philadelphia." *Pennsylvania Magazine of History and Biography*, Vol. 113, No. 4 (October 1989), 549–573.
Waldstreicher, David. "The Invention of the Fourth of July": http://hnn.us/roundup/entries/12527.html.
Wolford, Thorp Lanier. "Democratic-Republican Reaction in Massachusetts to the Embargo of 1807'" *New England Quarterly*, Vol. 15, No. 1 (March 1942), 35–61.

Newspapers
(Alphabetical by State)

Connecticut

American Mercury
Bee
Bridgeport Advertiser
Columbian Register
Connecticut Courant
Connecticut Gazette
Connecticut Herald
Journal of the Times
Litchfield Monitor
Middlesex Gazette
New-Haven Chronicle
Norwich Packet
Republican Farmer
Rural Gazette
True Republican
Weekly Oracle

Delaware

American Watchman
Mirror of the Times, and General Advertiser

Georgia

Augusta Chronicle
Columbian Museum
Farmer's Gazette
Public Intelligencer
Savannah Republican

Kentucky

Guardian of Freedom
Independent Gazetteer
Reporter
Stewart Kentucky Herald
Union
Western American
Western Citizen
Western World

Maine
(District of Massachusetts)

American Advocate
Eagle
Freeman's Friend
Gazette
Gazette Portland
Herald of Liberty
Kennebec Gazette
Oriental Trumpet
Russel's Echo
Weekly Eastern Argus

Maryland

Allegany Freeman
American and Commercial Daily Advertiser
Baltimore Patriot
Engine of Liberty and Uniontown Advertiser
Federal Gazette
Federal Intelligencer
Hagers-town Gazette
Hornet
Maryland Herald and Hager's Town Weekly Advertiser
Maryland Journal
North American and Mercantile Daily Advertiser

Bibliography

Republican Gazette and General Advertiser
Republican Star
Telegraphe and Daily Advertiser
Washington Spy

Massachusetts

Berkshire Gazette
Berkshire Star
Boston Commercial Gazette
Boston Evening-Post
Boston Gazette
Boston Gazette and Country Journal
Boston News-Letter
Boston Post-Boy
Constitutional Telegraph
Continental Journal
Democrat
Essex Gazette
Essex Journal
Franklin Herald
Hampden Federalist
Hampshire Gazette
Hive
Impartial Herald
Independent Chronicle
Independent Gazette
Independent Ledger
Massachusetts Centinel
Massachusetts Gazette
Massachusetts Mercury
Massachusetts Spy
Medley or Newbedford Marine Journal
Messenger
National Aegis
New-Bedford Mercury
New-England Palladium
Newbury Herald
Newburyport Herald
Political Atlas
Repertory
Russell's Gazette
Salem Gazette
Salem Mercury
Salem Register
Thomas's Massachusetts Spy, or Worcester Gazette
Wasp

New Hampshire

American Herald of Liberty
Amherst Village Messenger
Concord Gazette
Concord Herald
Constitutionalist

Courier of New-Hampshire
Dartmouth Gazette
Farmer's Weekly Museum
Freeman's Journal, Or, New-Hampshire Gazette
Mirrour
New-Hampshire Gazette
New-Hampshire Recorder
New-Hampshire Sentinel
New-Hampshire Spy
Oracle of the Day
Political Observatory
Portsmouth Oracle
Sun
United States Oracle

New Jersey

Centinel of Freedom
Federal Republican
Genius of Liberty
Jersey Chronicle
New-Jersey Gazette
New-Jersey Journal
Palladium of Liberty
Political Intelligencer
Trenton Federalist
True American
Wood's Newark Gazette

New York

Albany Centinel
Albany Citizen
Albany Gazette
Albany Register
American Citizen
American Minerva
Balance
Bee
Catskill Packet
Commercial Advertiser
Daily Advertiser
Diary
Evening Post
Gazette of the United States
Greenleaf's New-York Journal
Herald
Hudson Gazette
Impartial Gazetteer and Saturday's Evening Post
Independent Journal
Morning Chronicle
National Advocate
National Advocate for the Country
New York Aurora

Bibliography

New-York Chronicle
New-York Daily Gazette
New York Gazette
New-York Gazette and Weekly Mercury
New-York Herald
New-York Journal
New-York Mercury
New-York Packet
Northern Centinel
Northern Post
Northern Whig
Patriot
Patriotic and Commercial Register
Political and Commercial Daily Advertiser
Public Advertiser
Republican Watch-Tower
Rights of Man
Spectator
Suffolk Gazette
Weekly Museum

North Carolina

Carolina Federal Republican
Star

Ohio

American Friend
Liberty Hall
Scioto Gazette
Spirit of the West
Western Star

Pennsylvania

Aurora General Advertiser
Carey's Daily Advertiser a Literary, Political and Commercial Evening Gazette
Carey's United States Recorder
Carlisle Gazette
Chronicle
Chronicle, or Harrisburgh Visitor
Claypoole's American Daily Advertiser
Commonwealth
Democratic Press
Dunlap's American Daily Advertiser
Farmer's Register
Freeman's Journal
General Advertiser
Gleaner
Herald of Liberty
Mail
National Gazette
Oracle of Dauphin
Pennsylvania Chronicle
Pennsylvania Correspondent
Pennsylvania Correspondent and Farmer's Advertiser
Pennsylvania Evening Post
Pennsylvania Gazette
Pennsylvania Packet
Philadelphia Gazette
Pittsburgh Gazette
Political and Commercial Register
Porcupine's Gazette
Poulson's American Daily Advertiser
True American and Commercial Daily Advertiser
Weekly Aurora
Western Telegraphe

Rhode Island

Columbian Phoenix
Guardian of Liberty
Herald of the United States
Impartial Observer
Newport Herald
Newport Mercury
Providence Gazette
Providence Phoenix
Rhode-Island American
Rhode-Island Republican
United States Chronicle

South Carolina

Carolina Gazette
Charleston Courier
Charleston Morning Post
City Gazette
Columbian Herald
South-Carolina and General Advertiser
South-Carolina Weekly Gazette
State Gazette of South Carolina

Tennessee

Carthage Gazette
Nashville Examiner

Vermont

Bennington New-Letter
Burlington Gazette
Farmer's Library
The Farmer's Library: Or, Vermont Political & Historical Register
Federal Galaxy
Green Mountain Farmer

Bibliography

Herald of Vermont
Morning Ray, or, Impartial Oracle
Post-Boy
Rutland Herald
Spooner's Vermont Journal
Vergennes Gazette and Vermont and New-York Advertiser
Vermont Gazette
Vermont Republican
Washingtonian
Watchman
Weekly Wanderer

Virginia

Alexandria Advertiser
Alexandria Expositor
Alexandria Expositor for the Country
Alexandria Gazette
Alexandria Times
Columbian Mirror
Enquirer
Fincastle Weekly Advertiser
Petersburgh Intelligencer
Spirit of 'Seventy-Six
Virginia Argus
Virginia Chronicle
Virginia Gazette
Virginia Gazette, or American Advertiser
Virginia Herald
Virginia Patriot

Washington, D.C.

American Journal Argus
Centinel of Liberty
Courier
Daily National Intelligencer
Federal Republican
Independent American
Monitor
National Intelligencer
National Intelligencer and Washington Advertiser
Washington Federalist
Washington Gazette

Index

Numbers in **_bold italics_** indicate pages with illustrations

Adam and Eve story 197
Adams, Abigail 17–18, 37, 79, 84, 91, 106, 113, 174, 189, 195, **_196_**, 201
Adams, John 3, 10, 15, 28, 30, 37, 47, 53, 57–60, 63, 67, 71, 74, 81–85, **_85_**, 88–90, 93–95, 101–104, 106–110, 112–113, 117, 122–123, 125, 132, 141, 154, 162–163, 169, 174, 189, 195, 216–217
Adams, John Quincy 3, 17, 19, 91, 120, 152, 162, 166–167, 178, 183, 216
Adams, Samuel 19–20, 24, 26, 28, 45, 84
Adams, Thomas 113
An Address to the People of the United States 165
African Americans 3, 40, 209, 211, 214
African Society 215
The Age of Federalism: The Early American Republic, 1778-1800 54
Albany Centinel 103
Albany Gazette 90
Albion Benevolent Society of New York City 149
Alexander I, Czar 177–178, 180–181, 187
Alexandria Advertiser 127
Alexandria Expositor 122
Alexandria Gazette 165, 199
Algeria 211
Algiers 72
Alien Act of 1798 97
Alien and Sedition Acts 96, 98–99, 113, 134, 150, 217; *see also* Sedition Act of 1798
Allen, Ethan 33
"THE AMERICAN" 97
American Advocate 163, 175
"American Catiline" 144, 153; *see also* Burr, Aaron
American Citizen 127, 142, 196
American Coffee-House 33, 29

The American Crisis 40
American Republican Society of Philadelphia 159
American Watchman 185
"AMERICUS PATRIAE" 36
Amherst Village Messenger 92
André, John 38
Annapolis MD 43, 45, 153
Anniversary Day 15
anti-Hibernian Society 160
Antifederalists 1, 51
Antoinette, Queen Marie 65
Appalachians 121, 124
Arlington Sheep Shearing 160
Armstrong, John 162, 167
Army (US) 205
Arnold, Benedict 3, 33, 38–39, 63, 123, 171, 173
Articles of Confederation 43, 47–48
atheism 122
Attila the Hun 12
Aurora 106, 128, 114, 126, 133, 137

Bache, Benjamin Franklin 82–83, 106
Baltimore MD 49, 59, 90, 123, 173, 204
Baltimore Evening Post 161–162
Baltimore Patriot 178–180
Baltimore Union Greens 164
Bank of the United States 164
Barron, James 145
Barbary pirates 72–73, 116, 127, 130, 132, 154
Barbary States 116, 130, 212, 215
Bastille 54
Bastille Day 59–60, 63, 194
Bayard, James 109, 178, 183
Bayonne Decree 149
Bladensburg (Battle of) 182–183
Blennerhassett Island 142

255

Index

Bobolition Day 215
Bolivar, Simon 213
Bonaparte, Josephine 201
Bonaparte, Napoleon 3, 80, 86, 103–104, 115, 148, 156, 162, 167, 178, 180–181
Boston MA 23–25, 27–30, 33, 39, 47–48, 57, 73, 76, 79, 84, 108, 112, 130–131, 141, 147, 155, 157, 161–162, 174, 178, 190, 195, 214–215
Boston Cadets 179
Boston Chronicle 16
Boston Concert Hall 79–80, 108
Boston Fire Club 25
Boston Gazette, of Country Journal 34
Boston Massacre toast 28
Bourbon dynasty 181
HMS *Boxer* 179
British Independent Companies 176
Brown, Moses 16
Brunsman, Denver ix, 1–2, 166; *see also* impressment
bumper toast 12, 18, 192
Bunch of Grapes tavern 47
Bunker Hill 33, 62; anniversary 71–72
Bunker Hill Association 199
Burgoyne, Gen. John 37
Burke, Edmund 26, 31, 34
Burr, Aaron 3, 76, 93, 109–113, 115–116, 119–120, 123–124, 129, 131–134, 142–144, 125–154, 165, 217

Caesar, Augustus 12
Cain and Abel story 100
Calhoun, John C. 17
Callender, James T. 126
Canada 168–169, 171, 175, 179
Cape's Tavern 45
Carey, Matthew 18
Caribbean 213
Carlisle Gazette 51
Carolina Gazette 151
Catilina, Lucius Sergius (Catiline) 144
Celebrating the Fourth: Independence Day and the Rites of Nationalism in the Early Republic 3, 210
"CENSOR MORUM" 99, 101
Centinel 16, 117
Centinel of Freedom 169
Certificates 130
Cervantes, Miguel 199
Charleston SC 15, 32, 39, 58, 66, 70, 75–76, 93, 151, 213
Charleston Courier 9
CHARYBDIS 69
Chase, Samuel 126–127, 132, 135, 154
Chastellux, Marquis de 18–19

Cheetham, James 143
Cherokee nation 18, 205, 209
USS *Chesapeake* 145, 177
Christianity 207–208
Cincinnatus 41–42
Circular Letter 26
City Gazette 62, 75, 93
Clark, William 142
Clay, Henry 170, 183
Claypoole's American Daily Advertiser 79
Clinton, DeWitt 123, 143
Clinton, George 61–62, 131, 134, 158, 169–170
Clinton, Gen. Henry 35, 38
clodhopper 138–139
Cockburn, Adm./Sir George 176, 209
Coleman, William 125
Columbia (personification of liberty) 168, 179, 188, 192, 194–195, 198–199, 201
Columbian Centinel 78, 85, 204
Columbian Herald 57, 66
Columbian Society of New Haven 180
Commercial Advertiser 94, 190
Committee of Public Safety (Paris) 66
Common Sense 34, 38, 96
Confederation Congress 43, 52, 216
Confounding Father: Thomas Jefferson's Image in His Own Time 84, 118
Connecticut 27, 29, 33, 50, 67, 72, 78, 87–88, 98–99, 101, 103–104, 113, 117–118, 121, 128, 129, 135–136, 145, 153, 158, 173, 180, 186, 200
Connecticut blue lights 180
Connecticut Centinel 212
Connecticut Courant 119
Connecticut Gazette 27
"Conotacarius" (Town Destroyer) 207
The Constitution 50, 97–98, 123, 131, 211
USS *Constitution* ("Old Ironsides") 174
Constitutional Convention (Philadelphia 1787) 3, 6, 48–49, 216
Continental Congress: 1st 30–31; 2nd 33, 39, 43, 216
Convention of Montefontaine 109
Copenhagen 160–161
"Copenhagen bully" 160
Copley, John 85
Corday, Charlotte 195
Cornwallis, Lord Charles 39
Corsica 27, 29, 156
Cowpens (Battle) 39\
Craig, Sir James 171
Cranch, Mary Smith 106
Creek nation 18, 137, 205, 209
A Cultural History of the American Revolution 34

Index

Daily Advertiser 18, 70
Dartmoor Prison (Devonshire) 184
Davie, William 104
Day of St. Napoleon 148
Dearborn, Henry 170–171
Decatur, Stephen 127, 130, 180
"DECIUS" 123
Declaration of Independence 35, 37, 39, 61, 69, 83, 138–139, 172, 203, 210
Declaration of the Rights of Man 58
The Decline and Fall of the Roman Empire 12
De Grasse, Admiral 39
Delaware 41, 50, 109, 128–129, 135, 158, 170
Delaware River 128
Democratic Association of Gloucester 134
Democratic Press 147
Denmark 160
Derne 139
Diana 199, 201
Diary 62, 70
Dickinson, John 3, 26, 31; *see also* The Farmer
Dickson, Mary 191–192
Dickson, Paul 14
Dickson, William 191–192
District of Maine 55, 65, 80, 92, 98, 100, 105, 108, 122, 130–131, 163, 175, 181, 186, 199, 201
Don Quixote 171; book 199
Duane, William 114–115, 126, 137, 140
Duke of Brunswick 63
Dulcinea 199
Dumouriez, Gen. Charles Francois 62–63
Duval, Peter S. 179

Eagle Tavern 36
Eaton, William 139
Edenton Tea Party 190, *191*
Elkins, Stanley 54
Ellis, Joseph J. ix
Ellsworth, Oliver 104
Ely, William 129–130
"Ely's Amendment" 129–130
embargo 152, 156, 158, 199
Embargo Act 6, 133, 149–151, *151*, 154, 157, 167, 217
Empire of Liberty: A History of the Early Republic, 1789-1815 168
USS *Enterprise* 179
epiglottitis 105
Mr. Eppelle's Tavern 49
Essex Junto 128, 158, 164
Estates General 54
Evacuation Day (holiday in NY) 59, 74, 124

The Evil Necessity: British Naval Impressment in the Eighteenth Century 166
HMS *Experiment* 16

Fabius/Fabian strategy 12
Fallen Timbers (Battle) 206
Falmouth (Portland ME) 201
Faneuil Hall 23, 29, 87
Farewell Address (Washington) 82, 217
"The Farmer" 26, 28
Farmer's Library 21
Federal Gazette 60, 93
Federal Intelligencer 74
Federal Republican 173
Federalists (party) 2, 59–60, 63, 69, 71, 73–74, 78–80, 82–85, 87–88, 92, 94–101, 103–104, 106, 180–114, 118–124, 126, 128–129, 131–138, 140–143, 145–148, 150–153, 156, 158–159, 163–164, 166, 169, 172–176, 178, 182, 187, 194–195, 212, 217
Federalists (supporters of the Constitution) 51, 54
Fenno, John 61
Festival of the Sons of the Pilgrims 125
fisheries 17, 58, 87, 116, 133, 150, 160
Florida 136, 140, 142, 168–169, 179
Forefather's Day 14, 112, 133, 190, 203–204, 212
Fort Ticonderoga 33
Fourth of July holiday 35, 42, 44–48, 53, 55, 58, 62, 65, 67, 79–80, 82–83, 87, 90, 100–101, 106, 112, 115, 117, 123, 125, 127, 129–130, 145, 147, 149, 151, 153, 163, 166, 181, 194–196, 198–199, 210–212, 215–216
France 4, 13, 18, 27, 36, 38–39, 42, 45, 54–55, 58–68, 70–71, 73–77, 80–81, 83–97, 99–104, 108–111, 116–117, 121, 124, 133, 136, 148–149, 151–156, 159, 161–163, 173, 178, 181, 194, 196, 210–211, 213, 217
Franklin, Benjamin 12–13, 24, 31, 33, 36, 38–40, 58, 216
Fraunce's Tavern 41–42
Freemasons 44, 57
French and Indian War 23
French Directory 89, 92, 104
French Revolution 54, 59–61, 63, 65, 68, 72, 76, 80, 83, 193, 211, 213, 217
Freneau, Philip 82
Friends of Liberty 61

Gag Rule 214
Gage, Gen./Gov. Thomas 29, 33
Gallatin, Abraham Aflonso Albert 88–91, 93, 102–103, 115, 118, 123, 165, 178, 183
Gates, Gen. Horatio 37

258　Index

Gazette 131
Gazette Francais 74
Gazette of the United States 61, 88, 93, 117, 120
General Arnold 16
Genet, Edmund Charles Eduoard ("Citizen Genet") 66, 70, 80, 85, 152, 160, 71
George III, King 3, 15, 23, **24**, 34, 38, 40, 42–43, 76, 166, 203, 216; birthday celebrations 23–24, 67
Georgia 15, 27, 40, 47, 50, 90, 102, 112, 137, 142, 205
German Allied Armies 181
German Incorporated Society for the relief of Emigrants from Germany 77
Gerry, Elbridge 89, 93, 115, 172–173
Ghent, Belgium 183
Gibbons, Edward 12
Gilman, John T. 128
"Glorious Cause" 32, 191
Mr. Gordon's tavern 47
Gore, Gov. Christopher 128
Grand Army 148, 178, 180
Grand Lodge of Philadelphia 44
Mr. Gray's Public Gardens 59
Great Britain 6, 11, 22, 24, 27–28, 31, 34, 52, 54, 63, 73, 76–77, 80, 83, 87, 100, 109, 131, 136, 141, 146–149, 154–156, 158–161, 166–168, 170, 185, 187, 208
Great Lakes 183
Greeks 11, 198
Greene, Nathaniel 39, 58
Greenleaf's New York Journal 102
"Grito de Dolores" 163
HMS *Guerriere* 174

Haitian Rebellion 213
Hallowell Artillery 201
Hamilton, Alexander 3, 19, 58–59, 61, 63–65, 67, 71, 73, 88–89, 91, 102, 105–106, 108–110, 112, 114, 119, 123, 131, 133, 136–137, 139, 141–142, 159
Hampden Sidney College 113
Hampton VA (plunder of) 176, 200
Hancock, John 31
Hanson, Alexander Cote 173
Harrison, Gen. William Henry 3, 177, **179**, 187, 208, 217
Hartford Convention 185–187
Havre de Grace MD (sacking of) 176–177
health drinking 10
Henry, John 171–172
Henry Plot 171–172
Hibernian Provident Society 121, 180
Hidalgo y Costillo, Manuel 163

The History of Toasting, or Drinking of Healths in England 15
Hollis, Thomas Brand 60
Homer 11
Hooker, Edward 210
Hooker, Richard 10
Hopkinson, Francis 37
Hornet 134
Howe, Adm. Richard 38
Howe, Gen. William 38
Hutchinson, Gov. Thomas 29

Iberian Peninsula 156
The Illiad 11
Impartial Herald 99
impressment 140, 144, 166–167, 169
In the Midst of Perpetual Fetes: The Making of American Nationalism, 1776–1820 3
Independence Day 35, 37, 39, 41–42, 51, 58, 62, 69, 72, 79, 92, 94, 98, 105–106, 129–130, 138, 143, 145, 152, 155, 158, 162, 169–171, 176, 191, 194–195, 198–199, 210
Independent Chronicle 49
Independent Gazette 71
Independent Gazetteer 49
Independent Ledger 39
Indian 164, 175, 200, 202–209
Indiana Territory 208
Intelligencer Journal 191
Intolerable Acts 29, 190
Ireland 27, 31, 45, 65, 156, 160–161, 171, 173
Iroquois League 203–204
Isabella, Queen of Spain 190

Jackson, Gen. Andrew 3, 17, 62, 142, 168, 184, **185**, 186–187, 209, 217
Jackson, Francis James 160–161, 167, 173–174
Jacobins 60, 65, 71, 87, 92, 131
Jasper, Sgt. William 37
HMS *Java* 174
Jay, John 3, 61, 71, 73, 75, 87, 113, 159
Jay's Treaty 75–79, 82, 84, 87, 95, 131, 164, 217
Jefferson, Thomas 3, 17, 59, 61, 64–65, 69, 71, 83–85, 88, 90, 92–93, 97–100, 103, 107–111, 113, 115–117, 120–124, 127, 129, 132–134, 136, 140, 144, 149, 151, 153, 155–156, 162, 164, 169, 176, 181, 207–208, 213, 216–217
Johnson, Lady Arabella 190
Johnson, Samuel 36–37
Journal of the Times 103
Judiciary Act of 1801–1802 120

Index

Kentucky 55–56, 100–101, 105–106, 114, 124, 126–127, 136, 142, 164, 170, 175, 177, 208
Kentucky Resolution 100–101
King, Rufus 71, 141
King Philip/King Philip's War 203
Ki-on-twog-ky (Cornplanter) 204
Knox, Henry 48, 205–206

Lafayette, Marquis de 37, 39, 45, 54, 60, 65–66, 127, 216
Lake Champlain (Battle) 183
Lake Erie 136
Langdon, John 128–129
Lawrence, Capt. James 177
Leander 140
Lear, Tobias 139
Lee, Gen. "Lighthorse" Harry 173
Legion of the United States 206
HMS *Leopard* 145
A Letter from Alexander Hamilton, Concerning the Public Conduct and Character of John Adams, Esq., President of the United States 108, 125
Letters from a Farmer in Pennsylvania 26
Lewis, Merriwether 142
Lewis and Clark expedition 136–141
Lexington and Concord (Battles) 32–34
Liberty Hall 25, 169–170
Lies My Teacher Told Me: Everything Your American History Textbook Got Wrong 203
Lincoln, Gen. Benjamin 39, 48
Lingan, James M. 173
Livingston, Robert 124
Lloyd, Sen. James 98
Loewen, James 203
London 11, 15, 21, 24, 26, 29, 33, 36, 68, 73, 80, 106, 127
London Association 34
Louis XIV, King 13
Louis XVI, King 38–40, 45, 54–55, 59, 67–68, **68**, 86, 118, 181
Louisiana Purchase 111, 125, 127–128, 132, 135–136, 154, 217
Louisiana Territory 111, 142, 124–125, 128, 130, 135–136, 142, 144, 213
L'Ouverture, Francois Dominque Toussaint 213–214
Lucas, Dr. Charles 27
Lucretia 197
Lyon, Matthew 99

MacDonough, Commodore Thomas 183
Macedonian 180
Madison, Dolley 201

Madison, James 3, 69, 71, 93, 97–98, 100, 115, 151–155, 158–159, 165, 167, 169–172, 176, 180–185, 217
Marat, Jean Paul 195
Marbury v. Madison (1803) 166
MARCELLUS 69
Marshall, John 54, 89, 91, 143–144, 153, 166–167
Martin, Luther 144
Maryland 27, 45, 59, 90–91, 97, 100, 102, 119, 134–135, 144, 148, 152–153, 176, 182, 203
Maryland Journal 49
"MASSACHUSETTENSIS" 33
Massachusetts 2, 13, 21, 25–28, 30, 32, 40, 45, 47–50, 52, 55, 58, 65, 71, 74, 77–80, 82, 84–85, 87, 92, 100–102, 105, 113, 115–118, 125, 128–129, 134–135, 145, 147, 150, 155, 157, 161, 167, 169, 171–176, 178, 180–186, 190, 192, 195–197, 199, 203–204, 210
Massachusetts Centinel 45
Massachusetts Gazette 49
Massachusetts General Court 14
Massachusetts Mercury 74
Massasoit 3, 203, **204**
mastodon skeleton 117
Mather, Increase 13
Matlack, Timothy 138
Mazzei, Philip 92–93
McCullogh, David 108
McDonald, Robert M.S. 84, 118
McGillivray, Alexander 205
McKean, G. Thomas 139
McKittrick, Eric 54
Mechanic Hall 62
Mediterranean Sea 139
Merino wool 159–160
Michigan Territory 136–174
Milan Decree 148
Minerva 199, 201
Mississippi River 78, 121, 124, 136
Mississippi Territory 198
M'Kinsay, Capt. John 175
Mohawk Valley 204
Moncriefe, Margaret 189
Monmouth Courthouse (Battle) 37
Monroe, James 88, 93, 121–122, 124, 127, 140, 171
Montgomery, Gen. Richard 34, 58, 171
Monticello 153
Morellet, Andre 12–13
Morgan, Daniel 39
Morris, Gouverneur 119
"*Mort de Louis XVI; le 21 janvier 1793 Place de Concorde—on voit á gauche*

Index

le socle de la statue de Louis XV déboulonneé **68**
Moscow 180
Moses 53, 128
Moultrie, Gen. William 37
Mount Vernon 41, 53, 80, 105
Murray, William 104
The Mutual Assistant Society of Hair Dressers and Surgeon Barbers of Philadelphia 149

National Assembly (France) 54–55, 59–60
National Gazette 68–69, 82
National Intelligencer 126
Native Americans 3, 7, 137, 164, 200
Naturalization Act of 1795, 1798 97
Navy (British) 140
Navy Department 91, 164
"NESTOR" 92
Neutrality Proclamation 67, 217
New England 155, 169, 175, 177–178, 185, 217
New Hampshire 40, 46, 50–51, 53, 55, 76, 78, 90, 92, 101, 105, 126, 128–129, 134, 136, 152, 172
New Hampshire Gazette 36, 144, 190
New Hampshire Sentinel 106, 130–131
New-Hampshire Spy 51
New Jersey 19, 25, 41, 70–71, 100, 103, 112, 121, 123, 131, 134, 140, 146, 169, 180, 194, 199
New-Jersey Journal 71
New Orleans 124, 140
New Orleans (Battle) 184, 186, 217
New Spain (Mexico) 142
New York 17, 36, 41, 47, 51, 55, 61, 63, 70, 74, 76, 86, 101–102, 106, 108, 112–114, 124, 138, 141–143, 149, 160, 162, 173, 180, 190, 196, 198, 204–205, 209
New York Chronicle 13
New York City 34, 37–38, 41–42, 49, 53, 58–60, 62, 74, 84, 87, 111, 124, 127, 156, 160, 189, 194, 205
New-York Daily Gazette 99
New York Gazette 123
Newburgh 143, 162
Newburgh Address (1783) 162
Newman, Simon P. 3, 20
Newport Mercury 165, 203
Newsam, Albert 115
newspapers, role of 5, 20–21
Ninety-Two Rescinders 26, 31
Non-Importation Act (1806) 145, 147
North, Lord Frederick 29
North Carolina 53, 89, 190, 191
Norwich Packet 29

Oeller's Hotel 66
"Ograbme" political cartoon 157, **157**
Ohio 124, 127, 169–170, 177, 182, 198, 206
Ohio River 107, 136, 205
Oliver, Andrew 25
Orange County Republicans 143
Orders in Council 149
Oriental Trumpet 108
Otis, James 26, 28

Pacific Ocean 142
Paine, Thomas 34, 38, 40, 58, 61, 63, 96, 121–122, 124, 127
Palladium 117
Palmetto Day 37
Paoli, Paschal 27–28, 31
Parades and the Politics of the Street: Festive Culture in the Early American Republic 3
Paris 39, 54–55, 57, 60, 65, 89, 104, 106
Parliament 22, 24–26, 28–29, 31, 33, 36, 203, 214
Patriot 148
Patuxent River 148
"Peace Party" 175
Peale, Rembrandt 107, 117
Peninsula War 156
Penn, William 13
Pennsylvania 13, 15, 26–28, 40, 45, 49–51, 54, 61, 72, 83–84, 86, 93, 98, 113, 137, 139, 147, 156, 163, 173, 182, 193–194, 198, 202, 209, 212
Pennsylvania Assembly 113
Pennsylvania Gazette 24
Pennsylvania Society of the Cincinnati 209
Perry, Commodore Oliver 179
Petersburgh Intelligencer 24
Pether, William 24
Philadelphia PA 3, 6, 27, 30, 33, 37–38, 44–45, 47–49, 52, 59, 64–65, 67, 75, 77, 79, 83, 85–87, 94, 106, 114–115, 117, 120, 149, 159, 161, 179, 193, 204, 210
Philadelphia City-Tavern 30
Philadelphia Fusileers 123
Philadelphia Gazette 166
Philadelphia Republican Blues 128
"PHILOGENET" 69
Pickering, Timothy 87, 91, 106, 152, 158, 164–165
Pierce, John 140
Pike, Zebulon 177
Pilgrims 133
Pinckney, Charles Cotesworth 89, 132, 135, 152, 158
Piper, Col. G. 113

Index

Pitt, William 26
Pittsburgh Gazette 179
Plymouth MA 133
Poland 65
Political Atlas 145
Political Observatory 115, 131
Polly Packet 193
Pope's Day 14
Porcupine's Gazette 83, 85, 87, 96
Port Rosaway 147
Portsmouth Oracle 172
Portugal 156
Preble, Commodore Edward 130
Proctor, Commodore Henry 175
Prohibition 217
Providence Assembly 35
Providence Gazette 49
Purcell, Sarah J. 32
Puritans 13-14
Putnam, Israel 33, 189

Quaker (religion) 13
Quebec 29, 34, 171
Quebec Act 29
Queen's Head Tavern 34
Quids 137, 139, 143, 154

Randolph, John 137
Reign of Terror 65, 74, 96
Repeal of the Stamp Act 25
"REPUBESCO" 93
Republican (political party) 6, 59, 61, 63, 66, 69-73, 78-80, 82-89, 92, 95-96, 98-103, 105-106, 110-123, 126-129, 134-138, 143, 145-147, 149, 151-155, 157-157, 162-165, 167, 170, 172-173, 187, 191, 194, 207, 212-213, 217
Republican Citizens of Frederick-Town 194
Republican Ladies of Lancaster 196
Revere, Paul 28
"The Revolution Seen Through a Wine Glass" 10
Revolutionary Backlash: Women and Politics in the Early American Republic 192
Reynolds Pamphlet 119
Rhode Island 36, 41, 47-51, 53, 55-56, 63, 67, 72, 164, 203, 211
Mr. Richardet's Tavern 67-68
Richardson, Leonard 48
The Rights of Man 58
The Rituals of Dinner: The Origins, Evolutoin, Eccentricities, and Meanins of Table Manners 192
River Raisin Massacre/Battle 174-175

Roach, J. 10, 188
Robespierre, Maximilien 70, 74
Robin, Augustus 204
Rochambeau 39
Rodgers, Commodore John 171
Roman Catholicism 29, 54, 157
Romans 12, 198
The Royal Toast Master 10, *11*, 188
Russell, Jonathan 183
Russia 162, 177, 181
Rush, Benjamin 169

Sachem 44, 57, 103, 197-198, 203-205, 214
St. Clair, Brig. Gen. Arthur 205
St. Dominque 96, 213
St. John the Evangelist 44
St. Lawrence River 128
St. Louis 142
Salem Gazette 182
Sansculottes 60, 194
Saratoga 37, 62
savage (in reference to Indians) 6, 144, 168-169, 177, 179, 200, 203-204, 206-209, 217
SCIPIO 69
SCYLLA 69
Sealed with Blood: War, Sacrifice, and Memory in Revolutionary America 32
Second Embargo Act of 1807 149
Sedition Act of 1798 97-100
Seinfeld 9
Serious Considerations on the Election of a President: Addressed to the Citizens of the United States 111
Shakespeare Tavern 38
Shawnee nation 205
Shays, Daniel 48
Shays's Rebellion 3, 48, 52, 131
"Shaysites" 48, 179
sheep-shearing festivals 159
Shiply, Jonathan 33
Shirly, Gov. William 55
Siege of Yorktown tavern 119
Silverman, Kenneth 34
slavery 5, 7, 25-27, 33, 36, 40, 53, 58, 69, 139-140, 194, 202, 207, 210-212, 214-215, 217
slaves 7, 25, 36, 40, 72, 93, 96, 115, 129-130, 173, 194, 210-215, 217
smallpox 198
Smith, Robert 165, 167
Smith, William Stephens 174
Snyder, Simon 139
Society of Friends of Philadelphia 113
Society of the Cincinnati 41-42, 45, 47, 56, 98, 108, 193
Sons of Liberty 22, 24, 26, 28

Sons of St. Andrew 44
Sons of St. George 44
Sons of St. Patrick 27, 44
Sons of St. Tammany 44, 201
South America 163
South Carolina 9, 15, 17, 27–28, 32, 39, 57–58, 62, 66, 70, 75, 93, 132, 151–152, 199, 209–210, 212–213
Spain 38–40, 45, 121, 136, 140–142, 156–157, 163, 190
Spectator 124
Spooner's Vermont Journal 105
squaw 197–198
Stamp Act 24, 31, 34
Stanislaus, King 65
Stoddert, Benjamin 91
"STRICTURES ON CERTAIN TOASTS" 131
Strong, Gov. Caleb 176, 185
Stuart, Gilbert 196
Sullivan, Gen. John 204
Sullivan's Island (Battle) 37
Supreme Court 55, 73, 100, 105, 125–127, 135, 143, 166

Talleyrand-Perigord, Charles Maurice de 89, 92, 95, 101
Tammany Society 59–60, 77, 124, 127, 156, 173, 214
Tarquinias, Sextus 197
tea, destruction of 29
Tecumseh 177, 179, 208–209
Tennessee 78, 127, 209
"Terrapin System" 156–157
"*Tertium quid*" 137
Thames River (New London CT) 180
Third Toast controversy 131
Thomas, Gov. George 202
Thompson, Peter 10
Three-Fifths Compromise 112, 129, 132, 186, 212
Tippecanoe (Battle) 208
toasts, definition of 5, 9
Toasts: Over 1,500 of the Best Toasts, Sentiments, Blessings and Graces 14
Townshend, Charles 25
Townshend Acts 25
Travers, Len 3, 210
Treaty of Ghent 183–184, 187, 217
Treaty of Greenville, 1793 206, 208
Treaty of Lancaster 202
Treaty of New York, 1790 205
Treaty of Paris, 1783 40, 43
Tripoli 127, 130, 139
True American and *Commercial Daily Advertiser* 157

True Republican 145
Tudor, William, Sr. 108

Ugly Clubs 153
Union 175

Valmy (Battle) 62
Valpy, the Rev. Richard 15
Vergennes Gazette and Vermont New-York Advertiser 107
Vermont 21, 32, 36, 55–56, 59–60, 69, 78, 99, 101, 103, 123, 142, 186, 211
Versailles 40
A Vindication of the Rights of Women 197
Virginia 1, 21, 27–28, 39, 42, 51, 57, 76, 81–82, 84, 86, 88–89, 99–101, 112–114, 117, 122, 126, 128, 137, 143, 148, 154, 159–160, 165, 176, 190, 193, 197, 199–200, 202–203, 211–212
Virginia House of Burgesses 27–28
Virginia Journal 1
Virginia Resolution 100–101
Visser, Margaret 192
Vortigen, King 12

Wabash 205
Waldstreicher, David 3, 35, 215
Wallace, Sir James 16
War Hawks 170, 176
War of 1812 2, 3, 6, 16, 163, 168, 186, 200, 209, 213–214, 217
Warren, Dr. Joseph 3, 33–34, 58, 63, 216
Warren, Mercy Otis 189
Washington, George 10, 15–16, 19, 34, 37–45, 52–54, 56–59, 63–67, 69, 73–76, 78, 81, 93–96, 102, 105–107, **107**, 110, 113, 117, 120–121, 125–126, 133, 136–137, 154, 164, 169, 181, 188–189, 196, 204–206, 213, 216–217; birthday celebrations 65, 71, 82, 84–85, 100, 102–103, 119–120, 160, 169, 194–195, 210
Washington, Martha 3, 190, 195, 197, 201
Washington Benevolent Societies 172, 181
Washington, D.C. 142, 182
Washington Federalist 117, 125
Washington Juvenile Society 211
Watson, William 36
Wayne, "Mad" Anthony 206–207
Mr. Weed's Tavern 77
Weekly Aurora 182
West Point 41
Western Confederacy 206
Western World 142
Wheatley, Phyllis 189
Whiskey Rebellion 73, 103
White, Elizabeth 36

Wickham, John 143–144
Wilberforce, William 211–214
Wilkes, John 26, 31, 34
William's Inn 56
Winchester, Gen. James 174
Windham Herald 117
Windsor Light Infantry 211
Winthrop, John 13
Wise Tavern 1
Wolcott, Oliver, Jr. 109, 175
Wollstonecraft, Mary 197
Wood, Gordon S. 44, 168

Wood's Newark Gazette 78
Worrell, John K. 163

XYZ Affair 19, 89, **90**, 91–92, 95, 99, 110, 147, 195, 217

Yazoo land fraud 137, 140, 154
Yazoo River 137
yellow fever epidemic 87
Yorktown (Battle) 39, 42, 62

Zagarri, Rosemarie 192

www.ingramcontent.com/pod-product-compliance
Lightning Source LLC
Chambersburg PA
CBHW032034300426
44117CB00009B/1058